At the end of World War One, Government of India officials and Indian nationalist politicians began to recognize the need for an organized communications network that could reach out to a large and diverse Indian population. The challenge for Government and nationalists alike was to create an effective propaganda machine that could both disseminate news and at the same time elicit the desired political response. Milton Israel's book describes the role of the press, news services, and propaganda agencies in the last stage of the nationalist struggle in India before the departure of the British, emphasizing the media's participation in the development of a 'national' perspective. Within this context, the author informs on the significance of the encounter between imperialism and nationalism and the influence one had upon the other in achieving often conflicting objectives. *Communications and power* presents an original contribution to the study of nationalism and nation building which informed and constrained both Asian and African freedom movements in the twentieth century.

Cambridge South Asian Studies

Communications and power

Communications and power

Propaganda and the press in the Indian nationalist struggle, 1920–1947

Milton Israel
University of Toronto

CAMBRIDGE
UNIVERSITY PRESS

Published by the Press Syndicate of the University of Cambridge
The Pitt Building, Trumpington Street, Cambridge CB2 1RP
40 West 20th Street, New York, NY 10011–4211, USA
10 Stamford Road, Oakleigh, Melbourne 3166, Australia

First published 1994

Printed and Bound in Great Britain by
Athenaeum Press Ltd, Newcastle upon Tyne.

A catalogue record for this book is available from the British Library

Library of Congress cataloguing in publication data

Israel, Milton.
Communications and power: propaganda and the press in the Indian
nationalist struggle / Milton Israel.
   p. cm. – (Cambridge South Asian studies: 56)
Includes bibliographical references.,
ISBN 0 521 42037 7 (hc)
1. India – Politics and government – 1919–1947.
2. Press and propaganda – India.
I. Title. II. Series.
DS480.45.I84 1994   93–5226
954.03'5–dc20 CIP

ISBN 0 521 42037 7 hardback
ISBN 0 521 46763 2 paperback

CE

For Beverly

'The question is' said Alice, 'whether you can make
words mean different things.'
'The question is' said Humpty Dumpty, 'which is to
be Master – that's all.'   Lewis Carroll

'To support the official world and its garrison ... there
is, except Indian opinion, absolutely nothing.'   Meredith Townsend

'Irreverent boys, simply because you can scrawl a few
lines upon a piece of paper and get some fool to publish
them for you, you think you are the educators of the
world, the public opinion of India.'   Swami Vivekananda

Contents

Acknowledgements	*page* x
List of abbreviations	xi
Note on currency	xiii
Introduction: politics and the press in a colonial setting	1
1 The Government of India: images and messages in the defence of authority	26
2 The news services: 'impartial Reuters' or 'foreign pipes'	99
3 The Congress search for a common voice	156
4 *The Bombay Chronicle*: a case study	216
5 The struggle overseas	246
Conclusion	317
Bibliography	321
Index	329

Acknowledgements

This book has been in the making for many years and over this time a large number of obligations have been incurred. The research was carried out in the University of Toronto's Robarts Library, the Library of Congress in Washington, the National Archives and the Nehru Memorial Library in New Delhi, the British Library and the India Office Library and Records in London, the Cambridge University Library and the library of the University's Centre for South Asian Studies. The Nehru Library's collection of private papers and back runs of newspapers was especially valuable. I am very grateful for the help that was so generously provided by other historians, archivists and librarians in all of these institutions. In addition to the collection of materials for the book, my life continues to be enriched by the friendships made along the way. I have received financial support from the University of Toronto, the Social Sciences and Humanities Research Council of Canada and the Shastri Indo-Canadian Institute. I hope they will consider this book to be the product of a worthwhile investment. In addition, the University of Toronto has provided research leave and an environment that encourages individual scholarship. My obligation to other students of Indian nationalism and the history of the press is noted in the citations and bibliography. I am especially grateful to Shirly Uldall and Jenifer Esplin for their help in the preparation of various drafts of the manuscript. There are, as well, individual colleagues and friends who have made this a better book than it might have been without their critical advice and support. In this brief space I shall only mention John and Rani Drew in Cambridge, John and Nettie Youngman in London, and the Sham Lal family in New Delhi whose interest and friendship are especially appreciated. My wife, Beverly, has been my partner in every venture of our life together and this book is as much hers as my own. Its dedication to her is only a token expression of my appreciation, respect, and love.

MILTON ISRAEL

Abbreviations

AICC	All India Congress Committee
AICC (FD)	All India Congress Committee (Foreign Department)
APA	Associated Press of America
API	Associated Press of India
BLI	British Library of Information
BOW	British Official Wireless
CBI	Central Bureau of Information
CID	Central Intelligence Department
DCBI	Director, Central Bureau of Information
DPI	Director, Public Information
ENA	Eastern News Agency
F & P	Foreign and Political Papers
FO	Foreign Office
FPI	Free Press of India
GOI	Government of India
HBM	His Britannic Majesty
HE	His Excellency (the Viceroy)
HomePol	Home Political Papers
I	Information Department designation, India Office Records
ICS	Indian Civil Service
IENS	Indian and Eastern Newspaper Society
INA	Indian News Agency
INC	Indian National Congress
IO	India Office
L	generic designation for a department, India Office Records
NWFP	North West Frontier Province
P & J	Public and Judicial Papers
P & T	Post and Telegraph Department
PCC	Provincial Congress Committee
PSV	Private Secretary to the Viceroy

PTI   Press Trust of India
SGPC   Shiromani Gurdwara Prabandhak Committee
TUC   Trades Union Congress
UPA   United Press of America
UPI   United Press of India

Note on currency

1 lakh = Rs 100,000
1 crore = Rs 10,000,000 (100 lakhs)

Introduction: politics and the press in a colonial setting

On 7 February 1919, Motilal Nehru gave a dinner at Anand Bhavan, his Allahabad home, to celebrate the founding of the *Independent*; and in his toast to the paper, he spoke for a large and often competing fraternity of nationalist politicians, Government officials and professional news-papermen. The *Independent* would 'think aloud for India', Nehru declared, gathering together in a simple and potent phrase the emphasis on ideas, the presumption of an extraordinary representative role and awareness of the proselytising opportunities in the control of a newspaper. For politicians like Nehru, a paper provided an expanded platform, a public demonstration of influence, assured publicity for a particular perspective, as well as the opportunity to attack the views of others. The daily appearance of the paper provided the image of institutional stability for both the man and the viewpoint, a symbolic demonstration of the power to speak out – especially significant in the context of freedom struggle. Getting 'a good press' was considered to be essential support for a political career, and control of one's own newspaper clearly enhanced the odds in one's own favour.

Nehru's views regarding the role of the press in the nationalist move-ment were a legacy of the extraordinary syncretic nature of the British–Indian encounter and the colonial political culture that would provide the foundations of the modern Indian state. The conquest of a vast empire and its maintenance and administration for almost two hundred years were dependent on the acquiescence and participation of a range of indigenous groups. In the countryside, the primary British concerns for order and revenue were accommodated to the interests of the old princely and landed elites. In the European enclaves of Calcutta, Madras, and Bombay, a clutch of alien political appointees and senior bureaucrats determined policy and sought to control their Mughal inheritance. The basic institutions of the Raj were constructed largely in the space between: Government departments, councils, courts, universities, newspapers, business houses – operated jointly by Britons and a new Indian elite of English educated civil servants, academics, merchants, newspapermen,

1

lawyers, and judges. Directly or indirectly they served the Government of India by participating in the collaborative system on which it depended. And they would provide as well, generations of leaders of the Indian nationalist movement that threatened to displace it.

This 'space between' was both a barrier and a passage way. In no other place was the isolation of these 'two solitudes' more apparent. But it was as well an entrepôt for the exchange of ideas and perspective, angry attack, and defensive posturing among Indians and Englishmen who sought to construct ordinary lives in an extraordinary situation. And the ambiguity and paradox which informed their efforts was reflected in a multi-generational 'debate' about India's future and the role, place, and purpose of the British colonial enterprise.

Legacy: the press and the colonial system in the eighteenth and nineteenth centuries

The participation of the press in this critical enterprise began early, and prophetically in the context of an attack on Government, a repressive response, and an ambivalent debate about official relations with newspapermen. In 1780, James Hicky established the *Bengal Gazette*, the first weekly newspaper published in India. But his attacks on Warren Hastings' East India Company regime led to the seizure of his types and the closure of the paper in 1782. A series of deportations followed: William Deane in 1794, Dr Mclean in 1798, James Silk Buckingham in 1820 – each reflecting the Company's conviction that Government was not the public's business (a viewpoint that was not limited to colonial situations), and its determination to suppress critical comment in print. It was apparent, however, by the end of the eighteenth century that individual papers could be shut down but the press as an institution could only be controlled. The changing nature of these controls reflected differences of opinion among officials regarding the special circumstances of their situation and the appropriateness of a free press in a colonial setting.

Warren Hastings' Council had suppressed the *Bengal Gazette*, but it patronized its competitor, the *India Gazette*, recognizing the usefulness of a popular voice directed against its enemies.[1] But its successors rejected both the need for a 'voice' and for the publication of any news regarding the activities of the Government. The 1799 Wellesley Regulations initi-

---

[1] S. Natarajan, *A History of the Press in India*, Bombay: Asia Publishing House, 1962, p. 19. The term 'popular' referred only to the British or other 'Europeans' in late-eighteenth-century Calcutta. The maximum circulation of a paper among this group was approximately 200. Natarajan's book remains one of the best overviews of the history of the Indian press.

ated the institutionalization of constraints and banned virtually any discussion of Government in the press. In 1814, The Hastings Regulations introduced the cycle of conservative and liberal response to the press issue by establishing a more tolerant environment for newspaper activity. Although the ban on Government news was retained, a group of officials who opposed any loosening of control responded to the decision by establishing its own paper, *John Bull in the East*. By seeking to meet the enemy in its own camp, however, this group grudgingly recognized its significance and enhanced its vitality by its own participation.

In 1823, the Adam Regulations set a new standard for constraints on press freedom not to be surpassed by any subsequent Government. They reflected both the viewpoint of a very conservative regime and the new defensive concern that the debate was no longer confined to British protagonists, but included Indians as well. The first Indian-owned weekly appeared in 1816. Its survival was brief but Indian participation as newspapermen, readers of the press, and advocates of press freedom continued. The debate among Company officials preceding the intro-duction of the new regulations emphasized the alien nature of their regime and the danger of dealing with the press as if they were in England. Mountstuart Elphinstone noted the incongruence of a situation which attempted to bring together the 'more refined theories of Europe' and the 'prejudices and fanaticism of Asia'; while Thomas Munro insisted that 'a free press and the domination of strangers are things which are quite incompatible and which cannot long exist together'.[2] Another view, which clearly did not impress the Adam regime, but which would eventu-ally inform all future debate on the question was provided by the Bengali social and religious reformer, Raja Ram Mohan Roy. In his attack on the new regulations, Roy insisted that 'a free press and the domination of strangers' was in fact sustainable. And he associated this right with other examples of the positive and creative impact of British colonial rule in India.

The discussion concerning the Adam Regulations was the prelude to a decade of debate concerning British responsibility and mission in India, pitting 'orientalists', who argued for the development of Indian languages and institutions, against the 'anglicists', who insisted that only British institutions and the English language could set India on a progressive path. In the early thirties, the triumph of the latter was reflected in a liberal reformist programme including a new press law. T. B. Macaulay, the Law Member of the Governor-General's Executive Council, drafted the legislation and it was implemented in 1835 by Charles Metcalfe.

[2] *Ibid.*, p. 38.

Precensorship was abolished and the press was freed to print comment on Government action subject only to the laws of sedition. One reflection of the confidence of the Government was its willingness to depend on 'ordinary law' rather than arbitrary executive authority in dealing with its critics. Its successors sought to maintain both the confidence and the sense of ordinariness in their possession of power and position in India, but continuing reminders of the alien and arbitrary nature of their authority forced them back to defensive positions. From 1835 to 1947 and beyond, the Adam Regulations and the Metcalfe Press Law provided the parameters for official action, legislation, and perspective on the issue of freedom of the press. It was a wide space and there was regular reference to both precedents as required by the immediate political situation.

The 1857 Revolt shifted the control centre back toward the Adam restrictions with the introduction of the Canning Press Act. Throughout British India an enhanced environment of race consciousness and separation informed virtually all relationships. Although the educated Indian elites generally did not participate in the struggle, their press comments concerning the violent retribution of the victorious British forces were particularly noted in reference to the need for renewed constraints on freedom of the press. The provocative and racist Anglo-Indian publication and that in the British press at home, was generally passed over without comment. The Canning Act was short-lived, but the fear which produced renewed emphasis on the special and dangerous nature of the colonial context was not easily dissipated. In regard to the press, it entrenched the idea and perception of two distinct entities – an Indian and an Anglo-Indian press – sharing a common history, purpose, and ethos, but separated by some as yet ill-defined politicized communal loyalty.

In the second half of the nineteenth century, a number of Anglo-Indian and Indian-owned newspapers established in the major urban centres of British India became recognized as 'national' voices. Although their circulations were relatively small, they were read by an elite constituency; and those Anglo-Indians who held power and Indian politicians who sought it began to recognize the enhanced capacity of these papers to create environment and affect viewpoint. The *Times of India* in Bombay, the *Statesman* and the *Englishman* in Calcutta, the *Pioneer* in Allahabad, and the *Mail* and *Times* in Madras were influential Anglo-Indian voices supported by a range of merchants and planters, and indirectly by Government through purchase and advertisement. The Indian elite press was better off than its vernacular country cousins, but it too was denied the substantial support available to British-owned enterprises. Continuing financial problems both enhanced its separation from its more affluent Anglo-Indian 'contemporaries' and denied it the easy professional independence that economic security provides. But a combination of philanthropy, family enterprise, extraordinary individual sacrifice, and eventually the support of nationalist war chests produced over time another choir of 'national' voices which competed with increasing success. In Calcutta, the *Amrita Bazar Patrika* and the *Bengalee*, the *Tribune* in Lahore, and the *Hindu* in Madras represented the initial core of such papers. They were quoted and read beyond their provincial localities, and they were edited by men who perceived and wrote about events in an 'All-India' context. English was considered essential for any national role and the establishment or control of an English-language paper often signalled a politician's desire to move on to the All-India stage. B. G. Tilak's Mahrathi language paper, *Kesari*, had a large circulation and its profits were required to cover the losses regularly incurred by the *Mahratta*, its sister English-language publication. But Tilak wanted to reach out beyond his Marathi reading constitutency, to the English reading elite in other provinces and in Government. He apparently never doubted the *Mahratta*'s value, and made it a condition of the trust established to support the papers that the *Mahratta* be continued.[3]

There was little scope for any significant expansion of the Anglo-Indian press by the end of the century, but the potential for Indian-owned enterprise was boundless. The stagnation of the former and the growth of the latter was reflected as well in the range of viewpoint which created divisions within the two groups. While there was considerable difference between the fervent and defensive Anglo-Indian loyalty of the *Englishman* and the more judicious and balanced *Times of India*, there was consensus about the legitimacy of the Raj and its continuing creative role and mission. The Anglo-Indian press could be critical, but its opposition was always loyal. Among Indian newspapers, their shared nationalism was no constraint on a spacious range of views regarding means and ends. In its daily editorial comment and reporting of events, competing images of India present and India future reflected loyalties to a particular leader and the significance of ethnicity, language, local historical experience, and religion in any response to calls for unity of action and identity.

Increasing political institutionalization in the last quarter of the nineteenth century – both by British Government and Indian initiative, broadened this 'national' context. The Indian Councils Act of 1861 had initiated the development of legislative assemblies and enhanced Indian participation in Government.[4] Associational developments in major

---

[3] *Ibid.*, p. 194.
[4] Constitutional progress in India was marked by a series of such acts. The Indian Councils Act of 1861 was succeeded by two others in 1892 and 1909, and two Government of India Acts in 1919 and 1935.

urban centres provided a base for the subsequent establishment of the Indian National Congress in 1885.[5] The expanding political life of the country also stimulated increased and more combative press activity, especially in vernacular languages, and produced another round of press legislation in 1878. Rather than a response to direct attacks on their administration, British officials were now increasingly required to deal with 'local' situations that were only indirectly concerned with decisions and actions at the 'centre'. This form of independence threatened to undermine a system of control dependent as much upon a range of explicit and implied power-sharing agreements as on the Government of India's ability to enforce its rule. A Press Commissioner was appointed in 1877, to attempt an improvement in the 'tone of the press', but the passage of the Oriental Languages (Vernacular) Press Act in the following year reflected the perception of failure. An important element of the Act was the elimination of any judicial constraint on executive action concerning the press. This had been introduced in Metcalfe's 1835 Act, eliminated in Canning's 1857 legislation, and revived when that Act was repealed in the following year. The return to executive control in 1878, was also brief. Judicial review was reintroduced in 1881, when Lord Ripon's Council repealed the Vernacular Press Act and returned the situation to the 1835 status quo.

Stephen Koss has described the emergence of the modern press in Britain in the mid nineteenth century and the development of its intimate relationship with politicians and the political process. The abolition of various taxes released the British press from constraining state control; and technical advances gave it the tools to produce a better-looking product, distribute it efficiently, and through telegraph, cable, and international news agencies, quickly receive and pass on information from all parts of the world. This unprecedented independence and power, Koss argues, gave the press 'new respectability', a 'heightened self-consciousness', and led to the creation of 'a myth' regarding the institution of the 'Fourth Estate'.[6] Newspapers became 'The Press' and asserted more aggressively a unique position of freedom even within a free society. At the same time relations with individual parties and politicians were not perceived as a conflict of interest or restraint. Freedom of the press meant

---

[5] Such associations generally involved the participation of newspapermen. In Calcutta, Kristo Das Pal, the editor of the *Hindu Patriot* was active in the British India Association; the Ghose brothers, who owned and edited *Amrita Bazar Patrika* were involved in the India League; and Surendranath Banerjee, the editor of the *Bengalee*, participated in the Indian Association.

[6] Stephen Koss, *The Rise and Fall of the Political Press in Britain*, Vol. I, *The Nineteenth Century*, London: Hamish Hamilton, 1981, p. 2.

freedom to choose which idea, ideology, party, or Government to support. In Victorian England, Koss noted, 'partnership was the dominant characteristic of newspapers', and it remained so during most of the first half of the twentieth century.[7]

In India during the same period, the essential characteristics if not the whole context of this situation were replicated. Like Britain, politicians sought the control of newspapers and newspapermen went into politics. And in both societies there appeared to be an insatiable interest in political news. In 1865, the establishment of the cable link between Britain and India eliminated time and isolation as defensive weapons for a colonial regime that had always been aware of 'enemies' on both sides of the water. But the nature of the Anglo-Indian colonial society and the development of organized nationalist politics made the comparison difficult for the Government of India to accept. There were no proper political parties in India, only a Government that could not be turned out, its Anglo-Indian press supporters, and an Indian-owned press that had taken on the role of opposition – and increasingly only as loyal as the legal situation and their need for government cooperation and government news required. Many Indian papers and their editors were attacked for their allegiance to the Indian National Congress. They were accused of being unprofessional propagandists writing for political rags with no legitimate claim on freedom-of-the-press protection. But by the turn of the century, the elite press in Calcutta, Bombay and Madras had much in common with those in London, and official attack on their legitimacy required at least implicit recognition of the questionable nature of their own.

In the context of constitutional advances initiated in India in the 1861 Indian Councils Act, it was assumed that the development of representative institutions would lead to the establishment of parties and to a parallel development of an Indian party press. In both cases, it was argued, the inevitable divisions and competition would dilute the direct attack on the British regime and divert the attention of politicians and papers as they competed for place and power in the new India in the making. This optimistic scenario would allow 'legitimate' attack on the Government of the day without the need for 'illegitimate' assault on the bona fides of the British imperial state. But with or without parties, there were always divisions and competition among Indian politicians. While considerable attention was concentrated on the actions and policies of the Government of India in the Indian-owned press, there was as well a distinctive Indian agenda and frame of reference regarding relationships among Indian groups as well as with the British.

[7] *Ibid.*, p. 3.

Much of the attention of the Indian press in the early days was concentrated on social and educational issues, and these remained significant in the increasingly politicized environment of the late nineteenth century. The use of the press for a political campaign was preceded by and often inseparable from its use on behalf of social reform and the defence of traditional values and institutions. In 1890–1, B. M. Malabari, the Bombay editor and social activist, used his *Indian Spectator* to launch a successful campaign on behalf of a higher minimum age of marriage law. He was aided in Calcutta by K. C. Sen, an heir to Ram Mohan Roy's reformist legacy, who used tracts and the press to mobilize support. The combined assault from the east and west coasts gave the campaign an 'All-India' and 'national' quality which was not lost on their opponents. In Calcutta, the *Amrita Bazar Patrika* advocated the orthodox view on such issues as well as the nationalist cause, and 'the example of the *Patrika* first awakened in Tilak awareness of the possibilities of harnessing religious sentiment to political causes'.[8] In 1896, Tilak utilized the name and revitalized tradition of Shivaji, the seventeenth-century Maratha leader, to reach a mass audience through their religion and history. Much of Shivaji's fame rested on his courageous attacks on the Mughal Empire, and Tilak's two papers, *Kesari* and *Mahratta* advocated a reading of the past that attracted a large constituency among the Hindus of Maharashtra, although many Muslims were offended. The Shivaji symbol also attracted a 'national' audience. Within six years of the great king's reappearance in Poona and Bombay, Bengalis on the other side of the sub-continent were celebrating Shivaji festivals in honour of an 'Indian nation builder', despite his regional base and his bad reputation in Bengali history.

Hindu–Muslim relations were a subject that produced emotional and combative viewpoint and publication before Tilak's time, but his stature as a nationalist leader and the influence of his papers extended and politicized the debate. In 1911, Mohammed Ali's advocacy of Pan Islamic identity in *Comrade* would exacerbate the situation and add to the confusion. While urban-based English-language papers tended to be more restrained than the vernacular press in this regard, they set examples and suggested themes that often became violent and dangerous in translation. The British did not create these divisions, but where possible, they took advantage of them – often enhancing and entrenching in the process.

The possible uses of the past for the contemporary campaign were myriad since so much of it was still part of everyone's daily life; and the publicist delved selectively to find a symbolic life or event that could, with

---

[8] Natarajan, *The Press in India*, p. 135.

some writer's licence, be inducted into the movement. The editor of the influential Calcutta monthlies, *Prabasi* and *Modern Review*, Ramananda Chatterjee, chose his personal hero, Ram Mohan Roy, the founder of the Brahmo Samaj and the symbol of the positive and reformist approach to the presence of the British. David Kopf has described Chatterjee's adeptness in endowing Roy with those qualities he most appreciated in a national leader: a social reformer who emphasized the need for internal regeneration, a political and economic reformer, i.e., a nation builder and therefore a champion of Indian freedom.[9] Chatterjee's choice and views did not please the extremists in the first decade of the twentieth century when Calcutta in particular was noted for its terrorist activity and violent press, but it remained a potent message sent out in book form and reiterated continually for a generation in the pages of his journals.

In the decade preceding World War One, the Government of India perceived both danger and opportunity in a series of disturbances largely initiated in response to Lord Curzon's partition of Bengal, but reflecting as well divisions and malaise in the nationalist movement. Terrorist action in Bengal, peasant unrest in the Punjab, concern about disaffection in the army and an increasingly extreme voice in sections of the press produced the now-standard array of ordinance and legislation deemed necessary to defend the Raj. And the split within the Congress in 1907, which left the moderate leaders in temporary control attracted new adherents within the Government to a policy of reform that would rally support for their constitutional position and keep the extremists on the defensive. For both purposes a constrained press was considered essential and the Newspapers (Incitement to Offences) Act 1908, and in 1910, a Press Act shifted once again the context back to the Adam Regulations.

By 1914, virtually all of the major themes that reflected the intermingling of press and political history in India were evident. While the Indian-owned press was still weak, its potential significance was recognized. During the war, an elaborate information and publicity organization was established for the first time, and in addition to the activities of officials, it attracted the cooperation and collaboration of influential Anglo-Indian and Indian newspapermen. The honeymoon did not last very long after the shooting stopped, but the usefulness of such an organization and the continuing need for it after the war was apparent. Imperialism and nationalism in India confronted each other on a range of battle fields. The daily newspaper had become both one of the protagon-

[9] David Kopf, 'Rammohun Roy and the Bengal Renaissance: An Historiographical Essay', in V. C. Joshi, ed., *Rammohun Roy and the Process of Modernization in India*, Delhi: Vikas Publishing House, PVT Ltd, 1975.

ists and for most people, the primary source of information about the battle itself.

The endgame struggle for unity: 1918–1947

The context of advocacy and defence was remarkably different at the end of the war. The familiar world that had been dominated by European-centred empires and European-centred perspective about order and international relations remained largely in place, but increasingly defensive and susceptible to internal and external challenge. The leaders of the Russian Revolution committed themselves to the immediate export of their victory and adopted particular policies to deal with nationalist struggles in the colonial world. Lenin's chief adviser in this regard was M. N. Roy, a Bengali revolutionary who had left India like many others and who rejected anti-revolutionary accommodation made by the Congress leadership. Roy symbolized for the British the red menace that was the latest incarnation of Russian threat to their empire. An anti-communist theme became a permanent element in official propaganda campaigns against radicals and the Congress left. In addition, the final collapse and disposition of the remnants of the Ottoman Empire engaged the British in a confrontation with Pan Islamic viewpoint. In its Indian setting, the Khilafat Movement mobilized substantial Muslim support for the restoration of the Turkish Khilafa as the titular head of world Islam, and for Congress-sponsored confrontation with the British. Although there had been a rapprochement between the Muslim League and the Congress during the war, this new evidence of unified action was considered particularly dangerous by the Government. It also made an impact on some supporters of the Congress who were concerned about the introduction of a sectarian issue, particularly a Muslim issue, onto the agenda of the movement. In the far west, the new presence of the United States as a power able to influence world events turned the attention of nationalist leaders to the task of attracting American opinion to their cause. Officials in Britain and India recognized the need to respond to the new challenge and engage in the competitive dialogue on a new stage.

The call to defend the empire in 1914, had attracted a loyal response from politicians and the Indian army, but the defeat of the enemy released the leaders from their vows and the return of a large number of soldiers to a homeland destabilized by post-war political and economic malaise added to the potential for renewed trouble. In the Punjab, the dangerous tension was resolved in violent confrontation. On 19 April 1919, the slaughter of hundreds of unarmed civilians who had gathered for a public meeting at Jallianwalla Bagh in Amritsar was the result of an individual decision by a British officer made in misguided defence of the Raj. But the Government's success in suppressing information regarding this event for almost eight months made it an accomplice in the 'Punjab Wrong', which remained a rallying cry for nationalist demands for justice for much of the twenties. The Amritsar press gag both reflected the Government's increasing respect for the power of newsprint, and provided a lesson about the dangers in its misuse.

Financial constraint had always been a hallmark of British colonial administration, but the exigencies of the post-war British economy made 'retrenchment' the new catchword of choice for finance officials, and left little margin for creative response to a continuing and enhanced resistance. Throughout the war, those who remained outside the cooperative and loyal consensus that included most mainstream nationalist leaders were controlled by the omnibus Defence of India Act which allowed the Government virtually unrestrained use of executive authority. In response to the disturbances in north India and general concern about the renewed nationalist challenge, a substantial portion of these wartime powers were included in new legislation, the Rowlatt Acts. In addition to the 'Punjab Wrong' and the 'Khilafat Wrong', Rowlatt was added to the list of Government repressive actions against which the Congress would launch its first post-war campaign. On the other side of the scales, the Government met its pre-war commitment to major constitutional advance at the end of hostilities with the Government of India Act of 1919.[10] It provided for a substantial increase in Indian participation in Government. On the provincial level a diarchy system allocated certain portfolios to Indian ministers who would be responsible to an elected Indian majority in the legislatures. The changes were significant but far less than anticipated and in the context of the other sources of confrontation, 'the Reforms' too became an issue in the renewed nationalist debate.

---

[10] The 1919 Government of India Act marked a radical change in the pattern of Indian constitutional reform. The old arrangement established a quasi-parliamentary relationship between an irremovable executive and a legislature which was meant to represent an Indian opposition. The provision of separate electorates for Muslims and special representation arrangements for various interests created a forum for political debate in which members of the executive participated, but which they were free to ignore. In 1917, the Secretary of State for India, Edwin Montagu, declared that the new reforms would incorporate responsible Government as the context for constitutional relations in the future. When the reforms were finally legislated in the 1919 Act, however, the constraints on responsible Government that had been retained and the complexity of the new arrangements in the provinces produced disappointment and eventually strong opposition. Provincial executives were divided into two parts, a British part that remained irremovable, and an Indian part that was responsible to the legislature. The Act was a significant but flawed advance in power-sharing arrangements.

The Congress response to all of these challenges was profoundly influenced by the rise of a new group of leaders in the early twenties. The pre-war nationalist leadership had virtually disappeared by 1918, and the succession was marked by a sharp break with the past rather than a smooth transition. Both G. K. Gokhale and Pherozeshah Mehta died in 1915. Other pre-war moderate leaders still survived and their heirs would continue to play a role in national politics. But that role would be largely marginalized by the emergence of a new group of Congress policy makers and a more radical definition of moderation. In 1920, Tilak died and with him an older 'extremism' that in hindsight doubtless seemed quite tame to Raj officials.[11] In their place, M. K. Gandhi became the dominant leader in the Congress and his Non-cooperation programme fundamentally altered the context of political debate. In addition to his rejection of most forms of cooperative contact with the British regime, Gandhi reorganized the Congress, both expanding the opportunity for participation in a broadened popular base and tightening control at the top in a centralized high command. In this revitalized form, the Congress sought to portray itself as a 'parallel Government' and its leaders attracted new respect and attention from Government and a growing number of loyal supporters. Newsworthy events and personalities, once the monopoly of government, were increasingly the products of another political centre with a legitimacy and life of its own.

An important aspect of the new international status of men like Gandhi and eventually Nehru was the availability of new communications technology to those accustomed in the past to reading only other people's messages. The British were reluctant to share control, but they had little choice. Cable and wire services, air mail, new wealth from professions and more travel, massive funds raised to support the nationalist campaign, an increasing and sympathetic audience in Europe and North America – all tended to expand the range and purpose of users. Everard Cotes described his thirty-year career in India as a newspaperman and Reuters representative in a 1923 *Asiatic Review* article. He noted that the Anglo-Indian and Indian press had always been 'poles apart', but now they were served by the same news agencies.[12] Sir Edward Buck, reflecting on these changes in his reminiscences of an Indian Reuters career, recalled covering early Legislative Assembly meetings in the Viceroy's lodge in Simla. In 1905, only a room for sixteen was required and the press showed little interest.

[11] In the last years of his life, Tilak's 'extremism' had given way to more moderate extra-constitutional activities such as his patronage of the home rule movement. He also accepted the possible benefits of 'responsive cooperation', i.e., meeting the British halfway in the moves and counter-moves stimulated by the nationalist struggle.

[12] Everard Cotes, 'The Newspaper Press of India', *Asiatic Review*, n.s., 19 July 1923, 424.

By 1925, however, the legislators and an increasing press gallery had moved to a new wing, having settled briefly in the billiard room and dining room on the way.[13]

The emergence of Indians as personalities of note outside India clearly enhanced their importance among Anglo-Indian and India Office officials. The historian, Edward Thompson, suggested in 1932, that the British might profit from a rewriting and rereading of Indian history in which the activities and achievements of an earlier generation of Indian leaders could be studied.[14] That revisionist challenge was left to a future generation of scholars, but the role of the press and news services in carrying current Indian reputations abroad was clear and the Government accepted the need to respond to the challenge. The change in attitude was slow, but practical considerations determined the course. Within the Government of India there was increasing emphasis on image and concern about its ability to hold on to its distinctive role and place which had depended for so long on artful imagery. The struggle took place, however, on the middleground of accommodation and collaboration, for it was obvious that any defence founded on some absolute definition of unique role was an extreme position that could no longer be defended. Nationalist leaders were generally too engaged with their own imagery, their own role and place within the movement, to take notice of the internal traumas of the Raj establishment.

Gandhi's success in winning Congress support in 1920 for Non-cooperation and his leadership of the movement was not uncontested. There was substantial opposition at the Congress session which gave him his mandate, and from 1920 until his assassination in 1948, a range of individuals and groups, both within and outside the Congress, resisted his programme and rejected the religious and philosophical idealism at its base. Even among those who revered him and followed his lead for decades, there were few Gandhians – few who were prepared to accept or even able to understand the idealistic and spiritual components of his political activism and technique for confrontation with the British regime. Gandhi's call for unity was informed by a range of sub-texts: Hindu–Muslim partnership, Hindu social and religious reform, an economic programme symbolized by the spinning wheel and implying rejection of modern technology, a shift in the control of the nationalist movement from the old anglicised elite power centres in Calcutta and Bombay to north India, Gujarat, and the south. Each of these initiatives antagonized one constituency while attracting others.

[13] Sir Edward Buck, *Simla Past and Present*, Bombay: The Times Press, 1925, p. 102.
[14] Professor Edward Thompson, address at Welfare of India League reported in the *Times of India*, 15 January 1932.

The struggles between Congress 'moderates' and 'extremists' before World War One were significant, but far more measured and constrained than post 1920 confrontation. The Reforms, however disappointing, had appeared to present the 'moderates' with their long-sought opportunity for participation and power – only to be denied by Gandhi and his rejectionist idealogy. The new vision and technique created divisions that seemed far more permanent to those who had always assumed that their liberal viewpoint would continue to dominate the mainstream of Congress activity.[15] The changed situation was reflected in S. N. Banerjee's lament for his generation of nationalist workers: 'Their work lies buried in the forgotten columns of contemporary newspapers.'[16] In their view, Non-cooperation had produced violence, loss of control and the possibility of the scrapping of the whole British institutional inheritance. A new vision of free India had apparently supplanted theirs, and they rejected it. Gandhi's leadership produced as well disappointment and committed opposition on the far left, where his non-violence doctrine and defence of Hindu tradition were attacked as an idiosyncratic form of bourgeois reaction.

The debate stimulated by Gandhi's 1920 victory continued unabated in 1922, when the movement had apparently collapsed. There is a striking paradox in the new Gandhian-controlled 'centre' with its emphasis on unity and loyalty to a common means, goal, and programme stimulating a range of individuals and groups to affirm opposing views and identities. The new 'centre' leaders – Gandhi and then Nehru – were able to subsume a range of divisions and differences in a grand vision of fundamental unity and traditional solidarity.[17] For most others, viewpoint rested firmly on a less spacious base – regional, religious, social; and the command context of the political culture of this 'centre' presented challenges and difficulties no less significant to some than the British-dominated autocracy. Competing visions of free India reflected these differences – some merely defensive, others more fully realized and secure in a confident reading of past position and future opportunity. The possibilities and reality of such pluralism in the context of the struggle against a united enemy provided nationalist leaders with their most significant challenge.

---

[15] The 'moderates' left the Congress in 1918 and established the National Liberal Federation.

[16] Sir Surendranath Banerjee, *A Nation in Making*, Calcutta: Oxford University Press, 1925, preface.

[17] The relationship between tradition and 'solidarity makers' has been imaginatively described by Dietmar Rothermund, 'Traditionalism and National Solidarity in India', in R. J. Moore, ed., *Tradition and Politics in South Asia*, New Delhi: Vikas Publishing House PVT Ltd, 1979.

The twenties and thirties were marked by phases of intense Non-cooperation and Civil Disobedience activity separated by longer periods of withdrawal and participation in the Raj system. Whether the result of a policy of strategic retreat, Government repression, or internal pressures within the Congress, both the actions and the messages of the national campaign were mixed and confusing. The Government made assumptions about Congress weakness and Congress collapse that were always premature and too optimistic. But competing nationalist groups and leaders made the same error. The extraordinary attraction of the share of power available to those who chose to 'work the Reforms' in a 'cooperative' relationship with Government had not disappeared in the euphoria of the Non-cooperation campaign; and the slow process of return to the old playing field began in 1923, with the establishment of the Swarajist Party within the Congress. Its leaders declared their intention to wreck the reforms from within, but it was a beginning that led to a return to full participation. For the Government message makers, the shifts in Congress status from outlaw to central role in the system created special problems – in part because many officials could not decide which image they preferred and how well it represented reality. In the late twenties and early thirties, Congress and the Government jockeyed for position with the weapons and opportunities available to each. The Government always had the repression option and used it to crush the Civil Disobedience Movement in 1932 as it had dealt with Non-cooperation a decade earlier. But it utilized the olive branch of further reform and reasoned discussion when the timing seemed right.

In 1928, the Government miscalculated and announced a new round of constitutional advance to be initiated by a Statutory Commission headed by Sir John Simon. It handed the Congress a much-needed issue when the Commission turned out to be all British. Its visit to India, as in the case of the 1921 visit of the Prince of Wales, provided revitalizing opportunities for demonstrations and attacks on the Government. In response, the Congress appointed its own 'commission', chaired by Motilal Nehru, and the subsequent Nehru Report was an attempt to produce a made-in-India constitution. Both initiatives stimulated renewed debate regarding the divided communities of India; and Lord Irwin's declaration in the following year that 'dominion status' was the Government's goal for India's future produced further divisions within the Congress between a new generation of 'constitutionalists' led by Motilal Nehru who accepted dominion status, and those that called for full independence led by his son, Jawaharlal Nehru. The mixed messages continued to be sent in the following years: Civil Disobedience and Gandhi's Salt March in 1930, followed by the Gandhi-Irwin Pact and Congress participation in the

London Round Table talks in 1931, followed by Civil Disobedience again in 1932.

Throughout these years of alternating confrontation and cooperation, the Government attempted to take advantage of its victories and constitutional initiatives by launching propaganda campaigns that sought to project its image as a progressive and enlightened participant in the design of India's future, and that of the Congress as a spent force – unrepresentative of the 'peoples' of India who would find a more secure place under the Raj's umbrella. But even in moments of assumed triumph, senior members of the Government of India's bureaucracy remained defensive and frustrated by constraints on what they considered to be appropriate action. The 1919 Reforms expanded the Indian power base at their expense, significantly reducing the options available to them in times of crisis. They were required as well to act in the 'spirit of the reforms' and to keep in mind the elected assembly majority which needed to be convinced and was capable of rejecting proposed legislation. Executive certification was always available, but it was considered to be a last option after all else had failed. In regard to the press, the 1910 Press Act had been repealed in 1922, in keeping with the new spirit and the Metcalfe liberal standard was restored. By 1926, however, officials had become restive and there were discussions on the need for press control in response to the increase in vitriolic communal publication, especially in the vernacular papers. But nothing was done until 1930, when the renewed Civil Disobedience campaign strengthened the argument of the advocates of control and a Press Ordinance was proclaimed, followed by a new Press Act in 1931. But this time the swing back to controls was not complete. It was no longer possible to reinstitute the Adam Regulations and a denial of any role for the courts in dealing with a case against a newspaper. Such extreme legislation would not pass in the Assembly and on this issue, the Viceroy and senior officers in the Government rejected the possibility of certification. The legislation that eventually passed was as much a victory for press freedom as a constraint on it. Although the law was used in response to political as well as communal challenge, it was clearly designed to deal with those who advocated and stimulated violence and not political criticism of the Government.

Pat Lovett has described the decline of the British-owned newspaper establishment after World War One and the growth in numbers and significance of Indian-owned papers. In Calcutta, both the *Indian Daily News* and the *Empire* had passed into Indian hands, and the *Englishman's* days were numbered. Only the *Statesman* would survive the challenges of the new era. In Bombay, there was only the *Times of India*, and in Madras, only the *Mail*. It was clear that part of the reason was the post-war slump which caused as dramatic a decline in advertising and circulation as it did in the affairs of many British-owned companies. More important perhaps was the constraint on the size of their readership pools. 'In politics', noted Lovett, 'the British daily papers have come to represent one stereotyped view, so that more than one in any centre is an expensive superfluity.'[18] The growth of the Indian press in major urban centres and throughout the sub-continent reflected increasing desire to propagate viewpoint and join in the internal nationalist debate as well as in the struggle against the British. 'No Indian paper has a moral right to exist', insisted C. Y. Chintamani, the editor of the *Leader*, 'which was not an advocate of Swaraj.'[19] But the nature of that advocacy depended as always, upon personal perspective and local situation. Bombay was politically advanced, as was Calcutta, and supported papers like the *Bombay Chronicle* and the *Amrita Bazar Patrika*. Madras, more conservative, depended upon the *Hindu* to represent nationalist opinion. In the Punjab, Lahore supported the Congress, but critically, and the *Tribune* represented that viewpoint. All of these papers were nationalist, but they had to survive in their localities. It is in this context that Anil Seal has described the All-India Movement as a 'ramshackle coalition' and the clashes between colonial politicians 'struggling at the more humdrum levels where the pickings lay'.[20] Chintamani remained comfortable in his Victorian liberalism long after it was out of fashion with so-called advanced political opinion. But he felt compelled as well to assert a defensive Hindu identity in the pages of the *Leader*, both a reflection of local United Provinces viewpoint and his own concerns about decisions at the nationalist 'centre' which he considered dangerous and could not influence. In Poona, Tilak's heir, N. C. Kelkar, mobilized the editorial pages of *Kesari* and *Mahratta* in defence of Maharashtra's interests which seemed to be threatened by northerners in control of Congress.

The rejection of violent revolution by choice and necessity required nationalist leaders to concentrate on symbolic confrontation which would convince their adversaries that they represented a mass following, and convince that presumed following that they were capable of achieving power. Through such symbolic events as Gandhi's Salt March and Jawaharlal Nehru's 1930 celebration of 'Independence Day', images of leadership and power were evoked among both Indians and the British. They also had to attract votes in an election, thereby demonstrating their right

---

[18] Pat Lovett, *Journalism in India*, Calcutta: The Banna Publishing Co., 1928.
[19] C. Y. Chintamani, presidential address, All-India Journalists' Conference reported in the *Calcutta Forward*, 19 August 1935. India Office Information Department clipping file, L/I/1/335, File 131/5.
[20] Anil Seal, 'Imperialism and Nationalism in India', *Modern Asian Studies*, 7, 3 (1973), 321.

to power on British terms. That the electorate remained quite small, and Gandhi's march, a personal experience for a largely regional group, was resolved in the hands of the publicist and the propagandist, who turned both events into great victories and reflections of power achieved. In news stories, photographs, speeches, and even the negative attention of the Government of India, a 'national' event was produced in which millions participated.

Daniel Boorstin has noted that the 'power to make a reportable event is the power to make experience'[21] and Gandhi was a public-relations phenomenon. He produced the ideas and starred in their production, becoming himself the image of India's weakness and her resilient strength. His fasts were influential in large measure because they were well-publicized public events. Their vivid description, reiterated in the media throughout India and around the world demanded a response. 'By print', Marshall McLuhan declared, 'a people sees itself for the first time.'[22] The problem for all the protagonists involved in this great struggle, was that there were so many of them. Those who read the stories or had them read to them, and looked at the press pictures were required to choose from an array of viewpoints, all now fixed in print.

In order to achieve their goal, Congress leaders had to send out messages that depended on the reiteration of symbolic language equating the Congress with 'unity' and 'freedom' and at the same time tarring its enemies with the reverse. It was a package deal and the removal of one component meant the loss of the other. The stereotypes of the British campaign had to be attacked and replaced with a group of their own. Walter Lippman has noted that the successful conduct of a propaganda campaign requires 'some barrier between the public and the event'.[23] India clearly had no end to barriers, and there was ample opportunity for the element of artifice that allowed a 'vivid image' to 'overshadow pale reality'.[24] This was true for both the Government and the nationalists. The Punjab Wrong, the Khilafat Wrong, the ceremonial entrances of Congress presidents for the annual meeting, the fasts – all were messages made significant by an effective communications network.[25] A totali-

[21] Daniel Boorstin, *The Image*, New York: Harper Colophon Books, 1964, p. 10.
[22] Marshall McLuhan, *The Gutenberg Galaxy*, Toronto: The New American Library of Canada, 1969, p. 260.
[23] Walter Lippman, *Public Opinion*, New York: Harcourt Brace and Company, 1922, p. 43.
[24] Boorstin, *Image*, p. 13.
[25] There is a substantial literature concerning the significance of a communications network for national and social development. See Lucian W. Pye, ed., *Communications and Political Development*, Princeton University Press, 1963; Alan Casty, *Mass Media and Mass Man*, New York: Holt Rinehart and Winston Inc., 1968; and Karl W. Deutsch, *The Nerves of Government*, New York: The Free Press, 1966.

tarian regime might have prevented nationalist leaders from achieving such notoriety and suppressed as well news reports of embarrassing events. But the British Government of India lacked that absolute power. It could and did control at the margin, but in the main the communications system was extraordinarily free to use propaganda on behalf of any mission – as long as the attacks were not associated with violence. There were periods of greater official sensitivity, but absolute control was not even a subject for dreams among the diehards in the Home Department. The press provided prominence and exaggeration, and over time, despite division and defeats, the Congress was able to build its case against the Government's self-image and its portrayal of the nationalist opposition. The messages reiterated daily in newspapers, brochures, speeches, and acts of defiance produced a steady erosion of the British sense of legitimacy – so dependent upon the apparent willingness of India to have them.

This book concerns the 'national' communications institutions involved in the Indian nationalist struggle and the individual politicians, officials, newspapermen, and propagandists who participated in this enterprise during the inter-war years. In this penultimate period of Britain's two centuries of control in India, the Indian nation was still in the making. And the empowering opportunities provided by constitutional reform and the growing awareness that the endgame in the nationalist–imperialist contest had at last begun, stimulated a parallel struggle for a place at the table. This was not a new phenomenon, but the shift from nationalist movement to party and Government was a perilous passage. I focus on this competition and the role of the press and news services as media for the distribution of particular messages. In this context the book seeks to make a contribution to the study of nationalism and the nation-building mandate that informed and constrained Asian and African freedom movements in the twentieth century.

At the end of World War One, both Government of India officials and Indian nationalist politicians recognized the need to reach more of the Indian people in order to support their claim to speak for all of them. The challenge for the nationalists and for the Government was not only the creation of the messages and the communications network that would reach these large and diverse audiences, but to elicit as well the desired response. The goal had to be described, but without stimulating inordinate enthusiasm to achieve it, for no leader was confident that his voice commanded sufficient support for a safe passage. For the nationalists, the proliferation of newspapers – both vernacular and English language, the attempt to start an Indian-controlled news agency, the reorganization of propaganda and information activities within the Congress, and the search for non-British opportunities for contact with the West – all reflected a new commitment to control both the medium and the message. For the Government of India, the establishment of a new central information bureaucracy and maintenance of an enhanced association with the Reuters news agency were defensive measures from the beginning, reflecting its desire to contain the struggle within familiar and controllable bounds. For some officials, the willingness to accept increasing opposition on platforms and in the press represented a 'repressive tolerance'[26] view of a regime with sufficient power to ignore the attack. Others, however, were aware of the narrowing opportunities for independent action, and convinced of the need to inform and defend.

While the Government's ability to control the situation was eroding at an accelerated pace, the Indian National Congress sought to displace it with an alternative 'centre' of power – defined in terms of popular loyalty rather than constitutional construct. Law in India was clearly on the side of the Government which made it. The Congress assertion was an act of will and imagination. But the determination of its leaders to control the struggle – as the British sought to control the defence, produced its own internal opposition and reiteration of the rejection of centralized ordering encountered by all who have acquired sub-continental authority. The Congress sought monopoly control over the All-India campaign by accommodating a range of interests and viewpoint under its spacious umbrella. But competing groups and individuals – both within and outside the Congress, retained their distinctive identities and voice. The campaign against the Raj was strengthened, but incompatible images of nation and nationality were retained.

The dominance of the Congress in the nationalist struggle against the British regime gave it inevitable control over the parallel nation-building effort required to support it. And the demand for absolute unity in the immediate struggle informed as well the image of a free Indian state envisioned by the leaders. Since there was disagreement at the 'centre', the evolution of this ideal was slow and laborious. Within the high command, the differences between the Gandhian and Nehruvian utopias reflected the degree of possibility and of confusion that still informed the debate. But a hierarchy of viewpoint was eventually established which divided the Congress-controlled 'centre' from a range of 'localities'. The former was endowed with a progressive, secular, and unifying identity; the latter attacked as reactionary, communalist, and divisive. That the 'centre' was also the home of communalists and reactionaries was apparent, but the

---

[26] Herbert Marcuse's description of a situation in which people are free to attack the system, but not really free since the regime's residual power is sufficient to ignore any rhetorical challenge.

image making was in the hands of very few practitioners. Leaders in the 'localities' had the advantage of more limited interests and more homo-geneous constituencies. They lived in the 'centre' of their own utopias, where the Congress version was just another 'locality'. It all depended on perspective.

Throughout the period of nationalist struggle, India remained a col-lectivity of distinctive entities – languages, cultures, traditions, histories; and all of these produced their own illusions, myths, and utopias that competed and accommodated depending upon opportunity and power and images of the nation in place or the nation in making propagated in print. The Congress sought to convince Muslims that their interests were secure in the new India, and assure Hindus that Hindu–Muslim co-operation was not a sell out of majority interest. It had to convince Indian business and its own right wing that its social platform was an essential response to massive poverty, and the Americans that Indians were capable of administering their own Government. Revolutionaries had to be informed about the complexities of nationalist struggle, and 'sub-nationalities' of every kind had to be convinced that unity was not a threat.

This book emphasizes the significance of the All-India stage and its elite players in the media who participated in the development of national perspective. Benedict Anderson has noted the role of the English lan-guage in India in building 'particular solidarities' and that of the news-paper in 'representing the kind of imagined community that is the nation'.[27] In significant measure, the ideal of an All-India nation state that emerged out of the Indian nationalist struggle was imagined in English print. There were a variety of reasons to publish in English. It was the 'national' language, the only medium that reached beyond regional borders – especially those that separated the north and the south. It was also technically beneficial to publish in English since printing and the telegraph and wire services were more easily used. Important advertisers preferred English papers as their products were bought by people who read them. English was the officially subsidized language, making it far more difficult to run a paper in a professional competitive manner in a vernacular language.[28] Gandhi was reluctant to use English in his journal-ism, but recognized its necessity, in particular in regard to contact with the south.[29] He was also aware of the unique significance of the press both

[27] Benedict Anderson, *Imagined Communities: Reflections on the Origins and Spread of Nationalism*, London: Verso, 1983, pp. 30, 122.
[28] J. N. Sahni, interview, December 1970. See also S. N. Banerjee, *A Nation in Making*, Calcutta: Oxford University Press, 1925, p. 171.
[29] Natarajan, *The Press in India*, p. 194.

in practical terms as a means to communicate and in ideological terms as an institution with its own freedom identity. But Gandhi was not a newspaperman, although he edited or wrote for a newspaper throughout his public life. He was a user of the press and he clearly separated himself from those who considered themselves to be professionals, and the survival and improvement of their papers to be a priority. In 1919, in response to official pressure on an increasingly aggressive press, Gandhi suggested the use of handwritten or cyclostyled unregistered news-sheets that would transmit 'pure ideas in a concise manner'. But the editors and owners of the major nationalist press sought to protect their interests as business-men and professionals, insisting that they served the country at the same time.[30] A parallel theme here is the significance of this professional identity for the style and content of the national debate.

The emphasis on English-language abilities tended to limit the talent available in many regions and 'nationalize' the search for competent senior staff. T. B. Sapru noted that nine-tenths of the editors in northern India were 'semi-literate', and major papers like the *Leader*, *Tribune*, and the *National Herald* sought talent in Bengal and the south. In its short life, the *Independent*, which was meant to be the advanced nationalist voice of the United Provinces, was largely staffed with southerners. There were a handful of professionals moving about the country ready to serve the handful of papers that seemed appropriate to their talent and interests and would allow them to make a living. Of these, Pothan Joseph was the most celebrated. He was always in demand and he travelled from one paper to the next, accepting an appointment without political or ideo-logical consideration. Ramananda Chatterjee attempted to turn this phenomenon into a nation-building programme by institutionalizing a 'wander-jahre' for young journalists who would work in dailies in various provinces. 'Such All-India experience would stimulate our love for India as a whole', he suggested,'broaden our outlook and cure us of our provincial narrowness and angularities to a considerable extent.'[31] He failed to interest others in his scheme, but the process went on without organization.

While the circulation of these 'national' newspapers and news agencies was not large, their readership included opinion and decision makers in the nationalist movement and in the Government. In addition much of the material reappeared in some form in the vernaculars and in the

---

[30] S. N. Bhattacharyya, *Mahatma Gandhi: The Journalist*, London: Asia Publishing House, 1965, p. 161.

[31] Ramananda Chatterjee, *Modern Review*, January 1928, reproduced in *The Modern Review*, Ramananda Birth Centenary Number, June 1965, p. 33.

traditional idiom which allowed otherwise alien ideas to attract a broader response.[32] The significance of the massive flow of local, often sectarian literature is clear, but referred to here only as it touches more broad-based All-India activity. This was a political press and nationalist politics was the life's blood of virtually all Indian newspapers. But these particular papers shared as well a perception of themselves as distinctive national institutions. They identified with each other and regularly carried on a dialogue in the form of quotation from each other's editorials. 'What does India think?' in the *Indian Daily Mail* would present a range of such references on a particular topic of political significance, giving the paper an All-India representative quality.[33] They also warred with each other, competing for customers as well as adherents to the viewpoint they represented.

For the *Amrita Bazar Patrika*, the *Bengalee* was as much a legitimate target as the Government of India. In Bombay, the *Chronicle* and the *Times of India* often stated their positions by attacking the other's views. Although the *Times* was rich and shared the power of its Anglo-Indian patrons, when the *Chronicle* set its price at one anna, the *Times* felt compelled to reduce its single issue price from four annas in order to preserve its share of the market. After the 1937 elections, the new Congress Government in the United Provinces was denied the support of both of the major Indian-owned papers, the *Pioneer* and the *Leader*. It was necessary for Jawaharlal Nehru to patronize the establishment of a new paper, the *National Herald*, as a guarantee that the mainstream Congress view would have a substantial 'voice' in the provinces.

Membership in this elite fraternity was meant to be reflected in a particular orientation and style that distinguished them from the ordinary local press. J. N. Sahni, who served as editor of the *Hindustan Times*, noted that English tended to work in favour of conservatism and constraint.[34] J. Natarajan, an historian of the press, described the founding of Sachchidananda Sinha's *Searchlight* in 1918, as 'the beginning of national as opposed to sectarian journalism in Behar'.[35] It was in the same

[32] There are many examples of the well-travelled statement moving from written to oral and English to vernacular media. M. M. Malaviya's indictment of the Raj, 'Repression in India', was written in English exclusively for the legal press. It was found, however, in Hindi publications confiscated by the United Provinces Government. G. Pandey, 'Mobilization in a Mass Movement: Congress "Propaganda" in the United Provinces (India) 1930–1934', *Modern Asian Studies*, 9, 2 (1975), 219.

[33] The publication of a range of editorial viewpoint from papers across the sub-continent was common practice in most 'national' papers. It may have been a practice adopted from the major London press which regularly published a selection of views from newspapers in the country.

[34] J. N. Sahni, interview.

[35] Natarajan, *The Press in India*, p. 135.

context that Motilal Nehru noted the difference in the United Provinces between the 'national' and the 'gutter press'.[36] Those papers that were part of this 'national' group had significant, generally dominant reputations in their localities while reaching out to an All-India constituency. From this base, they were able to add the weight of their perceived prestige and influence to some national debate or consensus, subsuming their small but elite constituency in a broad national gathering of similar types.

On 26 November 1932, C. Y. Chintamani gave the convocation address at the University of Lucknow. Paraphrasing Gokhale, he urged the graduates to act as if power had been transferred and the responsibility was already theirs.[37] Another imaginative leap of faith is apparent in the perverse British understanding of the liberal nature of their administration reflected in their desire to rely on 'ordinary' law. Chintamani represented many others in his implicit argument for the possibility of an ordinary life as if the British had already left; while the British argued for an ordinary life as if they were not alien rulers. Both sought relief from the burdens of reality by imagining something better, in Spengler's phrase, by the 'actualizing of possible culture'.[38] The 'national' press encouraged this perspective by the daily reiteration in print – over generations – of stories about Indians and the British acting with and against each other. In the pages of nationalist and Anglo-Indian papers, stories about insurrection, jailed leaders and official repression shared space with descriptions of vice-regal visits, cricket matches, and news from England. An event like Gandhi's Dandi March was magnified by its replication in the press – but it was diminished as well by its association in print with more ordinary events. In some measure the struggle itself became normalized and 'ordinary', providing most of its leading participants a place where they could be 'at home'.

In 1881, Vishnu Krishna Chiplunkar, a Maharashtrian writer and journalist whose work inspired Tilak, wrote an essay in Marathi on the 'The State of our Country'. 'Crushed by English poetry', he declared, 'our freedom has been destroyed ... under their laws we have become bankrupt.' But in the same work, he also celebrated the boon of new ideas and liberal thinking. 'How lucky we are', he noted, 'that this vast body of knowledge from the West has just walked over into our land on its own.'[39]

[36] Motilal Nehru to editor of the *Pioneer*, 22 June 1929, Motilal Nehru Papers, P-6.
[37] C. Y. Chintamani, Convocation address, Lucknow University, 26 November 1932.
[38] Oswald Spengler, *The Decline of the West*, New York: Alfred Knopf, 1955, p. 55. See also Gabriel Marcel, *Men Against Humanity*, London: The Hawill Press Ltd, 1952, Chapter 1.
[39] Sudhir Chandra, *The Oppressive Present: Literature and Social Consciousness in Colonial India*, Delhi: Oxford University Press, 1992, pp. 18–19.

In Chiplunkar's life, and that of all these participants in this extra-ordinary exchange there was always ambiguity and tension, and, as Sudhir Chandra has noted, 'a determined exploitation of the little space available for action'.[40]

[40] *Ibid.*, p. 17.

1   The Government of India: images and messages in the defence of authority

The statue of John Lawrence which stood near the Lahore High Court at the Mall–Macleod Road crossing was not intended to be there. It had been commissioned in 1880 by friends of the late Governor-General and hero of the Mutiny to stand in London's Waterloo Place as a continuing reminder to future generations of Englishmen of the grandeur and achievements of their imperial heritage. But neither the patrons nor the sculptor liked the completed work when it was set in its place of honour in 1882; and a second statue was duly commissioned, completed, and erected on the same spot in 1884. The discarded original was stored away until 1887, when the sculptor, Sir Edgar Boehm, offered it to the city of Lahore. For all concerned, it seemed no less appropriate that Punjabis too, in generations to come, would pass by and remember.[1]

Over time when the memory of John Lawrence was recalled it seemed sufficiently respectful to satisfy those who had paid twice for his effigy; and in any case, the statue itself became familiar enough to Lahoris to be ignored by all but the most ardent anglophile or antiquarian. In 1920, however, Lawrence's statue, if not Lawrence himself, became the centre of a new confrontation between Britain and India. After years of inattention, someone took another look at its heroic bearing, its steady determined gaze, and in particular at the inscription carved into its pedestal, and was offended. This eight-and-a-half foot bronze giant held a sword in one hand and a pen in the other, and declaimed from its base: 'Will you be governed by the pen or the sword?'

This may well have been the only choice available to those who presumed to resist British power in the mid-nineteenth century; but in 1920 it was clear that if there were a brief message which Britain might choose to define her Indian mission, it certainly was not this. It was

[1] India Office note, 1923, IO L/P & J/6/1776. I am indebted to Mr A. Douglas Small, former Canadian Ambassador to Pakistan who sought out the present location of the statue during a visit to Lahore in 1980. He could not find it, but quoted a reference in Masud-ul-Hasan's *Guide* which noted that the statue had been removed to the Lahore Fort on 25 August 1951.

difficult, however, to find an acceptable substitute and to make the change without damage to the prestige of Government. A request by the Lahore Municipal Committee to remove the inscription, and a subsequent request in the following year to remove the statue marked the beginning of a six-year-battle, an apt reflection of the larger nationalist struggle in which symbol, message, and ceremony so often described and defined the anomalous constraint in purpose and method shared by most of the combatants.

While the initial request was virtually ignored by the Punjab Government Gandhi's arrival in the city in November 1921 turned an irritating problem into a major political issue. In a speech describing the new context of opposition to the British regime, he suggested that the removal of the Lawrence statue would be a good cause for offering Civil Disobedience. It was clear to both provincial and central Government officials that the concern about the inscription was shared by loyal and politically moderate Indians, and discussions took place at every level of administrative responsibility between Lahore and London. Within the India Office, the history of the statue's Indian journey was reviewed for Sir Arthur Hirtzel, emphasizing that the inscription was 'never meant to be seen in India'. Not only was the message not meant for India, it had never been sent by John Lawrence. The question and the challenge had in fact been authored in 1848, by a deputy commissioner of Hoshiarpur, R. N. Cust, in the campaign to pacify the Kangra Hill chiefs.[2]

Historical accuracy was, however, not the issue, nor even the symbolic assertion of British imperial power. Not far from Lawrence's statue, the late Queen-Empress sat passively and unchallenged on a great pedestal which appropriately dwarfed the declaiming Lawrence. But she sat in silent splendour. Had Lawrence's sword and pen been left to the imagination of passers-by, it is unlikely that those who sought to remove his successors would have found him either particularly offensive or useful in the struggle. It was the words – the presumption of all power made explicit and timeless. Boehm's error had been literally carved in stone, unresponsive to the new and evolving descriptions of a maturing relationship. What had once been accepted or ignored was now described by the editor of the *Bombay Chronicle* as 'humiliating to every Indian';[3] while Jawaharlal Nehru threatened to send volunteers from the United Provinces to deal with the statue.[4]

The Punjab Government satisfied itself that no disrespect to the memory of Lawrence was intended but refused to agree to the removal of the statue without a suitable replacement. During the years of confront-

[2] *Ibid.* India Office note, 1923.
[3] *Ibid.*
[4] *Ibid.*

ation, both the sword and pen were broken off, but the statue was repaired and a police guard provided to protect Lawrence from the depredations of overzealous satyagrahis (those who fought the British using M. K. Gandhi's non-violent, non-cooperation confrontational technique).[5] J. E. Ferrand produced a minute for his India Office colleagues noting his concern that the removal of the statue would itself be a wrong message, and encourage mischief-makers to cast around for some other statue or monument to which they might object. He recognized the significance of the attempt to destroy the Holwell Monument in Calcutta's Dalhousie Square as another attack on viewpoint as well as power. It had been erected by Lord Curzon in memory of those who had died in the 'Black Hole' of Calcutta, and as well of the 'barbarian' prince who had perpetrated the crime.[6] The Secretary of State, Lord Olivier, had little patience with these concerns. He considered the statue to be 'ridiculous and undignified', and the inscription 'irritating' and 'a complete anachronism'. He had no difficulty accepting the change in the situation and the need for new symbols and messages to reflect the change. The choice offered, he insisted, 'is now between the bureaucratic Pen and the reformed Government of India Act'; and suggested that an 'effigy of that document might be substituted for the sword and the inscription altered accordingly'.[7]

But rejecting the sword was easier than explaining the symbol of the pen. Olivier's explanation which cast the bureaucracy in the role of the harsh anachronistic alternative was clearly unacceptable to the covenanted mandarins of the Indian and Punjab Governments. What did the pen represent, queried H. D. Craik in the Punjab Legislative Council, except the rule of law? He reminded his colleagues that Englishmen had feelings, and that this demand was an insult to one of their greatest heroes. The Viceroy informed Olivier that a resolution to remove the statue would likely pass, but that his Government opposed this solution on principle. A confrontation was avoided, however, by a timely and discreet conversation between Sir Malcolm Hailey and some Muslim Members of the Punjab Legislative Council. The resolution was defeated but the Government committed itself to replace the inscription as an 'act of grace'.[8] The demonstration of its ability and willingness to act alone, gracefully or not, was meant to be another message in addition to the new words that patient Lawrence would now be made to speak: 'With pen and sword I served you.' On 20 May 1926, the Government of India was able to inform the India Office that 'the change was effected unostentatiously and has aroused little comment'.[9]

[5] *Ibid.*
[6] *Ibid.*
[7] *Ibid.*
[8] *Ibid.*
[9] *Ibid.*

For J. W. Hose, the whole problem was the result of a misunderstanding by 'touchy Indians' who interpreted the inscription to mean 'You are cowards, and a pen is weapon enough against you.' This was clearly not what was intended, for on the contrary, Hose insisted, it was 'an offer of friendship rather than war'. It was obvious to others, however, if not to Hose and many of his colleagues, that Indians were neither confused nor particularly 'touchy' about the issue. Cust's message described a choice which reflected the reality of British power in his time, and their view of their role and mission. In 1920, these verities of the Raj, its present role, its future mission, and the power to sustain both were matters for debate both within and outside Government.[10] The need to administer and control the situation remained, but now with the added requirement to describe and represent Government action in its most positive context. For this last generation of 'guardians', messages and argument would have to carry a heavy burden.

The Central Bureau of Information and the need to communicate

Publicity boards established throughout India during World War One reflected the Government's perception of the need for popular support; and the positive response of nationalist leaders and the Indian press convinced many officials that public relations had to become a permanent part of their responsibilities. 'The Bureaucracy for the first time in all its history', noted Pat Lovett, the editor of *Capital*, 'went out of its way to propitiate this "great instrument of propagandism".'[11] The instrument was the press and clearly Government had no monopoly on its use. A priority for the immediate post-war years was the establishment of an information system that would allow it to compete with other users, particularly with the developing communications network of the nationalist movement. Although the Government was in a better position to build an effective organization by using the various levels of the administrative system and its specialized departments, it shared with the Congress the problems of geographical, communal, and language division, financial constraints, differences of opinion among the leadership regarding both the message and the means of delivering it, and an inability to control the primary instruments of communication: the press and the news services.

[10] N. G. Barrier has noted that 'uncertainty over motives and goals of colonial government, not structural problems, probably contributed the most troublesome element affecting British political response'. *Banned, Controversial Literature and Political Control in British India 1907–1947*, Columbia: University of Missouri Press, 1974, p. 12.
[11] Pat Lovett, *Journalism in India*, Calcutta: Banna Publishing Co., 1928 (1926 lecture), p. 39.

Government could and did produce a prodigious amount of information, but most of it was for administrative use only; and it was assumed that the new target audience rarely read official messages deliberately prepared for it. Although the Government retained broad powers to suppress news and newspapers in the Indian Press Act of 1910,[12] their use could not produce a good press for a particular viceregal speech or piece of legislation. There was a range of views within the civil service regarding the priority that should be given to publicity and propaganda; but there was virtual concensus that it was no longer useful to assume as Lord Curzon had done: 'the right to decide when public opinion was an expression of views based on sober reasoning and supported by obvious justice, and when it was a mere frothy ebullition of irrational sentiment'.[13] Public opinion, whatever its perceived quality, had become important to the Government of India and it was determined to influence it. During the war, professional newspapermen like Stanley Reed, the editor of the *Times of India*, temporarily joined the Government to organize and preside over publicity operations.[14] In 1919, confronted by a range of post-war problems, political unrest, and the introduction of constitutional reforms, the Government of India established the Central Bureau of Information (CBI) within the Home Department.[15]

The immediate concern was the widespread opposition to the Rowlatt Bills, founded in their view on a successful propaganda campaign which misrepresented both the nature and intent of the legislation. From the beginning of this venture into systematic communications, those officials most involved, especially in the Home Department, oscillated between the euphoric glow of a pressman's scoop and the frustration of seeing a competitor achieve another victory. They were convinced of the quality of their message and critical of their own ineptness in not recognizing earlier the need to share it widely, tell the 'true facts' and reap the rewards of understanding and support. The establishment of the CBI reflected broad-based 'recognition of the fact that the Government of India suffered from its attitude of silent aloofness'.[16] That they might lose the struggle by default was a continuing theme throughout the inter-war period. The Joint Select Committee considering the 1918 Government of

---

[12] For a detailed description of press legislation see G. K. Ray, *A Handbook of the Laws Relating to Press in India*, Calcutta: Eastern Law House, 1932.

[13] Lord Ronaldshay, *The Life of Curzon*, Vol. II, London: Ernest Benn Ltd, 1928, p. 328.

[14] Reed directed the work of the Central Publicity Bureau at Simla for six months during the war.

[15] The CBI was formally established in 1 June 1919.

[16] Memorandum on publicity work in India, 29 July 1920, with quotations from a Home Department circular letter to Provincial Governments, 18 February 1919, IO L/P & J/6/1581.

India Act noted with concern that the case of the Government of India was unknown to the masses of Indians while the opposition case was 'becoming every day more widely disseminated by means of the vernacular press'.[17] When the new regulations under the act were debated in the House of Lords, the communications issue came up again, and the chairman of the Joint Committee expressed his regret that the Government of India was not responding to the challenge. It seemed clear that opposition success had been due to inaction in mounting a counter-propaganda campaign. It was also clear that the need for such a campaign had never been greater.

I hear from authority which I cannot doubt that at no moment of our connection with India has there been a greater, a more malignant, and a more persistent system of calumnies and lies than exists at the present moment, flooding India against the intentions of the Indian Government and of His Majesty's Government and the whole British policy towards India. I am told on authority which I cannot doubt, that these calumnies and lies are being believed.[18]

A decade later, the Simon Commission's recommendations concerning another constitutional advance would include a reference to the same problem. The vast majority of Indians had been left ignorant 'of all but one side of the case'. The problem now appeared to be far more significant since the lack of a fair presentation of policy and facts was no longer confined to India. In the view of the commissioners, public opinion throughout the world was being misled and 'the plant of self-government cannot be expected to exhibit healthy growth in an atmosphere so poisoned by misrepresentation'. It was essential to find methods to 'spread truthful information' and achieve the widest publication of 'a reasonable account' of the activities of the various Governments of India.[19]

In the early years of the CBI, it had appeared well within the powers of Government to meet the challenge. Senior officers in the Home Department retained their confidence in a potentially receptive audience for messages that would be carefully constructed and delivered. 'I am convinced', the Deputy Home Secretary insisted, 'that the solid mass of opinion in this country ... does support Government in the preservation of law and order. The difficulty is to get opinion of that type to express

[17] Report of the Joint Select Committee, para. 14, quoted by the Earl of Selborne, chairman of the Joint Committee of Parliament concerned with the new regulations under the Government of India Act, House of Lords Debates, 30 November 1920. Enclosure with Montagu to Reading letter 12 May 1921, GOI (HomePol) 225/1921.

[18] The Earl of Selborne, 30 November 1920, *ibid.*

[19] Simon Commission Report, quoted in 1933 Home Department memorandum, GOI (HomePol) 39/9/33.

itself.'[20] The new central managers of the communications system had other concerns as well. It was clear to them that it was unsafe to leave to the provinces All-India issues and the dissemination of news to Europe and the rest of the world; but their support in participating in an integrated information network could not be assumed.[21] In 1919, most of the provinces retained their own publicity organizations developed during the war, but each a little different, reflecting the unique local situation or the preferences of provincial officials. The Punjab and United Provinces Governments had established official newspapers and intended to keep them despite the opposition of officials at the centre. Madras had wanted to establish such an organ, but opposition from local non-official opinion, especially the *Hindu* and the *Mail*, concerned by the prospect of subsidized competition, restrained the Government. There were differences concerning the use of civil servants or professional newspapermen for this work; and some provinces such as the Central Provinces and Assam thought there was no benefit in their developing any official organization.[22]

It was recognized in the first exchange of correspondence between the Central and Provincial Governments that merely sending news to Indian-owned papers would not resolve the problem. There was general agreement that Indian newpapermen had become dependent on 'sedition and falsehood' in order to sustain their presses, and official news would be twisted and distorted to serve their purposes. It had, therefore, become essential to develop the capacity to orchestrate, if not absolutely control, the reporting of newsworthy events. The Government had to anticipate unfair criticism, know what the public wanted and develop the skills required to present its position effectively. It had to use its contacts and its power deftly, however, always sensitive to the professional concerns of newspapermen whose cooperation was essential. Little time was spent considering the paradox of officials of an alien oligarchy concerning themselves with such issues as the 'independence of the press' and the 'spirit of enterprise which ought to be the life and soul of Journalism'. The ideal was left in place and their discussion concentrated on how to use the system to advantage.[23]

The first Director of the CBI was L. F. Rushbrook Williams, who now

---

[20] H. D. Craik to S. P. O'Donnell, Home Secretary, 23 December 1921, GOI (HomePol) 784/1922.
[21] Home Department memorandum on publicity work in India, 29 July 1920, p. 2, IO L/P & J/6/1581.
[22] *Ibid.*, pp. 3–5.
[23] Secretary, GOI Home Department to Local Governments and administrations, except Coorg, 18 February 1919, IO L/P & J/6/1581.

added these general responsibilities to the preparation of the annual 'Moral and Material Progress Report'.[24] It was a temporary appointment, reflecting the defensive context of the decision to establish the new office. The omnipresent Retrenchment Committee, with a mandate to scrutinize any request for new expenditure, threatened to destroy the Bureau's capacity to serve its mandate before its competence could be tested. The sanction for the CBI and its Director was limited to a three-year trial, and Williams was required to engage the enemy both within and outside the Central Government. His 'Retrenchment File' contained the arguments that had been used to establish his office, and continually updated statistics regarding the number of words, messages, articles, and statements it produced. Care was taken to note any income from the sale of Government publications and the extraordinary cost–benefit ratio which had been achieved.

The need for a publicity officer at the headquarters of the GOI rests on the following grounds:

a. Information on matters on which public opinion is much exercised can in most cases be given only by the Central Government.
b. Information as to the general administration of the country can only be diseminated to Europe and especially America and outside India from the Central Government.
c. Provincial Bureaus, which are now in existence in most of the major provinces, need some office at headquarters to which they can look for information and assistance in their work in view of the fact that policy in regard to political movements is an All-India one.

Since the Bureau was established its work has developed considerably and may now be classified under the following detailed heads:

A. Information work in India, England and United States.
a. Articles are written explaining GOI policy in language which the public understand: News telegrams are prepared and despatched in large numbers. (Articles to newspapers average 10 per week)
b. Articles are placed in the daily press embodying a point of view which, while unsuitable in a formal communiqué is essential for proper appreciation by the public of a question at issue. (Telegrams average 5 per week)
c. The attention of the press is directed to the importance of particular

---

[24] Williams began his Indian career in 1914, as an historian at Allahabad University. From the beginning he combined academic teaching and research with literary and publicity services for the Government.

official pronouncements: and 'campaigns' of information conducted. (Private letters to Editors average 6 per week)

d. Misleading statements are contradicted in the locality from which they emanate. (Contradictions etc. to Provincial Publicity Officers average 18 per week)

e. Photographs and cinema films are circulated in England and America as well as in India. Very heavy demands are now made by the press and public upon the Official Photographer. (Photographs to India Papers 12 per week)

f. Assistance is given to, and material placed at the disposal of, manifold varieties of enquiries, editors, public men, travellers, Missionaries, lecturers, public bodies. (Foreigners etc. assisted average 1 per week in hot weather, 3 per in cold)

g. Close touch is maintained with those Foreign Office organs which are concerned to see the British Empire is not silent when slandered. (Communications to America etc. every mail)

B. Publication Work.

a. The M & MPR under its revised form is prepared and issued – an all-the-year-round task. (Average yearly sale – 10,000 copies)

b. Pamphlets and brochures are written dealing with current questions and widely distributed through India, England and America. (Average 2 per week from Central Bureau. Information supplied to Provinces for leaflet work an average 25 times a week)

c. Official reports are prepared without additional expense to Government i.e. 'India's Parliament' vols. 1.2.3. Lord Chelmsford's Administration Report. (These include, in addition to those mentioned, the writing of volumes of speeches by distinguished personages for wide circulation)

d. Leaflets for universal distribution in the vernacular are prepared. (Average monthly circulation during the past year 250,000 per month)

C. Newspaper Work

a. Government Departments are assisted to keep in close touch with public opinion. (To every Department cuttings are sent 6 times per week)

b. Classified cuttings, English and vernacular are placed at their disposal. (Average number of cuttings circulated 1500 per week)

c. An elaborate Press Cutting Index, used by every Department of Government enables particular cuttings to be traced readily. (Cuttings clamped and indexed every year averages 50,000)

D. Liaison Work
a. Close touch is maintained with the Provincial Publicity organs, the British Library of Information New York: the Information Officer India Office. (Newspapers, pamphlets, articles despatched in every mailing abroad)
b. All-India and Imperial matters are thus presented so far as possible in their right perspective, and their importance consistently stressed. (Communications to *every* province average individually 6 per week: total weekly communications to Provincial organs being 42)[25]

In addition to the question of paying for these activities, a more fundamental issue informed the exchanges between India and London. The duties of the CBI fell into two major categories: information work and propaganda; but Edwin Montagu, the Secretary of State, thought the latter activity was inappropriate for the British Government.[26] Williams emphasized that the need for propaganda work was temporary, and 'due to the special conditions which exist and will continue to exist in India for some time'; but principles and practicalities seemed to collide more pointedly when the press was involved.[27] Montagu insisted on the need for 'a clear definition of the legitimate functions of a government publicity department'. He recognized that Indian conditions were different from the situation in Western countries where party Government and opportunities to support official policy marked the essence of the political system. He also recognized the significance of extremist nationalist propaganda and the need to respond; but, he argued, such statements should 'never take the form of anonymous publications of a partisan character'. The Government of India should present a 'line of argument' to newspaper correspondents, 'but actual propaganda of a secret or anonymous nature should be studiously avoided'.[28]

The Members of Lord Reading's Council shared Montagu's principles but were generally bemused by the apparent *naïveté* and impracticality of their application in British India. W. H. Hailey was more cynical than most but his colleagues agreed with his proposed solution to the impasse.

I should advise that as a matter of tactics the despatch be rewritten; that we describe our present practice as 'supplying the press with material it can utilize in whole or in part as desired'; that we disclaim any intention of 'interfering with the

---

[25] Retrenchment File, Office of the Director, CBI, 12 July 1922, GOI (HomePol) 857/1922.
[26] India Office despatch, 12 May 1921, cited in *ibid.*
[27] *Ibid.*
[28] Montagu to Reading, 12 May 1921, GOI (HomePol) 225/1921.

independence or duties of the press'; that we are a little more guarded about the work of our private correspondents; and so forth. I believe that if this were done honour would be satisfied; and that we should not be interfered with in our present nefarious practices. The extent of our operations is probably perfectly well known to the India Office; but they would not look very well if openly avowed.[29]

Montagu responded cooperatively with a suspension of the paragraph in his despatch dealing with publicity,[30] and the Government of India's formal response[31] made the case as Hailey had suggested. But the presumed taint of any Government publication and, therefore, its diminished usefulness remained an issue for debate throughout this period. Virtually any publicity idea was assumed to require some external agent to attract the interest and resolve the concerns of officials. The Finance Member, Sir George Shuster, was convinced of the usefulness of a monthly magazine to give accurate economic data concerning the condition of the country. He assumed, however, that a Government publication would be suspect, and suggested to Bombay business man Purshotamdas Thakurdas that the Imperial Bank be the publisher.[32] But Thakurdas, although welcoming the suggestion, thought that the Bank was too close to Government to carry weight and 'inspire the same confidence in the Indian public as a similar magazine issued by a non-official agency'. He suggested that the Federation of Indian Chambers of Commerce and the Associated British Chambers do it jointly.[33] In a subsequent exchange with the industrialist G. D. Birla, however, it was agreed that the association with British Chambers would also be a problem and true public confidence would result only if the Indian Chambers produced their own publication.[34]

It seemed impossible to get far enough away from Government to meet such exacting criteria, and generally the contaminated product had to be used to the best advantage available. When Sir N. N. Sircar, the Law Member of Council, gave a particularly useful speech on the subject 'Congress and Terrorism', it was agreed to supply it to Provincial Governments for publicity purposes. It was assumed, however, that printing the speech in the Government press would reduce its value; and publication in the British-owned *Statesman* or *Times of India* would also

[29] H. D. Craik, Secretary, Home Department intra-department memorandum re. Montagu despatch of 12 May 1921, *ibid.*

[30] Secretary of State to Viceroy (telegram), 16 August 1921, *ibid.*

[31] Governor-General in Council to Secretary of State, despatch 6 November, 29 December 1921, *ibid.*

[32] Sir George Schuster to Pushotamdas Thakurdas, 5 August 1929, Thakurdas Papers, 42 (V).

[33] Thakurdas to Schuster, 10 August 1929, *ibid.*

[34] G. D. Birla to P. Thakurdas, 20 August 1929, *ibid.*

produce suspicion and in any case reach a small readership. The solution was a private press willing to do business with Government in return for a guarantee to purchase sufficient copies to ensure a profit, and aid with distribution as well. The Hindu Press in Calcutta did the job, and Barendra Kumar Ghose, Aurobindo's brother and 'ex-terrorist', agreed to write the preface. It was clearly the best send-off the Government of India could provide: 'If England conquered India she gave her a new outlook, a rebirth so to say, out of six centuries of creeping apathy and death. She was the chosen instrument of God for a new awakening.' Terrorism, Ghose concluded, was a 'blind ally' that would 'set us back'.[35] The Government agreed and bought half the publication run and arranged for an Urdu-language version published by the Tej Press. Provincial Governments joined in supporting the venture and Bengali and Hindi versions were produced.[36]

The questions of funding and the new powers of non-official members of the Legislative Assembly were closely linked. The budget of the CBI, including the salary of the Director, was now 'votable' and the whole enterprise could be lost if the Government could not make its case in the first instance to the elected members. Although the Viceroy retained the power to certify any legislation that failed to receive sufficient support, there was considerable concern about 'the spirit of the Government of India Act' and reluctance to use extraordinary authority. It was clear to the Home Member, W. H. Vincent, that the Government would require assistance in the conduct of publicity work and the protection of the CBI expenditure in the budget. The Madras Government had appointed a broadly representative committee to advise on issues and responses and, through the participation of unofficial Members of the Legislative Council, help secure the necessary funding. Vincent established a similar central Publicity Advisory Committee, agreeing with the Home Secretary that without it, 'there is no prospect of our obtaining funds next year.'[37]

The jeopardy had been made explicit on 12 March 1921, when a motion in the Punjab Legislative Council to omit from the budget Rs 119,000 for the provincial Publicity Board was passed by a vote of 46

[35] M. G. Hallett to S. N. Ray, Additional Secretary, Bengal Government, reprinting at the Hindu Press, Calcutta, of Sir N. N. Sircar's speech, 'Congress and Terrorism', given in the Legislative Assembly, 29 March 1935. Ray to Hallett, 6 April 1935, ibid.

[36] Ibid. The United Provinces Publicity Department brought out a vernacular translation of Sir Sankaran Nair's book, Gandhi and Anarchy, and copies were sent to all Local Governments. It was subsequently withdrawn when Sir Michael O'Dwyer sued Nair for libel regarding references to O'Dwyer in a chapter titled 'The Punjab Atrocities'. S. P. O'Donnell to A. W. Botham, Chief Secretary, Assam Government, 18 August 1922, GOI (HomePol) 585/III/1922.

[37] S. P. O'Donnell note, 28 March 1921, GOI (HomePol) 110/1923.

to 19.[38] In a subsequent debate in the United Provinces Legislative Council, a proposal to establish a standing publicity committee was defeated, the majority considering the activity a waste of public funds since no one appeared to read the leaflets produced by the Publicity Department.[39] Undaunted, Williams assumed there would be difficulties for some time, but was confident that Indian ministers and executive councillors would eventually agree 'that a powerful weapon lies at their command'.[40] As in the case of the Punjab and United Provinces Councils, Williams' budget was attacked in the Central Assembly but he managed to escape unscathed.[41]

The greater danger in 1922, came from within the Government, reflecting concerns that were similar to those expressed by Assembly critics: the cost and the possibility of misrepresentation. On 5 May, representatives of the major Departments met at Simla to consider their relationship with the CBI. It was agreed to cooperate in centralizing some communications with the press and news services, but the Finance delegate made it clear that his presence 'should not be taken as indicative of consent to any increase of expenditure . . . or even to the continuance of the existing scale of expenditure'.[42] The question of making the CBI permanent was under discussion, and the concerns of Finance were made explicit on every occasion it appeared on the agenda. An allocation of Rs 50,000 for provincial publicity work on central subjects received reluctant approval after considerable Home Department pressure, but the Finance Department insisted the decision was without prejudice to their right to challenge 'the whole of our expenditure on publicity on the ground that, although most useful and desirable, we must in the present critical state of our finances force ourselves to do without it.'[43]

Williams produced a flow of memoranda in support of his Bureau, and his job. Both were in jeopardy in the Assembly and in the Retrenchment Committee and his personal interests engaged the attention of officials in India and London. A number of suggestions were considered to place Williams in an All-India Service, where his salary would be 'non-votable'

---

[38] Extract from official report of the Punjab Legislative Council debates, 12 March 1921, pp. 336–46, IO L/P & J/6/1780.

[39] Extract from Official Report of the United Provinces Legislative Council debates, 24 October 1921, pp. 25–33, *ibid.*

[40] Rushbrook Williams, to J. W. Hose, Political and Judicial Department, India Office, 10 March 1921, IO L/P & J/6/1748.

[41] *Ibid.*, 17 March 1921.

[42] Memorandum: meeting at Simla of departments of the GOI re. relations with the CBI, 18 May 1922, GOI (HomePol) 225/III/1922.

[43] E. M. Cook, Finance Department, to Home Department, 18 July 1922. The 1922 CBI budget was Rs 1.5 lakhs including Rs 50,000 for the provinces.

and his position as secure as an officer of the Indian Civil Service (ICS); but the need to involve a Provincial Government and the Government of India's concern about potential embarrassment in the Assembly blocked all attempts.[44] Sir Basil Blackett, the Finance Member, reminded the Home Member of a 11 March 1922 debate in the Assembly in which Sir Malcolm Hailey rejected concerns regarding this kind of situation.

He (Mr Joshi) further suggests that we, I think somewhat more Machiavellian than we ever imagined ourselves to be, could, if we desired to do so, avoid bringing the question of a particular appointment before the Standing Finance Committee and the House by getting the Secretary of State to sanction a non-votable post that would remove it from the purview of the Committee and the Assembly ... Sir, it is possible for us to do a large number of improper acts which would offend the constitution laid down under the Government of India Act, against the proper feeling that should control our relations with the Legislative Assembly, and incidentally also against our conscience. We have no intention whatever of availing ourselves of the device which the Hon. Member suggests for the purpose which he implies, and I hope the House will accept my assurance that it is quite unnecessary to alter the terms of appointment of the Standing Finance Committee in order to provide against a contingency so remote, improbable, if not indeed so impossible.[45]

Hailey clearly left no room for manoeuvre and Williams could do no better than a new five-year contract when the Bureau was made permanent in 1923.

Although the Home Department was committed to the Bureau, Williams' spirited defence and his description of the future role and status of a Public Information Department raised other concerns. He foresaw it becoming 'the liaison between the executive and the people, explaining the acts, intentions and convictions of the one to the other'. It seemed clear to Williams that its central role would require the direction of a senior officer equivalent to the Director-General, Posts and Telegraphs, and a large and more highly paid staff.[46] But C. W. Gwynne, the Deputy Home Secretary, was wary of this grand vision and particularly concerned by the assumption of political expertise apparent in the Williams memorandum. 'The responsibility for political decisions will rest and must

---

[44] If Williams were transferred to the Indian Educational Service, a Local Government would have to agree to provide a post. Both the United Provinces and Punjab refused to accommodate a Home Department request, GOI (HomePol) 431/1924. The Secretary of State recognized an obligation to Williams and wanted 'to leave it on the record that we had been discussing proposals of this kind'. Secretary of State to Viceroy, 18 January 1924 *ibid.* Eventually Williams was given a promise of stability but without a legal commitment. Secretary of State to Viceroy, 9 October 1924, *ibid.*

[45] Sir Malcolm Hailey in Legislative Council debate, 11 March 1922, *ibid.*

[46] Williams memorandum on the future of publicity work in India, 9 June 1921, GOI (HomePol) 225/1921.

continue to rest on the Head of the Home Department', he insisted, 'and cannot in any shape or form be delegated to the Director of Information.'[47] The suggestion that the Director of the Bureau be made directly responsible to the Viceroy raised further concerns regarding a policy role,[48] and the Home Member spoke for his department and others in and outside Government.

in view of the fact that I shall shortly be resigning my office, I ought to sound a note of warning on one point, namely the tendency on the part of all publicity organizations 'amplificare jurisdictionem'. This tendency assumes various forms: sometimes there are attempts to secure a higher status for the DCBI than his length of service and his knowledge of administration warrant; sometimes attempts are made to secure unreasonably high remuneration and suggestions as to honours are made which do not always seem appropriate. More generally the tendency is to attempt to influence policy and secure power with the general public by creating an impression that the publicity authorities are in a position to exercise great influence over the Government or a particular Member. This danger will be the greater if the DCBI is allowed unrestricted access to HE by reason of the impression such a procedure will inevitably create in the public mind, and it is a great danger against which the Government of India should always be on its guard ... We do not want in India any publicity organization which can affect the policy or impair the authority of Government either directly or indirectly. As it is, the Publicity Bureau has very considerable opportunities of influencing Members of the Legislature, but I am glad to say that this influence has always been used on the side of Government and has been subjected to our direction. At the same time the personal ambition of a politically minded (if I may use such a term) DCBI is a factor which cannot be disregarded.[49]

The proposal to move Williams into a direct reporting relationship with the Viceroy was rejected[50] and the CBI was carefully monitored by the Deputy Home Secretary. The Home Department remained a strong supporter of Government publicity and propaganda; but the possibilities of the official news organization taking on a life of its own in response to its readers' perceived needs and tastes was troubling to a bureaucracy not yet comfortable with the new environment of debate and popular understanding. Gwynne and Vincent and their successors remained wary of these new experts in the CBI, the Anglo-Indian press, the 'responsible' Indian-owned press, Reuters, the *Times*, information officers in the India Office – all supposedly allies in the work of seeing India through her constitutional training, and in the meantime of maintaining order and administrative efficiency. They recognized, however, that they had become dependent on these professional communicators who might

[47] C. W. Gwynne, intra-departmental comment on Monatgu despatch of 21 May 1921, *ibid.*
[48] Vincent memorandum, 13 October 1922, GOI (HomePol) 854/1922.
[49] *Ibid.*
[50] C. W. Gwynne, Deputy Secretary, Home Department, memorandum, *ibid.*

break through the barrier between themselves and a large Indian constituency which they assumed was willing to hear their side of the story.

Considerable attention was given to the development of an 'oral propaganda' programme which could utilize the hundreds of leaflets and thematic 'lines for propaganda' which were prepared in the central and provincial secretariats. The personal contact of the district officer with the villager, which had attained legendary significance in the histories of the Raj, was clearly insufficient in the competitive environment of the 1920s. 'False information' had been spread by a growing army of propagandists; and the Government required an army of its own. In May 1922, the Home Department contacted Provincial Governments regarding the use of schoolmasters for the purpose of explaining the contents of CBI pamphlets to non-readers. At the same time it was suggested to the Governments of Bengal and Punjab that the services of maulvis might be utilized for 'propaganda on Muhammadan questions'.

In every region of India, local situation informed the nature and development of the national movement. In the United Provinces, agrarian unrest and the organization of peasants into leagues, Kisan Sabhas, paralleled the initiation of Non-cooperation and provided the focus for Congress–Government confrontation in the early 1920s. The Government continued to depend upon its old alliance with the landed aristocracy, while pressing it to accept tenure and rent legislation that would mitigate peasant grievances.[51] Moderate nationalists, Liberals since their 1918 exit from the Congress, were among the early organizers of the Sabhas, but they became increasingly concerned with Congress militancy that threatened to turn the peasant agitation into a revolutionary movement. The kisans were the 'bulwark of the nationalist movement', declared Motilal Nehru's *Independent*, and his election as president of the United Provinces Kisan Sabha provided a formal connection between local unrest and the national Non-cooperation campaign.[52]

In this context the Government pressed for counter-propaganda through its own local supporters and the formation of its own Sabhas to rally moderate opinion. The anti-revolutionary leagues were called Aman Sabhas. By August 1921 official reports noted that each of the forty-eight districts of the United Provinces had its own Aman Sabha, organized by district officers who utilized speakers, lantern slides, leaflets, and calls for loyalty pledges to carry the Government's message. The *Pioneer* referred to Aman Sabhas as 'loyalty leagues'.[53] The official message cast the

---

[51] Peter Reeves, 'The Politics of Order: "Anti-Non-Cooperation" in the United Provinces, 1921', *Journal of Asian Studies*, 25, 2 (February 1966).

[52] *Independent*, 13 January 1921, p. 4; cited in *ibid.*

[53] *Pioneer*, 31 January 1921, p. 10, cited in *ibid.*

Congress in the role of *badmash*, ruffian, and the Government in the role of provider. The success of the former, it was argued, was a threat to virtually all basic services: trains, canals, schools, hospitals. Peter Reeves has described the hierarchy of relationships: British support for land-lords, who in turn organized the 'loyalty leagues' – together insuring the maintenance of law and order.

Liberal viewpoint was reflected in C. Y. Chintamani's editorial comment in the *Leader*. 'Mobocracy is not democracy and lawlessness is not the road to liberty'.[54] Throughout the 1920s and 1930s, the fear of possible Congress patronage of revolution kept the Liberals on the margin of the nationalist campaign and their priority concern for 'law and order' made them loyal, if reluctant, partners of government. It was a choice between 'revolution which can only result in violence, ruin and devastation and an indefinite setting back of the hands of the clock of progress, or ... temporary reaction to stem the tide of social and political convulsion'.[55] The result in the United Provinces, Reeves notes, was the extraordinary 'alliance' of feudal landlords, Liberal politicians and British officials.

In the United Provinces, village schoolmasters had been employed in propaganda work since the end of the war. Aman Sabhas were the primary organizational units of the system in which district boards attempted to provide one schoolmaster in each *tahsil* for Sabha work. The teachers would travel around their *tahsil* with the appropriate literature and meet informally with individuals or in small gatherings. The system was slow to spread to all districts, however, no doubt due to the policy of requiring the Aman Sabhas to be self-supporting in this work.

The Central Provinces had an entirely different experience since officials were convinced that the use of schoolmasters for this purpose would lead to difficulties with village organizations which employed them. It seemed more likely that 'the local bodies will be more inclined to ask village schoolmasters to preach the gospel of non-cooperation than to explain Government pamphlets'. Madras had developed an elaborate system of 'non-official correspondents' to whom Publicity Bureau publi-cations were sent. In June 1922, there were 18,750 correspondents includ-ing 3,180 teachers. Success here and in United Provinces, Bihar and Orissa, and Delhi was generally measured on the basis of numbers of agents and numbers of copies of pamphlets sent out. 'There is no difficulty in disseminating pro-Government propaganda,' noted the Chief Commis-sioner of Delhi, 'it is the absence of such propaganda that is keenly felt'. The extent to which these 'true facts' reduced the size of a Non-cooper-

[54] *Leader*, 4 March 1921, p. 3; cited in *ibid.*
[55] *Leader*, 4 June 1921, p. 3; cited in *ibid.*

ation rally, prevented a communal confrontation, or actually won over an ally for the Government was suggested in the reports of schoolmasters to the secretaries of their Aman Sabhas, in weekly CID and press reviews, or in the range of personal contacts of local officials. Whether the linkage between message and action was accurately described seemed far more debatable than the larger question of the extreme nationalist messages and the response they were assumed to elicit.

Both Bengal and Punjab opposed the suggestions of the Central Government. Punjab officials viewed any religious propaganda as potentially dangerous and considered schoolmasters generally 'not bright enough to be useful'. They preferred to have such work done by carefully selected agents who would be able to combine it discretely with their own activities. Bengal officials noted that schoolmasters were often sympathetic to anti-Government movements; and those who might be used for this purpose would risk unpopularity in their villages and impair their usefulness as teachers. It was also assumed that this would be recognized by them and there would be little enthusiasm to take up the work. In regard to the use of maulvis, it seemed clear that it was too late to do much good. 'The Khilafat agitation had been too prolonged and has gone too deep to make it worth while.' If there were any maulvis not already affected it was assumed they were too insignificant to be useful to the Government. The Bengal Government preferred to keep its propaganda activities within its various departments rather than farm it out to doubtful unofficial allies.[56]

The General Staff, also involved in village level propaganda work, would have preferred to use British officers but the cost was too high for the Rs 32,000 budget they had been given for this purpose by the Home Department. Retired Indian officers and non-commissioned officers were hired for propaganda tours and the army was 'convinced that a great deal was being done by this system'. But the Home Department was as concerned about the General Staff's enthusiasm for this work as they were about the reluctance of some provinces.[57] Vincent insisted that it was not possible for the General Staff to publish a purely army viewpoint

---

[56] C. W. Gwynne to all Local Governments and administrations, 30 May 1922. Replies to Gwynne, 12 June–3 August 1922, *ibid.* The Superintendent of Education, Delhi and Ajmir-Merwara, informed the Chief Commissioner, Delhi, that Government-aided secondary schools had been warned that they risked withdrawal of their grants if any member of their management committee or teachers took part in propaganda or agitation in opposition to the Government, 11 April 1930, *ibid.*

[57] The Chief Secretary, North West Frontier Province rejected all written material as inappropriate for a largely illiterate population. He also rejected oral propaganda as unnecessary, Chief Secretary, NWFP, to C. W. Gwynne, 12 June 1922, GOI (HomePol) 225/III/1922.

unless it had been approved by the Government of India. In particular, he was concerned about statements issued regarding North West Frontier policy 'on which Government of India and HM Government did not see eye to eye'.[58]

Autocratic rule and a 'free press'

Throughout this period of increasingly volatile confrontation, the major nationalist press and the Government maintained continuing contact considered vital by both. A primary goal of information officials was to get their 'copy' published in Indian-owned newspapers that had substantial local circulation and a national reputation. A single story might move in stages from readers to narrators and make its way across a province. It might also be picked up by another paper in a distant province and the process would be repeated. The *Patrika*, the *Tribune*, the *Hindu*, the *Bombay Chronicle*, and the *Leader* received copies of each other's papers and regularly quoted editorial colleagues on issues of national significance. Translations appeared as well in a range of vernacular papers, the distance from elite centres often reflected in the accuracy and quality of the writing.

For the major Indian press, contact with Government officials was recognized as essential to the newspaper business. The Government produced news – sometimes in the form of general handouts, sometimes in the form of interviews and 'scoops' – and the political confrontation did not eliminate the appetite of these papers for professional success.

In one of his regular tours of major newspaper offices, Rushbrook Williams described the 'uniform kindness and courtesy' he received from editors who rarely missed an opportunity to attack the Government. He reported that even the extreme Non-cooperation press were quite willing to receive official material. There was a section of the press that remained very hostile, but the response was sufficiently positive to guarantee in Williams' view, widespread publication of material important to the Government. On the specific issue of the forthcoming visit of the Prince of Wales, he anticipated that only the *Bombay Chronicle* and the *Independent* among the influential Indian press would be hostile. The rest assured him they would either say nothing hostile or, as in the case of the *Basumati*, offered to organize 'a combine for the effective reporting of HRH's tour'. Williams was pleased with the results of his own tour, but cautioned his

---

[58] Response to remarks made by the General Staff representative Colonel Beach, during a meeting to discuss propaganda policies, 18 May 1922. Home Department memorandum, *ibid.*

colleagues that the situation could change quickly and 'constant touch' with the press by provincial publicity officers was essential if they were to be 'kept in a proper frame of mind'.[59]

The commitment to a range of professional interests and norms by the editors and proprietors of the major newspapers of India did not make them immune to the burdens of repressive executive action; but it set limits that preserved these papers both as business enterprises and key organizations in the nationalist campaign. The British regime had neither the totalitarian authority to constrain entirely the press attack, nor the desire. Officials were generally sympathetic to the tradition of press freedom and respectful of its power and influence. Although press legislation and overzealous bureaucrats could cast a wide net that endangered some of these papers, the effort tended to concentrate on influencing and restraining rather than destroying. Those papers that were forced out of business generally lacked sufficient financial backing and management skills, or were advocates of violence and communal confrontation.

On his death in 1922, Motilal Ghose, the editor–proprietor of the *Amrita Bazar Patrika*, was described as a man who 'had no party and no political opinions'.[60] He had spent a lifetime in the newspaper business, and a generation of officials would have agreed with Mortimer Durand's description of him as 'a low seditious scoundrel, who writes treason and the foulest Billingsgate issue after issue'.[61] But he attacked his own countrymen too and no party or section of the nationalist movement could claim him as their own. He was a nationalist and a newspaperman, and an individual with a range of interests and biases that were never wholly subsumed in the priorities of some 'high command'. His reputation with the British and with various nationalist camps reflected their perception of him and his paper's policy at any particular time. While Durand apparently despised him, Lord Ripon's private secretary, Primrose, maintained regular written and personal contact.[62] The *Patrika* was important to those who wanted to know what was going on in Bengal, and a key to its influence was Ghose's contact with officials.

His sources of inside information were seemingly complete. The Government of Bengal and the Secret Service knew this, and probably had a pretty good notion as to what the sources were. But there was no way of choking them. It was taken for granted that, roughly speaking, the *Patrika* knew everything that was going on in the Departments. The entire official world detested it, and read it.[63]

[59] Williams report on his tour, 20 July 1921, GOI (HomePol) 353/I/1922.
[60] S. K. Ratcliffe (former editor of the *Statesman* and editor of the *New Statesman*), 'An Indian Editor', *New Statesman*, Vol. XX, 7 October 1922, p. 10.
[61] Percy Sykes, *Mortimer Durand: A Biography*, London: Cassell, 1926, pp. 129–30.
[62] *Ibid.*
[63] Ratcliffe, 'Indian Editor', p. 9.

Ravinder Kumar has described the establishment by 1932 of 'a relationship of "confidence" between the British Government and the Congress', the result of a conservative determination to constrain worker and peasant interests in the mainstream nationalist programme.[64] A similar conservatism, personal and institutional, among the leaders of the Indian press, formed the basis of a much tried 'relationship of confidence' with the established Government. When Gandhi asked the editor of the *Hindu* to publish a proscribed book in 1919, he was told that they had made too large an investment in their presses to risk confiscation and ruin. As an alternative, an unregistered cyclostyled news sheet was produced, denouncing the Rowlatt Acts – serving both the *Hindu*'s nationalist principles and its business interests.[65] For those who became full-time political workers and participants in the national struggle, men like the *Hindu*'s publisher, Rangaswami Iyengar, often appeared to be 'vicarious nationalists'[66] allowing others to carry the burden. But Iyengar had no problem with his nationalist credentials and his paper was clearly a great national and nationalist institution. To serve these interests it needed to stay in business. At minimum the relationship with Government had to be 'responsive cooperation'.

Full-time nationalist leaders, although often frustrated by the lack of uncritical support in the press and the tendency of editors of major papers to editorial independence, recognized the value of a professionally edited and managed paper, and were sympathetic to the norms and values that were part of the alien legacy. For M. M. Malaviya, the press was a serious business. He was generally unhappy with lighter news or cartoons, and anything 'vulgar' such as sensational headlines. When J. N. Sahni took charge of the *Hindustan Times*, which Malaviya had parented with the aid of Birla money, he suggested *The Times* and *The Guardian* as appropriate models.[67] Motilal Nehru had established his own newspaper and sought the control of others. There was no question about the political master his paper was meant to serve, and he insisted on limits to confrontation and

[64] Ravinder Kumar, 'From Swaraj to Purna Swaraj: Nationalist Politics in the City of Bombay, 1920–1932' in D. A. Low, ed., *Congress and the Raj*, London: Heinemann, 1977, p. 105.

[65] Report of the Commissioner of Police, 25 March 1919, quoted in David Arnold, *The Congress in Tamilnadu: Nationalist Politics in South India, 1919–1937*, New Delhi: Manohar, 1977, p. 29.

[66] Bipin Chandra's phrase, 'Historians of Modern India', in B. Chandra, R. Thapar, and H. Mukhia, *Communalism in the Writing of Indian History*, New Delhi: People's Press, 1969, p. 44.

[67] J. N. Sahni, *The Truth About the Indian Press*, New Delhi: Allied Publishers, 1974, p. 37. In regard to the *Bombay Chronicle*, M. R. Jayakar advised the editor, S. A. Brelvi, that the language of the paper was to be 'chaste, dignified, courteous, and decorous'.

standards in journalism that he demanded in the *Independent* and on which he judged other papers. When he was attacked by a political opponent in a letter to the *Pioneer*, he responded:

Mr Hafiz Hidayat Hosain's choice of the *Pioneer* as a medium for the publication of his canard is unfortunate as I am a regular reader of that paper. He should have followed the practice of propagandists of his class and contented himself by circulating unfounded stories about me in packed gatherings or in a certain section of the Vernacular Press which no decent man ever reads. By rushing into the columns of the *Pioneer* he has deprived himself of the proverbial start necessary to prevent being overtaken.[68]

For a paper located in Delhi, there was a special opportunity to develop a useful relationship with Government and its news sources in the secretariat. J. N. Sahni has described the rapport established with Home Department officials and especially the Director of Public Information[69] who gave Sahni a scoop regarding the personnel of the Simon Commission.[70] In any case there were people at every level in the Government who would provide information to the press for one reason or another. One source was a former employee of the *Hindustan Times* who now worked for the Government press; but both Indian and British civil servants could be the source of useful information passed in an interview or at a party or club where newspapermen and officials met on a regular basis.[71] The confrontation between the elite nationalist press and Raj officials could often take on the quality of party debate in the House of Commons – vigorous, sometimes fierce, but generally followed by sociability. For Indian officials, the nationalist press could be an ally in the slow process of 'Indianizing' senior positions. Both S. N. Roy and R. S. Bajpai, Deputy Directors in the CBI, urged the press to agitate in favour of Indianization when their own careers seemed to be in jeopardy.[72]

In Madras, the editor of the *Hindu*, Kasturi Srinivasan, was particularly careful to maintain contact with the Provincial Government during periods of civil disobedience. In 1930, he asked his chief reporter, G. K. Vasudeva Aiyar, to keep him informed about official attitudes and 'how the bureaucracy's mind worked'.[73] He was aware that the Madras

---

[68] Motilal Nehru to editor of the *Pioneer*, 22 June 1929, Motilal Nehru Papers, p. 6.

[69] J. N. Sahni interview, December 1970. The Director, Central Bureau of Information became the Director, Public Information in 1923.

[70] *Ibid.* Sahni noted a personal indiscretion by Coatman produced a compromise useful to both. Sahni suppressed the information and Coatman fed him with daily information for twelve days regarding the make up of the Simon Commission published over the by-line 'Our London Correspondent'.

[71] *Ibid.*

[72] *Ibid.*

[73] Quoted in V. K. Narasimhan, *Kasturi Srinivasan*, Bombay: Popular Prakasan, 1969, p. 41.

Government was just as concerned to know the mind of the editor of the *Hindu*. 'They also know that our paper is too powerful to be trifled with.'[74] The *Hindu* and most of the major English-language Indian newspapers were served by an elite group of professionals who often moved from one paper to another seeking career advancement or in response to the call of a nationalist leader who needed an editor or correspondent for his paper. Among these Pothan Joseph was considered particularly skilled and he was always in demand. But Joseph had a primary concern to support a large family and use his professional talent to produce a good paper. If neither could be accommodated adequately by a particular nationalist paper, he moved on to a better offer. He maintained good relations with information officials and eventually joined the CBI. 'I do not think he cares a hoot about nationalist politics,' Ian Stephens noted, 'and believe he would be equally willing to edit the *Civil and Military Gazette*, the *Eastern Times*, or the *Tribune*.'[75]

Stephens was wrong about Joseph's nationalist credentials. He was a passionate participant in the struggle, but as an individual rather than the loyal follower of a particular leader or organization. The result was a body of professional writing that was critical, often witty, sometimes profound, but always engaged with the major events and issues of his time. In regard to Gandhi's fasts, he suggested the country required 'more logic and less magic',[76] and he tended to emphasize the complexity of India's divisions that competed with easy definitions of national identity and national action. As a Christian, Joseph was sensitive to the Hindu chauvinism that increasingly informed significant elements of the nationalist campaign.[77] His 'Over a Cup of Tea' column was required reading for many who sought intelligent and independent commentary. This was the platform from which he attacked Brahman tyranny over untouchables[78] and argued the creative nature of nationalist–British confrontation which would eventually produce Swaraj.[79] He was always concerned as well with the plight of the newspaperman. 'The journalist is the greatest sufferer in the proliferation of periodical reports', he declared, noting the mountain of paper generated by the Government. But 'useful or worthless the wretched thing has got to be reproduced for the benefit of the reader'. It appeared to be impossible, however, to satisfy anyone. 'The

[74] *Ibid.*, p. 42.
[75] Ian Stephens to Hugh MacGregor, information officer, India Office, 24 May 1936, IO L/I/1/1421, File 7.
[76] Quoted in T. J. S. George, *Pothan Josephs's India: A Biography*, New Delhi: Sanchar Publishing House, 1992, p. 157.
[77] *Ibid.*
[78] *Hindustan Times*, 20 January 1933, p. 8.
[79] *Ibid.*, 11 January 1933, p. 8.

Government are not pleased, the politician complains he is not fully reported. A plague on both your houses.'[80]

Another example of the elite correspondent who covered the headquarters of Government for a major paper was B. Shiva Rao of the *Hindu*. He maintained productive and informal relations with senior officials including the Viceroy of the time, Lord Linlithgow. The Government gave him information, and used him as an intermediary with nationalist leaders. In 1938, when S. Satyamurthi asked Rao to reconsider giving evidence to the Chatfield Committee regarding his experience on a visit to the frontier,[81] he regretted that 'it would be extremely difficult for me to explain why I was doing it especially as I do not belong either to the Congress or to any other political party. Also I have seen the Viceroy several times, dined at the Viceregal Lodge, etc. If I were now suddenly to change my attitude my work for the *Hindu* would certainly become more difficult.' Satyamurthi pressed him to consult with Srinivasan, which he did, and then gave his testimony *in camera* and a pledge not to report it. Rao became the Indian newspaperman of official dreams, professionally apolitical. In October 1939, he wrote to Srinivasan about a story he sent to the *Hindu* which Congress leader C. Rajagopalachari had criticized as apologetic regarding a viceregal declaration. He reminded his employer that it was necessary for the Government's views to find a place in the *Hindu*. 'After all as your correspondent here I have to keep all my avenues of information open. The creation of an impression that I am suppressing the official point of view will not be helpful from any point of view. It is because I have been regarded so far as fair and impartial', he concluded, 'that I am able to have access to official circles to an extent denied to other correspondents.'[82] Srinivasan did not disagree.

In 1921, the Government appointed a committee under the chairmanship of the Law Member of Council, T. B. Sapru, to examine the 1910 Press Act and other legislation concerning the control of publication. Although there was considerable debate regarding the wisdom of giving up this protection from slander and seditious writing, the Viceroy's Council generally agreed that the spirit of the new Government of India Act required them to rely more on the ordinary law and the courts rather than forms of executive action that, however legal and carefully administered, were considered arbitrary and inappropriate for a Government increasingly responsible to a largely elected Assembly.

In his testimony before the Committee, Kalinath Roy, the editor of the

---

[80] *Ibid.*, 8 March 1933, p. 10.
[81] B. Shiva Rao Papers, Nehru Memorial Museum and Library.
[82] *Ibid.*

Lahore *Tribune*, made that concern explicit by attacking the 1910 Act as a 'slur on the press'. While asserting his loyalty to the British colonial regime, he argued that the Press Act was an improper 'infringement of our liberty'.[83] Although approaching the issue from a different perspective, Roy, like the Members of the Viceroy's Executive Council, could concentrate his concern on a sector of freedom, however arbitrary the general hegemony of the alien Raj. Freedom of the press would not make British rule popular or even acceptable; but it was assumed that it would help to make it workable in a period of transition. In that context it provided support to both the nationalist movement and the expanding collaborative administration. Roy pointed out to the Committee that the 1910 law had not achieved its proposed goals; as the press was neither more bitter nor more pleasant than was the case ten or twelve years before when the legislation was passed. It was, he insisted, 'exactly what might be expected in the circumstances of the case'. The British Government simply could not have it both ways. It was an alien regime and would not receive popular and general support for anything other than an appropriate expansion of areas of freedom. He suggested, however, that there were opportunities in this situation for all concerned. The new constitution would stimulate the development of parties and with them the creation of party papers – at least as concerned with the need to support one set of leaders and attack another, as with the activities of the British Government.[84] Roy could have been reading from a script prepared in the Home Department, but the views were his own.

He agreed that there were problems with the extremist press, but he insisted, they could be dealt with by ordinary law rather than the executive action authorized by the Press Act. The Indian press, Roy noted, could be compared to the opposition in Britain, where opposition was not only legitimate, but essential for the proper working of the political system. When a member of the Committee pressed him to consider what was to be done with those papers that advocated the separation of India from the British Empire without the protecting powers available to Government under the Press Act, Roy responded with a description of the problem rather than a solution. 'If these articles are seditious, then under the ordinary law you can deal with them; if they are not seditious, you can leave them to themselves.'[85]

[83] Kalinath Roy testimony, Sapru Committee hearings, quoted in *The Press Law Commission Report and evidence*, 14 July 1921, pp. 68–89. See also GOI (HomePol) 4/IX/22.

[84] *Ibid.*

[85] *Ibid.* The increasing inability to suppress press attacks because legal opinion indicated the Government had 'no case' was a source of growing frustration among officials. While agreeing that the *Tribune*'s attack on the work of military and civil personnel after the

By 1921, the Government of India could not be certain what, in fact, was seditious; and how far it could go in accepting as natural, appropriate, or even legal, attacks on British rule made more dangerous by their spread through the press. At issue was the extent to which the British regime was capable of being an ordinary Government, administering ordinary laws to guide and control its hundreds of millions of Indian subjects. The extraordinary fact of their alienism had been less significant in an earlier time when law was promulgated, administered, and tested by executive action, and critical opposition was considered dangerous and simply rejected. What was extraordinary in 1920 was the extent of the Government of India's effort to be an ordinary Government, to found its administration on a deft mix of law and arbitrary power – each element allowing for the extension of the other as the situation required. If the Government wanted a better press, or at least a reduction in extreme attacks on its administration, it was necessary, as Roy and others asserted, to look again at the mix and move ahead with its programme of devolution of power to Indian politicians and parties. The press – or at least the sensible and responsible part of it, would then direct its attention to these new centres of power and decision as was the case in any free society. The 'irresponsible press' could then be dealt with by these Indian administrations as the ordinary law provided. Implicitly, Roy was telling the Government that Indian newspapers were not merely propaganda sheets published for the purpose of nationalist attacks on an alien regime. Indian newspapermen were professionals, who would work effectively and responsibly in a British-controlled system, if given the opportunity.[86]

If total freedom for India still lay in the future, freedom of the press could not be delayed. It was this particular freedom, many argued, that would allow the democratizing process to move ahead not only slowly, but safely for all concerned. A free press was at the same time the mouthpiece of nationalist opposition and an institution which reflected victories already won. Professional newspapermen employed by the elite national press lived and struggled in a competitive press world in addition to the larger context of the nationalist campaign. As a result, they often sought a place in that campaign on terms that would allow them a reasonable measure of autonomy. They perceived themselves to be far more than 'compradors' of the British regime, although they were surely workers of the imperial system. And however much they shared their

Quetta earthquake was insufficient to secure a conviction, the Commander-in-Chief lamented to Sir Henry Craik that 'we are the only country in the world who would allow its public servants to be so grossly maligned, and leave it at that'. 20 June 1935, GOI (HomePol) 88/II/1935.

[86] Kalinath Roy testimony, Sapru Committee, *ibid.*

goals, they were more than propagandists for the Congress or other nationalist organizations.

A newspaper career provided for some an opportunity to live an 'independent' life – a life of choices in the complex and constraining world of nationalist and loyalist pressures from the centres of Indian and British power. As newspapermen they could be critical freedom fighters and as well, critical subjects of the Crown. 'We were leaders in the nationalist struggle' asserted J. N. Sahni,[87] but 'we were careful to move only to the margin of sedition, to avoid breaking the law.'[88] It was the nature of that margin, its place and definition, that attracted the attention of both British officials and the mainstream nationalist leadership. Violent extremes having been rejected by both sides, both were left clinging to the space that they shared. 'This strange rivalry', Anil Seal has observed, 'was to continue in inconclusive fashion until 1947; two sides willing to wound, and yet afraid to strike.'[89] It was this mutual constraint which allowed life on the margin to flourish.

The Sapru Committee recommended the abolition of the 1910 Press Act and the 1908 Newspapers (Incitements to Offences) Act, and the Government of India agreed to accept their findings without amendment.[90] There was some concern in London that too much was being given up, but the necessary legislation was sanctioned with the provision that there be some form of protection for the princely states from propaganda attacks in British India.[91] In the presentation of its Report, the Committee concentrated on the 'altered circumstances' rising from the enactment of the Government of India Act which made the retention of the 1910 Press Act both unnecessary and 'incompatible with the increasing association of representatives of the people in the administration of the country'.[92] The Committee noted the opposition of most of the Provincial Governments, but insisted that the 'genuine popular demand', in the context of the new situation, made the advantages of repeal greater than any benefit that might be obtained from its retention.[93] One of those local officials, Sir Michael O'Dwyer, former Governor of the Punjab, remained convinced that sedition was fostered by certain sections of the

---

[87] J. N. Sahni was editor of the *Hindustan Times* from 1926 to 1933. He later founded the *National Call*.

[88] J. N. Sahni interview, December 1970.

[89] Anil Seal, *The Emergence of Indian Nationalism Competition and Collaboration in the Later Nineteenth Century*, Cambridge University Press, 1971, p. 350.

[90] Viceroy to Secretary of State, 5 July 1921, 28 August 1921, GOI (HomePol) 4/IX/1922.

[91] Secretary of State to Viceroy, 4 August 1921, *ibid.*

[92] Quoted from Press Law Commission Report in Home Department memorandum, 14 July 1921, GOI (HomePol) 4/IX/1922.

[93] *Ibid.*

press and that the law should have been retained. In 1923, commenting on the current political situation in India, he noted that the prescience of the Press Laws Committee 'may be judged by the fact that within a few weeks the Moplah rebellion broke out. That rebellion cost 10,000 lives and infinite suffering to $1\frac{1}{2}$ millions of people, a high price to pay for a formula – the liberty of the Press.'[94]

O'Dwyer's scepticism regarding the 'altered circumstances' was widely shared among officials, but the concept of new times and a new direction continued to dominate decision making at the centre of Government and to attract support in a variety of forms. K. C. Roy had represented the Associated Press of India (Reuters) at the Press Commission hearings and had urged on the Government both the new post-Reforms context and the special role of the press. He yearned to be an insider and his viewpoint may have been as much a product of that desire as of his position in the Reuters organization and of his good relations with officials. Like so many of his contemporaries, he had made the essential accommodation with both the reality of British power and the ideal of Indian self-rule that allowed him to be at home in the colonial system. Envelopes of freedom, limited opportunities for struggle, constrained alien hegemony – all were made to complement each other for those who chose to work the system. The new emphasis on the Government of India as a distinct entity separate from Britain was a powerful idea which attracted a constituency, both British and Indian, that believed or wished to believe that a significant measure of self-rule had been achieved.

Roy spent four months in London in the summer of 1922, and noted on his return the growing separation and conflict between Simla and Whitehall. In his view, the decisions and recommendations of the Government of India were not given sufficient respect in London and the new position acquired by India with the Reforms appeared to be ignored. It was no longer acceptable for the Imperial Cabinet to oppose the 'united voice of India both official and unofficial' reflected in legislation passed by the Legislative Assembly or in recommendations of the Governor-General in Council. Roy argued that when it was recognized in India that 'wholesome proposals of the Government of India', in particular regarding Indian revenues had been set aside in London, the Indian legislature would assert its authority over the financial proposals of the Government of India.[95] Like many officials within the Government he

---

[94] Sir Michael O'Dwyer, East Asia Association meeting, Caxton Hall, 9 April 1923, in *Asia Review*, n.s., 19 July 1923, 436–7.

[95] K. C. Roy, 'Simla vs Whitehall: A Conflict in Angle of Vision', *Leader*, 23 September 1922, p. 7.

attacked the continuing role of the London-based Council of India, now a 'third wheel in the coach', and insisted on a relationship between the Imperial and Indian Governments founded on respect for the changed situation. Unless Whitehall gave up its apparent reluctance to view the situation 'from an Indian standpoint', Roy predicted friction and constitutional deadlock.[96]

For senior officials in the Government of India, 'Indian standpoint' and the 'new situation' was translated into the new emphasis on ordinary law and constitutional normality. The desire to avoid repression and the use of extraordinary powers after the trauma of Jallianwalla Bagh and the revelations of the Hunter Committee Report, reflected a new sense of constitutional constraint as well as an appreciation of the benefit to Government of denying itself the use of the arbitrary executive authority which remained available to it. Sir William Vincent noted the connection between ordinary law and the Government's success in limiting the life and impact of the Non-cooperation Movement; and as D. A. Low had noted, this success 'conditioned the mind of the Government of India during the ensuing decade'.[97] It was in this context that the Government of India reviewed its press prosecution policy in 1921.

Concern regarding the 'recklessness and malignity' in articles published in some of the Indian papers remained,[98] but central officials were willing to prosecute only in cases where serious trouble was likely. Reliance on the ordinary law also required the Government to convince a judge of the validity of its case, and press prosecution was increasingly limited to cases 'reasonably certain of success'.[99] As an alternative to arbitrary control or an uncertain case, the Government sought to deal with lies and extremist editorials through the counter-propaganda of the central Publicity Bureau. In general, Local Governments agreed with this policy while sharing Thomas Munro's concern about the apparent irreconcilability of a free press and stable Government under alien control. The Home Department of the Government of India had urged Local Governments to 'prosecute vigorously' any paper inciting violence or undermining the loyalty of the army and police;[100] but it also pressed for restraint and noted 'the desire of the Secretary of State to see how India will respond to a free press'.[101] The Bombay Government noted its 'difficulty in combining

96 *Ibid.*
97 D. A. Low, 'Civil Martial Law: The Government of India and the Civil Disobedience Movements, 1930–34', in D. A. Low, ed., *Congress and the Raj*, London: Heineman, 1977, p. 166.
98 Secretary of State to Government of India, 17 August 1921, IO L/P & J/1760.
99 *Ibid.*
100 Home Department Note, 3 July 1920, *ibid.*
101 Government of India to Local Governments, 9 January 1920, *ibid.*

the experiment of a free press with an active campaign of prosecution', but its attempt to change the environment of Government–press relations was reflected in the decision to refund security deposits of 15 out of 19 papers, and 79 out or 87 presses.[102]

The significance of 'moral and psychological factors' in maintaining the stability of British rule in India was now related to the adept use of the ordinary law,[103] the effective 'working of the Reforms', and the dissemination of positive news about Government.[104] There was no perceived difficulty in simply describing the benefits of British rule. The Punjab Government responded to aggressive communal publication with a pamphlet on the growth of religious freedom in India under British rule. After a detailed description of Brahmanical attacks on Buddhism, persecution of Jains, the Portuguese inquisition in Goa, Islamic persecution of Hindus, and various Sikh atrocities, the enlightened nature of British religious policy seemed clear. 'Whatever changes might operate in the constitution and the Government of this country,' Punjab officials were confident that 'it will always be pleasant to reflect that the British rulers of India had never sought to impose impediments between the people and their God.'[105] But deciding on the most appropriate and politic response to antagonistic press stories in the Indian press was more difficult. The attempt to establish total censorship of all stories from the Punjab concerning Jallianwalla Bagh had caused almost as much difficulty for the Government as the event itself. 'The Nation Aghast' declared the *Bombay Chronicle* in December 1919, because the tragedy of Jallianwalla had 'managed to elude the knowledge of the British Public for the space of eight months'.[106] Much of the press in India and Britain agreed. The long delay may have helped to control the 'revolutionary situation in the Punjab', but it enhanced the status of the Punjab Wrong as a national symbol and antagonized the press which described and manipulated such symbols for a growing 'national' audience.

The abolition of the 1910 Press act required the Government to rely more on the courts when prosecution seemed essential and stimulated a debate among officials regarding ground rules that would guarantee

---

[102] Secretary of Government of Bombay to Secretary, GOI, Home Department, 24 December 1921, *ibid.*

[103] H. W. Emerson, Home Secretary, note, 17 June 1929, GOI (HomePol) 240/29, quoted in Low, 'Civil Martial Law', pp. 167–8.

[104] H. W. Haig, Acting Home Member, to Hotson, 25 May 1930, GOI (HomePol) 257/V/ 1930, *ibid.*, p. 169.

[105] Punjab Government to H. W. Emerson, 3 July 1930, re. 'Growth of Religious Freedom in India' compiled by the Punjab Publicity Department in the *Civil and Military Gazette*. An Urdu version was also published. GOI (HomePol) 35/28/31.

[106] *Bombay Chronicle*, 20 December 1919.

protection for the fundamental interests of the Raj. In regard to the press, such discussions and subsequent trials often involved the close analysis of words concerning British identity in India, and the separation of their over-arching power from Central and Local Governments with enhanced non-official participation. On occasion, the judiciary joined the Government in defending its institutional integrity against nationalist press attack.

On 6 May 1924, N. C. Kelkar published an editorial in the *Kesari*, concerning the acquittal of a British soldier who had shot and killed an Indian villager.

Both pans of the scale for weighing justice are not of the same colour, but one pan is black and the other white. What wonder is it then that the white pan being found heavier than the black one should sink down? It is indeed a matter for great shame that in this country there are some people blinded by partisan spirit who, considering the justice dealt out with such a false scale to be proper, remain satisfied. Those who say that the laws of Manu should be burnt, should raise a pillar of justice at Lohagoan[107] and engrave upon it the full details of this case, as a memorial showing what value is attached to the lives of the Indian subjects under the British Raj and how pure and impartial justice is meted out to them.[108]

While criticism of the decision was acceptable, the imputation of racial bias to the judges in the case was viewed as an attack on the whole judicial system of British India and could not be allowed to stand. Kelkar's defence that the bias might be unconscious, and that the reference to the balance and pans reflected a 'fatal fascination' for metaphors, did not prevent his conviction. Speaking for the court, Mr Justice Kincaid noted that at least 20,000 people had read Kelkar's remarks and that he had been convicted of the same crime in the past. A fine of Rs 5,000 was imposed.[109]

More difficult was the case of *Imperator* vs *Miss Maniben L. Kara*, who successfully appealed her conviction under sections 124A and 153A of the Indian Penal Code. The Bombay High Court held that 'imperialists', 'capitalists' and 'workers' were 'phrases too vague to denote definite and ascertainable classes of HM's subjects' in order to come within the scope of the Penal Code.[110] In such circumstances, officials recognized that a court case was 'very tricky'[111] and it was essential to make a case that an attack on 'Imperialism' was an attack on the legal Government of British

---

[107] The location of the incident, near Poona.
[108] *Kesari*, 6 May 1924. 'A true translation' by B. R. Pradhan, court translator, quoted in D. V. Gokhale, *The Contempt Case Against Mr. N. C. Kelkar, Editor of the Kesari*, Poona: K. R. Gondhalokar at the Jagadhitechu Press, 1924, pp. 5–6.
[109] *Ibid.*
[110] Maxwell to Hallett, 7 May 1934, GOI (HomePol) 33/3/34.
[111] *Ibid.*

India. A precedent had been set in the case of *Imperator* vs *B. T. Rana-dive*, the editor of *Railwayman*. He had been convicted of using the word 'imperialism' in the context of an illegal attack against the Government and the conviction had been upheld by the Bombay High Court. But Ranadive had been 'accommodating and linked up imperialism with the Government of India'.[112] In another such case concerning a speech by S. N. Tagore, officials agreed that his pejorative reference to 'imperialism' fell within the jurisdiction of the Penal Code, but he had not provided the linkage that the High Court would likely require. He had argued that by imperialism he meant capitalism, and an attack on the capitalist system remained fair criticism in the Government's arcane listing of dangerous nouns and adjectives. M. G. Hallett cautioned that attacks on imperialism should not generally be allowed to pass without Government action,[113] and H. D. Craik insisted that the speech was clearly seditious since he used 'the word "Imperialism" as synonymous with the existing form of Government in India'.[114] But the case was dropped since Tagore was already serving a one-year sentence for another offence.[115]

Throughout this period of constitutional reform and defence of authority, British officials in India strove to associate their rule with the progressive ideals and institutions described and partially implemented in 1919. But their alienness required a reserve of arbitrary power and the combination denied them the goodwill many thought they deserved. Lord Irwin lamented the Government's inability to attract a 'good' press in India but recognized that the general hostility of the press was a 'natural accompaniment of a Government not based on popular support'. The difficulty had only been exacerbated in 1919, when the Government was required to 'ask the Assembly to vote the funds which will to a large extent be used in countering the views of the majority'.[116]

But there was a job to do and powers available to repress and control the most dangerous challenges to their rule. These included mounting security charges which easily bankrupted marginal presses and papers, confiscation, and imprisonment. The Government was reluctant however, to use extreme measures in the case of large national papers where repression was generally counter-productive. Fines could be paid by these papers or their nationalist supporters; and a temporarily imprisoned editor made no lasting impact on the tone or policy of his paper. Working the Reforms in the 1920s meant, in the case of newspapers, attempting to

[112] He was tried and convicted, December 1929. Legislative Department note, 21 July 1936, GOI (HomePol) 134/36.
[113] M. G. Hallett note re. S. N. Tagore case, 22 July 1936, *ibid.*
[114] H. D. Craik note, 23 July 1936, *ibid.*
[115] *Ibid.*
[116] Viceroy to Secretary of State, 15 August 1932, GOI (HomePol) 35/28/31.

live with a generally free press. Open repression was concentrated on the small, usually vernacular papers whose encouragement of violence and sectarian bigotry often concerned nationalist leaders at the centre of the movement as much as local and central officials. For the major nationalist press, controls in the form of manipulation of essential press–Government relations were often more important. In this case, both the press and the Governments tacitly acknowledged their need to share the resources of the system; and their allegiance as well to the standards and norms summed up in the phrase 'freedom of the press'.

Diminishing sources of influence and control

While the Government could increase the financial burdens of a paper by demanding security deposits, there was some margin for support as well, through the manipulation of official advertising and a variety of informal and formal subsidy arrangements. But throughout the 1920s and 1930s, there was ongoing debate within the Government regarding the nature of these resources and the benefits achieved by their use. After the establishment of the CBI, there was continuing pressure from the directors, beginning with Rushbrook Williams, to centralize Government advertising in the Home Department's information branch in order to achieve maximum political benefit from the expenditure. There remained, however, strong resistance from those departments that had a pragmatic commercial interest or a legal requirement to inform the public, and increasingly constrained budgets. Others considered the attempt to use the Government's advertising budget for political purposes as a waste of funds. The most extreme vernacular press had no expectation of receiving such revenue, and those small papers that operated on the margin of financial and legal jeopardy wielded individually too little influence to serve official interests. Cumulatively, the small vernacular papers were important; but there were too many: too many papers, too many editors, too many sets of priorities, too much demand on meagre funding, and too little confidence in the usefulness of such relationships.

For the major national press, advertising revenue was important, although few papers other than the Anglo-Indian giants could attract a sufficient amount to allow for an ordinary commercial business operation. Government concentrated its advertising revenue in the major Anglo-Indian and Indian papers which would guarantee a reasonable circulation and readership. It was these papers whose editorial policies most interested the Home Department. For the Anglo-Indian press, the flow of such revenue was automatic. Similarly, for a portion of the Indian press elite – the *Leader, Hindu, Hindustan Times, Tribune,* even the

Bombay Chronicle – official advertising revenue generally formed a stable element in anticipated income. Whether there was a consequent impact on the editorial page was debatable.

R. S. Bajpai raised the subject of centrally organized official advertisement in 1921, in the context of supporting those papers which were helpful to Government or might be persuaded to be so. He emphasized that this form of support would not be a subsidy that might attract criticism in the legislature or from the press community. The judicious manipulation of Government advertising expenditure could form the base of a larger programme of assisting cooperative papers with 'well written articles on non-controversial subjects' and with circulation among schools, colleges, and other assisted institutions. There was a general flow of requests to the CBI for such advertising, but the lack of centralization made it difficult to create a powerful political tool. Bajpai advocated the establishment of an agreed list of papers for advertisement which would be revised from time to time. The Central and Provincial Governments could then confine the flow of advertising largesse only to these papers.[117]

Gwynne's concern for the political priorities of the Home Department was informed by sensitivity to the constraints on executive action under the Reforms. He insisted that advertisements to selected press amounted to subsidizing by the backdoor. It would also restrict publicity and work against the interests of departments anxious to advertise widely.[118] As a result, Rushbrook Williams and his CBI colleagues were required to act defensively within the Home Department and throughout the Government. The intersection of expertise and policy was a continuing point of conflict. Williams insisted that advertising was a technical business and departments required up-to-date information regarding circulation, cost, readership, etc., in order to make the best use of their expenditure. He pleaded for consultation with the CBI at minimum, if not total centralization in his office.[119] But decision making regarding advertising expenditure was neither centralized in a single office, nor within individual departments. Williams noted that the 'existing system puts considerable *dastur* into the pockets of the subordinate staff in certain offices';[120] and a Home Department memorandum pointed out with concern that in some provinces advertising decisions were placed in the hands of a clerk, such as the one who refused official patronage to an acceptable paper until the proprietor agreed to pay a 50 per cent commission.[121]

[117] R. S. Bajpai, Home Department memorandum, 22 November 1921, GOI (HomePol) 213/223/1923.
[118] *Ibid.*
[119] *Ibid.*
[120] *Ibid.*
[121] GOI (HomePol) 188/IV/1922.

Although the kind of coordination Williams advocated was never achieved, the Government of India did attempt to withhold advertisements from newspapers advocating Non-cooperation. Government lists of newspapers suitable or unsuitable to receive official advertisements and for reading by Indian troops were maintained in the Home Department and revised on a monthly basis. The 'A-1' list was appropriate for advertising while the 'A' papers were blacklisted.[122] Coordination between the central Government and the provinces was, however, a continuing difficulty from the beginning. The Punjab Government listed those papers appropriate for advertising, but kept no blacklist; and central Home Department officials could only send its blacklist for information and hope for cooperation.[123] Bengal kept no press lists since it assumed the financial value of its advertisements was too small to make a significant impact;[124] and the United Provinces also maintained no regular lists. Other provinces kept their two lists and updated them on a monthly basis.[125] Central departments were also asked to maintain advertising lists. While most of those which had an advertising budget used the Home Department lists, the Departments of Revenue and Agriculture, and Industries provided their own. The former's blacklist included in 1922, the *Amrita Bazar Patrika*, *Bombay Chronicle*, *Hindu*, *Independent*, *Young India*, and *Mahratta*.[126]

Monthly updating proved to be too burdensome for many provinces. Too many papers were out of business before reports could be circulated, while other candidates for 'A-1' or 'A' status were too new to achieve such official identity. Some papers managed to achieve an 'A' rating in one jurisdiction and an 'A-1' in another. Others ceased to advocate Non-cooperation too late to stop the press that listed them as inappropriate for official advertising. The Bombay Government decided to revise its lists on a quarterly basis,[127] reflecting the special burden of its large number of papers. In November 1923, Bombay listed seventy papers as 'A' (unsuitable). The next largest number (thirty-eight) was provided by Bengal.[128]

There was a special problem concerning the army which involved in particular the Punjab Government. While no general blacklist was main-

---

[122] *Ibid.*
[123] Home Department memorandum, 9 February 1923, *ibid*. After repeated argument, the Punjab agreed to accommodate the two-list policy in 1924.
[124] H. L. Stephenson, Chief Secretary, Bengal Government to Secretary, GOI, Home Department, 9 March 1922, *ibid*.
[125] *Ibid.*
[126] *Ibid.*
[127] Bombay Government, Home Department, 23 February 1922, *ibid*.
[128] In November 1923, 175 papers were included in the 'A' list: Assam 1, Bengal 38, Bihar and Orrisa 1, Bombay 70, Burma 9, Central Provinces 12, Delhi 6, Madras 11, Rajputana 1, U.P. 26. GOI (HomePol) 188/IV/1922.

tained in Lahore until 1924, Punjab officials did use three lists which confused and annoyed central authorities: (1) suitable for Government advertising; (2) suitable for troops; (3) unsuitable for troops. While it was noted that Local Governments were their own masters in this regard, the General Staff pursued the issue in association with the CBI and this difficulty was eventually resolved by rationalizing all papers into the 'A' and 'A-1' lists; the 'A-1' list to be suitable for both official advertisement and the troops.[129]

Throughout the 1920s, the various lists provided a context for debate and the perception of policy. Local Governments complained that the Government of India placed certain papers on one list or other without proper consultation, and each level of Government sought cooperation in designating a particular paper in accordance with its views. The exchanges took place at the highest levels of the civil service, resulting in accommodation or occasional confrontation. Both Local and Central Governments were also approached directly by newspapers seeking to increase their advertising revenue. The existence of a blacklist was officially denied but well known to the papers and politicians concerned.[130] The larger papers, however, attempted to work within the system and gain official cooperation rather than attack the Government directly. It was not always possible, however, for the CBI and Home Department to ensure that such cooperation would be rewarded.

In December 1924, F. E. Holsinger, the managing editor of the *Indian Daily Mail*, wrote to the Home Member concerning the paper's inability to attract Railway Board advertising. He noted the large circulation of the *Mail* in the Bombay area, and sought an explanation for such advertising in smaller papers. Holsinger invited the Home Member to consult the Director of the CBI who would be aware of the *Mail*'s influence.[131] Since the *Mail* was already on the 'A-1' list and the control of railway advertising rested with the Board, there was little that the Home Department could do other than to note the limitations of its powers in its response to Holsinger.[132] Many papers during these years would have some cause for

---

[129] Note from General Staff and correspondence with DCBI, 30 May 1923. Home Department memorandum, 9 February 1923; correspondence between the GOI and Provincial Governments, *ibid.*

[130] Chief Secretary, Government of Bihar and Orissa to Secretary, GOI Home Department, 8 January 1924, *ibid.* Acting Chief Secretary, Madras Government to Secretary, GOI Home Department, 30 January 1924, *ibid.* Punjab had placed the *Muslim Outlook* on its 'A-1' list, while the GOI had placed it on its 'A' list. Punjab requested the GOI to change its position and it obliged. Punjab Government to GOI Home Department, 5 August, 1925, GOI (HomePol) 174/1925.

[131] F. E. Holsinger to Home Member, 30 December 1924, GOI (HomePol) 174/1925.

[132] Home Department note, GOI (HomePol) 188/IV/1922.

regretting the inability of senior political officers to act arbitrarily in their support. In this context, the apparent availability of such authority caused confusion and frustration for both parties. The Home Department served as a clearing house for cooperating departments which sought advice regarding the appropriateness of advertising in a particular paper;[133] but without the central control sought by the CBI it was necessary to depend on the intersection of the commercial and political interests of the departments concerned. Even the most supportive papers could not assume success in the competition for these funds. The general manager of the *Leader* provided a list of government departments that would not advertise in his paper. He had approached the Central Publication Branch, the Controller of Printing and Stamps, and the Controller of Currency but received the same negative response from all of them. The *Leader* had a large circulation. It was influential and politically moderate. But the CBI could only lament its lack of influence with the departments concerned and the general lack of funds available for this purpose.[134]

In April 1925, the Home Department abandoned the 'A-1' list of acceptable papers and subsequently circulated the 'A' (black)list only. The army took the responsibility for its own list.[135] The flow of special cases remained, however, and CBI officers continued to solicit advertising support for particular papers that used the Bureau as an advocate for official interest and support. After discussion in the Home Department, a decision would be taken whether to support the request in a memorandum circulated to appropriate departments. When there was no obvious political benefit, this level of advocacy was rejected and the supplicant sent a letter of regret. Often, the same letter had to be sent when the internal advocacy did not produce an advertising contract.[136] In cases where the editor and paper were deemed particularly valuable to the priorities of the CBI and Home Department, carefully protected secret service funds were used.

By the end of the 1920s, there were few advocates left within Government who saw any significant benefit to be gained from the manipulation of advertising contracts, and the practical argument advanced by Mrinal Kanti Ghose on behalf of the *Amrita Bazar Patrika* attracted broad

---

[133] In June, the Home Department was asked for advice about advertising in the *Hindustan Times*. It was informed that the paper was not on the 'A' (black) list. A week later a decision was taken to put the paper on the 'A' list and the advertisement was withdrawn. Foreign and Political Department to Home Department, 10 June 1925. Home Department note, 17 June 1925, GOI (HomePol) 174/1925.

[134] General Manager, *Leader*, to R. S. Bajpai, 7 August 1925 and Bajpai note, *ibid*.

[135] Home Department memorandum, 18 April 1925, *ibid*.

[136] Coatman Note, 23 May 1927, GOI (HomePol) 129/1927.

support. The *Patrika* had been blacklisted and sought to regularize its relations with the Government. Ghose argued that the Government should regard his paper as 'their true friend, for we always endeavour to put the popular view of the questions before the Government so that they may take a proper and correct view of the matter'. He noted that the *Patrika* was not a party organ, criticizing the Swarajists and Moderates as well as Government when it seemed appropriate. It had a substantial circulation and it was unreasonable for Government to 'disfavour a journal which wields so great influence with and commands esteem and confidence of the people'.[137] The Home Department agreed and the *Patrika* was removed from the blacklist.[138]

Blacklisting had now become a revolving-door policy with the exception of the unredeemable communalist and revolutionary vernacular press. On 29 April 1929, the *Hindustan Times* sent a confidential circular to Government of India employees regarding the possibility of retrenchment of lower-paid employees. Since clerks in the Government could not press their own case, the *Hindustan Times* announced its intention to carry on a propaganda campaign on their behalf; and provided a questionnaire: 'Please state your personal and departmental grievances.'[139] When these circulars came to the attention of the officials in June, it was agreed that 'this wicked campaign to stir up trouble' had to be dealt with firmly and the paper was blacklisted. It was not clear to the Home Secretary, H. W. Emerson, whether this attempt to undermine the loyalty of Government employees was prompted by 'the desire to increase its circulation or by political motives'; but it was clearly essential for the Government to be united in its response. All departments were urged to rally to the defence of the Government's interests and deny any advertisements to the paper. By October, after the Home Member, Sir James Crerar, discussed the matter with J. N. Sahni, it was agreed that an apology and promise of good behaviour in the future would be exchanged for a withdrawal of the ban.[140] It had become clear that the Government's interests were better served by a critical *Hindustan Times* that regularly published Government news, than a major paper and editor with a professional grievance.

Throughout the 1930s, the pieces of the 1920 CBI plan remained in place. Blacklisting was neither eliminated nor administered with any optimism about the results to be gained. In 1938, the Director of Public

[137] Mrinal Kanti Ghose to Secretary, Home Department, 24 March 1925, GOI (HomePol) 174/1925.
[138] Home Department note, 16 April 1925, *ibid.*
[139] Jossleyn Hennessy, DPI, note 29 August 1938, GOI (HomePol) 33/9/1938.
[140] *Ibid.*

Information (DPI) , Jossleyn Hennessy, was still advocating some form of order in the Government's advertising policy, but the political priority had been discarded. Hennessy considered it unlikely that the use of the CBI as a central channel for advertising had achieved any significant influence over the editorial policy of the press with the exception of some small vernacular papers. As an alternative, he suggested that departments issue their advertisements directly to the press from a list selected on a commercial basis and sent to them by the Bureau twice a year.

In present day circumstances all newspapers can afford, on the one hand, to receive payment for Government advertisements and, on the other hand, feel completely free to criticise Government as they like. They know that should they be able to show that for a certain period they had received so many advertisements and that following certain criticisms of Government, the flow of advertisements suddenly stopped, they would be able to raise the most embarrassing questions in the Assembly.[141]

In the mid-1930s the DPI had pressed for greater centralization of distribution of advertising and selection of papers to receive contracts. But senior officers in the Home Department remained sceptical and Hennessey's rejection of such schemes removed the base for such advocacy within the Government of India.[142]

The idea of publishing a Government-owned paper such as the Punjab Government's *Haq* continued to attract official supporters. It was generally agreed in Delhi, however, that a paper known to be published or subsidized by Government was of little political use, and in any case too expensive in a period of fiscal retrenchment. Clandestine forms of official subsidization of loyalist papers were considered on a regular basis throughout this period, but the cost and political dangers generally weighed more heavily with Home Department officials than any public-relations benefit. Montagu had noted his opposition to such uses of secret service funds in 1920, and the Government of India, although never accepting the Secretary of State's idealism as policy, remained sceptical and concerned about such activities. In principle, tampering with the press and 'paying for loyalty' was unattractive; in practice, the benefit seemed marginal since the major Indian-owned papers were not willing to sell their editorial pages. And there were always the queries of Assembly Members to consider.

The question of subsidies was kept alive, however, by the petitions of Indian editors in addition to supporters within the Government. In July 1921, T. Beltie Shah Gilani, a director of the Dehradun–Mussoori Tramways, wrote to the Viceroy's private secretary concerning his proposal to

[141] GOI (HomePol) 18/3/1929.
[142] *Ibid.*

start a journal directed towards 'the education of the masses'. It was agreed that counter-propaganda among the middle classes was needed during the early stages of the Non-cooperation Movement, but discussions with the United Provinces and Punjab Governments had been disappointing. Both Governments noted that an Urdu or Hindi organ would be more useful, but that there could be no guarantee to purchase a large number of copies since it was too expensive in present circumstances. A frustrated Beltie Shah complained that any journal, English or otherwise, which opposed Non-cooperation and supported the Government could not survive without some form of subsidy. If there could be no guarantee of a minimum purchase, then some other form of official support for a 'ministerial paper' was requested.[143]

In the subsequent discussion within the Home Department, the question of subsidies was reviewed. The policy of disseminating official propaganda through subsidized journals had been tried earlier, but largely abandoned in response to the opposition of the Secretary of State in 1911. Because of the particularly difficult situation in Bengal at the time, the practice was maintained only in that province. In 1912, Sir Henry Wheeler had noted that the practice had produced 'three schools': (1) whole-hearted supporters, (2) those who thought it 'contemptible, indefensible, and absolutely useless', and (3) those who considered it useful in some parts of India. The *War Journal* in United Provinces and the *Haq* in the Punjab were considered useful for a time, but in 1922, there was no enthusiasm among Home Department officials for either official newspapers or secretly subsidized papers. S. P. O'Donnell noted that subsidies had been 'tried, failed, and discredited', and was unwilling to go beyond the supply of material for publication, preference in advertisement, and contracts for the printing of leaflets and pamphlets.[144]

It was clear to these officials that semi-official status for a paper was not possible; and any form of subsidy would soon become public and prejudice circulation. Buying a 'good press' might be possible in some circumstances, but not very useful in achieving the public-relations goals of the Government. In any case, it was essential to spend the limited funds available for publicity where the guarantee of a large readership would provide an economic as well as a political rationale. Small projects such as that advanced by Beltie Shah did not meet this criterion. An array of Beltie Shahs, and there were many, were encouraged to go ahead with their ventures, but without special guarantees. As was often the case, the

---

[143] Mr T.Beltie Shah (Gilani) to PSV, 2 July 1921, re. scheme for a political journal for 'Ministerial Propaganda', GOI (HomePol) 878/1921.
[144] S. P. O'Donnell Note re. press subsidies, 13 June 1922, *ibid.*

'experts' in the CBI disagreed. Rushbrook Williams supported the proposal, arguing that past failures had been due to bad papers and not subsidization, which was a good idea in principle. But this project and many others were rejected.[145]

In 1925, the *Indian Mirror* of Calcutta had completed more than sixty years of 'unswerving loyalty' to the Raj, and its editor, Satyendranath Sen, considered that sufficient reason to seek some form of subsidy in order to keep the paper alive. Lord Reading had cancelled Government subscriptions as an economy measure; but Sen argued that the Government of India had an obligation to provide some support for his paper since its financial troubles were the result of its 'loyal and moderate political views and pro-government tendencies'.[146] Sen complained that English journalists had been knighted or decorated for far less service and urged Reading to save his paper. He warned the Viceroy that the Government had to help its loyal supporters. 'The way in which my loyal and devoted services have been treated by a great and mighty government will create a more unfortunate impression and the fate of the *Indian Mirror* will serve as a warning to those who are loyally inclined.'[147] Sen's loyalty was recognized within the Home Department and CBI officials felt he deserved support; but it was agreed that there could be no subsidy and no special advertising treatment since the *Mirror*'s small circulation (c. 700) made such expenditure uneconomical.[148]

The danger of the wrong kind of publicity resulting from illicit press–Government relations was demonstrated in 1928, when a subsidy arrangement for the *Aligarh Mail* was revealed in the nationalist *Forward*.[149] The editor, Rauf Jafri, had resigned and provided a statement for the *Forward* in addition to a copy of a letter from Ziauddin Ahmed, pro-vice-chancellor of Aligarh Muslim University to John Coatman, the Government of India's senior publicity officer. Ahmed asked in the letter for payment to Jafri of the agreed support for September 1927 to January 1928, and also solicited general advice and 'practical tips' regarding the running of the paper. The *Mail* was owned by Nawab Muzam mil-ullah Khan, a zamindar and vice-chancellor of Aligarh Muslim University, and the subsidy had been negotiated with Coatman by Ziauddin Ahmed who had promised a paper conducted on the lines of the *Leader*. The Government denied that a subsidy had been provided or that there had been any such

---

[145] Home Department discussion re. press subsidies, 13 June 1922–19 June 1922, *ibid.*
[146] Satyendranath Sen, ed., *Indian Mirror* (Calcutta) to Reading, 23 March 1925, GOI (HomePol) 219/1925.
[147] *Ibid.*
[148] Home Department discussion re. *Indian Mirror*, 7 September 1925, *ibid.*
[149] *Forward*, 11 January 1928, IO L/P & J/6/1956.

contact with Coatman; while privately lamenting that the ex-editor had 'let the cat out of the bag'.[150]

Some petitions for support did attract the interest of officials and an effort was made to respond positively. In 1930, B. C. Pal requested some form of Government patronage for his proposed English weekly, *Freedom and Fellowship*. In a letter to Sir Bhupendra Nath Mitra, Pal noted his work in his 'Through Indian Eyes' columns for the *Englishman*, and the general lack of organization among those who desired peaceful advance to political freedom within the British Empire. Although he anticipated a small circulation, it would be on an all All-India basis, and Mitra was asked to commend the project to the various departments of Government.[151] A generation had passed since the words 'Lal–Bal–Pal' (Lala Lajpat Rai, Bal Gangadhar Tilak, Bipin Chandra Pal – three nationalist leaders associated with early extremist activity) had summed up extremist opposition to the Raj. By 1930, Pal's views had changed and he needed a professional livelihood. It was clear to Home Department officials that Pal was capable of 'delivering the goods' and producing an influential moderate paper.[152] The Deputy Secretary, S. N. Roy, argued that 'we should help him help us', and wrote to W. S. Hopkins, the Chief Secretary, Bengal Government, regarding the project. But the project was still-born.[153]

A similar enterprise in Calcutta reached a more advanced state of relationship with Government. K. P. Thomas had contacted the Home Member, Sir Henry Craik, in the spring of 1935, seeking financial assistance for the *Modern Student* which provided educational propaganda against subversive activities among young people. The Bengal Government had provided a monthly grant of Rs 500 and Thomas now sought the aid of the Government of India. 'The one great advantage of it,' he noted to Craik, 'is that the public do not suspect it to be a propaganda scheme.'[154]

The Bengal Government endorsed the request for a grant of Rs 10,000 or Rs 1,000 per month from the Government of India. It was noted in Home Department discussions that Thomas had raised this matter with them two years earlier and had been referred to Bengal authorities since the mandate of the paper was anti-terrorist. Local Government funding had allowed the project to start and the paper had been recommended to other Local Governments, some of which subscribed to a number of copies. Some small funding had been provided on a one time basis by the

---

[150] India Office internal note and discussion, *ibid.*
[151] B. C. Pal to Sir Bhupendra Nath Mitra, 5 March 1930, GOI (HomePol) 24/7/1931.
[152] S. N. Roy, Deputy Secretary (Home Department) memorandum 20 May 1930, *ibid.*
[153] S. N. Roy to W. S. Hopkins, Chief Secretary (Bombay), 22 May 1930, *ibid.*
[154] K. P. Thomas to Sir Henry Craik, 18 May 1935, GOI (HomePol) 33/10/35.

CBI, but the decision had been made to leave any regular subsidy to Bengal. Home Department officials were particularly sensitive to the increasing frequency of Assembly questions, the response to which was always 'no subsidy'. By 1935, the Bengal Government had provided more than Rs 10,000, but Thomas argued that the danger from socialists and communists was particularly acute in that province; and in any case the funding was for the scheme of anti-revolutionary publicity and not for the paper.[155] However beneficial the *Modern Student* appeared to be, the Government of India considered itself unable to help, and the Bengal Government, after this exchange, decided to cut off the paper following the provision of six additional monthly payments to cover Thomas' deficit.[156]

By 1926, many of those in Government who had supported the abolition of the 1910 Press Act, were actively engaged in discussions concerning the adequacy of existing press constraints. Of particular concern was the accelerating politicization of communal identity and the often virulent advocacy of these interests in the press. Sumit Sarkar has noted that the rise of communalist identity and competition was 'in the very logic of participation in the post-1919 political structure'.[157] The combination of a more-broad-based franchise, separate electorates, an increase in the number of the educated without adequate opportunities to use newly acquired skills and expectations, and post-war economic readjustment with the inevitable component of social unrest – all produced a responsive audience for quick solutions to contemporary problems cast in personal and traditional moulds. To meet the need for organization and platforms, 'the link between elite and popular communalism was provided by the rapid growth of communal associations and ideologies'.[158]

The proliferation or revitalization of such groups in the 1920s[159] provided both opportunities and dangers for the British regime. Some officials seemed to discover in the confusion the beginnings of a party system – the hoped-for solution to Congress dominance and the concentration of opposition on the Raj administration. Others, unaware of any long-term institutional benefits, sought opportunities and allies for

[155] *Ibid.*, 20 June 1935.
[156] A. S. Hands, Deputy Secretary (Home Department) to G. P. Hogg, Chief Secretary (Bengal), 18 July 1935; Hogg to Hands, 14 August 1935, *ibid.*
[157] Sumit Sarkar, *Modern India 1885–1947*, Delhi: Macmillan India Ltd, 1983, p. 234.
[158] *Ibid.*, p. 235.
[159] The Hindu Mahasabha was founded in 1915 and became increasingly popular by the early 1920s. There were in addition: the Sanatan Dharma Sabha, the Shruddhi and Sangatham movements of the Arya Samaj, the Rashtriya Swayan Sevak, and the communal politics of Pandit M. M. Malaviya.

this undetermined period of transition. Muslim officials, such as Nawab Muzaffar Khan, the Director of the Punjab Information Bureau, were deputed to work with publicists within their community in order to gather information regarding viewpoint on a particular issue, and to influence it. In 1930, the Government was concerned with the attitudes of Punjab Muslims toward the Simon Commission, and Muzaffar Khan arranged for discussions with the editors of four Muslim papers in the office of the *Muslim Outlook*. He told the editors that 'the Report had once for all shattered the dream of Hindu Raj and had saved the Mussalmans from being politically swallowed by the Hindus'. The federal system in the Central Government, indirect Assembly elections, separate electorates, the creation of a separate Muslim majority province in Sind, and the reforms for the New West Frontier Province were all noted as supportive of Muslim interests and reason to support the Government and the Commission's work. In response, the editors noted the gains in principle, but generally felt that Muslims had been thrown at the mercy of non-Muslims. Especially in regard to the scheme for provincial autonomy, they perceived a Hindu Raj under British protection. Muzaffar Khan found growing resentment that so little reward had resulted from Muslim loyalty. He noted that the papers would continue to be anti-Congress, but this did not make them supporters of the next dollop of reforms. 'I personally would prefer hundred times real British Raj', noted one editor, 'to this sort of self-government'.[160]

In Bengal in the early 1930s, the Government attempted to use the talents of traditional Muslim leaders in an environment of terrorist actions and community confrontation. Sufi Abdul Qadir was deputed to Bengal at the end of 1932, and had worked closely with Bengal authorities for nine months. The line apparently preached among Bengali Muslims emphasized that the terrorist movement was directed against the British Government because it stood between Hindus and the achievement of Hindu Raj. When the present system of Government changed, the terrorists would turn against Muslims, who would then be the main obstacle to Hindu Raj. British officials were anxious to find allies in their campaigns against terrorist activity, and Bengali Muslims were saturated with pro-Government arguments to counter anti-Government propaganda. But Qadir's description of his work on their behalf received a sceptical response in the Home Department. While approving the message, the Director of the Information Bureau was convinced that Qadir could not have delivered it. The Bengali Muslim peasant was too dependent, in his

---

[160] Note re. Nawab Muzaffar Khan on the attitude of Punjab Muslims towards the Simon Commission, 4 July 1930, GOI (HomePol) 346/1930.

view, upon Hindu zamindars and moneylenders to allow for the open preaching of the dangers of Hindu Raj. It was also noted that Qadir was a Qadiani preacher working in an area where the majority of Muslims were either followers of the Deoband school of thought or of Maulvi Abu Bakr of Ferfera, both anti-Qadiani. There was no consideration of the foolishness of the choice of messenger, only the futility of the message.[161]

Competition and accommodation

Life was becoming increasingly complex for those responsible for the defence and advocacy of the Reforms agenda laid down in 1918. The perceived 'enemies of progress' were now dividing into so many camps that the control of the battleground itself seemed in jeopardy. British officials had satisfied themselves by the mid-1920s, that Non-cooperation, while still dangerous, had been largely neutralized and absorbed into a system of relationship with the Raj which limited confrontation and danger within acceptable boundaries. This apparent success was viewed as a victory of both idea and muscle. The Government had committed itself to 'dominion status' for India, and had been prepared to defend the goal as well as the time-table from the pressures of those it perceived as either naïve, impatient, or malevolent – who sought to rush the pace and endanger the achievement. But communal incitement and terrorist conspiracy recognized no limits and forced the Government to consider the retrieval of executive powers given up at the beginning of the decade.

In the spring of 1926, the Members of the Viceroy's Executive Council searched for a formula that would allow the Government to revive limited press controls with special reference to communal incitement. It was clear that many bridges had been burned with the total repeal of the 1910 Press Act, and there was no easy way to go back. However 'imprudent and precipitate' many believed that decision may have been, it was recognized that renewed controls would be difficult to defend among those who had been 'working the reforms' and had assumed the entrenchment of a fundamental change in the relationship between the British regime and its Indian subjects. The Government was now concerned about the forthcoming elections and had no wish to undermine loyal candidates. It was clear to central officials that a case had to be built, but they could not do it. The demand had to come from Local Governments and their more popularly based legislatures, but it seemed unlikely that Delhi's willingness to differentiate between communal and seditious writing would be accepted.

---

[161] Home Department note, 10 August 1933 re. propaganda work of Sufi Abdul Qadir in Bengal. Also, DIB note, 19 August 1933, GOI (HomePol) 39/11/1933.

I do not think it can be disputed that without some revival of these powers, there can be no effective control of communal incitements in the Press. On the other hand any attempt to revive these powers would be attacked as a Machiavellian plot to get the principle of the control of the Press accepted during the panic caused by communal animosity, with a view to its subsequent extension to seditious writings.[162]

The response from Local Governments was, as anticipated, not very helpful. Madras, Bombay, Assam, and the Central Provinces thought existing powers were adequate for their situations. Bengal and Punjab wanted far more drastic action than the Government of India had suggested. The rest of the Governments supported the revival of the powers under the 1910 Act. It was decided to limit immediate action to an amendment to the Criminal Law Procedures Code to provide for forfeiture powers against publishers who incited communal violence. It was agreed, however, that press legislation that would really control inflammatory communal writing would have to be so autocratic and confer such extensive powers on the executive that the alienation of supporters would be far more significant than any benefit that might be achieved. And in any case it was recognized that control of the press would not solve the problem.[163]

For the balance of the decade, the issue of press controls was continually introduced into discussions concerning communalism and communism, and the violence associated with both.[164] Revolutionary pamphleteers were becoming increasingly inventive in circumventing existing laws. The Chief Commissioner of the North West Frontier Province complained that seditious literature was being sent into his province by train from Lahore or Rawalpindi. Since no use had been made of the mail, the Post Office Act could not be invoked to seize and censor.[165] Similarly, the use of ranks of 'dummy editors' had involved the Government in useless and expensive prosecutions.[166]

The challenges to Congress unity in the mid-1920s – as No-Changers and Pro-Changers, Swarajists and Responsive Cooperators competed for control of the nationalist centre – had provided a measure of peace and a return of confidence to the beleaguered British regime. But the decision to initiate the next round of constitutional advance revitalized the nation-

---

[162] H. G. Haig, 26 July 1926, GOI (HomePol) 236/26 and KW.
[163] Executive Council re. adequacy of existing law to deal with communal incitement, 25 May 1926–11 September 1926, ibid.
[164] 1922–7, 5 Peshawar conspiracy cases; 1924, Kanpur Bolshevik conspiracy case; 1929–33, Meerut conspiracy trial.
[165] Sir Norman Bolton, Chief Commissioner, NWFP, to Secretary (Home Department) 5 April 1930, GOI (HomePol) 168 and KW 1930.
[166] Home Department note, 22 April 1930, ibid.

alist campaign. No Indians were appointed to the Statutory Commission chaired by Sir John Simon, and when it arrived in India in 1928, there was almost universal condemnation of the apparent commitment to an All-British, 'made in England' process. In response the Congress organized an All-Parties Conference that brought together representatives of a range of divergent groups and interests. And a committee, chaired by Motilal Nehru, was charged with the task of producing a 'made in India' constitution. The effort to create a united 'voice', however, tended to enhance concern for individual and divergent interests. The Nehru Report called for the termination of 'separate electorates' for Muslims; and communal struggle in the context of Hindu–Muslim confrontation, moved to the centre stage. This was an old theme in the rhetorical battle, but by the end of the 1920s it threatened to displace all others in determining freedom-struggle priorities.

The combined British and Indian efforts at constitution making stimulated another source of division within the Congress. A new generation of 'moderates' and 'extremists' fought for the right to define the freedom goal for which they struggled together. The Nehru Report called for dominion status, but Congress radicals insisted on a deadline of 31 December 1929 for its achievement. If the Government did not accept this demand it was agreed that a new non-cooperation campaign would be initiated. While the Nehru Report symbolized the 'moderate', cooperative constitutional path; a 'Declaration of Independence' on 26 January 1930, and the demand for complete separation from the British Empire was the message of the 'extremists'. In addition, a series of conspiracy trials, terrorist attacks, and continuing communal turmoil had increased the defensiveness of officials. Determined to demonstrate the legitimacy of their regime by making Government work, they confronted this new challenge with a mixture of power and accommodation. The existing law was used without restraint to crack down on dissidents who advocated violence, and Lord Irwin returned from a mid-term leave with a call for Round Table discussion in Britain and a declaration of dominion status as 'the goal'.

The Government had no option other than the constitutional path envisioned in the Round Table proposal; and its rejection by the Congress at its Lahore meeting in December 1929, was a challenge that concentrated the minds of a range of officials on developing the right messages to attract support for the defence of their position. The radical programme outlined by the new Congress President, Jawaharlal Nehru, provided all the ammunition they required; and vindicated the 'red scare' image in which he had been cast by those who had tracked him across Europe and Russia, noting carefully the socialists and communists with whom he associated. In a document specially prepared for propaganda purposes immediately after the Lahore session of the Congress, the Punjab Chief Secretary outlined suggested lines of discussion to be taken up with non-officials throughout the province. After a list of general observations noting Congress opposition to a peaceful settlement, the thrust of the argument was to highlight the apparent surrender of leadership to young revolutionaries. In a section entitled 'Communist and Socialist Aspect', Nehru is described as an enemy of landed proprietors whose vision of independent India included nationalization, the collapse of property rights, division of land among peasants, and economic ruin. Although, it was noted, the Russian experience was a failure and her economy was in chaos, Nehru was clearly leading the Congress into the 3rd International, and the country to a similar fate.

The document specifically directed local officials to use material regarding Russian troubles that had been published in the *Tribune*, and to emphasize the *Tribune* source. In turn, every conceivable occupation or class interest, with the exception of the professional revolutionary, was described as at risk. No Government would construct canals for the benefit of farmers, nor landlords sink wells and make other improvements, unless property rights were certain and there was no risk of confiscation. It was essential for landlords to organize and fight for their legitimate rights or they would lose their property, as would be the case for *banias* and moneylenders whose wealth 'would similarly be divided among the have-nots'. Industrialists would suffer with the decline of capital enterprise, as would labourers whose jobs depended on enterprise and confidence.

A special caution was to be directed to the middle and professional classes. It was apparent that Nehru was carefully avoiding a direct attack on their interests, but it was clear that his revolution would eventually displace them as well, in favour of the masses. The menace to India's stability was broadened to an international state. Debts would be repudiated, credit withdrawn, money would become increasingly expensive, and the inevitable result would be the 'economic and industrial ruin of the country'. Unless, it was argued, the enterprising and competent came forward to reject the Congress programme and support the Government's effort to achieve a workable settlement and further constitutional advance, the fruits of their labours would be 'divided among the idle and incompetent'.[167]

---

[167] H. W. Emerson, Chief Secretary (Punjab), to all commissioners of divisions, inspectors-general of police, deputy inspectors-general of police, Eastern-Central and Western Ranges, deputy commissioners, superintendents of police, 14 January 1930 (secret), GOI (HomePol) 176/1930.

It was clear to officials at the centre and in Local Governments that counter-agitation and propaganda had to be carried out on different lines. Paid propagandists were too expensive and, in any case, legislative councils would not vote the funds. The Governor of Bombay, Sir Frederick Sykes, urged the Viceroy to carry the struggle to the Congress camp rather than wait to react with a rejoinder to a campaign that had already done its damage. He shared with many of his colleagues a concern that the Government was losing the battle against the idea and image of the Congress as the legitimate representative of the Indian people; and a conviction that it was a battle that still could be won. His recommendation, however, was not very imaginative. As an alternative to funded professionals, Sykes proposed voluntary propagandists to be rewarded with minor honours, and Indian titles, but distributed on a much larger scale.[168]

The Governor of Madras re-established the Information Bureau that had been allowed to run down during the more confident mid-1920s. He agreed with Sykes that the campaign had to be pro-active, and instructed collectors in all districts to 'make themselves aware of anything that is disturbing the minds of the people'. On the basis of their reports, leaflets were to be prepared by the Information Bureau before the Congress had the opportunity to take advantage of the situation. He emphasized, however, that the whole plan remained confidential. Even his Cabinet could not be told until the scheme was virtually in place, since the money would have to come from the Council.[169]

Sir Fazl-i-Hussain urged Irwin to emphasize the communist source behind the renewed Congress challenge, and 'therefore all those who stand for property and for religion will have to combine in order to fight this movement'. Hussain was convinced that the publication of the facts would attract a positive response and eliminate the need for organizing expensive and often useless pro-Government institutions like *Aman Sabhas*. 'This movement should be essentially public-spirited,' he argued, 'and not a put-up-job.'[170] The Director of the Information Bureau, John Coatman, agreed with Hussain that the Government had put too much emphasis in gaining satisfactory comments in the press, and too little on shaping and using the events themselves. As an example, he referred to a recent vote in the Assembly on Pandit Malaviya's adjournment motion. Only Hindus of 'one particular political complexion' had supported Gandhi and his movement. 'The complete abstention of Muhammadans

[168] Sir Frederick Sykes to Irwin, 12 February 1930, GOI (HomePol) 35/28/1931.
[169] Governor of Madras to Irwin, 26 February 1930, *ibid*.
[170] Sir Fazl-i-Hussain to Irwin, 5 March 1930, *ibid*.

from the pro-Gandhi lobby is a fact of the highest significance,' he noted, 'and one which will arrest attention wherever the news of the assembly proceedings of yesterday goes.'[171] Coatman suggested that whenever important Municipal or District Board meetings, or gatherings of well-known communal bodies pass resolutions against the Gandhian programme, 'the value of that one event, as broadcast in the newspapers, is worth reams of mere controversial writing'. He was not content, however, to rely on such meetings being called by local initiative alone. When necessary, influential officials and non-officials were to call representative meetings of Hindus, Muslims, and Sikhs in Lahore and pass resolutions in opposition to the independence movement. It would then be useless, in Coatman's view, for newspapers like the *Tribune* to report decisions of small extremist bodies or insignificant college meetings, since these inspired meetings would represent the 'expression of the authentic opinion of the people of Lahore'.[172]

Increasingly, 'authentic opinion' was sought at more and more local levels of society, either following Congress organizers or blazing their own trail with the aid of link figures who represented old and still vital relationships. In the traditional army recruiting areas, officers on special propaganda tours moved through the districts, showing the flag and the Sahib – still considered a solution to local problems and anti-Government agitation.[173] While convinced of the general loyalty of the military, both serving and retired, the General Staff sought to check on any participation of army or ex-army personnel in Congress activities, and when necessary issued warnings or cut pensions. Meetings were organized with instructions to circulate loyalist declarations, and ex-soldiers were encouraged to break up Congress gatherings. An attempt was made to establish a precise roster of individual soldiers, reservists, and pensioners district by district, and this took the touring officers into the villages – often for the first time in many years.[174]

As in other areas, the army considered itself the underdog in regard to propaganda and local organization. Both in terms of the spread of nationalist news and viewpoint, and pressure for financial contributions to the cause, the Congress machine was viewed by many as a model to be emulated. Officers were convinced that Raj representatives had been away too long and there was a need to re-establish a personal relationship by more touring and long stays in each place.

[171] Coatman note, 11 March, 1930.
[172] *Ibid.*
[173] Note re. special propaganda tours carried on by recruiting officers and other officers of the Army, April–December 1930, GOI (HomePol) 265/1930.
[174] Report on a tour of Sialkot District by Major L. W. H. Mathias, DSO, 10 July–8 August 1930, *ibid.*

Pensioners and ex-sepoys are not disloyal and are very pleased to see a Sahib who will take the trouble to talk to them. The trouble is that once they leave a regiment they hardly ever see a Sahib again. Several old villagers talked of the days when the Deputy Commissioner was a real get-atable person and mentioned names of various Colonels and Majors who had been Deputy Commissioners 20 or 30 years back.[175]

Whether reality or myth or faulty memory, a continuing personal relationship between British officers and Indian soldiers was no longer possible; and it was considered necessary to rely on a 'gesture from us' in the form of jobs for pensioners and demonstrations of strong rule. Touring officers were quick to generalize from an individual encounter with loyalty and a reference to an old and mutually admired relationship. During his tour of Rohtak and Bulandshahr Districts, Major C. O'B. Daunt encountered an old Jat *rais* of wealth and position who recalled his visit to England in 1911, as an Honorary Risaldar for the King's Coronation. Daunt noted that such men thought that the Raj in the old military sense would come again, and although he insisted that he was not retelling his experience 'in any die-hard vein', Daunt was convinced that anyone listening to this old man describe a Congress regime as 'Bilkul Absolute Ruin Hoga', would have 'been made furiously to think'.[176]

While Daunt was 'thinking furiously' of older and better times, and the countless Indians represented by the old Jat who presumably yearned for the good old days; his colleagues touring other districts were generally less romantic in describing the problem and more pragmatic in suggesting solutions. In Amritsar District, the touring officer had no hesitation in suggesting that a large number of ex-soldiers would join the Congress if offered better pensions than available from Government, 'for an Indian has no sense of patriotism and doesn't mind who he serves under so long as he gets fair treatment and regular meals'.[177] Such competing perspectives produced arguments for different messages designed to maintain and extend local centres of loyalty; and the Home Department responded with individual packages for selected groups. All Local Governments were asked to submit lists of approximately four hundred names divided into 'waverers', 'reconcilables', 'suitable candidates for the ensuing elections', and 'government-supported who would likely make propaganda use of the literature', who would receive material directly from the centre.[178]

[175] *Ibid.*
[176] Tour of Rohtak and Bulandshahr by Major G. O. B. Daunt, July–August 1930, *ibid.*
[177] F. Adams, Amritsar District tour, July–August 1930, *ibid.*
[178] D. Gladding to all Local Governments re. supply of propaganda literature to selected members of the public in different provinces, 6 August 1930, GOI (HomePol) 35/318/1932.

Within provinces, pamphlets, and leaflets were distributed on a much
larger scale with an emphasis on vernacular material issued by private
presses. The Home Department sought to induce a competitive spirit
among the Local Governments by noting one province which had
distributed 30,000 such leaflets, or another which had an especially
effective propaganda technique.[179] On occasion, the response was
annoyance rather than enthusiasm. The Central Provinces refused to send
any list of individuals to the centre, arguing that the responsibility to
maintain law and order rested with the Local Government.[180] And the
Home Department, reminded that its messages to the provinces often had
to be as sensitively constructed as those for nationalist consumption,
decided not to circulate a Bengal leaflet considered especially useful 'lest
we create the impression anywhere ... that we are not giving credit for the
efforts of other provinces'.[181]

Every department of the Government of India participated in the
propaganda campaign in terms of defending its own programme and
areas of responsibility. Although information officers were never entirely
successful in centralizing all such activity in the Information Bureau, in
periods of major confrontation the Home Department acted as a clearing
house for leaflets, press stories, and proposals for propagandist activity.
Materials were often passed from one department to another with the
Home Secretary seeking the right balance of information and argument.
Overzealous defenders required careful vetting when the pressure of a
particular Congress campaign unleashed biases and epithets generally
held in control. The Finance Department produced one such pamphlet in
June 1930, in response to the Congress boycott of foreign goods. It began
with a general description of the sources of the boycott 'based upon a
diseased mentality which is unfortunately a characteristic of India today'.
The argument continued that India was primarily suitable for the production of tropical goods, and trade would remain largely an exchange of
the products of Indian agriculture for the manufactures of Europe.[182]

Officers in the Commerce Department began to dissect the work of
their Finance colleagues from the first sentence. Beginning with the
obvious, they suggested that 'to tell the person you desire to convince that
he suffers from a diseased mind is likely to defeat the object in view; it is
bad tactics'. It was also noted that the suggestion that India could not
become an industrialized nation was impolitic and clearly 'unappealing to

[179] D. Gladding (Home Department) to Local Governments, 21 August 1930, *ibid.*
[180] *Ibid.*
[181] *Ibid.*, 4 November 1930.
[182] H. W. Emerson Note re. Government propaganda re. Congress boycott of foreign goods
and Commerce Department reply, 16 June 1930, GOI (HomePol) 507/1930.

national sentiment'. To the Finance draft's reference to a time when unfortunate European consumers were exploited by India in the early days of the East India Company, Commerce simply noted that it betrayed 'an inadequate appreciation of the term "exploitation" as used in India'. Where Finance described boycott propaganda as a blow to Britain, Commerce suggested that any analysis of the motives behind the boycott was dangerous since it drew attention to the political strength of the weapon. In order to demonstrate the positive role played by the Government of India in India's industrial development, Finance had described Government of India efforts as being 'often in the teeth of strong opposition from the Home Government'. Commerce responded with a warning that such differences of opinion should not be disclosed in an 'inspired article'. Point by point, the ineptness of the Finance effort was demonstrated and its suppression, with the exception of some economic data, was inevitable.[183]

The Information Bureau had been founded by an historian and a preference for historical reference and perspective informed much of its product. While some considered the effort to be pedantic and useless, others were convinced that it helped to place the British regime in legitimate relationship with earlier dynasties, always an attractive argument for a Government which sought to defend itself on the basis of moral right and legal precedent. In reference to the Salt Tax, which Gandhi had turned into a powerful symbol of oppression, it was noted that this ancient method of raising revenue was not a 'satanic' British creation. Taxes had always been necessary and, referring to Gandhi's advocacy of sacrifice, the Salt Tax was described as the one contribution that all citizens made in return for the benefits of peace and order. This was no oppressive tax, it was asserted, since it reached all without unduly burdening any one.

After a detailed analysis and simple description of the tax, its sources and rationale – i.e., the Government made no profit on salt manufacture, only the duty, and without Government control on prices, the consumer would pay more – the historical context was established with quotations from the *Mahabharata* and Kautilya's *Arthashastra*.

For the protection of his subjects the King should realize from them one-sixth of the produce as tax. (Sloka, 25, p. 1445, Chapter 70)

With regard to the gold mines and the like, the sources of rivers and the herd of elephants, the King should appoint reliable ministers to decide the question of imposition of taxes, taking into consideration the profit and loss. (Sloka, 29, p. 1446, Chapter 70)

[183] *Ibid.*

Soon after the crystalisation of salt is over, the superintendent of salt shall in time collect both the money rent and the quantity of the shares of salt due to the Government and by the sale of salt he shall realize not only its value but also the premium of 5 per cent.

Imported salt shall pay one-sixth portion to the King. The sale of this portion shall fetch the premium of 5% or the 8% in cash. The purchasers shall pay not only the toll but also the compensation equivalent to the loss entailed on the King's commerce. In default of the above payment he shall be compelled to pay a fine of 600 panas.

Adulteration of salt shall be punished with the highest amercement; likewise persons other than hermits manufacturing salt without a licence. (*Arthashastra*, pp. 95–6, Chapter 12, R.Shama Shastri, trans.)[184]

The scholarship was impressive, but as Gandhi had demonstrated six months earlier, effective propaganda required imagination and flare. Accurate information was no substitute for an argument that would be read or an event that would attract wide attention. In his long march to Dandi on the Gujerat coast, Gandhi wrested the high ground from the Raj in an obvious and public way that left no room for rationalization. The legal case shorn of any moral content appeared especially inadequate in opposition to the Mahatma's simple and powerful message staged in an event covered by the world's press. The *Times of India* noted the futility of Gandhi's campaign, but it also provided publicity. Its 4 March edition included a photograph and description. 'An excellent impression of Mr Gandhi in pensive mood as he set forth on Wednesday morning from his Ashram at Sabarmati with 79 followers on his march towards an Independent India via the salt of Gujerat.'[185] The gentle mockery was obvious, but Gandhi's personal courage and determination were also publicized.

As had been the case in Bardoli in 1928, dramatic press coverage had highlighted a local revenue-assessment problem, turning it into a direct confrontation between an embattled peasantry and an arbitrary alien regime. Although the agitations were on a limited scale, 'their importance lay in the effect they had on the rest of India. At the time it seemed as if the "Indian peasant" was battling with the might of imperialism.'[186] Vallabhbhai Patel's campaign described daily in the press produced a 'a propaganda victory out of all proportion to its size'.[187] Gandhi's open

---

[184] Home Department British memorandum re. lines of propaganda, September 1930, GOI (HomePol) 5/X/1931.
[185] *Times of India*, 13 March 1930.
[186] David Hardiman, 'The Crisis of the Lesser Patidars: Peasant Agitations in Kheda District, Gujarat, 1917–1934', in D. A. Low, ed., *Congress and the Raj*, London: Heinemann, 1977, p. 71.
[187] Dennis Dalton, 'The Dandi March', in B. R. Nanda, *Essays in Modern Indian History*, Delhi: Oxford University Press, 1980, p. 86. The *Satyagraha Patrika* had a daily run of 10,000.

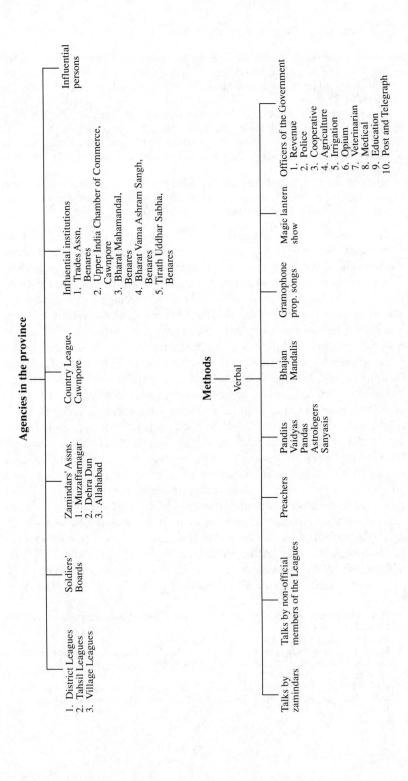

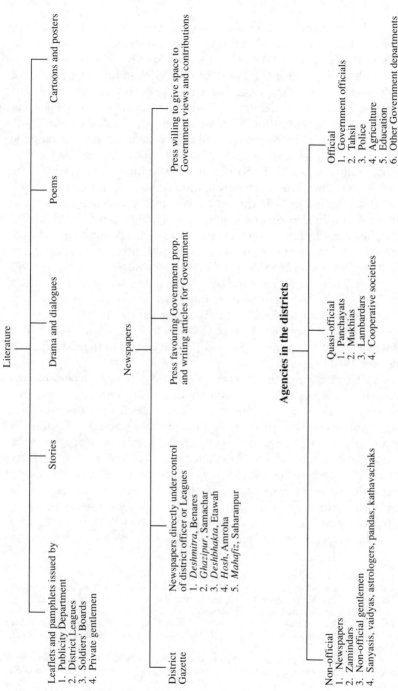

Literature

Leaflets and pamphlets issued by
1. Publicity Department
2. District Leagues
3. Soldiers' Boards
4. Private gentlemen

Stories

Drama and dialogues

Poems

Cartoons and posters

Newspapers

District
Gazette

Newspapers directly under control
of district officer or Leagues
1. *Deshmitra*, Benares
2. *Ghazipur*, Samachar
3. *Deshbhakta*, Etawah
4. *Hosh*, Amroha
5. *Mahafiz*, Saharanpur

Press favouring Government prop.
and writing articles for Government

Press willing to give space to
Government views and contributions

Agencies in the districts

Non-official
1. Newspapers
2. Zamindars
3. Non-official gentlemen
4. Sanyasis, vaidyas, astrologers, pandas, kathavachaks

Quasi-official
1. Panchayats
2. Mukhias
3. Lambardars
4. Cooperative societies

Official
1. Government officials
2. Tahsil
3. Police
4. Agriculture
5. Education
6. Other Government departments

Figure 1 *A bird's-eye view of the propaganda work by Ram Babu Saksena, MA, LLB, publicity and propaganda officer, United Provinces*
Source: GOI (HomePol) 35/28/1931.

letter to Irwin laying out the reasons for the return to Civil Disobedience was acclaimed and attacked, but it was covered in any case, with publication of the full text and detailed editorial comment.[188]

From the Lahore ultimatum in December 1929, to the renewal of Civil Disobedience in January 1932, the nationalist–Government confrontation was focused in a series of events which reflected the priority given in both camps to mobilization of popular opinion; and the difficulties, particularly for the Government of India, in accommodating the message to the immediate relationship. The Irwin Declaration and call to the Round Table, the Dandi Satyagraha, Government repression, the Gandhi–Irwin Pact, renewed confrontation and emergency powers – each event and situation in turn attracted widespread press coverage and the need to maximize benefits or contain the damage. Beyond the drama being played out by the lead actors on centre stage, a continuing chorus of communalist incitement, terrorist action, and rising rural discontent forced the debate between those officials who insisted that the Government must 'continue to make the best of the power we have'; and others who had been insisting for some time that emergency powers were essential to meet the challenge. Finally, in the spring of 1930, the experiment with 'press freedom' was ended with a Press Ordinance, which restored most of the powers that had been available to the Government under the 1910 Press Act.[189]

A Sub-Committee of the Viceroy's Executive Council was established to consider propaganda and publicity issues in connection with the renewed Civil Disobedience Movement, but its discussions did not move beyond policies and programmes that had become standard responses in the previous decade. Special arrangements for news distribution were made with Reuters and the Associated Press of India, new lines for propaganda were issued, the Army Department was encouraged to increase its publicity activity, and a range of unofficial contacts were called in to help support the campaign.[190] Local Government publicity organizations which had been dismantled in the mid-1920s in response to retrenchment pressures or legislative votes, were now reconstituted to

---

188 *Ibid.*, pp. 100–2. The *Pioneer* and *Times of India* published the full text of Gandhi's letter and devoted editorials to a critique. The *Leader* noted that most moderates opposed Gandhi, but on this occasion he was not wrong. Gandhi 'is in truth a Mahatma by reason of his unusual and spiritual greatness'.

189 The 1930 Ordinance was a holding strategy. A new Press Act was passed in 1931. See S. Natarajan, *A History of the Press in India*, Bombay, Asia Publishing House, 1962, Appendix I, Press Legislation, pp. 325–77.

190 Note re. publicity and propaganda in connection with the Civil Disobedience Movement – Viceroy's Executive Council Sub-Committee meeting, 29 May 1930, GOI (HomePol) 5/X/1931.

meet the renewed challenge[191] with some, at least on an organization chart, achieving extraordinary comprehensiveness.

In December 1930, however, the Home Department reluctantly advised the Viceroy that central press legislation would be required to control press incitement to violence and communalist agitation. The Chittagong armoury raid had concentrated the centre's attention on Bengal, and an attempt had been made to contain the situation through local legislation. But it seemed clear that reluctance to confront the non-official majority in the central legislature with an unpopular Press Bill was no longer tenable in the context of Local Government demands for support. Home Department officials thought there was a 'fair chance' for the Bill to pass without certification[192] since the Criminal Law Amendment Bill had passed in the Bengal legislature. They were prepared to certify the legislation if necessary, but hoped to attract support by asking for a five-year term and settling for one year with power to extend one year at a time to a five-year maximum.[193]

The Government prepared its case with extraordinary care for detail and strategy. Before the Bill was presented to a Select Committee, the Viceroy reduced the proposed time frame to three years and a mass of materials was collected to support the need for action. A calendar of terrorist acts prepared by the Bengal Government in support of their Criminal Law Amendment Bill was attached to specimens of terrorist leaflets, *Congress Bulletins*, extracts from the Bengal and Punjab press, and terrorist statements noting that they were incited to join the movement by newspaper writings.[194] The Government insisted that no general attack on the press was intended, and a Bill restricted to incitement to murder and violence replaced a more general proposal that had been introduced on 1 January and withdrawn in September. It was this restricted Bill that was referred to the Select Committee with an argument that Government was entitled to support in such a situation since both political power and responsibility had been transferred to non-official legislators.[195]

---

191 In Bombay the legislature threw out the Publicity Department's grant in 1924, and the Government amalgamated the Directorates of Information and Labour. Judith M. Brown, *Modern India: The Origins of An Asian Democracy*, Delhi: Oxford, 1985, p. 237. In 1930, a separate office for the Director of Information was re-established in Bombay. Home Department (Bombay) to H. W. Emerson (Home Department GOI), 8 July 1930, GOI (HomePol) 35/2/1931.

192 Home Department Note to PSV, 30 December 1930, re-enacting a Bill in the Legislative Assembly to control the press on the lines of the India Press and Unauthorised News Sheets Ordinance X of 1931, GOI (HomePol) 22/29 and KW I and II.

193 *Ibid.*

194 *Ibid.*

195 Crerar memorandum re. enactment of Indian Press (Emergency Powers) Act, 1931, 11 September 1931, GOI (HomePol) 4/36/1931.

The major changes made in the Bill by the Select Committee and accepted by the Government reflected a shared concern for constitutional process and press freedom. The title of the Bill was changed to emphasize the emergency nature of the legislation; and its life was limited to one year with executive power to extend for only one additional year rather than the original three to five. A number of changes protected the non-offending press. Security deposits were to be refunded after three months without offence for a new press, a maximum security was set, and most important, in any appeal to the High Court, a Local Government was required to describe the offending matter on which it based its demand for security. The precise definition of what constituted offending matter was to be left to the court if necessary. Finally any offending press which furnished a security deposit was not to be subject to forfeiture. After a lengthy debate, the Bill was adopted with a thirty-one vote majority; officials, non-official British, and Muslim Members generally supporting the legislation. In a minute of dissent, five Members attacked the Bill because it remained in their view too broad a challenge to press freedom and did not go far enough in limiting arbitrary executive action by extending the power of the High Court.[196] Within the Home Department, however, the enhanced powers of judicial review appeared to deny them the essential authority they had sought to meet the emergency.

These suggestions strike at the very root principle of the Bill, which is designed to give power to the Executive to demand and forfeit security. The power to demand security is likely to lose all its preventive and deterrent value if restricted in this manner and the acceptance of the proposals would be likely to make the Bill entirely ineffective for the purposes in view. As the Bill stands an appeal lies to the High Court against the forfeiture of security and this secures the depositor against any financial loss due to arbitrary executive action.[197]

Between the initiation of the first Press Act proposal and the passage of legislation nine months later, the political situation at the centre moved dramatically away from confrontation. The Delhi Pact of 5 March 1931, ended the current round of Non-cooperation but created a range of ambiguities and problems for both camps. For the official propagandist, the unrestrained anti-Congress message was no longer available to a Government that wanted the settlement to last and had invested much of its diminishing financial and political capital in the success of the Round Table process. New and elaborate plans had been formulated,[198] but they

---

[196] Minute of Dissent: H. S. Gour, B. Sitaramaya Raju, B. R. Puri, C. S. Ranga Iyer, A. Hoon, *ibid.*

[197] Home Department note, 22 September 1931, *ibid.*

[198] The proposals were drafted by H. J. Davis, former advertising manager, *Times of India*: (1) Greater use of Official District Gazettes, (2) greater use of village officers or

were stored away for the inevitable return to battle.[199] Although it was assumed that the Congress would continue to publish reports on the 1930–1 Civil Disobedience Movement for both domestic and foreign consumption that would keep up the 'war mentality' and 'create more enmity against Government',[200] Home Department officials limited themselves to correction or contradicting accounts they considered untrue or exaggerated.[201]

The India Office agreed that 'propaganda directed against the Congress is of course out of the question'. The Government would be accused of advancing a 'partisan argument', no longer acceptable under the informal guidelines Lord Irwin had established. The new challenge was to get out the information and point of view that would serve the Government's interests without attacking Congress. Information officers were urged to describe the better atmosphere, the benefits of peace, and the renewed opportunities for trade with the end of Civil Disobedience. It was now necessary to find ways to weaken the case of diehards in the Congress who wanted a fight to the finish, while avoiding 'the weakness of appearing to argue for the status quo and oppose National feelings'.[202] Anything connected with the Round Table Conference was considered good, since it reflected the Government's determination to move ahead with constitutional reforms whatever the provocation.[203]

The burden of these constraints was made explicit in the following year

---

headmen, (3) a special department of the CID to deal with the vernacular press, (4) greater use of Government printing presses, (5) overhaul of present publicity departments of Government: Central and Provincial, enlarging their scope, (6) greater use of reliable press in India with Government paying regular rates for advertisement, (7) greater aid by CID and DPI to political officers in native states, (8) enlargement of oriental translating departments and greater attention to illiterates, (9) greater use of public meeting places, i.e., railway stations, post and telegraph offices, (10) less dependence on Secretariats and more on local officials, (11) greater cooperation among services: police, forests, agriculture, etc., (12) need to gain support from unofficial Europeans: 'Sympathy and understanding by all Europeans', (13) greater use of posters, news sheets, pamphlets, (14) cinema lecture tours, (15) publicizing non-political issues: health, livestock, etc. H. J. Davis to Sir Findlater Stewart (IO), 27 January 1931, GOI (HomePol) 35/31/1932. While the India Office was generally supportive, the Home Department was sceptical. The response emphasized the inexperience of local officers with publicity responsibilities, constrained funding, an uneducated public, packaging appropriate materials, differences of opinion among officials, Assembly overview, and concern about the loyalty of local Indian officials. There was agreement to move slowly, recognizing that the whole process was new to India. Home Department note, 11 April 1931, *ibid.*

[199] Emerson to Findlater Stewart, 26 May 1931, GOI (HomePol) 35/3/1932.

[200] H. William (DIB) note, 22 June 1931, re. copies of PCC reports on the Civil Disobedience Movement, 1930–1, GOI (HomePol) 5/62/1932.

[201] *Ibid.*, 23 June 1931.

[202] Note on propaganda enclosed with Secretary of State to Viceroy, 26 June 1931, GOI (HomePol) 35/3/1932.

[203] *Ibid.*

after the renewal of Civil Disobedience allowed for a return to business as usual in the Home Department. The Home Secretary noted that the Delhi Pact had made propaganda work difficult in 1931, but now with the Government fighting the Congress as an unlawful association, 'this propaganda is comparatively easy'.[204] He recognized, however, that the political role determined for the Congress in the Government's own forecasts would bring problems in the future. At an earlier stage in the process, initiated with the 1919 Government of India Act, many had argued that the development of political parties would create a new arena for constitutional debate, and redirect attacks on the British regime to an opposition competing for seats and power. But the Congress's dominant position had made many officials less sanguine about such a scenario. 'When and if Congress abandons its present hostile attitude, it becomes merely a political party, and this makes it difficult for Government officers to combat it.'[205] It was clear that the need for official neutrality would make non-official work more important, especially in elections; but their marginal success in rallying this kind of support was reflected in the Home Secretary's lament, 'how can we help those who will not help themselves'.[206]

In 'peacetime' the continuing financial constraints were also made worse. As long as the Congress was associated with subversive activities, expenses could be justified to both the legislatures and the Finance Department. But a Congress Party contesting an election had some institutional protections unplanned in anyone's scenario. The recurrent demand to 'take a leaf out of the Congress book and spend money',[207] seemed less an option than ever before. To the Secretary of State's suggestion that one or two first rate press officers be sent out from England, the Home Secretary noted the unlikelihood of their being useful, 'unless they appreciated fully the peculiar conditions prevailing here, of an alien Government in a position of splendid isolation'.[208]

The truce was broken in January 1932, with the return of the Congress to Civil Disobedience and of the Government to emergency powers and overwhelming force. Although this round of confrontation would not be formally withdrawn until April 1934, official determination to crush the

---

[204] M. G. Hallett note, 25 July 1932, GOI (HomePol) 35/17 and KW, 1932.
[205] *Ibid.*
[206] *Ibid.*
[207] Chief Commissioner, Delhi to H. W. Emerson, 28 January 1930, GOI (HomePol) 489/1930.
[208] M. G. Hallett note, 25 July 1932, GOI (HomePol) 35/17 and KW 1932.

movement led to its decline by the end of 1932.[209] As had been the case in the past, information officers rose to the occasion, again released from the constraints of constitutional practice. It would be the last time before the outbreak of World War Two allowed an easy conscience for those responsible for controlling the exchange of information and viewpoint within India, and between India and the rest of the world. Throughout the Civil Disobedience campaign, however, preparations for a return to collaboration with the Congress in the context of councils and ministries and another round of elections remained a high priority for the Government and its publicity staff, who concentrated their attention on describing the place and role of the various players in the constitutional endgame which was about to begin.

In addition to the more obvious forms for propagandizing the Government's position, officials engaged in intense lobbying to gain the support of influential Indian leaders for the preservation of specific areas of executive authority. During the preparation of the Joint Select Committee Report on the new reforms, Sir Reginald Clark urged Purshotamdas Thakurdas, 'in the interest of India', to insist on some arrangement in the White Paper by which there would be no interference from ministers in either the Central or Provincial Governments regarding the CBI at Delhi and Simla. Clark was particularly concerned that the Director of the CBI not be required to divulge the sources of information essential for its work.[210] Although this attempt to establish an arms-length relationship would have very mixed success, it reflected a developing consensus among officials that its relationship with the press and news services had to become professional and disinterested.

The publication of the Report presented a new challenge, the creation of a positive environment for its reception both in India and in Britain. A 'chorus of disapproval' was anticipated by the Secretary of State and he urged the Government of India to join the India Office in organizing 'an effective counterblast'.[211] Officials in India, confident that the country

---

[209] B. R. Sen, Additional Deputy Secretary (Bengal) to all District Officers, 13 April 1932, IO L/I/1 424, File 171/4.

[210] Purshotamdas Thakurdas, *London Diary*, 29 May 1933. Thakurdas Papers, 140. During this visit to London to participate in the Joint Committee hearings, Thakurdas dined with Rushbrook Williams, who reminded him that Thakurdas' intervention in support of the retention of the CBI in 1922 had helped his career. Thakurdas noted in his diary that the CBI 'was then supposed to be at least neutral in its outlook and not anti-nationalist. Since then that Department has gradually got into the Home Department atmosphere, and I do not think it did any service from the Indian point of view.'

[211] Secretary of State to Viceroy, 1 February 1934, GOI (HomePol) 39/18/34.

was tired of agitation and the Congress too disorganized to mount a successful campaign, seemed concerned that opposition editorials in the Indian press would strengthen conservative anti-reform forces in England.[212] It was assumed that the English-owned press, some of the Muslim press, and papers like the *Hindu* would publish articles supporting the Report, and their efforts were concentrated on minimizing the risk of a bad press from the rest. They were especially concerned with the English-language press which could be easily quoted in speeches in Westminster and contrived to ensure that the initial coverage would be full and the response positive or at least non-committal.[213]

The India Office took the responsibility for preparing a summary of the Report especially for Indian consumption, another was prepared for England; and the Home Department contrived to issue the summary to the Indian press and news agencies without advance notice in order to obviate the preparation of an alternative. On the basis of previous experience with this technique, the Home Member was confident that 'practically every English written newspaper in the country, irrespective of its political views', would publish the India Office material without change.[214] Findlater Stewart, the Under-Secretary of State, was reminded about the need for secrecy and the danger of leakages, especially in Britain, where it was assumed that the India Office would have to battle opposition on both the right and the left.[215]

The preparation of 'lines of action' reflected the new confidence of information officers about the situation in India. Ian Stephens suggested three possible approaches: (1) to refute Congress misrepresentation of the White Paper generally; (2) to deride the Congress proposal for a 'Constituent Assembly'; and (3) to emphasize inconsistencies in the Congress attitude towards the 'Communal Award'. After reflection, however, he thought it appropriate to pass up the opportunity to use the Assembly and Communal issues since there appeared to be adequate opposition within the Congress and in the national press.[216] Stephens' optimism reflected the growing divisions and communalizing of the debate within the nationalist movement and reflected at the Round Table meetings. The inclusion of the princes and their states in a new Indian federation appeared to provide sufficient conservative ballast to ensure the stability of the state. Separate electorates for Muslims and untouchables institu-

[212] M. G. Hallett note re. the Joint Select Committee Report, 14 February 1934, *ibid.*
[213] *Ibid.*
[214] Home Member to Sir Findlater Stewart (IO) 14 March 1934, *ibid.*
[215] *Ibid.*
[216] I. M. Stephens note, 4 August 1934, GOI (HomePol) 51/14/36.

tionalized social and religious distinctions as an additional guarantee against a united nationalist campaign.

The 1932 Communal Award which was meant to entrench a separate political identity for untouchables, produced strong opposition and a successful campaign led by Gandhi to compel the Prime Minister to accept a compromise. But caste Hindu defensiveness also produced a revitalized message – 'Hinduism in danger'. The Congress might reject 'playing the communal card' and insist on its secular character and principles, but its All-India umbrella remained a refuge for many with their own game on the side. Divisions among nationalists continued to force the main game back to the British field of play. In 1934, M. M. Malaviya and his Congress Nationalist Party were pressing their campaign for election to the Councils and ignoring the Congress Parliamentary Board's opposition to participation in elections and taking office under the British regime. Attempts to revive the Swarajya Party were underway and the Hindu Mahasabha, with its Congress adherents, symbolized the renaissant communal content of political debate. While the *Hindu* and the *Bombay Chronicle* supported the Congress position, the *Tribune* and the *Amrita Bazar Patrika* opposed it.[217]

The apparent arrival of party politics further enhanced the Government's confidence and made officials more restrained regarding their role in the debate. After orchestrating the publication of the White Paper, publicity was confined in the first instance to the correction of misrepresentation.[218] The impending constitutional changes had clearly made an impact, especially on local officials as Hyde Gowan, the Governor of the Central Provinces, noted in his response to Lord Willingdon's general letter concerning reforms propaganda. He quoted the Central Provinces Home Member, Raghavendra Rao, who argued that propaganda activities by Government servants might be considered justified now but turn out to be a serious political danger under a more responsible system of Government. 'Once the practice is sanctioned and becomes crystallised,' he suggested, 'the lower services would be increasingly utilised for doing propaganda for the Government of the day and keeping it going. Nothing would be more suicidal to the healthy growth of 'responsible' Government'.[219]

The Bengal Government's press officer described the reticence of local officers in organizing propaganda, noting that it was foreign to past

---

[217] *Ibid.*
[218] Home Member note, 19 June 1934, re. propaganda in favour of the White Paper and against a constitutional Assembly, *ibid.*
[219] Hyde Gowan to Willingdon, 18 October 1934, GOI (HomePol) 39/18/34.

traditions and many were 'yet unable to accommodate themselves to the changed circumstances in the country'. But he remained committed to 'traditional' practice. In his view, relations between the press and the Bengal Government had been one of continuous struggle since Lytton's 1878 Press Act, and he described the more forceful 'traditional' style used during the recent Civil Disobedience campaign. 'It was clear that so long as the back of the nationalist press was not broken, it would refuse to be fed.' Official pressure had, however, produced visible benefits. The *Patrika* and *Basumati* to some extent, and *Hitavadi* and *Bangabasi* to a larger extent were now willing to publish material supplied by the press officer.[220]

In regard to the 1934 Central Legislative Assembly elections, it was not a question of choosing between Central Provinces constitutional reticence and Bengal aggressiveness. Home Department officials had difficulty in stimulating any interest at all. Local Governments were now urged to combine a campaign of support for the White Paper and the attraction of good candidates. Although the difficulties in working through the agency of Government servants were obvious, there appeared to be no other way to influence the elections. Officials were pressed to have private conversations with provincial ministers, who did not share their constitutional disability, and urge them to canvass constituencies and influence candidate selection. Lord Willingdon suggested to Provincial Governors that discrete conversations with orthodox Hindu representatives might emphasize changes in religious institutions advocated by the Congress, and noted the Temple Entry Bill as evidence of the Government's opposition to revolutionary changes and willingness to assist them if they defended themselves.[221]

The challenge from Delhi that the battle should not be lost by default had little effect. Malcolm Hailey noted that there was little enthusiasm for the central Assembly elections in the United Provinces, where the provincial legislature was viewed as the place 'where one can do something for himself and his friends'. Assembly elections were expensive and the return did not seem worth the investment. The United Provinces Government had managed to get a group of landlords to form two associations to select and assist candidates, but there were clearly too many All-India candidates in the United Provinces to fight all the seats. Hailey reminded the Viceroy of the United Provinces Government's effective anti-Congress publicity work during the non-cooperation period, but the

---

[220] Report on propaganda and publicity in Bengal during the period January 1932 to March 1933, 12 May 1933, GOI (HomePol) 39/9/1933.

[221] Willingdon to Provincial Governors, 15 September 1934, GOI (HomePol) 39/16/34.

change in Congress policy had 'raised awkward questions'. Landlords who had always supported the Government wanted support for their candidates, but the new situation had produced new rules. He assumed, however, that it was still legitimate to oppose socialism and communism and therefore by implication the Congress left.[222] The situation was not unlike that which had once constrained nationalist critics of Government when their attack on 'Imperialism' and 'Capitalism' was carefully scrutinized, often in the courts, for a direct challenge to the legitimacy of the Government of India. To the extent that finesse remained the primary attribute of the successful player, the game remained the same; only the sides had changed.

The Bihar and Central Provinces Governments reiterated the local lack of interest, and the Governor of Bengal assumed there would be a Congress sweep. Lord Brabourne, like Hailey, referred to the days of enthusiastic activity during the Civil Disobedience Movement, noting in contrast the collapse of Bombay's propaganda organization and the concerns about anti-Congress bias that would be raised by any attempt to rebuild it. The Governor assumed that Willingdon would agree that an official propaganda agency had now become 'a highly dangerous precedent for the future'.[223] The Governor of Assam summarized the problem and identified its source. The solid conservative leadership in the province had no interest in the central Legislative Assembly and always won in local elections. As a result, the Congress and Malaviya Nationalist candidates had no serious opposition. In these circumstances, he insisted, there was simply no role for Government. The same scenario applied to the White Paper debate.

If we could conceive of circumstances in which the country would be called on to decide such an issue as 'This Bill or else back to autocracy', then a party could arise to fight for the Bill entire or modified. As it is, the Bill, is safe and represents the minimum. The obvious line for anyone is to go into opposition and demand the maximum, secure in the knowledge that there is nothing to lose.

Keane assumed, however, that the Government could 'take care of itself'.[224]

Within the Central Government, there was growing concern that a Congress victory would likely be misunderstood by the British public unless the press prepared the ground for the election results. Ian Stephens,

---

[222] M. Hailey, Governor of United Provinces to Willingdon, 18 September 1934, *ibid.*

[223] J. D. Sifton (Bihar) to Willingdon, 21 September 1934; Hyde Gowan (Central Provinces) to Willingdon, 24 September 1934; J. A. Woodhead (Bengal) to Willingdon, 30 September 1934, *ibid.*

[224] M. Keane (Assam) to Willingdon, 24 September 1934, *ibid.*

the senior information officer, cautioned the Simla representative of the *Times* about the tendency to view the situation as a 'test match between the Government and the Congress, on whose result the political future of India will largely depend'. This was, he insisted, fundamentally wrong, since unlike England, general elections in India made no impact on 'an irremovable Executive'. The Government, therefore, should not be perceived as participating in the struggle, but rather as an umpire whose conduct was constrained by the requirement for strict neutrality. In addition, Stephens noted, the Government had no reason to deplore Congress participation in the elections since it reflected the success of constitutionalism in contrast to the futility of non-cooperation. He was also clearly in agreement with local officials about the futility of any constitutional campaign against the Congress' All-India position ('under the existing constitution there has always been something essentially unreal about Assembly elections'), and directed the attention of the *Times* to Provincial Councils for a much closer parallel to the British House of Commons. It was at this level, he insisted, where the 'active, vital participation of representative elements takes place'. If the *Times* would 'put this all across for British consumption,' Stephens concluded, 'we shall be much obliged'.[225]

On 23 March 1929, Lord Irwin had written to the Provincial Governors about the need to look again at some form of press legislation to control communal incitement and the advocacy of violence. The exchange led eventually to the Press Ordinance of 1930, and a new Press Act in the following year. It is clear from his letter, however, and a detailed note prepared by the DCBI, John Coatman,[226] that the solution to the Government's political problem as reflected in its continuing inability to attract a good press was presumed to be found in a further significant development of self-government. 'A popular Government will not be able to maintain itself without support in the press, and the present phase of having practically all newspapers ranged in opposition to Government need hardly be expected to survive the introduction of more popular machinery, if this be the outcome of the present enquiry'.[227]

The emergence of the Swarayja and Responsivist Parties in the 1920s gave support to those in and out of Government who looked forward to the evolution of modern party politics without the overarching presence of the Congress. In 1934, there were still some official believers in a

[225] I. M. Stephens to Alexander Inglis, representative of the *Times*, 15 October 1934, *ibid.*
[226] John Coatman note on the 'Tone of Certain Sections of the Press and the Policy to be adopted towards it', 1 January 1929, GOI (HomePol) 178/29/1929 and KW.
[227] Irwin to Governors, 23 March 1929, *ibid.*

non-Congress afterlife, who looked to the 'localities' to provide a more malleable alternative. But others had made their peace with a Congress future in which the left, represented by Jawaharlal Nehru and Subhas Bose, by Kisan Sabhas and a socialist mandate, would be contained and controlled by practical pro-business, anti-communist leaders like Sardar Patel and C. R. Rajagopalachari. The elections of 1937 produced a range of winners not always apparent in the victory speeches of the candidates. 'The election which will take place will be controlled by the "Vallabhbhai Group", and if Lord Linlithgow handles the situation properly, there is every likelihood of the Congressmen coming into office'.[228]

During the 1937 election campaign, the question of an official propaganda effort to respond to the All Indian Congress Committee (AICC) was raised by Information officials, but never given serious consideration. 'The matter may be allowed to drop', declared the Deputy Home Secretary, R. M. Maxwell. 'The Bureau is always on doubtful ground if it tries to score propaganda points.'[229] Ian Stephens agreed and noted in addition that AICC statements were not always antagonistic to the Government's interests. Always adept at finding something positive to support a progressive image for the Government of India, Stephens quoted an AICC election bulletin which seemed to suggest that democracy had arrived without the necessity for the removal of the British administration: 'This is the greatest election that India has ever seen. The ballot-box has reached the fringe of the village and the city-slum, and with it, democracy in various garbs has come nosing round unfrequented spots.'[230] A 1938 review of the impact on the press of the 1937 elections and the introduction of provincial autonomy provided further cause for optimism. It appeared that the only section of the press that Indian ministries could count on was the Anglo-Indian press. The *Statesman* was generally friendly to Congress Governments and supportive of the non-Congress Government in Bengal. The *Times of India* was only 'slightly more critical'; and the *Madras Mail* concentrated on local issues on their merit. The leading nationalist press was, however, strongly critical of Congress Governments' resort to 'repressive' measures such as the enforcement of the Criminal Law Amendment Act in Madras, and the continuing demand for securities from newspapers in Bombay and in the Central Provinces. In regard to the crisis in the Central Provinces in which the premier, Dr Khare, was forced out by the Congress leadership, the

---

[228] J. D. Birla to P. Thakurdas, 20 April 1936, quoted in Sunmit Sarkar, *Modern India, 1885–1947*, p. 348.

[229] R. M. Maxwell, 28 February 1937, GOI (HomePol) 4/4/37.

[230] AICC (Department of Political and Economic Information) *Bulletin*, quoted by Ian Stephens, 8 February 1937, *ibid.*

Patrika, Tribune, and *Hindu* were strongly critical of the 'fascist methods' of the Congress Working Committee. While the left-leaning section of the nationalist press was critical of this apparent business as usual policy of Local Governments, Liberal papers like the *Leader* were equally uncompromising in their criticism of such Congress Government actions.[231]

The Congress leadership could still depend on S. A. Brelvi and his *Bombay Chronicle* to give them the benefit of the doubt and consistent support. And the *Hindustan Times,* though unenthusiastic about labour legislation that affected owner G. D. Birla's business interests, could still call itself a Congress paper. But the new leaders, like those they succeeded, wanted loyalty, not criticism. In response to a pledge of support 'when they were right' from Swaminath Sadanand of the Free Press of India (FPI) Vallabhbhai Patel declared the interest of all Governments: 'We are interested in newspapers which will support us wholeheartedly. To say you will support us when we are right is meaningless. For why should anyone oppose us then?'[232] With the achievement of power and office in the provinces, the Congress leadership felt the need more than ever before for a loyal party press. The lack of a guarantee that nationalist Indian-owned papers would support Congress Governments resulted in the establishment of the *National Herald* in Lucknow, founded by Jawaharlal Nehru and pledged to support the policy of the Congress High Command; and the *Indian Express* in Madras, the mouthpiece of the Premier, C. Rajagopalachari.

While the Indian ministries in the provinces settled into new roles and responsibilities, Government at the centre sought to accommodate the new situation while exploring the margins of its retained authority. The possibility of war in Europe and an inevitable role for the Indian army caused the Home Department to raise the question of press censorship under the Defence of India Act. Under the Act passed in 1915 by the central legislature, censorship powers were vested in the Governor-General; but the Government of India Act of 1935, contained no entry 'Defence of India' as an exclusively federal subject. It was possible to have an Act passed in the central legislature on the lines of the old Defence of India Act, but the presence of newspapers as an item in the concurrent legislative list placed the executive authority in this regard with the provinces. It was clearly no longer possible for the Home Department to centralize all executive authority in respect of newspaper censorship. If

---

[231] Survey of the policy of newspapers in India since the introduction of provincial autonomy, Bureau of Public Information (GOI) November 1938, GOI (HomePol) 53/2/1938. Also IO L/I/1/332, File 131/2.
[232] Quoted in Natarajan, *History of the Press in India,* p. 313.

any system was to be effective, it would have to depend on provincial cooperation.[233]

V. P. Menon, then an official in the Reforms Office, could not imagine any situation in which such cooperation would not be offered in wartime 'for the sake of their own self-interest, if for no other reason';[234] but the continual discovery of the intimate relationship between the transfer of areas of authority within India, and Britain's general world interests concentrated the minds of officials on what still could be done. Rumours began to spread about the flow of German, Japanese, and Italian funds to the Indian press. An Indo-German news exchange was apparently entirely funded by private German money. The Bombay Press Service run by R. Krishnamachari, originally an anti-communist venture financed by Sir Cowasji Jehangir and other Bombay businessmen, appeared to be working for the Germans and with their money.[235] Reports of a Rs 1,000 per month retainer for the *Hindustan Times* in return for pro-Nazi articles and the transfer of Italian firms' advertising from the *Statesman* to the *Patrika* for some pro-Italian propaganda were given some credence in the Home Department, although proof was elusive. It was also assumed that the Japanese Government funded *New Asia* and the *Eastern Economist*, and provided as well an additional Rs 12,000 for general propaganda and espionage in India.[236] The restoration of broad executive powers during the war and the demise of Congress Governments in the provinces, however, removed 'for the duration' concerns in Delhi about constitutional constraints.

The passage of the 1935 Government of India Act had evoked a range of responses from officials in India responsible for its implementation. In regard to information policy and Government relations with the press, the most influential transition figure was A. H. Joyce. He was an official in the Simla CBI in 1935, and transferred to the India Office the following year as an assistant information officer. He returned to India for a six-month deputation in 1936, and in 1937, returned again as DPI for another six months at the request of the Viceroy.[237] During his initial appointment, Joyce prepared a memorandum for the Home Department,[238] predicated

233 V. P. Menon note, 24 July 1937, GOI (HomePol) 21/13/138.
234 *Ibid.*
235 R. Krishnamachari, editor of the *Indian Mirror* (Bombay) started the Bombay Press Service in 1936. It was anti-communist and anti-Congress socialist and it achieved a measure of success with weekly bulletins and leaflets published with a range of Anglo-Indian and Indian papers. In 1937, he sought support from the Home Department but after a brief consideration was refused, GOI (HomePol) 16/39/36 and 39/9/36.
236 DIB note on expenditure of foreign money in India on subversive propaganda, GOI (HomePol) 23/37/39.
237 GOI (HomePol) 16/25/36.
238 A. H. Joyce memorandum of relations with the press, 7 May 1935, IO L/P & J/7/896.

on the assumption that party Government was virtually at hand and the Government of India was required finally to change both its viewpoint and practice in its relations with the press. He recognized that this had been the direction of Government planning for some time, but a new system seemed essential to carry the administration through this transitional period and on to a future relationship with an independent Indian Government not yet determined.

Joyce advocated an open, even-handed, professional relationship centred in an Information Bureau that recognized its responsibility to safeguard the interests of Government, but respected as well the interests and priorities of the press. This would require, he insisted, that the Government treat its own senior information officer as a member of its inner circle, informed about matters available to the public, and about confidential issues as well. His advocacy had many similarities to arguments that had been made by Rushbrook Williams in 1920, but in 1935 a professional press argument attracted a positive response.

If a Publicity Officer is kept in touch with such questions he has a grip of the situation if news should break suddenly, he can act with knowledge if there is a leakage, and if matters take a normal course he has the advantage of background which will enable him to deal more efficiently with any question of publicity if and when it arises.

Every journalist goes about with his eyes and ears open. He gets a hint here and a hint there, and from the unlimited sources open to him, he eventually strikes an item of first class news. Time is the all important factor with him and it will be appreciated that a great deal may depend upon a Publicity Officer from whom an enquiry is made or from whom guidance is sought, being able to handle a situation at once with at least some knowledge of the circumstances.[239]

Joyce insisted that all communiqués and statements to the press should come through the DPI's office, but noted as well that such official statements were rarely sufficient to satisfy the need of editors and correspondents for 'background and guidance'. In such cases he suggested three possible responses: an unofficial note that could be made available at the discretion of the DPI; a press conference conducted by the DPI or on occasion by a Member of Council or department secretary; or in delicate circumstances a private briefing of a few reliable correspondents. Joyce noted that all three methods were now used with success in England and there no longer appeared to be any reason not to develop similar responses in India.

The core of Joyce's proposals was a commitment to equality of treatment of the press as a whole in the supply of general information.

[239] *Ibid.*

There is nothing that a journalist fears most in the exercise of his profession than that he may be 'scooped' by a competitor and it is of the greatest importance that every accredited journalist shall feel that in his relations with the official world, he will not be let down as a result of preferential treatment to a rival. Only by the strict application of this principle in the dissemination of news can the personal element of good will, so essential to effective contact and influence with the Press, be established and maintained.[240]

Joyce reiterated his views in 1937, during his temporary appointment as Director of the Public Information Bureau.

I am not in favour of any attempt to influence public opinion through the Press except by open methods of publicity. What the Government of India may lack, in present circumstances, in public support for their policies or in power to guide and influence the Press, cannot in my view be made good in any degree of reality, by recourse to any other means.[241]

By March 1938, the Home Department could inform the India Office that the Government of India was 'seeking to close down the subterranean side of our Information Bureau in consonance with Joyce's recommendations'.[242] There remained, however, in Joyce's view one major problem that prevented both the efficient propagation of Government news, and the fair and equitable treatment of the press generally. India required, he insisted, a reliable news service, and the continuing relationship of the Government of India with the indirectly subsidized Reuters–Associated Press of India (API) organization seemed to serve only the interests of that agency. Both in India and in England, Joyce campaigned for an independent and apolitical news service similar to England's Press Association, itself the progeny of Reuters. Joyce was not alone in this enterprise. Reuters had been at the hub of the British-controlled communications network in India, and throughout the world, for more than half a century. Since the end of World War One, however, the company's interests had tended to drift in an independent direction, without however, any severance of its intimate connections with the Government of India. A range of protagonists in the Government, the nationalist leadership, and the Indian and Anglo-Indian press had developed a relationship with Reuters founded on a mixture of necessity, admiration, and distrust. While officials suspected that the company's Indian news coverage had fallen into antagonistic nationalist hands, nationalist leaders and the Indian press viewed it as virtually a department of the Government. Reuters itself had begun to turn its attention toward survival

---

[240] *Ibid.*
[241] A. H. Joyce report, 16 October 1937, IO L/P & J/7/1840.
[242] W. Thorn, Home Department (GOI) to R. T. Peel, Secretary, Public and Judicial Department (IO) 15 March 1938, *ibid.*

in India, whatever the party in control, from the early 1920s. The story of the evolution of its 'Indian' identity, in parallel but quite separate from the Government's efforts, and the attempts to establish an alternative news service are important aspects of the history of the press and the development of an indigenous communications network in this period.

2 The news services: 'impartial Reuters' or 'foreign pipes'

Reuters

When Henry Collins established the first Reuters office in India in 1866, his company had already become one of the dominant communications powers in the world. Through reciprocal news exchanges which would be enshrined in agency treaties in 1879, Reuters shared with its two major competitors, Havas and Wolff, a division of the world into 'spheres of influence', reflecting the positions and priorities of their national sponsors. The strategic interests of Germany and Wolff were on the continent, and that company received exclusive right to exploit Austria, the Scandinavian countries, and Russia. In return for their abstinence in Northern Europe, the others were amply compensated. Havas was granted the French Empire by right, and received as well the countries of Latin Europe and eventually South America. Reuters obtained the monopoly for the British Empire and the Far East.[1]

Like the founders of British interests in India, Reuters' agents came to do business, to carry commercial news from Britain to the merchants on the spot, and to share in their financial success. The need for speed and accuracy had never been more important than in the mid-1860s, when the American Civil War had caused a dramatic rise in cotton prices and the chance for quick profits. By 1865, the first Indo-European overland line was in place. Four years later, the Indian Submarine Company's cable completed the final link between Aden and Bombay, providing a half-hour telegraph exchange between London and Simla.[2] Although the service was expensive, £1 per word with a minimum of £20 per cable, there was no lack of subscribers. Forty clients were required in order to make the commercial service viable. By the end of the first year, Collins had

---

[1] The best general history of Reuters is Graham Storey's *Reuters' Century*, London: Max Parrish, 1951. See also Henry Collins, *From Pigeon Post to Wireless*, London: Hodder and Stoughton Ltd, 1925.

[2] Storey, *Reuters' Century*, p. 67. See also F. J. Brown, *The Cable and Wireless Communications of the World*, London: Sir Isaac Pitman and Sons, Ltd, 1930.

signed up fifty.[3] From the beginning, there was no question regarding which agency would service India only whether anyone could afford it.[4] Happily for Reuters, there were many who could not afford to be without it. Neither was there any substantive consideration of the political significance of the little Bombay office with the flat above the shop, where Collins, with the assistance of one Parsee clerk and a messenger, laid the foundations of yet another British Empire in the East.

When Collins returned to England in 1872, Reuters had expanded its interests and services throughout the Far East, using fully the mandate allotted to the company in the Agency treaties. From Bombay to Yokahama, the company's writ was unchallenged; and to the end of World War One the business continued to grow throughout the world.[5] At times it required aggressive entrepreneurship, as in the case of the ill-fated Persian Concession of 1872.[6] In other areas, however, the company merely settled into place as one of the natural results of British conquest. Soon after the arrival of British forces in Egypt in 1882, Havas responded to the demise of French power and influence by closing its Cairo office; recognizing without debate Egypt's passage into the Reuters sphere of influence.[7]

A special relationship between the Government of India and Reuters had been initiated almost immediately after the first meeting between Collins and the Viceroy, Lord Lawrence. Each assumed that their particular interests would be served by the activity of the other and, as a beginning, Reuters telegrams were provided free to the Viceroy in exchange for early receipt of official Government of India news. Although this intimacy would one day be reviled as dangerous and unethical, in the

---

[3] Storey, *Reuters' Century*, p. 62.
[4] High cable charges remained a controversial issue until the cost was reduced to one penny per word as a World War Two priority. The focus for the cable charges debate was the Imperial Press Conference which met in 1909, 1920, 1935, and 1946. See Thomas H. Hardman, *A Parliament of the Press, the First Imperial Press Conference*, London: Horace Marshall and Son, 1909; Robert Donald, *The Imperial Press Conference in Canada*, London: Hodder and Stoughton, 1920; H. E. Turner, *The Fourth Imperial Press Conference (Britain) 1930*, London: The Empire Press Union, 1931; T. W. Mackenzie, *The Fifth Imperial Press Conference (South Africa) 1935*, London: The Empire Press Union, 1936; H. E. Turner, *The Sixth Imperial Press Conference (Britain) 1946*, London: The Empire Press Union, 1947.
[5] Storey, *Reuters' Century*, p. 43.
[6] The 'Persian Concession' was meant to mean no less than the opening up of Persia to the West. Reuters received major railway, mining, customs, industrial, and investment opportunities. The deal was described in the House of Commons as based 'on thoroughly English principles', but 'extraordinary' and 'dangerous'. It was abrogated in 1874. Storey, *Reuters' Century*, p. 78.
[7] *Ibid.*, p. 96.

mid-nineteenth century, both at home and in India, it seemed the natural result of success and well-earned status.[8]

The Government of India entered into its first formal agreement with Reuters in 1873. For a payment of Rs 600 per month, copies of foreign press telegrams were distributed to a number of Government officials. It was an indefinite arrangement, neither the number of copies nor the number of words being specified.[9] In succeeding years the relationship expanded: Government payments increased; post- and telegraph-rate concessions were granted; special services were introduced; and both merchant and client were clearly satisfied with the results of their association.[10] Political and official news, never a priority for Reuters unless some business interest was involved, had become essential to the administration of the Raj; its increasing burdens and complexity reflected in the increase in the minimum number of words deemed necessary to guarantee adequate linkage with London and the rest of the world. In 1878, the subsidy was raised to Rs 1,200 per month and a minimum of 2,400 words per month from London was required. The number of words and level of subsidy rose again during the South African War. By 1914, no less than 219,500 words were required by the Government of India to ensure that officials at the centre and in the provinces were properly informed.[11]

The value of the special relationship was further demonstrated during World War One. A Reuters special service account was established to finance the distribution of messages, at actual cost of transmission, to any part of the Empire. Reuters was given an advance of Rs 5,000 and bills were submitted periodically to be adjusted against the advance. The Government of India had become concerned about reports circulating in the British press suggesting that India had not been doing its share to support the war effort; and the always-sensitive Home Department was quick to respond with more words to ensure the contradiction of 'baseless reports circulated from anti-British sources'.[12] The Government's need was good for Reuters' business since it allowed the company to send much of its regular Indian news to imperial customers at marginal cost beyond the official subsidy.

---

[8] In regard to this form of official press collaboration, Storey notes that: 'It was the sort of relationship between Press and Government which successive great editors of the *Times* in the nineteenth century felt to be essential to the paper.' *Ibid.*, p. 65. See also Stephen Koss, *The Rise and Fall of the Political Press in Britain*, Vol. I: *The Nineteenth Century*, London: Hamish Hamilton, 1981.

[9] *Ibid.* See also GOI (HomePol) 402/1922.

[10] In addition to commercial information, there was significantly increased interest in political news from India after the 1878 Afghan War, Storey, *Reuters' Century*, p. 93.

[11] GOI (HomePol) 402/1922.

[12] C. W. Gwynne, Deputy Secretary, Home Department memorandum, 24 March 1921, GOI (HomePol) 78/1922.

The war also produced a change in the working relationship between the company and the British Government which, although temporary, set a standard and precedent that lasted until 1945. The control of the Reuters Telegraph Company passed into the hands of Roderick Jones and Mark Napier in 1916, and Reuters Limited was established. It was agreed by the new owners that the company should adopt 'a new and explicitly patriotic role' during the war but, notwithstanding the extraordinary need of the moment, many were concerned about this apparent loss of principle. Although Jones remained active as managing director of the company during the war, he accepted a supervisory role in the Department of Information, which became the Ministry of Information in 1918. John Buchan, also a Reuters director, became Director of Intelligence for the ministry. Although Buchan left Reuters during his ministry service, the new intimacy between the company and the Government was noted in the House of Commons and in the British and American press. The enemy was no less concerned: 'Mightier and more dangerous than fleet or army is Reuters', lamented the *Berliner Tageblatt* in 1918.[13]

At the end of the war, the Government of India began to dismantle its extraordinary publicity apparatus, but it recognized the necessity of maintaining some of it to meet new post-war circumstances. When the Reuters' agent in Simla, E. J. Buck ('Bucky' to his friends, who included everyone worth knowing in the civil service, the army, and among businessmen and the princes), approached the Government for a continuation of the special service arrangement. He was strongly supported by the Home Department.[14] R. S. Bajpai, Deputy Director of the CBI, argued that this service could not be considered merely a war measure, since the 'contradiction of baseless reports' would continue to engage the attention of the Government and the assistance of Reuters would be necessary.[15] It seemed clear that no government was more in need of efficient publicity machinery, but, lamented the Home Secretary, the Government of India was 'perhaps of all civilised Governments the worst-equipped in this respect'.[16]

It is in this context that one writer of the time emphasized the role of London as the 'greatest news entrepôt' in the world. The control of the description of British enterprises around the world was an essential element in its success. London was 'the nerve centre of the Empire and the

---

[13] Storey, *Reuters' Century*, pp. 158–171. See also Cooper, *Barriers Down*, 1942.
[14] Sir Roderick Jones, *A Life in Reuters*, London: Hodder and Stoughton, 1951, p. 283. See also Sir Edward Buck, *Simla Past and Present*, Bombay: The Times Press, 1925, p. 255.
[15] R. S. Bajpai, Deputy Director, CBI, memorandum, 16 June 1921, GOI (HomePol) 78/1922.
[16] C. W. Gwynne, memorandum, 24 March 1921, GOI (HomePol) 78/1922.

vibration of those nerves is faithfully recorded on the conscientious and impartial Reuters instrument'. It was essential that news 'pass through British channels and not be coloured or even contaminated by passing through foreign pipes'.[17]

Until the end of World War One, it was taken for granted that the combination of Reuters and British pipes would suffice to ensure British interests in this regard, and that, in fact, impartiality in news service was synonymous with those interests. The company had glided easily in and out of an official role, serving the Government and itself as well. It appeared that this easy relationship would survive the new challenge undiminished. But this was not to be the case. While the spread of Reuters' enterprises paralleled and complemented British imperial interests there had been no cause for debate. But challenges to those interests, with subsequent impact on the company's affairs, brought different responses. It became increasingly clear that the needs and priorities of the Government of India were often different from those of the company; that there was a Reuters empire that had a life of its own, and a small army of Reuters men who marched to a different drummer. Eventually the company, like the Govenment itself, was required to give increasing attention to the question of the survival of its monopoly interests in India, and it became clear that the company had a chance to survive, even if the Raj did not.

An occasional Reuters story, offensive to Government or the India Office and apparently supportive of the 'extremist' nationalist cause, had always been assumed to be an aberration in an otherwise solid family relationship. A brief exchange of letters or a lunch with a company director was sufficient to note the concern and receive a reaffirmation of loyalty and shared commitment. By the mid-1920s, however, officials in India and at home began to detect a more sinister deviation of interest. The frequency of stories considered unfriendly or at least insensitive to the interests of Government could no longer be ascribed to a correspondent's error or the pressure of work in Bombay or London. It seemed clear to many officials, that Reuters was in business in India only for the money, and that the company's major customer, the Government of India, was no longer getting its money's worth.

It had been agreed to continue the special war service in 1919, but by 1921 the Home Department was pressing its case for termination and a new arrangement. The occasions when Reuters 'let us down very badly'

---

[17] J. Saxon Mills, *The Press and Communications of the Empire*, London: W. Collins and Co., Ltd, 1924, pp. 79, 126–7. See also Charles Bright, *Imperial Telegraphic Communication*, London: P. S. King and Son, 1911; and Brown, *Cable and Wireless Communications*, p. 101.

were becoming too significant. Stories about peasant unrest in Rae Bareli and the development of Kisan Sabhas in the United Provinces were considered fuller than necessary and to have placed far too much emphasis on their economic rather than their political cause.[18] As significant and frustrating was the Government's inability to obtain information concerning the content of subsidized messages. E. J. Buck would send out those messages he considered desirable, and draw an advance from time to time from the authorized subsidy. The Accountant-General, Central Revenues, would check the company's books at regular intervals but whether the Government received value for the expenditure remained a mystery.[19]

It had been an easy relationship founded on trust; but clearly both the trust and the ease were in jeopardy. Although the general service to India was considered to be unsatisfactory and the number of complaints by officials and the Anglo-Indian press increased, the search for a viable alternative only intensified the frustration. It was agreed within the Home Department that all subsidized messages would be funnelled through the office of the DCBI rather than allowing each department to deal with Buck directly as in the past.[20] There was clearly no way to avoid a working arrangement with Reuters but it was assumed by Home Department officials that they were the senior partner in the relationship. Officials in the India Office were less sanguine. There appeared in their veiw, to be a shift in the balance of power. Lloyd Evans reminded his colleagues that Reuters had 'practically a monopoly in India', making it advisable for Government 'to keep on friendly terms, if possible'.[21] The Home Member, Sir William Vincent, also recognized the difficulty. While agreeing to the new centralized relationship with the company, he assumed Reuters would object and that the issue would have to be reconsidered when the Government reassembled at Simla.[22]

The debate continued within Government and between officials and company officers concerning Reuters' obligations to itself as a commercial business and news agency, and the possibility and appropriateness of agreed constraints as part of its relationship with its special clients in Simla and London. J. W. Hose rejected the complaints of his India Office and Government of India colleagues. The problem, he argued, was in the relationship itself. By providing a subsidy to the company to send a fuller report of events considered important by Government, 'we upset the

[18] C. W. Gwynne, memorandum, 8 February 1921, GOI (HomePol) 78/1922.
[19] *Ibid.*
[20] *Ibid.*
[21] Lloyd Evans note, 6 October 1923, IO, L/P & J/6/1958.
[22] Sir William Vincent, 29 March 1921, GOI (HomePol) 78/1922.

balance of their messages and we trespass on the duty of the news agency'. It was clear to Hose that as long as this practice continued, Reuters would not increase the content of Indian news in its own service. Implicit in Hose's argument was the good sense in allowing the news itself to attract the interest of the company and its customers, and the futility of seeking to pad and control the product. Hose recognized that particular crisis situations such as the war and the 1919 Amritsar violence required special measures; but he insisted that these were extraordinary and should not inform ordinary relations with the company. The Government could not edit Reuters' copy, and therefore the company should be employed as professionals and be given a free hand.[23]

In January 1923, when the periodical renewal of the special Reuters agreement was under discussion, the Government of India requested its termination and the arrangement was stopped on 15 April. Officials were unwilling, however, to deny themselves any opportunity to influence the flow of news, and it was agreed that they might ask occasionally that a special despatch be sent. In addition, when the company thought that a particular situation required coverage beyond the ordinary service that was commercially feasible, it could bring the matter to the attention of Government.[24] This limited and apparently controlled relationship also was troublesome. Hose noted that Reuters began to press the Government with regular and substantial requests for special despatches, averaging in one six-week period in the summer of 1923 more than 4,000 words per month. What was particularly galling to officials was an apparent decision to remove any reference in Reuters' regular service to a subject which had received Government special-despatch agreement. As an example, Hose noted the 2,000 words authorized for reporting the Kenya White paper. Reuters sent a total of 2,024 words and charged only 24 to their regular service.[25]

Concern had hardened into conviction that the company was neither patriotic nor fair in an ordinary business context. An India Office request for a reduction in the 8d per word rate for special messages produced a renewed pledge to send any despatch desired by Government but no bargain rates. John Buchan, now back as the company's deputy director, noted with regret that such messages produced no 'enhanced prestige or gratitude from our customers'.[26] It was, in fact, those customers that

[23] J. W. Hose note, 26 October 1923, IO, L/P & J/6/1858.
[24] J. W. Hose review memorandum, 17 December 1924, *ibid.*
[25] *Ibid.*
[26] John Buchan to Sir Malcolm Seton, 13 December 1923, IO, L/P & J/6/1858. The concern for fiscal retrenchment became a permanent part of official life after the war. The need to justify the budget of the Post and Telegraph Department to the legislature under the

caused the greatest concern. 'Throughout this business', noted Sir William Duke, 'Reuters' endeavour has been to obtain from this office the cost of making their service more acceptable to their Indian clients and to avoid incurring any expenditure in this respect themselves.'[27]

The company's offer to provide the India Office with copies of its Indian service for a nominal subscription of £150 per year only enhanced official dismay. Sir Malcolm Seton wondered whether Buchan had really meant shillings, and noted that certain correspondents of Indian newspapers received this material for only £8 8s 0d per year. Buchan's explanation brought no satisfaction. 'I fear we are getting a most sinister reputation with you – the ravening commercial wolf and the innocent official lamb!' He went on to explain that the Indian newspapers in question took Reuters' service and were regular customers. The India Office was not in that position. In similar cases with such 'private customers' the company charged £200–£300. The £150 was a marginal charge covering only the cost of the messengers and additional copies. He agreed, however, to reduce the charge to £120 since the India Office, though not a subscriber, was 'a frequent customer'. Since the India Office only wanted the service in order to decide if more news was necessary, the offer was rejected.[28]

Buchan provided a lengthy memorandum defending the company's record of service in India. In a detailed critical response prepared for discussion within the India Office, Duke built a case against an apparently faithless ally. He rejected the argument that Reuters had established an independent reputation in India, separate from Government. It was also not correct, he insisted, that Reuters was 'now a household word in India for accurate and unbiased news'. Finding it convenient to use an argument that would have been rejected in any public forum, Duke noted that for some years, the Indian press 'has doubted it and may be said fairly to have regarded it as a department of the Government whose duty was to concoct news favourable to the Government for the Indian public'. Duke attached as support for his view, an extract from a recent issue of the *Bombay Chronicle*.[29] It is unclear whether he was suggesting that Reuters might as well live up to that reputation and serve the Government loyally; or that the well-known loss of innocence had decisively diminished the usefulness and value of their services. He might have cited numerous

---

Reform scheme created an additional problem for publishing/propaganda officers in the Home Department. GOI (HomePol) 100/VIII; 789/1922.

[27] Sir William Duke, minute, 24 January 1924, IO, L/P & J/6/1858.

[28] Exchange between William Duke and John Buchan, 13 December 1923 and 9 January 1924, *ibid.*

[29] Sir William Duke minute, 24 January 1924, *ibid.*

critical references to the Reuters monopoly in the press and the provincial reports on Indian newspapers which were prepared each week and sum- marized in annual collections. More significant were the enquiries by members of the reformed Legislative Assembly and Council of State regarding official subsidies,[30] regularly reminding officials that times had changed.

It seemed clear to Duke that the Indian Government had created a 'Frankenstein monster' by allowing Reuters a monopoly control of the Indian market. It had even placed at the company's disposal all messages received in India from the Foreign Office wireless, eliminating a possible competitor with the Reuters' Service. Finally the messages themselves, whoever the paymaster, were frequently 'of a dangerous character'. This was particularly the case in regard to Turkey. The Government of India had protested and the company had apologized; but the added ammu- nition for the Khilafat cause and its non-cooperation allies could not be withdrawn.[31]

It was in this context that a new and more critical relationship devel- oped between Reuters and the Government. The collaboration continued – there was clearly no choice, but press messages were rigorously scruti- nized for signs of disloyalty. Both the scepticism and the fatalism were shared by the Indian press; but the company and its product also repre- sented the essential connection to a world-wide communication network, and the key to a professional standard. The *Hindu*, in a 1925 story about Reuters,[32] noted the importance of the 30,000 to 40,000 words received in India from abroad each month. Its enthusiasm reflected a continuing commitment to technological improvement and competition both with other Indian papers and the Anglo-Indian press. The first teleprinter installed in the *Hindu* offices in 1939, facilitated its cooperative relation- ship with Reuters. More important, as its editor, Kasturi Srinivasan, noted: 'We are now in the happy position of getting the news right into our own office simultaneously with the rest of the world.'[33]

It was not merely the increase in the number and quality of its Indian customers that had affected the company's product. Far more important was the increase in the number of Indian newsmakers most often in what was considered to be the extreme nationalist camp; and the change in the nature of the issues and incidents which interested the reading public in India and Britain. While the company was willing to help the Government

---

[30] GOI (HomePol) 402/1922; 47/1924.
[31] Sir William Duke, minute, 24 January 1924, IO, L/P & J/6/1858.
[32] V. K. Narasimhan, *Kasturi Srinivasan*, Bombay: Popular Prakasan, 1969, p. 18.
[33] *Ibid.*, p. 56.

make news, it could not restrain its reporting to this source if it wanted to
sell it. The Government recognized the problem and accepted the need to
present a reasonably balanced picture, but too often Reuters appeared to
go out of its way to offend.

Like an ageing actor who resents the loss of public interest and the
press attention given to a young rival, Government and its supporters
condemned the company's apparent perfidy. Edwin Haward[34] was a
particular sensitive and exacting critic. In a steady flow of letters to the
India Office, he denounced the general tenor of Reuters' messages. It was
not only the particular information provided in any message, Haward
noted, but the image it left with the reader. In his view, Reuters generally
gave the impression that the Indian National Congress was stronger and
more representative than it was. His examples reflected the acute sensitivity of all parties to the legitimising authority of the printed word,
especially when it was widely distributed. A reference to Gandhi as 'the
Mahatma'; to Patel as 'the ex-speaker of the Legislative Assembly'; to the
anniversary of the Indian Mutiny – all appeared to be deliberate and
unnecessary recognition of new and independent status, or, at least, a
description of a situation from the wrong perspective.[35]

Keeping order meant maintaining individuals and organizations in
their proper categories and presenting them in that context in news-
service stories. Haward pointed out the impropriety of a Reuters telegram
which noted both Sarojini Naidu's leadership of the Civil Disobedience
Movement and the death of the Begum of Bhopal. It seemed clear to him
that the writer of the story had not the slightest knowledge of Indian
sentiment in associating in one story a Muslim leader with 'a protagonist
of Hindu domination'. In Haward's view, there were far too many such
messages to consider them either inept or accidental. To him, they
'savoured very strongly of anti-government propaganda'.[36]

A similar attack was launched by the *Times of India* in a July 1930
editorial titled 'Propagandist News', attacking Reuters for reporting a
meeting in London where Indian politicians spoke against the Statutory
(Simon) Commission Report. 'We have rarely seen a more propagandist
effort', asserted the paper, 'masquerading as news.' The lack of space
given to those who supported the Report was another example of anti-
Government political bias which they had detected regularly in Reuters'
messages. Like so many others in Government, nationalist politics, and

[34] Edwin Haward had a brief newspaper career in India and China and served as an
information officer in the Indian office.
[35] Edwin Haward to J. R. Pendrigh, Reuters' dominion editor, 14 May 1930, IO, L/I/1/260,
File 99.
[36] *Ibid.*

the press – both Indian and British – the premier Anglo-Indian journal had decided that Reuters had lost its judgement and perhaps its principles. It apparently could find only negative comment that was worth reporting in reference to the Statutory Commission, rather than the 'fair and unbiassed reporting which we have a right to expect from an agency in whose business political bias ought to have no place'.[37] The range of the company's critics suggests that it may have been doing a better job under the circumstances than seemed apparent to its committed customers. But in the view of the *Times of India*, Reuters sent opinions on Indian affairs of the *Daily Herald* kind, more frequently than those of the *Times*.[38]

The preparations for the Round Table Conference in the late summer of 1930 produced media problems to complement the more obvious political concerns. The London location would attract a larger press audience in Britain and the United States, in addition to the Indian press which would receive stories from correspondents and news services. Although the conference would be closed and there would be little official news during the sessions, it was apparent to Home Department officials that delegates would talk freely outside the conference hall and stories would flow back to India that would serve the Congress cause. It was agreed that the best defence was a full and regular service of 'authentic news', and to achieve that end a reliable Indian journalist had to be sent to England.[39] It was decided within the Government of India that the travel and expenses of an Indian press representative and a subsidy for a special Reuters' service should be funded and the Viceroy informed the Secretary of State of their plan.[40] The India Office was sceptical. It seemed doubtful whether messages sent to India by a 'subsidized semi-official observer' would carry more weight with the Indian press than the 'news they would receive through their own channels'. And, in regard to Reuters, the Secretary of State insisted that any subsidy for enhanced coverage would have to be given to the press as a whole.[41]

It was clear to the Home Department that India Office officials did not understand the situation. It was not merely the information that would be supplied, but the 'atmosphere created in India' by its presentation that had to be considered. The Viceroy noted in response that Indian correspondents would 'naturally be more familiar than any others with the most

---

[37] *Times of India*, 'Propagandist News', 24 July 1930, quoted in *ibid*.
[38] *The Daily Herald* was a left-wing London paper, often critical of the Government of India.
[39] Haig note, 11 August 1930, GOI (HomePol) 48/II and KW, 1931.
[40] Viceroy to Secretary of State, 24 August 1930, *ibid*.
[41] Secretary of State to Viceroy, 25 August 1930 *ibid*.

effective way of presenting matter to Indian readers'; and unless the
Indian Government's plan was carried out, the only Indian press representatives would be those of the Free Press of India[42] and nationalist
papers. In addition, it was reiterated that the ordinary Reuters service
would be inadequate to counteract the array of coverage that would likely
be antagonistic to British interests.[43]

The exchange continued and eventually the India Office yielded to the
Government of India's position. It was agreed that U. N. Sen[44] would be
sent to London but the subsidized expense arrangements were to be
'strictly confidential', at least until the end of the conference in order to
avoid trouble from the British and American press as well as from the
FPI.[45] Sen would be sent as a member to Reuters' staff and therefore the
payment of his expenses would be a subsidy to the company. There was
greater reluctance to approve the direct subsidy for an extended service.
In the view of the India Office, the company should be prepared to expand
its coverage for such a special occasion on a purely commercial basis; but
the Viceroy insisted that conditions in India required this support. The
recent enactment of the Press Ordinance[46] had restricted the market and a
possible boycott by some newspapers would lead to further contraction
and a decline in Reuters' revenue. It was also assumed that it would
produce an increasingly hostile press requiring the counter-measures
which the Government of India had proposed. There was clearly sufficient precedent for such subsidies to Reuters and this too could be kept
confidential at least for the duration of the conference.[47] The Secretary of
State agreed, but their hard won success left the Home Member with a
feeling of unease.

If we do give a subsidy to Reuters, then we have the right to expect that Reuters
would keep in touch with the Publicity Officer and would within reason accept his
advice in regard to the news to be sent to India. This does not mean that Reuters'
messages would be censored or even scrutinized before they were despatched, but
that Reuters would let the Publicity Officer have copies of messages and would
accept suggestions regarding the character of the news to be sent.[48]

---

[42] Nationalist news agency established by S. Sadanand in 1924.
[43] Viceroy to Secretary of State, 9 September 1930, *ibid.*
[44] U. N. Sen was K. C. Roy's deputy in the API.
[45] Secretary of State to Viceroy, 19 September 1930, GOI (HomePol) 48/II and KW, 1931.
[46] By 1930, repressive press ordinances and legislation might bring some relief from the
publication of extreme viewpoint and calls for violence, but the involvement of the
mainstream Indian press also constrained the Government's effort to propagate
viewpoint and reach a wider audience.
[47] Viceroy to Secretary of State, 28 September 1930, GOI (HomePol) 48/II and KW,
1931.
[48] Emerson note, October 1930, *ibid.*

One of Edwin Haward's regular critiques of Reuters' cables made the difficulties apparent. In a message announcing the British Indian representatives to the first Round Table Conference, it was noted that the delegation included forty-six representatives reflecting all religious, geographical, class, and political views, 'except the nationalist view'. It went on to point out that the notables included Mohammed Ali Jinnah, 'who was one of the organizers of the boycott against the Simon Commission'.[49]

Throughout the early 1930s, the India Office and the Government of India engaged in a continuous exchange of correspondence concerning the failures, the errors of judgement, and the mismanagement of Reuters, followed by a further exchange between Government and company executives. It had become an old problem for both and the repetitive response would follow. While the frustration was no less burdensome, a developing sensitivity to each other's needs and concerns is evident. Constitutional constraints after the Reforms had made arbitrary action in this area, and in particular funding it secretly, more difficult. Indian Government officials were now more inclined to accept the view argued by J. W. Hose a decade earlier that full news coverage was more important than controlled news. It seemed clear to many that the Government's case was a good one, and would inevitably attract support if only it were effectively told.[50]

Reflecting this new attitude as well as the experience of Round Table coverage, Hugh MacGregor, an information officer in the India Office, contacted the company in March 1933 to note the Government's recognition that messages would be sent from time to time to which they could not attach official approval. Clearly the 'exercise of newspaper enterprise' and 'agency requirements' preclude absolute unanimity all of the time. He suggested, however, that differences could be minimized if someone with Indian knowledge could vet India-bound news and make certain that messages were shaped with the clients in mind. William Turner, the overseas general manager of Reuters, readily agreed, offering in addition the possibility of comment on such material by MacGregor himself.[51] But too many words and messages now flowed between London and India to allow for any fail-safe system.

In May 1935, the Royal Jubilee appeared to provide the ideal occasion for useful and uncontroversial news and the subsidy system was invoked

[49] E. Haward to Hugh MacGregor, 12 September 1930, IO (InfoDept), L/I/1/260, File 99.
[50] IO (InfoDept), *ibid.*; also L/I/1/264, File 99B; GOI (HomePol) 48/II and KW, 1931.
[51] Hugh MacGregor to William Turner, Reuters' overseas general manager, 28 March 1933, IO (InfoDept) L/I/1/264, File 99B. The informed consultant was H. B. Edwards.

to provide maximum coverage. But the Indian press gave prominent attention to a Reuters' message which was not useful to those who paid the bill.

Deplorable piece communist propaganda enacted Fleet Street near Ludgate stop Banner stretched across road inscribed long may they reign suddenly changed its character as majesties passing stop it was released disclosing inside sign of hammer and sickle and inscription quote workers of all lands unite unquote police rushed buildings where from banner suspended . . .[52]

Within two days the Government of India's concern was cabled to the India Office, suggesting that they 'inspire a message putting the incident in proper perspective'.[53] On the same day the India Office passed on the request to Reuters,[54] and a revised message was sent out to India on the following morning.

Communist banner momentarily unfurled Fleet Street passed practically unnoticed indeed regarded so trivial that no further action taken stop attitude of labourites evinced their unreserved support yesterdays motion Commons . . .[55]

Whether the first message would have suggested to many Indian readers that the revolution had begun in Britain and India's freedom would be one of the results of the workers' victory was clearly not the point; but the increasing tension in sections of the Indian bureaucracy produced quick defensive reaction, and hypersensitivity regarding the stability of the regime and the *izzat* (honour) of its officials. In his subsequent apology to MacGregor, William Turner noted that Reuters was often accused by Indians of obscuring unpleasant facts and the company was under pressure to provide as balanced coverage as possible. He agreed that their judgement was wrong in this case, 'but there it is'.[56]

Since the second message was 'for educative purposes' rather than news content, the India Office paid the bill, as would be increasingly necessary in the troubled years ahead. Those officials in the Home Department and the India Office responsible for the Government's image appeared to lose none of their enthusiasm for the job. But the environment of 'Retrenchment' which had settled in after the war made it more difficult. The debates within the Government of India in the early 1920s which had led to a significant reduction in the number of copies of Reuters' messages purchased for officials[57] were succeeded by increasingly closer scrutiny of individual messages and accounts. Referring to the transmission of a

---

52 Reuters' message, 6 May 1935, IO (InfoDept) L/I/1/260, File 99.
53 A. H. Joyce to H. MacGregor, 8 May 1935, *ibid.*
54 H. MacGregor to H. B. Edwards, 8 May 1935, *ibid.*
55 Reuters' message, 9 May 1935, *ibid.*
56 W. Turner to H. MacGregor, 9 May 1935, *ibid.*
57 Throughout the 1920s, fiscal retrenchment constrained all official expenditure.

speech by the Secretary of State at a Bombay dinner in 1938, A. H. Joyce, the India Office's senior information officer, reminded Reuters that they had been 'charged for 448 words but, according to our calculations, the figure should be approximately 415 less 20%'.[58]

They had come a long way from the days of large advances when neither the cost nor the content concerned the Government. In 1932, one Government of India official noted to his India Office counterpart: 'Our first conundrum is – How do you at the other end know the difference between a subsidized Reuters' message and an unsubsidized message?'[59] By the end of the decade this was no longer a problem. Government paid for messages it wrote itself or closely vetted. The symbiotic relationship survived, but in a tacitly agreed new context. Reuters officials continually reminded Government of the access the company provided to the Indian press. 'The display of our news is quite amazing.' W. J. Moloney[60] noted to Joyce, attaching copies of the *Hindustan Times*, *Amrita Bazar Patrika*, the *Hindu*, and the *Leader*.[61] In response, the Government was prepared to accept the situation in which Reuters would do their 'utmost to help us consistent with safeguarding their interests from a business point of view.'[62]

Although injudicious press reporting from England continued to cause concern, it was the reverse traffic, and Indian news circulated within India, that was clearly more important. The growing opposition to this portion of the company's business involved much of the Indian and Anglo-Indian press, nationalist leaders, and Government officials – all of whom saw dangers and opportunities in the company's Indian operations.

The Associated Press of India

While Reuters provided an international service, the principal distributor of news within India was the Associated Press. It was founded in 1899 by K. C. Roy, who subsequently established a Press Bureau in 1910, with regional offices in Bombay, Calcutta, and Madras. Since Indian papers could not afford to pay separate telegraph rates, news was sent to these regional centres where messages were copied and distributed to the bureau's customers. In addition to his news service, Roy and his

[58] A. H. Joyce to A. E. Watson (Reuters) 7 June 1938, IO (InfoDept) L/I/1/260, File 99.
[59] Sir Evelyn Howell, Foreign and Political Department, Government of India to D. T. Monteath, India Office, 5 May 1932, GOI (F & P) 119–X.
[60] William Moloney was Reuters' general manager in India, 1923–37.
[61] W. T. Moloney to A. H. Joyce, 24 October 1938, IO (InfoDept) L/I/1/260, File 99.
[62] A. H. Joyce to W. Moloney, 14 June 1939, *ibid.*

associate, U. N. Sen, represented in Simla a number of Indian news-papers, a curious mix of responsibilities which would remain a part of the API operation until 1935. The business remained financially weak, however, with Indian newspapers haggling over the service and the rates, and Anglo-Indian papers remaining aloof until the *Statesman* and the *Madras Times* finally took it on.[63] It was Everard Cotes of the *Statesman*, however, who delivered the *coup de grace* in 1913, with the establishment of the Indian News Agency (INA) in competition with Roy's service. Cotes was also associated with Reuters and was supported in this venture by a Government subsidy. In 1914, he invited Roy to cooperate and the INA and API were amalgamated into the Eastern News Agency (ENA).[64] The Associated Press name was retained, but Cotes became managing director until Reuters bought him out and took control. The headquarters of the new company was established in Delhi, and with the investment of Reuters capital, the first teleprinters in India were installed and there was an immediate growth in the service.[65] Roy became a director of the ENA, the correspondent of the API at Delhi and Simla, and until his death in 1931, the dominant influence in editorial policy.

The organization of Reuters' Indian operation appeared complex, but it was ideally suited to serve the needs of a large and varied clientele and as well to maximize profits and fend off competition. It provided in addition a division of responsibilities into discrete legal entities which allowed for useful cover in the political struggle between nationalists and the Government of India. There were four constituent parts although the personnel, machinery, and basic news product remained the same. The ENA distributed foreign news to the press in India, while the API distributed Indian news in India. The INA distributed Indian news to Government, and the Reuters name was used for the distribution of Indian news to London. In each of these avatars, Reuters' Indian identity was declared, attracting supporters and enemies as well as clients in any one particular case, but never providing an opportunity for a unified challenge.

Beyond the interior life of this mix of companies, an essential nation-building role was being performed. Roy and the senior Indian reporting staff clearly viewed themselves as nationalists, sharing the goal if not the methods of those on the front line. They were also convinced that they had a particular professional talent and opportunity that made their role

63 *Vidura*, Vol. III, August 1966, pp. 10–12. See also A. S. Iyengar, *All Through the Gandhian Era*, Bombay: Hind Kitabs Ltd, 1950, pp. 133–7.
64 *Ibid.*
65 *Ibid.*

significant and useful. That opportunity was the API, its existence, and the communications process it organized. If it was not owned and controlled by nationalists, neither was it held in check by a totalitarian British regime seeking a monopoly on all means of communication. In the transitional world of the inter-war years the API facilitated the linking of a range of local and central action and ideas into some semblance of presumed order and relationship. While merely a camp follower, it was able to find a place in the headquarters of all the belligerents, serving at one time individual clients and the continuing collaborative consensus which lasted until the final stage of power transfer. Profit, professionalism, loyalty to the company and to the empire, a shared nationalist goal but opposition to the more aggressive means to achieve it, a commitment to individual careers – all of these could and were subsumed in this extraordinary organization under the patronage of a Government and a nationalist movement that needed to communicate and had no easy alternative.

With more than a bit of hyperbole, J. N. Sahni has described 'the manner in which the Delhi–Simla set-up operated in gathering news and syphoning it through different channels, giving it at the same time different tints and hues'. It constituted in his view, 'a type of racket unknown in the profession of journalism anywhere in the world'.[66] But Sahni could not deny grudging respect to Roy who was at the head of this 'octopus-tentacled establishment'. When the Government was in Delhi, Roy's office was in the Maidans Hotel close to the old Secretariat where he made his daily rounds.[67] In Simla, Roy kept a pemanent groundfloor suite in the Cecil Hotel annex just opposite 'Holcombe', Everard Cotes' house and headquarters.[68] Sahni provides a rare personal profile of Roy, the suave and soft-spoken bachelor,[69] generally in 'silk pyjamas in garish stripes, relaxing behind a window overlooking the main road'. It was at this 'checkpost' that Roy held court for officials, newspaperman and nationalist politicians. Befitting the complex role he had created for himself, 'K. C. was a friend of the nationalists, a confidant of the communalists, a liberal by political affiliation and a trusted loyalist where Government was concerned'.[70]

In a discussion concerning journalism in India at a 1933 meeting of the Royal Empire Society, William Turner, Reuters' overseas manager, noted the special problems confronting his company in the selection of news

[66] Sahni, *The Indian Press*, pp. 54–64.
[67] Iyengar, *Gandhian Era*, p. 139.
[68] Buck, *Simla*, p. 172.
[69] Roy married in 1928.
[70] Sahni, *The Indian Press*, pp. 54–64.

which was suitable for both Anglo-Indian and Indian-owned newspaper clients. The 100 per cent increase in the number of the latter and the stagnant or declining situation of the former over the previous eight years had required adjustments in Reuters as well.[71] Roy's strategic position at the centre of the API allowed him to respond to a range of clients whose interests and priorities were often very different. Sahni notes that Roy produced four different reports of Assembly proceedings each day: a routine agency report, one with an Anglo-Indian angle, one liberal, and one with a strong nationalist bias. Occasionally he would add another for the Muslim press.[72] It was an impressive performance and outrageous at the same time.

The Associated Press was one of the many platforms shared by the Government and the nationalists, and the dominance of senior Indian personnel in the reporting and editing staff provided special opportunities for an extraordinary kind of professional collaboration. Durga Das became the agency's chief correspondent in 1919, and he was joined five months later by A. S. Iyengar, who had worked briefly for the *Independent* and the Congress Punjab Enquiry Committee.[73] In addition to their API work, they provided special correspondent reports for most of the major nationalist press until 1934, when Reuters responded to Government pressure and banned this particular form of moonlighting. Sahni notes that he and other Indian editors did not like Roy's loyalist politics but appreciated his willingness to allow Das and Iyengar to work for the Indian press. They also recognized Roy's power and attempted to use him and his organization as much as possible.[74]

In 1921, the only reporters allowed access to the AICC preparatory sessions for the annual Congress meeting were Das and Iyengar. A report was prepared for Gandhi's approval and subsequently released to the general press.[75] At the next session in Gaya the following year, the press was not allowed access to the Swarajist–Gandhian debates; and was again barred from the special Delhi meeting of the AICC, although Iyengar notes, 'Still, every bit of the proceedings was available from every delegate soon after the day's sitting was over'.[76] The meetings were open to the whole press in 1923, but the API continued to play a unique role. A special service was arranged for the Congress annual meeting at a controlled subscription rate in order to attract the maximum number of

[71] Sir Alfred Watson, 'Journalism in India', *The Asiatic Review*, n.s., April 1933, 269–70.
[72] Sahni, *The Indian Press*, pp. 54–64.
[73] Iyengar, *Gandhian Era*, pp. 138–9; interview with Durga Das, 1970.
[74] J. N. Sahni interview 1970.
[75] Iyengar, *Gandhian Era*, p. 99; Durga Das interview, 1970.
[76] Iyengar, *Gandhian Era*.

clients. For the flat Rs 40 fee, telegrams were sent directly to the subscribing papers. Roy was apparently particularly concerned that Anglo-Indian papers might reject a price rise and Congress in turn would lose important publicity outlets.[77]

In an earlier period, one of the weapons in the Government armoury was denial of access to newsmakers. But far too many Indian personalities without any direct relationship to the great secretariats in Simla and Delhi were now making news and participating in newsworthy events. The press section of the Congress *pandal* (pavilion) in the 1930s generally filled one-third of the space; and the opportunities for a good story were limited only by a reporter's energy and talent. Leading Congress personalities developed press reputations. Srinivasa Iyengar 'could be interviewed at any time'; while Motilal Nehru tended to be more 'cautious and deliberate in every word that he uttered'. Gandhi was 'excellent copy', but it was essential to tell him in advance the subject for the interview.[78]

India Office officials generally ascribed the Hindu bias they detected in API messages to Das and Iyengar, but they found it difficult to make a case.[79] Their API positions gave them access to leaders of virtually every political persuasion who recognized their usefulness. Sahni again captures the breadth of their contacts in a typically ironic description.

In the Congress camp they sought confidence as patriots ... With Sapru and Jayakar they claimed to be the only friends of the lost Liberal cause. They assured Jinah, Fazl-i-Hussain, and the League leaders that they were the most serviceable channel to reach the favourable Anglo-Indian and Muslim press. In Government circles they emphasized the impression that not only Government publication was safe in their hands, but that with their all-round intimate contacts they were its best and most dependable informants.[80]

The key to the success of this multifaceted operation was the extraordinary partnership of Roy and William Moloney, Reuters' general manager in the East from 1923 to 1937.[81] Moloney was more businessman than newspaperman and his primary concern for the company's financial success combined with sympathy for India's nationalist aspirations allowed him to leave much of the political fine tuning to Roy. And Roy was the master tuner, pitching his messages with sensitive appreciation of

[77] *Ibid.*, p. 100.
[78] *Ibid.*, pp. 89–90, 102.
[79] M. MacGregor cable to Ian Stephens re. Hindu bias of API correspondents, 26 November 1932. Stephens asked MacGregor to send a copy of the message since he could not find 'much Hindu bias in the text Reuters has shown me here'. IO (InfoDept) L/I/1/260, File 99.
[80] Sahni, *The Indian Press*, p. 62.
[81] W. Moloney's former title was managing director.

the capabilities of the delicate instrument on which he played. Although often grudging because of the nature of the base which had given him so much power, the admiration for his professional skills was apparent in all camps. Most significantly he was useful, for many, an essential connection to the national communications network. Pat Lovett[82] has described Roy's influence on the development of the modern press in India, declaring his 'genius for the staple of news has proved a more potent factor in bringing Indian journalism up-to-date according to western notions than any editor in the last forty years'.[83] For Pothan Joseph,[84] Roy's success in breaking the 'cordons of the British monopoly by capturing a supreme appointment in the charmed circle' was an extraordinary achievement, often used for the benefit of young Indian journalists like himself.[85]

In addition to his ordinary responsibilities with the API, Roy chose to use his place in the 'charmed circle' in the service of his profession, and thereby meeting in his view both his obligations to Indian nationalism and to a political system which held his respect. Freedom of the press was the key to that relationship and he pressed the Government to repeal legislation that constrained the press and to develop a positive relationship with the press generally. He urged officials to convene meetings of newspapermen, to reward them for distinguished service and performance, and, above all, to 'recognize the profession'.[86] His own easy access to officials, especially in the Home Department and his nomination to membership in the Legislative Assembly, suggests a positive response. But his position was virtually unique[87] and, as Durga Das has noted, he was trusted but not overloved, and denied the knighthood he thought he deserved.[88]

Between the interests of the national campaign and the British regime, Roy carved for himself a role and place which, by serving its own master, could be useful to the nationalist cause as well. Achieving success as an individual, as a professional in a competitive business with an international standard and ethos of its own, was for him, the key to the

---

[82] Pat Lovett was a well-known Anglo-Indian newspaperman. He worked for a number of papers and edited the Calcutta Weekly, *Capital*, for which he wrote a popular column, 'Ditcher's Diary'.

[83] Lovett, *Journalism*, p. 45.

[84] Pothan Joseph was probably the best-known newspaperman in India. He worked for twenty-six papers throughout the sub-continent in a fifty-year career.

[85] Pothan Joseph, *Glimpses of Yesterday*, Madras: The Madras Premier Co., 1959, p. 34. Joseph described the Cecil Hotel in Simla, Roy's headquarters, as 'the hub of the Universe'.

[86] K. C. Roy, oral evidence, Press Law Committee, *Report and Evidence*, 14 July 1921, p. 44.

[87] Both Surendranath Banerjee (the *Bengalee*) and C. Y. Chintamani (the *Leader*) were influential editors and served briefly as provincial ministers.

[88] Durga Das, interview, 1970.

working-out of his national identity and place in the struggle which dominated his professional life. It was a job which had to be done; which was clearly an intrinsic part of national progress; which could not be left to the British, but could not be wrested away. To practise his profession in this context, he could not choose a side in the sense of serving only Government or the nationalist cause. There was a practical as well as a principled constraint. He argued that the degree to which the press was allowed to do its job free from undue restraint of any kind would reflect the progress of constitutional change and developing freedom generally. Although most nationalist leaders preferred loyalty and a less constrained endorsement of their views, many of those at the centre generally had little use for the press that did not maintain reasonably professional standards; for those papers tended to emphasize parochial, often communal, interests antagonistic to national priorities.

Clearly Roy's methods and goals accommodated exactly the needs of the company. There were in addition, however, central issues which attracted the opposition of those who rejected the appropriateness of Reuters' Indian persona. Questions in the Legislative Assembly or Council of State regarding Government funding of Reuters' services generally received an itemized response and a brief comment regarding a simple payment for service and an ordinary business relationship. Questions which concerned any specific subsidy for the API were always rejected on the basis of a standard response prepared for the Home Member after an exchange of letters between Roy and the Home Secretary. There were payments for INA telegrams, since this service was designed to provide Indian news to Government. No payments went to the API since it was a distinct corporation.[89] Such answers were generally accepted with weary resignation although outside the Assembly nationalist press and politicians might vent their anger in a strongly worded speech or editorial. The Anglo-Indian establishment was often no less concerned.

On 27 September 1929, the annual meeting of the India and Ceylon Newspapers London Committee was held at the *Statesman* offices. These representatives of English-owned Indian papers had gathered to discuss a new agreement with Reuters for the supply of news to India. The future of the API was their central concern. The editor of the *Times of India* insisted that there should be no clause regarding the API in the new contract and that they should be able to take their Indian news from any agency or start one themselves. The prohibitive clause in the current contract denied them this alternative. Although it was indirectly

[89] IO (HomePol) 47/1924; 205/1925; 402/1922.

subsidized by the Government of India, it was clear to them that the API was 'largely propagandist'; and in any case, it was noted, the lack of competition had allowed Reuters to carry on 'in their old indifferent way'. In addition, it was asserted, their sporting news was particularly poor.[90]

The API clause was slipped into the contract at the last moment, lamented Sir Stanley Reed, a former editor of the *Times of India* and the chairman of the meeting. As a result the Indian press had drifted into the dangerous position of being dependent on Reuters for practically the whole of their foreign and internal news service. This meant dependence on the API, a service that was 'most inefficiently run', was often 'blatantly propagandist', and was 'most untrustworthy'. It was clear to Reed that Anglo-Indian papers needed a certain amount of control over news agencies distributing news in India, and he wanted to tell Reuters that the Anglo-Indian press would establish a cooperative service unless they were allowed to acquire a proprietary share in the control of the API, a director on the Board, and a constant supervision of news.[91]

Since the number of Indian-owned papers was increasing and their collective influence and power would soon be more important than the Anglo-Indian press, it seemed imperative to move quickly. It was clear to these editors and proprietors that Anglo-Indian press interests would receive scant attention when they no longer dominated the field. While the others agreed with Reed's analysis of the situation, there was no consensus about what action to take. For one, it was clear that Anglo-Indian press control over the API would never be accepted by the Indian press, and unfortunately, he noted, 'howls from the Indian Press were now heard in high quarters – an insurmountable obstacle'. The meeting ended with agreement to seek support for an attack on the API clause.[92]

The opposition to the API continued throughout the 1930s. The Anglo-Indian press shared its concerns with the Government and these were added to the files of grievances generated among officials. In July 1933, Hugh MacGregor cabled Ian Stephens, the DCBI, with a complaint about a recent Reuters' message received from India. He noted that Samuel Hoare's evidence presented to the Joint Select Committee received a favourable response from Indian delegates, and that the Reuters' message sent from London was accurate and well done. But the Reuters' report from India regarding Hoare's evidence emphasized the unhappiness of the Indian participants and the possibility of protests

---

90 Samuel Sheppard, editor of the *Times of India*, confidential report, annual meeting of the Indian and Ceylon Newspapers London Committee, 27 September 1929, IO (InfoDept) L/I/1/260, File 99.
91 *Ibid.*, Sir Stanley Reed.
92 *Ibid.*

against the decline of provincial autonomy. Although MacGregor concluded by noting that the 'basis for this perturbation is, therefore, to us a mystery', it was generally assumed in such situations that the API was working for one of its non-official clients.[93]

Others resented the unfair competition. In a series of letters to Government of India officials, Geoffrey Dawson, the editor of the *Times*, complained that the API arrangement with the Government created a distorted context for professional press activity. It appeared that the Department of Public Information thought primarily of the needs of the Indian press and ignored its larger responsibilities. The *Times* did not want to be required to do business with the API, which meant Reuters to them, in order to do business in India. Dawson provided long lists of examples which illustrated the impact of the Reuter–API monopoly and the Government's continued support for the old arrangement. The handling of press coverage for the Gandhi–Irwin talks was particularly disturbing. After Gandhi's third interview with the Viceroy, a brief communiqué was issued from Viceroy's House but handed only to the API representative. When it became known that the Government of India planned to give the text of the agreement between Gandhi and the Viceroy to the API for general distribution to its customers, only considerable pressure from the *Times* correspondent produced a copy for it as well.[94]

It was obviously easier for the information officers in the Home Department to pass material to Roy or Sen, confident that it would get out to the desired market, and in a form that respected the Government's intentions. Although the Government had its own problems with Reuters and API, in general the company responded well at critical moments. By using it in this way the Government hoped to beat the newspaperman at his own game, getting their view out first and perhaps denying a readership to less supportive papers or agencies who would come in late. At times, however, the API appeared to be the Government's information department, and both were embarrassed by the lecture from Fleet Street. When a *Times* correspondent asked the Census Bureau for rough figures regarding the 1931 census, he was told that they were available through the API which had distributed the data to the press.[95]

The India Office supported Dawson's demands and, in an April 1931 letter to the Home Secretary in the Indian Government, noted that no preferential treatment was given to any agency in England. It suggested that the Government of India consider the possibility of treating the

[93] H. MacGregor to I. Stephens, 14 July 1933, IO (InfoDept) L/I/1/260, File 99.
[94] Geoffrey Dawson to India Office, April 1931, quoted in Iyengar, *Gandhian Era*, p. 148.
[95] *Ibid.*, pp. 148–9.

representatives of the prominent British and American papers directly and not through the API.[96] Officials in India disagreed. Gerald Barrier has noted that the Government of India 'had neither the will nor the power necessary to maintain extensive controls when emergencies subsided'.[97] In 1931, it was not only a question of controlling API–Reuters, or protecting the Indian market for a useful ally. Serious competition from the Americans would not develop for a decade. If API could not guarantee that all of its news products would be pleasing to Government, it did ensure access to the national communications system for the Government's messages. For a Government that still believed it had a good case to make and it was essential for the largest possible audience to hear it, in India, Britain, the United States, and Europe, access was not insignificant.

As the pressure increased to do something about the API monopoly, the Government of India initiated a series of exchanges with the India Office with the goal of eliminating the special correspondent services to the national press which had been provided by Das and Iyengar since 1919. Roderick Jones, the managing director of the company, was contacted and he agreed to act. In July 1931, he requested Roy to terminate the service; but it was difficult to ignore Roy's response. He noted that the special correspondent work had kept out other news competition and preserved the API–Reuters monopoly. If the service were ended, Roy argued, API control over independent news services would pass to others.[98] 'Independent' meant purely nationalist such as the FPI, against which Roy had fought since its founding in 1924. Its style offended Roy's professional standards, and its politics offended Roy's liberal views. Its founder Swaminath Sadanand, also offended Roy's taste in colleagues or friends. Happily for Roy, Sadanand and the FPI offended the Government of India as well. Through the private correspondent services of Das and Iyengar, generally appearing in the nationalist press under a 'by our correspondent' byline, an informal dyarchical arrangement was sufficiently useful to both parties to avoid serious challenge.

Durga Das agreed that the API was the instrument of government, but insisted that there was ample space for the other side in terms of pure news. Since nationalist news could sell itself, that was enough. It could be picked up by nationalist editors and then used in a more committed manner. The Government news was obviously official and would go down or not according to the audience.[99] Das and Iyengar had a personal

---

[96] *Ibid.*, p. 150.
[97] Barrier, *Banned*, p. 60.
[98] Quoted in Iyengar, *Gandhian Era*, pp. 144–5.
[99] Durga Das interview, 1970.

interest in the special services as well since it provided a significant addition to their income. When Das came to the API, his starting salary placed him instantly among the highest paid newspapermen in India.[100] The combination of salary and private income, some of which flowed back to the API directly or in terms of guaranteed clientage, was too significant to give up easily.

Roy, in his exchange with Jones, emphasized the likelihood of a substantial fall in revenue. He also reminded him that the sources of news at Simla and Delhi were becoming more and more unofficial, and that the connections and relations established by API staff with the major Indian papers had given the company a considerable advantage in maintaining regular contact with public men throughout the country. Jones' cabled order was clearly not in the interest of the company, and Jones had to agree. The service was allowed to continue, although Roy was warned that the pressure from all sides was building up and that he was to make certain that the special services were only to supplement the API regular service, and not to compete with its other customers.[101]

The Government accepted Jones' decision, but continued to build a dossier for the future. The next major encounter concerned two Reuters' telegrams to London describing 'Muslim murderers in Calcutta' and 'Muslim propaganda to support boycott'. Reuters was immediately informed that the India Office was unhappy, although MacGregor was prepared to let it pass since the company had clearly been more careful with its messages than in the past. He assumed that the occasional slip was due to the unsettled question of the editorship of the API.[102] Roy had died in September 1931, and Sen had succeeded, although not yet confirmed by the company. Sahni described Sen as an innocent, sweet bachelor, who inherited Roy's throne without either his talent and toughness or his influence and connections.[103] And Durga Das, not an unbiased witness, insisted Sen had no politics and no nationalism, and in addition was not a professional newspaperman. He was simply Roy's assistant.[104]

It was assumed in the Home Department that Sen would not be able to give a satisfactory explanation regarding the 'Muslim messages', but their discussion with him produced information that was more troubling than anticipated. Sen insisted that no Reuters' message about the Muslim meeting was sent from India to London on the 21st. There were telegrams sent on the 20th, but these were quite free of the Hindu bias often

[100] *Ibid.*
[101] Iyengar, *Gandhian Era*, p. 145.
[102] R. S. Bajpai, 11 March 1932, IO (InfoDept) L/I/1/264, File 99B.
[103] J. N. Sahni interview, 1970.
[104] Durga Das interview, 1970.

perceived in API material. Ian Stephens thought it might just be conceivable that the FPI 'have been up to some hanky panky in the matter', but he admitted there was no proof to back up his suspicions.[105]

It was generally agreed in the Home Department that Sen was not responsible for the two questionable telegrams but the source was nevertheless the API. 'The inference–and an alarming one', suggested the Home Member, 'is that Reuters are publishing propaganda matter on behalf of outside parties as their own. There is the further inference', he lamented, 'that they are probably drawing money from these parties at the same time as they are drawing money from us.'[106] Sen was emphatic that no Reuters telegrams were sent on the 21st, but in fact the messages were sent and never shown to Sen, and no copy was placed in the ordinary API office file. Stephens reminded MacGregor that they had long believed Sen to be a 'good and reliable fellow' but he was clearly not in command of his own office. The source of the problem was likely Durga Das and Iyengar, 'both of whom are perhaps in some ways cleverer and more energetic than he is, and who from time to time are unable to resist the temptation of misapplying their abilities and the organization of the API in nationalist or Hindu propaganda'.[107]

As has been the case in the past, Sen supported his staff and took responsibility for the error. The Home Department took up the matter with Moloney, who attempted to preserve the current arrangements but at the same time began a series of discussions with various clients in India who were antagonistic to the API.[108] Joyce remained sceptical about Reuters' apparent support and cooperation. 'Personally I suspect that the Government of India and the India Office are not the only people from whom Reuters receive "subvention". I do hope I may prove to be unduly suspicious.'[109]

By 1935, the Government of India had reached the end of its patience regarding the private business of the API. The Viceroy, Lord Willingdon, noticed its tendency to 'distort information obtained in their "Jekyll" capacities and propagate it in a form more suitable to "Hyde"'.[110] The message was relayed to Jones more forcefully than in the past, and he agreed. The decision also initiated a renewed effort to develop an alternative agency that would compete effectively with Reuters. The same

[105] Ian Stephens to H. MacGregor, 28 November 1932, IO (InfoDept) L/I/1/264, File 99B.
[106] Home Member to Croft, 12 December 1932, *ibid.*
[107] Ian Stephens to H. MacGregor, 19 December 1932, *ibid.*
[108] Discussions were held with J. N. Sahni, Cowley, (*Statesman*), and others re. API's 'private business', Sahni, *The Indian Press*, p. 64.
[109] A. H. Joyce to I. Stephens, 11 January 1933, IO (InfoDept) L/I/1/264, File 99B.
[110] Willingdon to Zetland, 17 May 1935, IO (InfoDept) L/P & J/7/896.

possibility appeared to open up for Durga Das and Iyengar, who had received substantial raises to compensate for the loss of their private contracts but were unhappy with the reorganization within the company. They talked with Jinnah and Purshotamdas Thakurdas, and the latter offered to finance a news agency if papers like the *Hindu* promised to subscribe. A scheme was prepared and submitted to Thakurdas, and then to Kasturi Srinivasan of the *Hindu*. There was, however, 'an abundant degree of caution' evident in their conversation and the proposal was dropped.[111]

The Government was no more successful. The abandonment of the API special service was only a part of the problem. Reuters repeatedly sent messages from India to London which tended to emphasize comments adverse to the Government and suppress material indicating another viewpoint. 'This may be sound "business" so far as their Indian clients are concerned,' noted Joyce, 'but it is very unfortunate politically.'[112] It has been assumed that the problem would be resolved in part by an agreement to send messages through Reuters that had been drafted in the Home Department. But some of these had been 'emasculated' in transit without any reference to the Government. Stephens noted as an example messages concerning Indian reactions to the Joint Parliamentary Committee Report. The 'alteration of emphasis' had produced over two pages of P. N. Sapru's critical view, and less than two lines given to the favourable reaction of men like the Maharaja of Darbhanga and Sir Mohammad Usman.[113]

The India Office could do little more than sympathize with the Indian Government's problem. 'The beastly thing about it,' noted Hugh Mac-Gregor, 'is our ultimate helplessness.'

To introduce a new or to expand our official news service is little or no good from the newspaper point of view; to introduce an existing commercial British service into India probably is impracticable in that the Central News is really American-owned and the Exchange Telegraph Company has not a sufficiently comprehensive world service, and to secure the Exchange Telegraph Company and expand it requires money which won't be forthcoming.[114]

The extent of their weakness was made explicit by the Governor of the Central Provinces in a lengthy anti-Reuters lament. The cost of their

---

[111] Iyengar, *Gandhian Era*, pp. 152–3. Durga Das described these negotiations in a December 1970 interview.

[112] I. Stephens to H. MacGregor, 9 November 1932, IO (InfoDept) L/I/1/264, File 99B.

[113] I. Stephens to J. S. Barnes, Reuters/API correspondent at Simla, 17 December 1934, *ibid.*

[114] H. MacGregor, to I. Stephens, 4 January 1935, *ibid.*

contact with Reuters to receive fifteen copies of INA messages a day was Rs 5,400 per year. Since the material was considered practically useless and pressure to make economies had increased, it was decided to dispense with the service. It soon became clear, however, that INA agents had been instructed to publish only unfavourable information concerning the Central Provinces Government. As a result, Sir Hyde Gowan felt compelled to resume the service although he assumed most of his officials would toss the telegrams out without bothering to read them. 'If there is any distinction between this sort of thing and blackmail,' he declared, 'I find it difficult to detect it.'[115]

There was a changing hierarchy of influence and circumstance pressing on this carefully contrived system reflecting a similar rearrangement in the status of the various reluctant partners. Reuters had used B. B. R. Chaudhury as a representative in order to remain in touch with Congress activities in London. When the messages that flowed from this arrangement became too much of a burden for the Government of India, the company was pressured into firing him. The need for such a person on Reuters' staff remained, and in the company's view became more important as conditions changed in India. They attempted to replace Chaudhury but could not find a satisfactory substitute. It was clear to Reuters that the Congress would take their business to a competing agency if their service did not cover all facets of the political situation in Britain and India, and in any case they wanted to avoid complaints from their Indian clients. As a last resort they sought agreement from the Government of India to rehire Chaudhury on the condition that he would not describe himself as a Reuters representative and his copy would be carefully vetted before being sent to India. Reuters admitted that Chaudhury still held advanced political views, but noted that he was less active than in the past.[116] By the end of the decade, the war would resolve all such problems with an undeniable demand for patriotism by writ; but in 1936, the India Office made a last effort to press Reuters to regain direct control of the API by suggesting that Sen be replaced by an Englishman who would guarantee loyal coverage of Indian affairs. Jones' response was immediate and uncompromising. The API had to 'be Indian otherwise it could not survive'.[117]

---

[115] Sir Hyde Gowan, Governor of the Central Provinces, to Sir Henry Craik, Home Member, GOI, 16 September 1935, IO (InfoDept) L/P & J/7/896.
[116] Home member to Mr Johnston, 22 November 1935, IO (InfoDept) L/I/1/264, File 99B.
[117] H. MacGregor note, 22 June 1936, following lunch with Jones, IO (InfoDept) L/I/1/264, File 99B.

The Free Press of India

Many of those who had cheered the demise of the old *Pioneer* monopoly
and the rise of K. C. Roy and his API were looking about in the
mid-1920s for a challenger to the new monopoly that had been established.[118] In 1914, it had been a family struggle between the ageing and
old-fashioned *Pioneer*, its well-connected Simla reporter and pristine
loyal pages; and the *Statesman*'s Cotes with the patronage of Reuters, and
the subsidized approval of the Government.[119] The context of association
was meant to remain substantially unchanged. But the India, or at least
the Anglo-India of the *Pioneer* ascendancy could not be recreated after
the shared effort of the war years. The newsmakers tended to wear white
khaddar rather than khaki drill, and newsworthy events were less likely to
have been planned in the Delhi or Simla Secretariat. Rowlatt became an
epithet for tyranny in the pages of the Indian press. The bureaucracy
could still make the law, but could not control its presentation and,
therefore, its impact. Beyond the tragedy of the people directly involved,
Jallianwalla Bagh became a massacre for those who read the bold headlines and detailed stories, and then talked about them and passed them
on. Frank Moraes has described the feeling of 'horror, frustration and
rage' as he and his school-friends discussed the event. When he returned
home on holiday some months later, the impact of that event had not
dissipated among his parents and their friends. 'My father, a mild-
tempered man, was almost speechless with indignation on reading in a
newspaper of the presentation of a gold sword to General Dyer by "the
Ladies of England"'.[120]

Swaminath Sadanand worked with Durga Das as a reporter for the
API and both covered the Amristar meeting of the Congress in 1919. Das
noted that Sadanand was so overwhelmed by the events of the meeting
and the tragedy that preceeded it, that his utility as a newspaperman was
diminished. The API was clearly not a place for a reporter who allowed
his emotional involvement to effect his professional standards, and in
particular to make him 'oblivious of the practical aspects of the situation'.[121] Almost as significant as the event itself was the Government's
suppression of the story,[122] and the API's great sin of omission was never

---

[118] George Joseph to K. M. Panikkar, 22 March 1924, AICC Paper, 1924, Pt 1.
[119] Lovett, *Journalism*, pp. 44–5.
[120] Frank Moraes, *Witness to an Era*, London: Weidenfeld and Nicolson, 1973, p. 7, e.g.,
Bombay Chronicle, 19 and 20 December 1919.
[121] Durga Das interview, 1970.
[122] The press in Britain and in India covered this point extensively. See *Bombay Chronicle*,
19 December 1919 headlines, 'Concealment By Government Most Shocking Feature'.

forgotten. Sadanand left soon after and devoted much of his professional career to the destruction of its monopoly.

The idea of the Free Press was circulated around Congress circles in the spring of 1924. Gandhi had apparently noted his interest and the information concerning start-up costs had been submitted to him. The most important question that concerned him, and most others involved in the project was whether the API could be beaten.[123] Although Indian politicians and businessmen had a range of competing agendas they desired to publicize, there was no debate among them or in the Indian press about the need for the kind of news service Sadanand described in his 12 September announcement and appeal: 'An independent news agency which will collect and disseminate news with accuracy and impartiality from the Indian view-point is a long-felt public want'.[124] It was of course the relationship between 'viewpoint' and 'impartiality' that concerned the protagonists.

API–Reuters was efficient, dependable, and generally accurate. Its perspective was, however, more alien than disinterested despite its recognition of the need to accommodate the changing press world in the sub-continent. Roderick Jones noted with admiration the extraordinary aptitude which men like Edward Buck shared with his counterparts posted for long periods of time in foreign lands, 'for getting under the skin of an alien way of living and of an alien thought'. As a result they became, in Jones' view, 'equipped and qualified to interpret the peoples of these lands to the rest of the world, and they do so without in any sense clouding or sacrificing their marked British character and principles'.[125]

The *Bombay Chronicle* announcement of the opening of the FPI office described a mission far more daunting than the mere rendering of 'Indian viewpoint'. It had to discover it as well. The *Chronicle* described the increasing tendency of public bodies and publicists to organize their activities on a communal or sectional basis and the need to coordinate the range of national action in order to achieve tolerance and understanding of the various conflicting viewpoints.[126] The FPI was to be nothing less than the publicity organ of the whole nation. Sadanand had imagination and energy, and 'a one-track mind once he made a decision'.[127] But he would also require financial backing and a shared commitment from the Indian press in order to achieve his goal.

[123] George Joseph to K. M. Panikkar, 22 March 1924, AICC Papers, Pt 1, 1924.
[124] Swaminath Sadanand, 'Announcement and Appeal', 12 September 1924, Jayakar Papers, 398.
[125] Jones, *Life in Reuters*, p. 360.
[126] *Bombay Chronicle*, 8 January 1925, clipping in Jayakar Papers, 398.
[127] Durga Das interview, 1970.

It seemed to some of his potential backers in the Bombay business community that the agency would require years of private subsidy in order to survive, and in any case was unlikely to compete successfully with the API. J. B. Petit, who had helped Pherozeshah Mehta launch the *Bombay Chronicle* and now controlled the *Indian Daily Mail*, was invited to invest in the FPI and join the first Board. He declined, noting that estimated expenses seemed too low and estimated revenues considerably overstated. While Sadanand anticipated a self-supporting FPI in the second year of operation, Petit foresaw large losses for at least five years. He had asked F. H. Holsinger, the managing editor of the *Mail*, to go over Sadanand's figures, and his response was unequivocal. There was no scope for a second news agency in India since there were not enough papers. Indian papers were finding it difficult enough to pay for the API service; and although another service would produce rate competition, the API–Reuters organization would always be able to underquote the FPI.

It was clear to Holsinger that the Anglo-Indian press would not give up the API and that there was no possibility for a news service in India to survive without it. He reminded Petit that it had been their refusal to support Roy and Sen in 1910, that ensured the collapse of the Press Bureau and required their association with Cotes and subsequent absorption into the Reuters empire. There was more to the news business than politics, Holsinger insisted, and neither the Anglo-Indian press nor Indian papers like the *Mail* which sought to be full professional enterprises 'could afford to subscribe to a news service which will probably not be able to provide much more than political news'.[128]

For the first five years of its existence, the FPI was committed by Sadanand to the service of those who were willing to pay to keep it alive: Indian business and commercial interests, the Swarajist Party, and subsequently the Responsive Cooperationists led by the Bombay Swarajist leader, M. R. Jayakar, one of his early patrons and a director of his company. The war had generally benefited Indian business, the cotton textile industry in particular stimulated by enhanced protection without any increase in the countervailing excise. In the post-war period, the general decline and malaise was widely shared, but Indian businessmen were not inclined to give up their gains to allow their Anglo-Indian or

---

[128] Jehangir Petit to M. R. Jayakar, 18 November 1924 with enclosure: F. E. Holsinger to Petit, 3 November 1924, Jayakar Papers, 398. Petit was briefly on the FPI board. For a brief overview of M. R. Jayakar's role in the establishment of the FPI, see M. Israel 'M. R. Jayakar and the Bombay National Press: The Struggle for Identity within a Nationalist Movement', in N. K. Wagle, ed., *Images of Maharashtra*, London: Curzon Press, 1980, pp. 9–28.

British competitors to receive benefits which were detrimental to Indian-controlled interests. It is in this context that many businessmen moved beyond the stage of 'vicarious nationalism'[129] and became active participants in the struggle, although generally on their own terms. They contributed generously to Congress funding campaigns, although the establishment of the Anti-Non-cooperation Association reflected the limit of their enthusiasm.[130]

In addition to their support for the nationalist political campaign, it became clear to these businessmen that they would have to organize themselves into an effective lobby in order to protect and give priority to their interests among politicians as well as with Government. G. D. Birla reminded Purshotamdas Thakurdas that his earlier suggestion of a federation of Indian chambers of commerce had attracted little interest, but the aggressive anti-protection stance of the European-controlled Association of Chambers of Commerce of India and Ceylon required a response. Birla was convinced that the cause of protection had 'already suffered a good deal on account of their organised propaganda', and insisted that Bombay had to add an interest in economics to its new commitment to politics.[131] Thakurdas agreed but lamented the lack of public interest in commercial and industrial matters. It was the Non-cooperation Movement, he insisted, that was largely responsible for the situation as it had 'given the masses the very dreary and dangerous satisfaction of resting content only with destructive work'.[132]

The establishment of the Swaraj Party in 1923, provided an opportunity for cooperation and both Party and business leaders sought to achieve maximum benefit for their own priorities, while serving the less-well-defined general cause. In October 1924, Motilal Nehru wrote to Thakurdas about the futility of Gandhi's recently ended fast and the need for practical men like themselves to get on with the 'real political work in the country'. Nehru assumed that 'Gandhiji will either convert the Congress into a spinners association or else stick to his ... boycotts.' It was apparent, however, that neither was likely to produce useful results.[133] The immediate necessity was for money and publicity, and Nehru pressed for promised instalments of pledges made by the Bombay business com-

---

[129] This is Bipin Chandra's phrase.

[130] See Sumit Sarkar, *Modern India 1885–1947*, Delhi: Macmillan India, 1983. He notes that Bombay alone contributed 372 lakhs of the crore of rupees raised for the Tilak Swaraj Fund. The Anti-Non-cooperation Association was established in 1920 and included among its founders: P. Thakurdas, Jamnadas Dwarkadas, Cowasji Jehangir, and Pheroze Sethna. *Ibid.*, pp. 207–8.

[131] G. D. Birla to P. Thakurdas, 7 December 1923, Thakurdas Papers, 42(II).

[132] P. Thakurdas to G. D. Birla, 11 December 1923, *ibid.*

[133] Motilal Nehru to P. Thakurdas, 8 October 1924, Thakurdas Papers, 40–1.

munity. In subsequent correspondence, Nehru reiterated the relationship between effective work in the Assembly in the interests of Indian business and financial support for the Party, insisting that there was 'little doubt left that Commerce cannot have better or stronger allies in the political sphere than the Swarajists'.[134] A. D. D. Gordon has described the development of close links between Bombay industrialists and Swarajists, culminating in the currency exchange debate in 1925–6. The Indian Currency League, founded by forty industrialists at a garden party in 1926, was essentially a vehicle of propaganda. It was also a 'synthesiser of the Bombay and Ahmedabad industrialists and the Swarajists'.[135]

From its establishment in 1924, the FPI had been 'run by a coalition of Bombay industrialists and journalists'.[136] It helped to propagate Walchand Hirachand's claim on behalf of his Scindia Steam Navigation Company for reservation of coastal traffic to Indian-owned vessels,[137] and by 1926 it had attracted increased funding and commitments of support from businessmen who perceived a need for such a publicity outlet.[138] From October 1926 to February 1927, the FPI transmitted 86,755 words of propaganda for the Currency League in return for a Rs 2,500 per month stipend and an additional contribution of Rs 5,000 from the Millowners Association of Bombay.[139] Birla and Thakurdas had joined the Board and contributed an additional Rs 5,000 to its working capital. Looking to the future, Jayakar urged Sadanand to take advantage of the presence of these men to attract others of their kind and create a 'first-class businessman board'. Perhaps reflecting his concern about Sadanand's uncontrolled enthusiasms, he noted that such a Board would avoid 'dumping funds into a pit again'.[140]

Throughout the Swarajist years, Sadanand attempted to serve the interests of the Party and of the FPI as well. He was a patriot and a newspaperman, and viewed the achievement of success in his profession

---

[134] Motilal Nehru to P. Thakurdas, Thakurdas Papers, 8 October 1924, 40–2. Regarding Congress support for business interests, Nehru cautioned Thakurdas: 'As you are aware we have socialists, communists and demagogues in our Party and each wishes to distinguish himself in his own line. It will be a hard job to keep them together.'

[135] A. D. D. Gordon, *Businessmen and Politics: Rising Nationalism and a Modernizing Economy in Bombay, 1918–1933*, Australia National University Monographs on South Asia, No. 3, Delhi: Manohar, 1978. The British insisted on the 1s 6d rupee in order to achieve savings in their sterling expenses. India business wanted a 1s 4d ratio.

[136] *Ibid.*, p. 184.

[137] Iyengar, *Gandhian Era*, p. 140.

[138] Natarajan, *History of the Press*, p. 210. See also Jayakar Papers, File 398 re. the establishment of the Indian Currency League.

[139] Gordon, *Businessmen and Politics*, p. 184, quoted from Sadanand to Jayakar, 9 March 1927, Jayakar Papers.

[140] Jayakar to Sadanand, 12 April 1927, Jayakar Papers, 398.

as the best way to contribute to the nationalist goal. In this regard he and
K. C. Roy were much alike, although neither would have likely accepted
that observation. Each pressed the margin of professional initiative that
was possible in the constrained environment of the Raj. But Roy pressed
deftly from the inside, while Sadanand struggled for recognition and the
opportunity to compete on reasonable terms. The API and Roy did
everything possible to defeat Sadanand's challenge which they considered
unprofessional, and dangerous to their monopoly.[141]

Publicity work for the Swaraj Party provided contacts throughout
India and the possibility of increasing the number of papers subscribing
to the FPI service. The impressive makeup of his Board, however, was not
reflected in Sadanand's personal lifestyle or the staff and facilities of his
company. J. N. Sahni has described this 'Robin Hood' who wrote,
managed, edited, and sought support for his agency, 'wearing a khadi
lungi and a khadi shirt, his feet and legs swollen with elephantiasis, living
on a simple fare of rice and *rassam* . . . '[142] His initial salary was Rs 100 per
month, rising to Rs 200 per month after the formal start of business in
January 1925. To this he was able to add Rs 150 per month by writing
leaders for the *Advocate*, which also provided free office space for the FPI
in the *Advocate* building.[143] It was clear from the beginning that the
long-term future of the FPI was going to be Sadanand's problem; and the
willingness of his affluent backers to continue more than marginal philanthropy would depend on his success in becoming a stable competitor in
the professional press world. They were never willing, however, to under-
write the high cost that might have made it possible to achieve that goal.

Sadanand used Jayakar's contacts by writing directly or asking Jayakar
to intercede on behalf of the agency. Rangaswami Iyengar promised to
secure the *Hindu* and the *Swadesamitran* in Madras and Lajpat Rai was
pressed to bring in the *Bande Mataram*. Sadanand had secured a commission to write a weekly letter for the *Bengalee* but making that paper a
customer for his service was more difficult. An indirect contact with
Kalinath Roy produced only a commitment to see what he could do.[144] In
February 1925, Sadanand asked Jayakar to arrange a yearly grant of Rs
2,000 for Swaraj Party publicity work since the 'poverty of the Indian
press' made it impossible to sustain the agency without a subsidy. He
agreed to cover all Bombay Council activities in addition to Swaraj Party
affairs and requested all members of the Council to provide him with

[141] Durga Das interview, 1970.
[142] Sahni, *The Indian Press*, p. 123.
[143] Jayakar Papers, 398.
[144] Sadanand to Jayakar, 28 January 1925, *ibid.*

information on a regular basis.[145] In general he carefully catered to these priorities and covered the activities of his chief patron.

In the first three months of the FPI service, thirty-six papers received local and provincial news but, with the exception of the *Advocate* which made a contribution in addition to free office space, the service was free. Sadanand planned to set up a telegraphic service from Bombay and contact nationalist newspapers with a full range of activities including a foreign department 'for the dissemination of foreign news from the radical standpoint in India and for supply of selected Indian activities from the nationalist viewpoint to papers in England and other foreign countries'. To achieve this goal, however, he needed money, and again his patrons were pressed for support.[146]

With a staff of two reporters and one *sepoy* in the Bombay office and nine correspondents in major centres, Sadanand began to issue the *Free Press Bulletin* in February 1925, in addition to the FPI service. Lacking a sufficient number of customers to take his messages – even at no charge – the *Bulletins* served as outlets, self-generated vehicles and advertisements for his service. Eventually they would be replaced with a chain of news-papers established by Sadanand to become customers of the FPI service as well. Regrettably these papers were perceived by other clients as competitors and their patriotic commitment to the FPI was eroded.[147]

Although the Swaraj Party work and publicity for Bombay business interests allowed the FPI to survive, there did not appear to be a future in the news agency business. In mid April 1925, Jayakar wrote to A. Rangaswami Iyengar seeking some alternative employment for Sadanand. His father had been a newspaperman in the Tamil press, and it semed best that he return to Madras. 'The poor man is struggling very hard to keep his head above water. Can you give him some work in honest journalism ...? He is a nice, capable youth who ruined what might have been a fine career in journalism. He is picking up his threads and wishes to do something useful and good'.[148] Sadanand, however, had no intention of giving up the FPI. In May he wrote optimistically to Jayakar that Iyengar had agreed that *Swadesamitran* would subscribe to the service, and

---

[145] Sadanand to Jayakar, 13 February 1925; Sadanand to members of the Bombay legisla-ture, 19 March 1925, *ibid.*

[146] March 1925, *ibid.*

[147] In the first three months of operation, Sadanand issued the following bulletins: Dr Besant, All Parties Conference, February 1925; C. F. Andrews, Indians in Africa, February 1925; Radindranath Tagore, World Unity, March 1925; B. F. Bharucha, Liquor Auction in City, March 1925; An English Trade Unionist, Indian Labour Movement, April 1925. In addition, ninety-two 'special News Bulletins' were sent out in the same period.

[148] Jayakar to A. Rangaswami Iyengar, 14 April 1925, Jayakar Papers, 398.

promised to induce the *Hindu* and the *Andhra Patrika* to subscribe as well as assisting Sadanand with a Madras office for the FPI. But in another letter three days later he noted his concern that neither of these papers had responded, nor had he received a response from the *Tribune*, *Swarajya* or *Forward*. The separate publication of the *Bulletin* had also become too expensive and it was now a supplement to the Sunday *Advocate of India*.[149] All such letters included a plea for money in a tone of alternating desperation and anger.

In July, Sadanand toured Madras and Calcutta and returned with seven subscriptions to his supplementary telegraphic service and the possibility of four more customers in these two cities. But he remained troubled by the apparent lack of patriotism which continued to deny him a measure of financial stability. 'I am not, however, elated as my faith in the character of the Indian Press is not much.'[150] In September, the *Bulletin* was suspended 'pending arrangements for expansion and stability', and in December Sadanand was off on another tour to get support for an All-India free press service. As would be the case throughout his career, the solution to financial troubles was expansion. It was clear to him that the supplementary service was no longer adequate, and the FPI would either have to expand or confine itself to a very narrow field of activity. Since this narrow field was not even self-sustaining, there was no choice.[151] On 1 January 1926, the new All-India free press service was supported by seventeen out of the forty-five Indian-owned dailies, and at the end of March it was incorporated as a limited company.[152]

In October 1925, Jayakar began his move toward Responsive Co-operation and separation from the Swarajya Party, which remained committed to wrecking the Reforms from within the legislatures. Sadanand went with him. He pressed Jayakar to include the FPI as an important item on the agenda of the Akola meeting of the new Party, stressing that 'Responsive Cooperation had no chance without adequate publicity'.[153] Although there was apparently no mention of the FPI at Akola, Jayakar assured Sadanand that he could be the official publicity agent for the Bombay branch, and suggested that he become the organiz-

[149] Sadanand to Jayakar, 8 and 11 May 1925, *ibid.*
[150] Sadanand to Jayakar, 27 July 1925, *ibid.*
[151] Sadanand to Jayakar, 14 September and 18 December 1925, *ibid.*
[152] Sadanand, 1 January 1926. The FPI service was taken in part or in whole by: the *Tribune*, *Bande Mataram*, and *Pratap* (Lahore); the *Hindustan Times* and *Tej* (Delhi); the *Indian Daily Telegraph* (Lucknow); *Aj* (Banares); the *Servant*, *Basumati*, *Anand Bazar Patrika*, *Swatantra*, *Viswamitra*, and *Bhararamitra* (Calcutta); *Andhrapatrika* (Madras); and the *Advocate of India*, *Hindustan*, *Lokomanya*, and *Navakl* (Bombay), Jayakar Papers, 398.
[153] Sadanand to Jayakar, 9 February 1926, *ibid.*

ing secretary of the Party in Bombay.[154] The first Board of the newly incorporated FPI reflected its responsivist loyalties: Jayakar, N. C. Kelkar, and Sadanand. Jayakar wrote letters to associates and friends in every part of India, and Sadanand returned to his touring in Delhi, Madras, and Bombay to raise funds for the Party and the service.[155]

Sadanand recognized the possibility of a windfall for the FPI in the Rs 50,000 fund collected by M. M. Malaviya from G. D. Birla and his friends. There were a variety of groups associated with the Responsivists, Malaviya's Independent Congress Party and the Hindu Mahasabha who were making claims for support, and Sadanand suggested that Rs 5,000 be reserved for the FPI. But Malaviya rejected the request and resisted further pressure from Jayakar and Kelkar. Sadanand also talked directly to Birla, who supported his claim to part of the fund but refused to make any additional contribution.[156]

The lack of extraordinary support for the FPI during the 1926 election campaign was particularly frustrating to Sadanand, since his Responsivist loyalties had cost him clients who had remained loyal Swarajists. Rangaswami Iyengar and his associates in Madras had apparently boycotted the FPI and Sadanand responded with a directive to his Madras office to 'leave the Swarajists alone until they show a contrary inclination'. The opposition from the Swarajists had spread to other parts of the country as well, leaving the FPI dependent on Responsivist support. But Malaviya had no money for him, and other independents such as the Liberals and landowning classes could not be penetrated because prominent men among them showed no interest. He had, however, received some encouragement from Bengal Responsivists led by B. Chakravarty; and B. K. Lahiri finally agreed to get twenty shares subscribed by friends and took four shares himself.[157]

Sadanand proposed a grand plan to Lahiri, typical of his optimism and tactics when under stress. It was typical also of his identification of the FPI with the larger patriotic mission of the nationalist campaign. He suggested that the burden of contributions to the capital of the FPI should be distributed among the major provinces, that is, Bombay, Bengal, Madras, and Punjab. Each province would be represented on the Board of Directors. Of the Rs 50,000 that was required to get the FPI started properly, it semed appropriate that Bombay pay Rs 20,000 and others Rs 10,000 each. He asked Lahiri to join the Board as the Bengal

---

[154] Jayakar to Sadanand, 18 February 1926, *ibid.*
[155] Memorandum, n.d. *ibid.*
[156] Sadanand to Jayakar, 1 July 1926, 2 July 1926; Jayakar telegram to M. M. Malaviya, 6 July 1926, *ibid.*
[157] Sadanand to Jayakar, 6 July 1926, *ibid.*

member and get the Rs 10,000 subscribed among his friends.[158] Like so many other of Sadanand's proposals, it was stillborn.

During the last six months of 1926, the affairs of the company remained on the margin of survival. The pleas for funding continued, including a request to the directors that his honorarium be increased to Rs 200 per month. Jayakar wrote more letters soliciting support, and Sadanand continued his lonely travels in search of clients.[159] His appeal letters reiterated the story of the founding of the FPI, provided financial data on the amount of money Indian-owned papers were currently spending on news services, noted the relatively small amount of revenue the FPI required to break even, and reminded these newspaper editors and owners who called themselves nationalists of the need for an Indian-controlled news agency.[160] During each of these cycles, a few more clients would be added to the roster, almost always preceded by bargaining for a special rate which ensured virtually no profit to the FPI. By February, 1927, there were twenty-two subscribers bringing Rs 2,205 per month in revenue against expenses of Rs 5,348 per month.[161]

It was clearly time for expansion. Sadanand noted that the FPI was not yet covering the Government of India and now required offices in Delhi and Lahore. With this expansion, expenses would increase to Rs 8,000 per month, but revenues would increase to Rs 5,750 with the addition of an anticipated twelve new subscribers from the new centres. There would be increased revenue from old subscribers who would benefit from the expanded service, but it would be necessary to cover the anticipated Rs 2,250 monthly deficit until all forty-three Indian papers became subscribers.[162] He assumed that the majority of vernacular papers would rely on the FPI entirely, while the English-language papers would continue with both the API and FPI. He also assumed that the Anglo-Indian press would have no interest in his service, although he did not entirely exclude the possibility that one or two might take it on. The new plan was taken to his Board and received the usual cautious support, and this time another Rs 5,000 from a group of millowners.[163]

By 1928, Sadanand's relationship with Jayakar and the Responsivists was becoming too burdensome for both. Although he had always

---

[158] Sadanand to B. K. Lahiri, 16 July 1926, *ibid.*
[159] Sadanand to Jayakar, 31 July 1926, Jayakar to Lahiri, 17 August 1926; Jayakar to T. Tamagaki, 7 September 1926, Sadanand to directors, 22 November 1926; Jayakar to Lajpat Rai, 9 December 1926, *ibid.*
[160] Sadanand, 'Free Press of India', for private circulation, *ibid.*
[161] Sadanand memorandum, 23 February 1927, Jayakar Papers, 400.
[162] Those Indian papers subscribing to a news service in 1926.
[163] Sadanand memorandum, 23 February 1927; Jayakar to Sadanand, 16 July 1927, Jayakar Papers, 400.

managed to work for the Party and his company as well throughout this period, the FPI was widely perceived as the mouthpiece of one particular camp of the nationalist movement. In addition, his work as a publicist for the Bombay business elite had identified him with another special interest outside of the Gandhian mainstream of nationalist activity. After almost four years of news service activity, Sadanand and the FPI remained marginal to the interests of the major Indian and Anglo-Indian press, the nationalist political leadership, and the Government of India. K. C. Roy and his API colleagues had been watching the development of his organization and were clearly concerned about the potential competition, but everyone who knew anything about the FPI in 1928 recognized the likelihood that it would probably not survive until the end of the year. With the exception of the 'Royists',[164] however, and notwithstanding his 'knack for antagonizing people – friends as well as enemies',[165] most of those who recognized what he was trying to do wanted him to succeed.

In May 1928, Sadanand wrote to the General Secretary of the AICC concerning the role that the FPI might play as a publicity agent for the Congress. He now described his company as the nationalist news agency and offered his facilities to the office-bearers and committees of the Congress. It was suggested that the secretary of each Provincial Congress Committee (PCC) be informed of the desire of the FPI to serve the cause and that all accounts of their activities should be sent to the nearest FPI office. He received a positive response from Jawaharlal Nehru, who promised to circulate copies of his letters to all PCCs.[166] Sadanand was in the process of breaking away from his initial and still primary source of support, but was not yet in a position to survive without their patronage. He was convinced that the requirements of the Anglo-Indian and Indian-owned press were 'entirely different', but continued to have difficulty convincing the major newspapers in the latter group that this was in fact the case – especially in regard to the use of a news service.

In Sadanand's view, Reuters was maintained chiefly from the standpoint of the Anglo-Indian press, and any competitive service would have to adapt itself to the needs of the Indian press. In the case of most of the vernacular press, this argument could be sustained, but not with the major English-language papers. They were concerned with the British and official bias often observable in Reuters' and API messages, but they had generally learned to live with it and use it for their own purposes. The special correspondent services of the API provided a partial corrective,

[164] J. N. Sahni's term.
[165] J. N. Sahni interview, 1970.
[166] Sadanand to General Secretary, AICC, 8 May 1928, AICC G-15/1928.

and the larger papers had at least informal correspondents who sent them regular messages – although usually by mail rather than cable. Smaller papers, English language or vernacular, which wanted Reuters' messages could always get them secondhand. Everard Cotes once noted in a speech to the East India Association that he had not had much to do with 'vernacular sheets ... and the weird characters in which they are printed',[167] but he had done more than he knew. K. D. Umrigar, who ended his newspaper career at the *Times of India*, recalled an early reporting job on the staff of the Gujerati *Sanj Vartaman*, where his work involved translating API and Reuters' messages into Gujerati. He was told that was the main work of reporters of Gujerati papers and he rarely did any actual reporting.[168]

In July 1928, G. D. Birla lamented that the company's affairs continued to be disappointing and recognized that it would continue to require help from friends like himself for some time. There was some consolation, he suggested to Sadanand, that he was doing a great service and particularly that 'one does not find the name of the Associated Press in various Indian papers'.[169] Purshotamdas Thakurdas was less sanguine, suggesting at the August Board meeting that the FPI should close down voluntarily unless additional funding could be found.[170] But in September, the Board 'resolved that the continuance of the Free Press of India with unimpaired efficiency is a national necessity and that it be continued'. The FPI was converted from a public to a private limited liability company and the number of shareholders increased. It was assumed that there would be an annual deficit of approximately Rs 70,000 for the next three years, to be met by contributions towards capital as well as revenue. A list of potential

---

[167] Everard Cotes, 'The Newspaper Press of India', *Asiatic Review*, n.s. 19, July 1923, 417–41.

[168] K. D. Umrigar, *Lest I Forget*, Bombay: The Popular Book Depot, 1949, pp. 28, 31, 41.

[169] G. D. Birla to S. Sadanand, 18 July 1928, Jayakar Papers, 400. In Lahore, *Pratap*, *Milap*, *Bandemataram*, and *Siyasat* gave notice of discontinuance to the API. The *Forward* subscribed to the whole FPI service and left the question of cancelling its API subscription for the future. In Bombay, the *Indian National Herald* and the *Hindustan* indicated they would rely only on the FPI from 27 July 1928, as did the *Swatantra* and *Basumati* in Calcutta. Jayakar Papers, 400. The FPI's relationship with its subscribers tended to be unstable and a monthly review would indicate the addition of new customers and the loss of others. The lower cost of the FPI service was of primary significance to many of its customers, especially among the vernacular papers. For Sadanand, any loss to the API was a victory. There were in fact few of these. Prior to the establishment of the FPI, the Indian press paid approximately Rs 600,000 with no apparent reduction in API revenue. The FPI service was either additional for those who could afford it or considered it a patriotic duty; or the only service for those not able or interested in competing with major papers. Sadanand always insisted that the 'big switch to the Free Press was only a question of time', Jayakar Papers, 400.

[170] Sir P. Thakurdas, seventh meeting of the Board of Directors, 3 August 1928, *ibid*.

donors was drawn up and as a beginning, Birla, Thakurdas, and Phiroze Sethna, all directors, agreed to subscribe Rs 5,000 each towards share capital for the current year. In addition, Birla Brothers would make a contribution.[171]

A year later the financial condition of the FPI had not improved and Thakurdas was again talking about liquidation. He told Birla that Sadanand had difficulty paying a Rs 50 bill, and had received little response from the continuing advertisement of his service. Birla remained reluctant to allow the company to collapse and sent another Rs 5,000 to get it through another month.[172] But this time, Thakurdas was determined to end what he considered to be a poor investment and a wasted philanthropy. He had become convinced that a national news service could become virtually self-sustaining, but not with Sadanand in control. It was a management problem, and he and Birla, with Jayakar's agreement, had decided to make a last attempt to save the FPI if control could be transferred to a more businesslike management.

On 19 September Sadanand was informed that the present Board[173] could no longer take responsibility for collecting the capital required to meet the annual deficit and the choice was either liquidation or transfer. If the FPI were transferred to parties approved by the Board, and managed along lines that were also approved, Birla and Thakurdas agreed to pledge Rs 5,000 each for the next two years. There appeared to be three possibilities for transfer. Jayakar had actively sought control of a newspaper to publicize his views for almost a decade, and had been the most loyal supporter. Alternatively, N. C. Kelkar, perhaps with the participation of Motilal Nehru, might take charge. Finally, Sadanand might take over control and attempt to run the business himself.

Sadanand pressed for the status quo, insisting that the FPI had a bright future, but received no support.[174] It was agreed that Jayakar would consult Kelkar and report back in a few days. The result was an elaborate set of proposals,[175] all of which challenged Sadanand's methods and

---

[171] The eighth meeting of the Board of Directors, 19 September 1928, *ibid.* Shares were purchased by: G. D. Birla (10), Sir Phiroze Sethna (10), Sir P. Thakurdas (10), D. K. Lahiri Chowdry (1), and Sir Dorab Tata (30). *Ibid.*

[172] G. D. Birla, *Ibid.*

[173] The new Board: Birla, Jayakar, Thakurdas, and Sadanand.

[174] Minutes, Board of Directors, FPI, 19 September 1929, Jayakar Papers, 401.

[175] Jayakar reported his conversation with Kelkar and presented the following proposals:
  1. Present Board continue with additions.
  2. The deficit for the current year be reduced by Rs 15,000.
  3. Current debts to be paid by Rs 10,000 donations promised by P. Thakurdas and G. D. Birla.
  4. Thakurdas and Birla to find Rs 15,000 to reduce deficit.
  5. Jayakar to guide editorial side.

day-to-day control and were unacceptable to him. It was finally agreed to transfer control to Sadanand. Birla and Thakurdas committed a last Rs 10,000, specifically for the clearing of the current debt, and Jayakar eventually agreed to convert a Rs 5,000 note into shares. And with this final show of generosity, they all resigned from the Board and left the company and its future in the hands of its founder.[176]

The drift toward more radical editorializing, which in addition to Sadanand's erratic management style had antagonized the businessmen of his old Board, continued to move the FPI into the Congress mainstream, and therefore into increasing confrontation with the Government, The FPI also became a much more aggressive competitor for API–Reuters' customers. When the Board was recast in 1930, Sadanand had managed to attract the participation of one businessman, Sir Phiroze Sethna. Although the company had become virtually self-supporting, its deficit in the six-month period April to September being less than Rs 2,000, Sethna could not cope with the style and policies that had apparently produced the miracle. He resigned in February 1931. In his view, Sadanand was 'going from bad to worse for whilst he does not openly support these Bolshevists, the headings he gives to his paragraphs clearly indicate that he does not approve of the Irwin–Gandhi agreement'.[177]

Reuters had become increasingly defensive regarding its Indian monopoly in the late 1920s, although it generally discounted the FPI as a serious challenge. In 1926, Reuters had given its customers in India six months to conclude contracts with the company for the supply of news from London. The major new condition of these contracts was a commitment not to use any other news service from London. There was little complaint from the India press since few could afford or thought they required additional London messages, and Reuters had agreed that it could continue to receive news from its own correspondents. In addition, the London committee representing the major Anglo-Indian press agreed to play a watchdog role regarding messages sent out to India. There was not, however, universal approval, especially from the British United Press Agency which was doing some business in India and would now be virtually cut out.

British United Press suggested to the India Office that Reuters worked

6. Another director to guide business side.
7. Sadanand to remain, but under supervision.
8. There should be an attempt to reach an understanding with the API.
Ibid.
[176] Minutes, Board of Directors, FPI, 21 September 1929; Sadanand to Jayakar, *ibid.*
[177] Phiroze Sethna to Mrs Barns, 26 March 1931, Sethna Papers (1931), 186–7; FPI Directors' Report, 31 March 1931, Jayakar Papers, 399.

very closely with European agencies which were controlled by foreign governments,[178] and inevitably alien official bias would influence Reuters messages. The nature of the Reuters monopoly was reiterated and the role that the Government of India continued to play in ensuring that position in India. There had been three potential rivals for Indian business. The Australian Cable Service had lost its best client, the *Times of India*, and it was no longer a contender. Under the new Reuters arrangements, the *Statesman* service and the British United Press service would also lose. The *Indian Daily Mail* had arranged for a London service with the Central News Agency, but this too would have to end.[179]

The British United Press had been established in 1924 by its parent company in the United States and had become a major channel into the Indian market. In 1926, there were ten United Press correspondents in India and the *Times of India* was one of their clients. They were strong enemies of Reuters in Canada and Australia as well. The United Press's mention of Reuters' European connections was sufficiently disturbing to the India Office, always anticipating an embarrassing question in the House of Commons, to raise the matter with officials in India. The Home Department contacted the editor of the *Statesman* who reminded them that Reuters was the only complete service available in India and agreed that Reuters had a good financial case for insisting on a monopoly. Although Reuters had sent questionable telegrams in the past, the *Statesman* assumed that the combination of the Press Committee and the India Office would suffice to control the situation. It was also noted that supplementary agencies like British United Press had only commercial motives, and it seemed clear they had been given 'orders from their office in New York to fight Reuters "politically".'[180]

In 1927, Sadanand began a direct campaign against the API–Reuters monopoly. As a first step he sought recognition for the FPI as a news agency and eligible for the grant of normal press privileges by the Government. In response to his request, the Press Committee met on 14 February. Its membership did not guarantee Sadanand a disinterested hearing. In addition to the Home Secretary, H. G. Haig, and the DPI, John Coatman, the press was represented by Reuters' Edward Buck and U. N. Sen from the API. There were degrees of privilege available to pressmen at the centre of Government. The minimum offering was

---

[178] Reuters had treaty agreements with Havas (France), Wolf (Germany), and Stephanie (Italy).

[179] J. E. Ferrand, Secretary Public and Judicial Department, India Office, to H. G. Haig, Secretary, Home Department, GOI: two confidential notes, 29 and 30 June 1926, GOI (HomePol) 186/26.

[180] *Ibid.*

admission to the press gallery, already available to Sadanand. An additional privilege was admission to the press room, and finally admission to department officials in the Secretariat and receipt of Government communiqués and publications before publication time. Both Haig and Coatman thought it quite reasonable to allow Sadanand press-room privileges, but Buck objected, noting that 'Mr Sadanand was personally objectionable and his agency was a mushroom agency.' But Sen agreed with Coatman and the privilege was granted. Access to advance copies of Government papers, however, was unanimously rejected. Sadanand reminded Haig that the FPI could not compete with the API unless he received material at the same time. His clients would be required to subscribe to an additional service for this material. Haig did not disagree but neither did he grant the request.[181]

In November, Sadanand established the FPI foreign service and appointed a series of London representatives. None of them were satisfactory to him and the service remained weak. But it strengthened the FPI in his view, as did his new status in Delhi and Simla; and some London papers and more on the continent began using FPI telegrams.[182] He also challenged the Congress to end its own special relationship with the API when a Working Committee resolution was given to the API which passed on an 'exclusive' to the *Times of India*.[183] It was not possible to challenge the API without challenging as well powerful patrons who were either committed to the old arrangements or convinced there was no adequate alternative.

In March 1928, the *Pioneer*, briefly radical under the editorship of F. W. Wilson, published an FPI-inspired article entitled 'A Mischievous Monopoly'.[184] Sadanand had provided a detailed analysis of the Government's budget estimates under the 'miscellaneous demand' account which

---

[181] Home Department memorandum re. the admission of Sadanand to the press room of the Government of India, 14 February 1927; J. Coatman note, 11 March 1927; Sadanand to Haig, 26 February 1927; Haig to Sadanand, 30 March 1927, GOI (HomePol) 19/II/1927.

[182] Sadanand memorandum, n.d., Jayakar Papers, 400. The FPI Foreign Service was established in November 1927. The first London representative was Mr Karandikar of the INS. British news was sent to India and Indian news to England, the continent, and America. But he proved to be 'very unbusinesslike and unsteady', and was replaced by Charles Barnes, who had been associated with Major Graham Pole, a long-time member of the British Committee of the Indian National Congress. But as usual, there were difficulties with Sadanand. 'He was journalistically less efficient than Mr. Karandikar and tried to bleed the Free Press.' The third and current representative was Mr Pulin Seal, but, lamented Sadanand, he was 'most inefficient and is costly and greedy'. The service was weak and always on the verge of collapse. Jayakar Papers, 400.

[183] Sunder Kabadi (FPI) and K. Natarajan (*Indian Daily Mail*) to Working Committee, 21 May 1927, Sreenivasa Iyengar Papers.

[184] *Pioneer*, 23 March, 1928.

was devoted to news-agency expenses. The cost of the API–Reuters' service to the Central and Provincial Governments was reviewed, and the *Pioneer* questioned whether an annual expenditure of approximately Rs 172,000 to supply news to officials was justified. It agreed that twenty years ago the Government might have felt it could not depend on the underdeveloped press, but that was no longer the case. The wide distribution of news at Government expense had now become 'a wholly unwarranted interference with legitimate newspaper enterprise'. It concluded by noting that for all practical purposes, all the money went to the same place, the Reuters–ENA monopoly. In April, Sadanand's patrons in the Bombay Indian Merchants' Chamber contacted the Home Department regarding the *Pioneer* story. The current news-service arrangements were questioned, but the Home Department refused to provide a full response, noting that the Chamber's business was not related to the subject. It suggested as an alternative that the question might be raised in the Assembly by the Chamber's representative, and immediately began an internal review in order to prepare the answer. It would be the same as in the past: there were no papers showing that Reuters and the ENA were under one control. Payments by Government for news services were made on a commercial basis and were not a subsidy. Government officials required news as quickly as possible.[185]

Sadanand's allegations were circulated to Assembly members and published in the *Hindustan Times* on 6 April 1929.[186] In addition to the familiar story of the Government of India–Reuters relationship, information was provided regarding such special privileges as free first-class travel on the Indian railway system, free use of trunk telephones, reduced telegraph charges, and favoured treatment in regard to Government news. In every case, the FPI had asked for equal treatment and been refused.[187] The Home Department had anticipated an Assembly question, but not the detailed analysis of Reuters' privileges. In the subsequent discussions within the Department it was recognized that the large lump-sum allocated under '74–Miscellaneous – Books and Periodicals' attracted attention and should be distributed among the budgets of the individual departments using API–Reuters services. In regard to the free first-class travel concession, it was noted that the matter rested with the Railway Board, which had refused a free pass to the FPI 'at our suggestion'. It was generally agreed that the inferior quality of the FPI service

[185] Indian Merchants' Chamber, Bombay, to Home Department, 19 April 1928, GOI (HomePol) 22/V/1928.
[186] 'Note on Relations between the Government of India and News Agencies', 11 March 1929, Jayakar Papers, 399.
[187] *Ibid.*

allowed the Government to ignore any charge of discrimination, but each time the issue came up, there was increasing defensiveness and a small move toward accommodation. Where the word 'subsidy' had been typed in the note describing these Home Department discussions, someone had crossed it out with a pen and written 'payment'. For the FPI it was agreed that the Department should be prepared to give in on the question of an advance copy of the honours list if the request were made again.[188] It was obviously not a significant gesture, but still difficult for some members of the Department who in earlier considerations of the question allowed their imaginations great flight regarding the damage Sadanand could perpetrate with the material.

By the end of the 1920s, the Government was becoming increasingly ambivalent about the FPI. As the capability of the agency and number of its customers increased, Sadanand's presumed potential to make trouble and to compete with the API became evident to those who seemed to note down quite regularly his movements as well as the more-forceful leaders in his messages. There was always a debate about an FPI request. In July 1928, the grant of press telegram facilities between India and Sweden, Norway and Austria was considered normal but passed on to the Home Department for comment. John Coatman immediately agreed, but noted that the messages sent from these countries should be watched. Others were more concerned. An exchange of letters between Sadanand and Shapurji Saklatwala[189] had 'come into our hands', which appeared to make clear 'the character of Sadanand's Free Press agency'. Saklatwala had advised Sadanand to build up his service in order to exchange news 'of a certain kind' between England and India and therefore provide 'political information as well as political education'. The news from India was to be 'of different spirit if not in substance from what Reuter may be sending'.[190] It seemed obvious to some officials that Sadanand was a specialist in anti-Government news and his association with Saklatwala made it clear that the FPI was to be used for the dissemination of Bolshevik propaganda. The Home Secretary, H. H. Haig, was not convinced. He had read the Saklatwala–Sadanand correspondence and in his view Sadanand was resisting proposals to turn the FPI into a communist propaganda agency. It was obvious that Sadanand did not want to endanger the position of the FPI, and it was clearly not in the interests of Thakurdas, Birla, and Jayakar (still directors of the company) that the

---

[188] Deputy Secretary, Home Department, note, 19 August 1929, GOI (HomePol) 19/19/1929.

[189] Saklatwala was a Parsi expatriate living in London. He was a member of the Communist Party, and was twice elected to the House of Commons.

[190] S. Saklatwala to Sadanand, January 1928, quoted in GOI (HomePol) 172/28.

FPI be captured by the communists. It was agreed to 'say yes and watch closely'.[191]

By 1927, when 'beam' routes were established between England and various parts of the empire, including India, competition with cable routes became a serious matter for discussion among the companies concerned and the Government. It seemed clear that unrestricted beam wireless services would undermine the ability of cable operators to maintain their business on a paying basis. The solution to both the practical and political problem was the amalgamation, as far as possible, of all cable and wireless interests conducting communications between various parts of the empire 'so as to secure unity of control and unity of direction'.[192] A holding company, Cable and Wireless Ltd, was established to take control of all the ordinary shares and stock of the Eastern and Associated Companies, and all the ordinary shares and preferential shares and debentures of the Marconi Company. The better-established cable interests retained control of this company. In addition, an operating company, Imperial and International Communications Ltd, with the same directorate, was assigned all the 'communications assets' of the holding company, although not the investment and manufacturing interests. This company also received ownership of the imperial cables formerly controlled by the British Post Office, the Pacific and West Indies systems formerly worked by the Pacific Cable Board, and a 25-year lease of beam stations formerly controlled by the Post Office. The British Government approved two directors of the companies and government control of the whole operation was guaranteed in the event of war or emergency. Throughout the empire, advisory committees were established by the Governments concerned.[193]

The new technology created a more difficult control problem for the Government of India but it attempted to maintain its dominance by limiting the establishment of wireless stations. The Indian Post and Telegraph Department maintained a station at Jutogh, near Simla, for receiving British Official Wireless (BOW) messages. These were supplied to Reuters and then distributed to the company's customers in India for a fee. The arrangement reflected well the careful balancing of commercial and political interests on the pattern established in London. 'On the spot', however, it was a more tenuous balance and a target for 'colonial upstarts' like Swaminath Sadanand.

[191] Memorandum re. grant to the FPI of press telegram facilities between India and Sweden, Norway, and Austria, GOI (HomePol) 172/28.
[192] Brown, *Cable and Wireless Communications*, p. 101.
[193] *Ibid.*, pp. 101–2.

In response to Sadanand's initial complaint regarding the Reuters monopoly on distribution of the BOW messages, the Home Secretary merely noted that the present arrangement was working well and the Government was not prepared to make any changes.[194] Sadanand insisted that Haig had missed the point of his argument. It was not a question of whether the Government was satisfied with the publicity it received for these messages or whether the existing system should be changed. The issue concerned the maintenance of a wireless press service by the Telegraph Department in collaboration with Reuters. The service, he insisted, should be provided directly to every newspaper and news agency in India on payment of the same fee that Reuters was charged. Since the Telegraph Department was a public utility, it could not act to benefit a particular private agency to the exclusion of all others.[195] The Home Department pointed out in response that the BOW was an official service and therefore decisions regarding its distribution were clearly the responsibility of the Government. If the FPI wanted these messages it could take them from Reuters at the Rs 60 fee charged to its Bombay customers.[196]

Sadanand reminded officials that the British Post Office had declared that the BOW was broadcast for universal dissemination and consequently was meant to be available to the world press, including, he assumed, India. But he allowed that issue to pass and concentrated on the commercial aspect of the issue where the Government and Reuters were more vulnerable. Since Reuters had only one official office in Bombay, BOW services to its customers in other parts of India were more expensive. Sadanand noted that Reuters had insisted that the FPI pay the Simla rate (Rs 60 plus Rs 90 for inland telegraph charges), and a similar demand was made to *Prajamitra*, a Bombay Gujerati daily. He then threw out a challenge which the Government had to take seriously.

You cannot be unaware that Reuters is not the only news agency in India and that there are other news agencies which have a larger number of offices in different parts of India than Reuters, and which would, therefore, be in a better position to supply the British Official Wireless for an inclusive monthly subscription of Rs 60, to a much larger number of papers than Reuters could reach.

Both the API and FPI, he insisted, should receive BOW on the condition that they make it available to all newspapers at their centres at the Rs 60 price. Sadanand assured the Government that the FPI was prepared to

[194] Haig to Sadanand, 31 March 1928, Jayakar Papers, 400.
[195] Sadanand to H. G. Haig, 8 June 1928, *ibid.*
[196] H. G. Haig to Sadanand, 20 July 1928, J. D. V. Hodge, Deputy Secretary, Home Department to Sadanand, 20 July 1928, *ibid.* The charge for the BOW–Reuters service was Rs 60 for Bombay customers because Reuters had an office there. All others

take on the responsibility, noting that only twenty-one papers took the Reuters service although more than sixty daily papers subscribed to some news service. When the Home Secretary noted that the rest of the press could take the messages from papers that had paid for the service, Sadanand suggested that it was desirable to discourage such free copying in the interests of the profession.[197]

Sadanand called in his Bombay backers for support, and in August 1928, the secretary of the Bombay Merchants' Chamber wrote to the Home Department concerning the unfairness of the two-fee system. Haig passed the letter on to K. C. Roy, noting that an earlier complaint from B. G. Horniman's *Indian National Herald* had resulted in Roy's agreeing in that case to a Rs 60 charge. Roy responded with a detailed analysis of the Chamber's charges. In the Home Department document describing this exchange there is a notation 'correct' after each charge, followed by Roy's rejection.

It was 'not quite correct', he insisted, that the BOW was broadcast for universal distribution. There was an 'inherent right' vested in a Government on the spot to regulate its dissemination. It was also misleading to suggest that the Government of India was intercepting BOW in India at its cost, since Reuters paid terminal charges and other costs which he did not describe. The Chambers' suggestion that sixty papers might take the service at the Rs 60 rate was considered wildly exaggerated as it overlooked entirely 'the economic condition of the Press in India and their political predilections'. To suggest that Reuters did not have any distribution offices in India outside Bombay, was, he insisted, entirely untrue and 'does a great deal of injustice to the premier world news agency of Great Britain'. There were in fact nine centres.[198] This argument was not, however, very useful to the Department which had always insisted that the API and Reuters were separate companies.

Roy's response to the two-tier payment system issue reflected the mixture of priorities that informed his attitudes toward the nationalist struggle and the newspaper profession. He was convinced that BOW messages were of no interest to nationalist politicians or newspapermen who had a surfeit of official news. This was a matter of professional competition – of maintaining the revenue of his company and the official patronage that preserved its advantageous position, and of beating the FPI. He argued that the Chamber's concern about the Rs 150 fee reflected

received the service directly from Simla via telegraph for Rs 60 plus Rs 90 for inland telegraph charges.

[197] Sadanand to H. G. Haig, 30 July 1928, Jayakar Papers, 400.
[198] There were API offices throughout the country, but only one designated Reuters office, in Bombay.

its ignorance of the newspaper business. Papers like the *Statesman* or *Pioneer* would pay any cost to bring BOW the fastest way, and would reject receiving the service through an agency's office which would involve three to six hours delay. First-class newspapers, Roy insisted, would consider the Rs 60 rate a waste in that context. It was clear to Roy that the Chamber 'have allowed themselves to be used as an instrument for the promotion of a special interest without ascertaining the correct position, both commercial and professional'. He concluded with a challenge to Home Department officials.

It is for the Government of India to consider whether it would be wise to destroy the existing uniformity of distribution which gets the BOW the very best market it can, and place the service in the hands of all and sundry, but in my opinion it should distinguish between news agencies and views agencies and should hesitate before breaking away from a practice which has served them so well in the past and which ensures the fullest scope for development in the future on a genuine commercial and professional basis.[199]

Roy's apparent antagonism to the Federation of Indian Chambers was noted by Walchand Hirachand in a letter to Purshotamdas Thakurdas. 'He is getting extremely pro-Bengali and to achieve that end anti-Marwari or something of that sort.' Thakurdas passed on the remark to G. D. Birla who insisted that Roy was neither anti-Federation nor anti-Marwari. He was merely anti-Free Press. Birla assumed that in the next Assembly Roy would be out – neither the Government nor 'any decent party' would nominate him, and 'therefore, he is anti-everything'. In Birla's view, Roy was exploiting anti-Marwari feeling or rather pro-Bengali feeling in order to get elected to the next Assembly from the Bengal National Chamber of Commerce.[200]

Within the Home Department, discussions centered on how to maintain the relationship with Reuters but accommodate the demands of the Mechants' Chamber and the FPI. It was agreed that if the FPI could do the job for Rs 60, then Reuters should be able to do the same. Roy and Moloney were contacted and after a brief but argumentative exchange, it was agreed to establish a new distribution scheme by setting up facilities in Calcutta, Madras, and Karachi. Haig had pointed out to Moloney that it was essential for the Government to consider public criticism, and that Reuters' reasons for the differential rates simply 'will not carry weight

[199] Secretary, Indian Merchants' Chamber, Bombay, to Secretary, Home Department, Government of India, 18 August 1928, Jayakar Papers, 400; K. C. Roy to H. C. Haig, 29 August 1928, GOI (HomePol) 241/128.
[200] Walchand Hirachand to P. Thakurdas, 6 June 1929; G. D. Birla to P. Thakurdas, 13 June 1929, Thakurdas Papers, 42 (III).

with the public'. When he was informed of the decision, Sadanand thanked the Department for its positive response.[201]

The Bombay office of the FPI was raided by the police on 20 March 1929. The Home Department had authorized the confiscation of records, particularly concerning the foreign contacts of the company.[202] Sadanand contacted Thakurdas, the chairman of the Free Press Board, who subsequently pointed out to Haig that he, Birla, and Jayakar had been in New Delhi at the time and the Home Department might have talked with them. The required papers, he noted, would have been handed over on request without the need for a search warrant.[203] Although there was a polite exchange and an offer to pass on additional papers that were available in New Delhi, the incident and further conversations with officials complemented and enhanced Thakurdas' unease regarding the financial stability of the FPI and the appro-priateness of Birla, Jayakar, and himself remaining on the Board. The incident marked as well the beginning of a period of virtually con-tinuous confrontation between the FPI and the Government as the brief Gandhi–Irwin peace came to an end and Congress returned to Civil Disobedience. Paradoxically, one of the results of Government repress-ion was the expansion of Sadanand's organization with the estab-lishment of the *Free Press Journal* in 1930.

The promulgation of the Press ordinance in that year had resulted in the closing of a number of papers and subsequent loss of subscribers to the FPI service. The decline in revenue forced Sadanand to bring in additional income, first from the *Bulletin*, run off on a gestetner machine and then from the *Journal*, established on 13 June. In the context of the 1930s press crisis and the aggressive nationalist stance of these papers, only the Government objected. Rs 500 security was demanded from both

---

[201] Home Department memorandum re. BOW services in India including: H. G. Haig discussion with W. Moloney, 11 September 1928; Moloney to Haig, 18 September 1928; Haig to Moloney, 5 October 1928; Moloney to Haig, 9 October 1928; Moloney to Haig, 15 October 1928, K. C. Roy to Haig, 1 November 1928; Sadanand to Haig, 5 December 1928, GOI (HomePol) 241/28.

[202] Sadanand noted the files taken from this office:
1. Foreign Service and foreign correspondents.
2. Account books.
3. Press cutting book containing *Daily Telegraph* (London) clippings on Russia.
4. Materials received from the League Against Imperialism (most had not been published by the FPI).
5. Certain foreign telegrams.
6. Books about socialism by Upton Sinclair, etc.
7. Annual reports of the FPI.
Sadanand to P. Thakurdas as chairman of the Board, 20 March 1929, Jayakar Papers, 401.

[203] P. Thakurdas to H. G. Haig, 21 March 1929, *ibid.*

by the end of the first week,[204] and rose incrementally over the next four years. The agency was 'clearly an agent for the dissemination of Congress propaganda', and developed a reputation among officials for unscrupulously distorting facts. The Punjab Government noted in December 1930 that 'practically every message published by it is false'.[205]

Sadanand was prosecuted under the Criminal Law Amendment Act[206] and two of his reporters were convicted of seditious activities. Frustrated officials discussed the difficulties of stopping or censoring propagandist press messages, insisting that the rules be amended at least to stop this going on at concessional press rates. Sadanand's perennial financial difficulties eased the problem, by allowing the Post and Telegraph Department to deny him the privilege of receiving bearing press telegrams when he failed to pay his bills. But he could still receive prepaid messages. The Home Member reminded his colleagues that the Secretary of State had ruled out censorship of foreign telegrams, but with certain exceptions such as the telegrams of the Free Press Agency.

By 1932, the monthly reports of objectional FPI clippings[207] filled a sizable niche in Home Department files and the level of forfeited security had reached Rs 6,000. But the *Journal* had achieved a circulation of 25,000 and a new paper, the *Nav Bharat*, had begun publishing in August. An array of well-known names were included in the list of FPI correspondents in India, Britain, Japan, and the United States.[208] Sadanand was briefly imprisoned but the FPI organization survived. The Government noted that there seemed to be no lack of funds and worked hard to find the source.

The Bombay Government ordered the forfeiture of yet another security

---

[204] Sadanand circular letter, 17 June 1930, Jayakar Papers, 399.
[205] Sadanand successfully appealed his conviction and three month sentence to the High Court, 3 February 1931, *ibid.*
[206] D. J. Boyd, Secretary, Punjab Government to H. A. Sarus, Director-General, Post and Telegraph (copy to Emerson), 1 December 1930, GOI (HomePol) 21/13/1931.
[207] The Home Secretary asked the DPI to submit FPI material specifically, 24 February 1932, GOI (HomePol) 228/1932.
[208] Outside of India there were a range of agreements with: Pulin Behari Seal (Orient Press Service, London); Margarita and Charles Barns (accredited FPI representatives in London); S. D. Saklatwala (communist politician); Vishnu Karandikar (Indian News Service, London); Bernard Houghton (communist, ex-ICS, associate of Saklatwala and M. N. Roy); Agnes Smedley (revolutionary journalist and associate of like-minded Indians); A. C. Nambiar (Berlin correspondent of FPI, covers Berlin, Moscow, and Central Europe); V. Chattopadhyaya (joint secretary, League Against Imperialism, Berlin); C. P. Dutt (communist now in Berlin, used FPI service when on staff of *Daily Worker* in London); A. M. Sahay (influential Indian in Kobe and apparently accredited FPI agent in Japan); S. N. Ghose (American branch of the Indian National Congress, temporary relationship with FPI to cover Vithalbhai Patel's American tour); Veltass, London (London branch of Russian agency), GOI (HomePol) 228/1932.

deposit in August 1932, and hoped it might make a positive impact on the *Journal* but the establishment of the *Nav Bharat* and the good supply of European news made them pessimistic. 'I have for the last few months inflicted on myself the duty of reading daily this horrible newspaper and can safely say that practically everything which it prints is directed towards envenoming the minds of its readers against Government in every conceivable manner'. It was clear to Home Department officials that the *Journal*'s productions in the previous seven months were proof positive that there was no muzzling of the press by the Government of India. In practically no country, lamented one official, was such licence allowed to the press by a Government engaged in 'what is really a war with those who are working or advocating civil disobedience as well as in a separate war of terrorism'. In regard to the FPI agency, the Government could not take action unless it intercepted its telegrams, and the Home Member did not see sufficient justification for that, noting that 'some telegrams are true'.[209]

In November 1932, the *Journal* was required to pay a security deposit of Rs 20,000 and by August of the following year Rs 10,000 of that amount had been taken bringing the total forfeiture to date to Rs 26,000. But Sadanand responded philosophically in a *Journal* editorial: 'Considering that we are living in war times, and that the "Journal" has always been putting itself in the forefront of the firing line, in the discharge of its duties, I have come to the conclusion that allowances must be made for the onslaughts which the Executive have made'.[210] The Home Department acted in a similar fashion. The FPI was readmitted to the Government press room at the end of 1932, while officials in India and London monitored its extraordinary growth. An FPI world news service was established in October, through arrangements with the Exchange telegraph, the Central News, and British United Press. News was supplied to the FPI London office for selection and transmission to India. Hugh MacGregor informed the Home Department that the FPI had opened an office at Ludgate House in London, provided it with adequate staff, and was ready to provide a full and regular service in competition with Reuters. There were already twenty subscribers in India, and MacGregor anticipated that others would join as soon as they were able to get out of their restrictive Reuters contracts regarding supplementary London services.

The *Journal* was buying heavy equipment in London and incurring significant financial commitments, and there was some concern in the

---

[209] Home Department note, August 1932, *ibid.*
[210] *Free Press Journal*, 6 November 1932, clipping in Jayakar Papers, 399.

India Office regarding the kind of impact all this would make on Reuters. MacGregor wondered whether Reuters might begin sending more Congress material than was desirable; but he assumed that Government financial pressure would be able to control the situation.[211] In response, Ian Stephens noted the spread of the *Journal* in north India and gossip about Sadanand's plans to set up four new nationalist papers in Delhi, Calcutta, Lucknow, and Lahore.[212] Sadanand had apparently told Stephens that a 'friend' had provided the money to pay off all his debts as well as a loan for expansion. Stephens thought the 'friend' was Bombay businessman, Mathradas Vissanji Khimji, which was in fact the case. It all sounded fantastic to Stephens, but he noted that only four nationalist papers were run on sound business lines, the *Hindu*, *Amrita Bazar Patrika*, *Leader*, and *Tribune*, and he assumed Sadanand could rout his inefficient rivals.[213]

While the *Journal* was showing a substantial profit in 1933, the agency was losing money,[214] and the planned expansion was meant to increase profits in order to carry the FPI. A third paper, the *Indian Express*, had been established in 1932, and although many of Sadanand's plans were stillborn, in 1934 he established the *Dinamani* in Madras and the *Navasakti* in Bombay. The *Free India* ran briefly in Calcutta.[215] Sadanand's apparent success, however, added to his old enemies, the API and the Government of India, a substantial number of Indian newspapermen. His desire to maintain an Indian-controlled news agency was laudable, but not at the price of competing with his customers by establishing his own papers. In Calcutta, there was already too much competition among nationalist papers and the increasing pressure on the agency led to the desertion of the *Free Press* Calcutta editor, B. Sen Gupta, who established the United Press of India in 1933.[216]

At the end of 1932, however, the FPI gave the impression it might survive the struggle and Reuters and the Government took it seriously. In December, Roderick Jones wrote to the Secretary of State requesting early copies of important answers to parliamentary questions about India

---

[211] H. MacGregor to I. M. Stephens, 28 September 1930, GOI (HomePol) 35/33/1932.

[212] *The Guardian* (Delhi), *Free India* (Calcutta), *The People* (Lucknow), *United India* (Lahore).

[213] I. M. Stephens to H. MacGregor, 25 November 1933, GOI (HomePol) 33/6/1923.

[214] J. F. Glennings, Director of Information, Bombay to I. M. Stephens, 23 November 1933, *ibid*.

[215] Natarajan, *The Press in India*, p. 214.

[216] Sushila Agrawal, *Press, Public Opinion and Government in India*, Jaipur: Asha Publishing House, 1970, pp. 187–88. J. N. Sahni also emphasized the competition problem. Interview, 1970. In Bombay, the *Chronicle* became an enemy of the *Journal* in self-defence.

in order to make certain they would get their messages to India ahead of the FPI. Hoare wanted to help, but he was cautious about providing special treatment in favour of Reuters unless he was certain of a good case against the FPI. He indicated that he was having FPI messages examined and also took the opportunity to note the India Office's displeasure with some recent Reuters messages. He was particularly concerned about the 'pro-Hindu tinge' which had been noted from time to time in regard to the API.[217]

On the following day, Jones responded, describing the howls of his India editor-in-charge regarding the number of corrections to Hoare's answers in the House of Commons when official copies arrived forty-five minutes after the answers were given. He noted that the Secretary of State had read very rapidly from his script with his back half-turned to the Reuters representatives covering the debate, and 'thus facing the *Free Press* correspondent in the front row of the Strangers gallery opposite'. While Reuters waited for the corrections, the FPI correspondent left immediately after the last Indian question and sent his story to India.

Speed is of the very essence of the matter if we are to forestall and frustrate, as it is in the public interest and in your interest that we should, the activities of a correspondent or correspondents, bitterly hostile to the British connection and concerned, not with accuracy and the honest representation of the Imperial point of view, but with the making of mischief and the sowing of discord ... A gap of 45 minutes is fraught with danger.[218]

Two days later, Jones wrote again, this time regarding Hoare's criticism of Reuters' messages.

The Free Press and its associates are declared enemies of the British connection. Surely such people, wholly unfit to be trusted, are not entitled to the same consideration from a department of state as that which fairly may be claimed by a responsible organization like Reuters whose sole aim and purpose are faithfully and dispassionately to represent to the people of India facts as they are and not as Congress propagandists strive to make them out to be? Without for one moment taking sides in any controversy Reuters are in *effect* fighting your fight.[219]

But Hoare remained concerned about those mysterious cables that Sen had not seen and suggested a lack of sufficient control of the company's operations in India. Jones reiterated the need for Reuters to report on incidents and meetings that the India Office might prefer to ignore, and suggested that the lack of such material in Reuters' messages would be the *raison d'être* for the FPI. If such news were repressed in the company's

---

[217] Hoare to Sir Roderick Jones, 5 December 1932, IO (InfoDept) L/I/1/264, File 99B.
[218] R. Jones to Hoare, 6 December 1932, *ibid*.
[219] Jones to Hoare, 8 December 1932, *ibid*.

messages, the nationalist press in India would move to the FPI and Reuters would lose power.[220] The combined pressure from the India Office and the FPI did, however, result in the reorganization of the API which ended the special correspondent services and brought Turner out to manage the company's affairs.

By the middle of 1933, the FPI's financial problems were too burdensome for Sadanand's clients and his own newspapers to carry. Charles and Mary Barns, FPI representatives in London, contacted Thakurdas, who was there at the time, to seek new funding. Thakurdas responded with a suggestion that the FPI be transformed into a new company controlled by the Indian press that subscribed to the service. Rangaswami Iyengar also participated in the discussions, but they ended inconclusively.[221] By 1934, the circulation of the *Journal* was down to 15,000[222] and the goodwill of Sadanand's 'secret patron', Mathradas Vissanji Khimji, was exhausted. In October, Vissanji Sons and Company launched a series of mortgage cases against the FPI which carried over into July of 1935. Charges and counter-charges of libel and 'gross waste and mismanagement' were exchanged and the final days of the court hearings filled the pages of the press. The *Bombay Chronicle*, long resentful of the *Journal*'s competition, devoted most of its 10 July front page to the story, without a hint of sympathy for the plight of the only Indian-owned news service.[223] In the previous month, Sadanand had published a final plea in the *Journal*.

The Hour of Test is come – should the FPI live or die? The ultimate choice, however, rests with you, dear reader who has put faith in the Free Press and stood by its newspapers in tens of thousands, through the darkest days. The message of the FP is carried every day to 30,000 homes in the whole of western India. It is no mean achievement. The answer rests with you.[224]

The case was lost and with it the Rotary machines and a substantial settlement to the plaintiffs.[225] The FPI, without any financial base, simply disappeared, with no apparent shedding of tears by the Indian press or the Congress. The view of the Government of India and Reuters was never in doubt.

Not surprisingly, Sadanand had the last word. He had no intention of

[220] Hoare to Jones, 9 December 1932; Jones to Hoare, 12 December 1932; Jones to Hoare, 15 December 1932, *ibid.*
[221] P. Thakurdas, Diary, 1 and 2 July 1932, Thakurdas Papers, 140.
[222] Home Department note, 15 August 1934, GOI (HomePol) 34/10/34.
[223] *Bombay Chronicle*, 10 July 1935.
[224] *Free Press Journal*, 28 June 1935. Two security deposits were forfeited bringing the total of Rs 46,000, Jayakar Papers, 399.
[225] Sadanand owned Rs 16,473-134-9 plus interest to Vissanjii and Sons.

ending his newspaper career at the age of thirty-five. On 26 July 1935, a few days after the loss of his paper and news service, he published the following letter in the *Daily Sun*.

Dear Friends,

You have at last won. Your insistence on the resurrection of the *Free Press Journal* without enriching the Government has prevailed. As a result, by the courtesy and kindness of the States People Ltd., especially Mr. Amritlal D. Seth, the *Daily Sun* will issue regularly from today even like the *Free Press Journal* in all respects until such time as circumstances render the resumption of the *FPJ* or the *FPB* possible. All steps have been taken to preserve the continuity of service to the regular readers and advertisers of the *FPJ*. With a view that these arrangements may not prove a burden to *FP* as a business concern. I have undertaken entire personal responsibility for this venture.

S. Sadanand[226]

[226] *Daily Sun*, 26 July 1935, Jayakar Papers, 399.

3   The Congress search for a common voice

Competing viewpoints and the question of unity

In his 1937 review of Indian politics in the eighty years since the Mutiny, C. Y. Chintamini described the Congress as a propaganda organization 'in which there is no room for more parties than one'. It was committed to the advocacy of particular opinions, he insisted, and its programme would be crippled by the inclusion of parties 'speaking in different voices'.[1] In the early 1920s, Chintamini had attacked the Non-cooperation Movement and an intolerant Gandhi-controlled Congress. In the late 1930s, still on the margins of nationalist action, he attacked Jawaharlal Nehru's socialist ideology and a Congress which remained, in his view, intolerant of other viewpoints. Chintamani was particularly offended by Congress insistence that it alone represented the views and interests of the Indian people; and that such an argument was sufficient to reject alternative positions and demand unity and loyal support. 'Vox populi, vox Dei is a doctrine not less dangerous', he insisted, 'than the counter-doctrine of the divine right of kings.'[2] In the Congress, as it had developed since the end of World War One, to outsiders like Chintamani, both phenomena seemed apparent.

Throughout the 1920s and 1930s, as the endgame of the nationalist struggle approached, the search for a 'voice' that would be perceived as widely shared and representative reflected renewed concern within the Congress about both the divide-and-rule tactics of the British regime, and the reality of the range of divisions among Indians that might be mobilized by a different vision of freedom, a different 'voice'. A struggle within the evolving Indian polity paralleled the confrontation with the British, reflecting an increasingly enhanced sense of personal and group jeopardy – not the result of Government action but a response to the programmes

---

[1] C. Y. Chintamani, *Indian Politics Since the Mutiny*, Waltair: Andra University, 1937, p. 89.
[2] *Ibid.*, p. 217.

156

and policies of the Gandhi–Nehru-dominated Congress. Chintamani's concern with Nehru's radical rhetoric in the 1930s – clearly evident in Congress propaganda campaigns – was shared by the liberal and independent heirs to the 'moderate' nationalist legacy. 'As regards the Congress, the less said the better' noted T. B. Sapru in a letter to M. R. Jayakar. 'I wonder what you think of Jawaharlal's views and his fond love of communism.'[3] Sapru knew what Jayakar thought and the two attempted to pacify each other in a substantial correspondence reflecting a shared sense of the struggle lost – however successful the general campaign against British rule.[4]

Within the Congress there had always been a debate at the centre and in the years since Gandhi's rise to power entrenched differences were no less significant than the new and broadened unity of purpose and action reflected in his charismatic dominance and ability to mobilize a mass following. Neither Gandhi nor Nehru was satisfied with a simple confrontational nationalist struggle. For both, there was a particular social and economic agenda which informed their definitions of political unity and their envisionings of a free India. As a result, they attracted and antagonized, requiring the Congress centre to launch a multi-layered propaganda campaign in support of a Congress–unity–freedom–progress package, not only in opposition to the British, but as a means to mobilize support for the India of their dreams.

Chintamani's concern about the intolerance of the Congress campaign which had marginalized moderate viewpoint was reflective of a broader concern that leaders at the centre of the movement might be willing to sacrifice a range of interests which they deemed parochial or reactionary in order to maintain their design for Indian nationhood. Regional, communal, landed, princely, untouchable – interests defined and advocated by subsets of leaders attracted loyalty and competed for power and position both within the mainstream Congress and outside it. The challenge for the Congress as it evolved from movement to parallel Government to the presumed successor to the British regime was convincing these interests within India as well as the British and other influential parties in the West of its suitability to govern – confirming its presumed representative role as the voice of the Indian people.

By the mid 1930s the Government of India had accepted the inevitability of power transfer but was slow to identify its successor in the Congress. In response to the publication of brochures in 1937, to mark

---

[3] T. B. Sapru to M. R. Jayakar, 21 April 1936, Jayakar Papers, 433.
[4] There is an extensive correspondence in both the Jayakar and Sapru Papers concerning their differences with both Gandhi and Nehru.

the fiftieth jubilee of the Congress, the Home Department contacted the India Office Information Department to note its concern about the success of the Congress publicity campaign. M. G. Hallett was impressed with the quality of the writing and it was clear to him that the reputation of the Congress had been enhanced. While he assumed that such propaganda would not have much impact in London, he was less sanguine about American 'sentimentalists' who were likely to be uncritical in their response. 'It is very important to avoid the impression gaining ground at home', he insisted, 'that Congress is really a "nice" organization.' He cautioned India Office officials about the activities of those in England 'who are always doing all they can to show that the Congress is not as black as we paint it'.[5] For Home Department officials, a 'nice' Congress meant that the British Government of India was not. It also suggested that the Congress had attained the stature, competence, and representativeness to succeed to power.

On 6 October 1921, in the midst of the Non-cooperation campaign, Gandhi published a 'Manifesto of Freedom of Opinion' in *Young India*. He noted that the rejection of violence meant that the struggle against the British had become 'a propaganda movement of the purest type'; and that the regime's efforts to repress it was, therefore, an 'attempt to crush public opinion.'[6] The identification of specific Congress programmes with a presumed Indian opinion intensified throughout the decade. While the founding generation of Congress leaders also assumed a representative role, they were more conscious of their isolation from that popular constituency, and less willing to test the validity of the relationship. Pre-war Congress programmes – whether 'moderate' or 'extremist' in inspiration generally were variations of a 'work the system' theme and certainly lacked any sense of the Congress as Government-in-waiting. But Gandhi demanded hard choices by recasting the confrontation on a different stage and defining action in uncompromising terms. It was Non-cooperation or cooperation, rejection of the colonial relationship, or collaboration with the alien regime.

While attempting to destroy the context of accommodation that had allowed the Congress and the Government to evolve a symbiotic relationship which constrained the threat to both, Gandhi recognized the need to propagate his views and sell his programme to leaders being asked to subordinate power and interests to a new overarching commander, and to

---

[5] M. G. Hallett note, 18 December 1935, GOI (Home Pol) 414/36; Hallett to H. Macgregor, 21 December 1935, *ibid.*

[6] S. N. Bhattacharyya, *Mahatma Gandhi: The Journalist*, London: Asia Publishing House, 1965, p. 43.

a mass constituency unused to any form of participation. 'I believe that a struggle which chiefly relies upon internal strength', he noted, 'cannot be wholly carried on without a newspaper.'[7] And *Indian Opinion* in South Africa, and subsequently *Young India* and *Navajivan* in India became principal weapons in the struggle, the vanguard of a massive publicity campaign. Gandhi rejected a press career as a means to earn a living.[8] In his view, his own writing, the Congress publicity campaign, and all nationalist newspapers were meant to serve the mission of freedom struggle by educating the Indian people and drawing them into the movement. For Gandhi, the idea and the educating mission were inseparable; and his extraordinary stature as a national leader was dependent in significant measure on his ability to publicize himself and his actions in a manner that required response.

Press comment on the abandonment of Non-cooperation in 1922, after the violent confrontation at Chauri Chaura reflect the new and intrusive force of the Congress as Gandhi's instrument and the presumed 'voice' of all Indians. For loyal Congress papers like the *Bombay Chronicle* and *Swarajya*, the decision was only a strategic retreat. After a period of discipline and training the movement would be reactivated and eventually win Swaraj for India. For others, there was relief that it was possible again to be good nationalists and congressmen, and to work the official system as well. The *Hindu* applauded the Bardoli Programme of constructive work which Gandhi had substituted for Civil Disobedience, noting that it had 'the outstanding merit' that it included nothing to which a 'sensible Government could reasonably take exception'. The independent *Tribune*, which had opposed much of the Non-cooperation programme, approved its termination and called on the Government to make a creative response. Chintamani's *Leader* reflected Liberal opposition, noting the 'dawn of reason', but cautioning its readers that the abandonment of the Non-cooperation programme had not removed the 'fundamental objection that the aim of the Congress activities is to destroy the existing system'.[9]

There was a publicity element to virtually every Congress action, reflecting the continuing need to establish credentials, assert leadership, and create a track record of success at the centre where denizens of the Raj and the nationalist elite confronted and collaborated, and in the provinces and localities where most Indians lived. Every action needed to

[7] *Ibid.*, p. 8.
[8] *Ibid.*, p. 33.
[9] All of these press comments were reprinted in the *Indian Social Reformer*, 19 February 1922. See also the *Leader*, 9 July 1918 and 11 July 1918 for discussion of the reforms and the nature of Gandhi's concerns.

be explained to some constituency since the purpose was often elusive and to some groups offensive. Congress publicity was spread throughout the sub-continent in a variety of forms. The AICC and PCCs published and arranged for distribution of statements, reports, bulletins, information, and directions for workers. There was also coverage in Congress newspapers controlled by leaders. This was no guarantee that the campaign would be described with one 'voice'. Gandhi's *Young India* or C. R. Das' *Forward*, or Motilal Nehru's *Independent* had much in common, but often approached fundamental issues regarding means and goals from different perspectives. Their distinctive localities and readership were not unimportant in this regard. There was also the large vernacular press, increasingly influential and much more sensitive to local constituency viewpoint and interest. The great campaigns carefully designed at the centre were often unrecognizable in these parochial settings. The major Indian-owned papers which considered themselves nationalist if not necessarily Congress reported events and commented on them in their editorial columns. Whether supportive or critical, the coverage enhanced the event – made it more important by its commitment to print and availability in every part of India. The Anglo-Indian press and the Government of India also provided unintended support by attacking a particular Congress position or activity and therefore publicizing it as well. And the news services facilitated an All-India debate and extended awareness of the event throughout the world.

As in the case of the Government, there was general agreement about the need to publicize and educate, and constrained resources to meet the cost of the campaigns. In 1921, the Tilak Memorial Swarajya Fund was established and collections in the first years exceeded one crore. But there was a long list of activities which required support and competing interests at the centre and in the provinces. It was widely assumed by many in the movement and in the Government of India that a handful of central leaders controlled this huge fund and in the area of publicity in particular, it appeared that the Congress could now compete successfully with official propaganda activities. Officials within the Home Department often used this argument in their own search for dwindling Government resources. And the requests and demands for funding which came into the central offices of the Congress also reflected this view. In fact, the AICC quota from general donations was only 25 per cent of the total, the balance being retained in the provinces where the funds were raised. In the second and third year of the campaign for support, collections were considerably reduced, and the Congress centre's quota was reduced as well, to 5 per cent.[10]

[10] Complaints about expenditure from Tilak Memorial Swarajya Fund (1924), AICC Statement, AICC 28/1924, Pt 2.

There were also a large number of specific grants and pledges which committed funds to spinning, ashrams, national education, or famine relief. Their inability to set priorities was sometimes discouraging to national leaders. In response to a gift of Rs 25 lakhs, and the promise of an additional Rs 75 lakhs, to propagandize cow protection, Motilal Nehru noted his concern for human beings as a higher priority.[11] When his son donated his personal war bonds to the Tilak Fund, Nehru was unhappy and asked that the Nehru women be given some consideration. If the bonds had to be committed to the nationalist effort, he suggested that they be designated for his *Independent* newspaper. 'I see people doing all sorts of fantastic things under cover of the fund', he pointed out to Jawaharlal, reflecting a widespread view that money was being misappropriated.[12] Stories of theft and malfeasance in provincial Congress offices led to the publication of a detailed financial report in 1924, and the establishment of new rules for collection, custody, and expenditure.[13] There was also increasing reluctance to share meagre central funds with local bodies. When a Rs 25,000 fund was established for central publicity work, Provincial Committees which asked for part of it were generally refused.[14]

This fund was largely committed to the 1926 election campaign and designated for leaflets, press propaganda, and the touring costs of central leaders. In order to increase the support for this work, the Publicity Sub-committee of the AICC decided to require individual candidates to contribute Rs 50 to the central propaganda fund. It was a good idea, but the response was generally disappointing. There was clearly an assumption that the money was meant to flow in the other direction. However impoverished central committees might be, provincial bodies were generally poorer, and in any case often assumed that funds were available at the centre but designated to some other priority not of their making. The United Provinces and Andhra Congress Committees noted they had no funds and had intended to seek support from the centre. Karnataka agreed to pay the Rs 50 for each candidate, while Kerala Congress leaders provided detailed accounts of the poverty of most candidates. They preferred not to ask for the individual donations but agreed to do it and in case there was a positive response they indicated that the funds would be sent. There was an extensive correspondence and a flow of reminders, but little money in the return mail.[15] The requests for financial support from

[11] Motilal Nehru to Jawaharlal Nehru, 16 May 1920, Motilal Nehru Papers.
[12] M. Nehru to J. Nehru, 27 June 1921, Motilal Nehru Papers.
[13] Tilak Memorial Fund Statement re. expenditures, AICC 28/1924, Pt 2.
[14] The fund was established on 10 March 1926, AICC G-47.
[15] A. Rangaswami Iyengar, General Secretary, AICC to all candidates, 17 May 1926, AICC F-23.

all levels of Congress organization seemed as unreasonable to some would-be candidates, as it was clearly essential from the perspective of those who were organizing the campaign.

You demand Rs 50 while the Bengal PCC demand Rs 5000. I am not a moneyed man and won't be able to pay anything. So if you like you may strike my name from the list of selected candidates and publish the matter accordingly. This sort of intimation I have submitted to the BPCC. You are at liberty to select any other candidate in my place.[16]

The Bengal PCC noted that this candidate was a staunch non-cooperator and urged the AICC to exempt him from the payment. It was a difficult argument to resist.[17]

There was a steady and increasing flow of Congress publication and the files of the AICC and the private papers of leaders reflect the extraordinary effort as well as the frustrations involved in writing, printing, funding, and distributing the material.[18] There were always unpaid bills from a number of presses and regular correspondence seeking a reduction in the cost as a reflection of a heightened patriotic awareness.[19] But this second line of patriots had to pay bills in order to serve the leaders who had become full-time politicians with little or no private income. There was also a continuing marketing problem which left hundreds of copies of a report in central or provincial offices. And when the material was distributed there were complaints about both the price and the content.[20] The Congress also provided a distribution opportunity for the personal writings of leaders. There was always a selection of Congress publications as well as the works of Gandhi, Jawaharlal Nehru, and others on sale at Congress meetings. In the case of Nehru's book describing his 1927 visit to Russia, the AICC received a 25 per cent commission on the 123 copies of the book that were sold in this way.[21] There was also financial support for Congress newspapers – either those established by leaders like Motilal Nehru's *Independent* or Jawaharlal Nehru's *National Herald*; or for less ambitious vernacular papers with a specific propaganda mission. In 1926, Motilal Nehru arranged a Rs 4,000 grant for M. V. Abhyankar to establish a Marathi paper in Nagpur. Subsequently an additional Rs 1,500 were allocated from the Rs 25,000 propaganda fund of the AICC 'which

16 Umesh Chandra Chatterjee, Member of the Legislative Council (Bengal) to AICC, 2 August 1926, AICC F-23.
17 Bengal Congress Committee to AICC, 20 September 1926, *ibid.*
18 Mohanlal Nehru to J. Nehru, 2 April 1928, AICC G-61; AICC F-7/1927, Pts 1, 2, 3.
19 *Ibid.*
20 Secretary, AICC to Mr Kauhaiyalal, 1 October 1927, *ibid.*
21 Law Journal Press (K. P. Dhar, manager) to Under-Secretary, AICC, 5 December 1928; AICC memorandum, 12 January 1929, AICC G-61.

is no doubt intended for your carrying on of work on behalf of the Central Committee; but which practically will be available to you for election work for use for propagandists, leaflets and other purposes'.[22]

The API provided important opportunities to get a message out at no expense. The increasing newsworthiness of Congress-sponsored events and the statements of leaders who had become national and international personalities reduced the effort required to obtain publicity. As in the case of the Government of India, the Congress Working Committee regularly gave its resolutions to the API for distribution to its customers throughout India and via Reuters throughout the world. In the late 1920s this practice was attacked by the FPI service which considered the Congress as well as the Government to be uncritical patrons of API–Reuters.[23] But API could deliver a professional service to a larger audience. The FPI plea to support an Indian institution was not considered compelling in these circumstances. The AICC also requested free subscriptions to all major papers and in return distributed Congress literature at no charge. This exchange included both the Anglo-Indian and Indian-owned press, but those critical of Congress policies made their reservations apparent in their responses. *Justice* rejected the request, while the *Leader* offered only a half-price subscription.

Coverage of annual Congress meetings in the press became so thorough by the mid 1920s, that the Government of India decided to reduce its own 'covert' but widely recognized activities. During the sessions, officers of the Special Branch of the CID and a 'short hand force' submitted daily reports to the Government of India and the appropriate local government. In 1924, however, CID officials in Bombay noted the high cost of this activity and questioned its worth. It was pointed out to Home Department officials that no prosecutions had ever been initiated as a result of such verbatim reporting except for one speech at a 1921 Khilafat Conference in Ahmedabad. Since papers like the *Bombay Chronicle* published full speeches within two days, the CID's work seemed redundant and might be better reserved for private meetings where its particular expertise was required. The Bombay deputy inspector of police, CID, also argued a beneficial 'moral effect' if the verbatim coverage were discontinued. 'The mere fact that Government goes to the trouble and expense of securing immediate verbatim reports of what goes on, in itself lends an importance and weight to this gathering of which it is by no means worthy.' Information officers in Home Department resisted reduced

[22] A. Rangaswami Iyengar to M. V. Abhyankar, 22 May 1926, AICC G-547/1926.
[23] K. P. Kabadi, *Free Press of India* and K. Natarajan, *Indian Daily Mail* to Sreenivasa Iyengar, 21 May 1927, Sreenivasa Iyengar Papers.

official coverage, but cost and opportunity were irresistible to the retrenchers in the Government.[24]

The Congress needed and vigorously sought publicity for all its activities, and generally there was no problem getting 'coverage'. But the publication of the speeches of leaders and the decisions of the annual meeting and the high command was meant to attract active support as well as to inform, and it was recognized that these messages needed to be amplified by further action. In addition to the normal print outlets utilized by Congress leaders, propaganda organizations keyed to particular issues were established that attempted to link policy and programme with a mass constituency. The Non-Cooperation Movement of 1920–2, had demonstrated the ability of the Congress to mobilize massive participation in such a centre-designed programme. It also demonstrated the mixed response that all such initiatives received, and the difficulty in maintaining loyalty to a particular policy and principle, once it was widely shared. The kind of unity sought by Congress leaders at the centre was far easier to describe than attain. Whenever possible, leaders would do double duty, participating in decision making at the centre, and then, wearing their provincial hats, actively organizing the implementation of that decision without significant change from the original design.

At the conclusion of the Central Legislative Assembly session on 28 March 1928, a meeting of Congress leaders agreed to organize a general movement in the country to boycott both the Simon Commission and the use of foreign cloth. It was agreed that central and provincial boards would be established to direct the movement and mobilize support. The central board was to include such Congress luminaries as Jawaharlal Nehru, Pandit Malaviya, Jinnah, Jayakar, Lajpat Rai, and Motilal Nehru, and these leaders would also participate in the provincial boards in their provinces.[25] Within a week, however, the difficulties in achieving agreement on organization, goal, and message had become apparent. T. Prakasam, the editor of *Swarajya*, expressed his concern that central and provincial boards with separate funding would be destructive to Congress organization and constrain the opportunity to send out a single agreed message in support of a united Programme.[26] In response, Jawaharlal Nehru reluctantly agreed that many Congress members opposed the boycott of foreign cloth and the association of the two campaigns against the cloth and the Commission would likely weaken both efforts.

[24] Recommendation of deputy-inspector of police, CID, Bombay, 19 September 1924 (Home Pol) 391/24.
[25] Note re. Boycott Meeting, 28 March 1928, AICC G-64.
[26] T. Prakasan to J. Nehru, 9 April 1928, *ibid.*

Sarojini Naidu suggested the establishment of separate boards in order to allow individuals to make a choice. It was assumed that there would be no problem attracting large support for the statutory commission boycott. But Nehru, often quick to respond angrily in such situations, rejected the compromise and the boards were never established.[27]

Unity and cooperation, especially from millowners in a Swadeshi campaign that damaged their business interests, remained a problem for Congress organizers throughout the nationalist struggle. In 1931, when the Swadeshi issue was joined with that of industrial workers' conditions and wages, the internal struggle became more intense. At the December 1931 annual meeting of the Congress in Karachi, a resolution was passed concerning the working conditions of industrial workers. The result was the establishment of the Congress Textile Mills Exemption committee. Circular letters were sent to millowners demanding that they sign a Congress declaration regarding minimum working conditions and the boycott of foreign cloth. Many signed, but the inclusion of the boycott provision stimulated continuing opposition. Gandhi was urged to reconsider the boycott clause, but he refused. It was agreed that publicity was the only weapon available to the Congress to be used against those who refused to cooperate in the nationalist cause. A directory was prepared which listed only those mills which had signed the declaration. Those which refused or subsequently did not give a satisfactory response regarding working conditions and Swadeshi were not listed or removed from the list.[28]

The Bombay *Congress Bulletin* as well as other local Congress publications and the press were utilized to extend the publicity campaign against blacklisted firms. For those who agreed to cooperate as a result of such Congress pressure, the *Bulletin* would note the addition of the firm to the approved list.[29] The Bombay *Bulletin* was also available to attack individuals who continued to do 'business as usual' with the British and were particularly successful at it. In an editorial titled 'Suffering is Not Over', Purshotamdas Thakurdas and G. D. Birla were attacked for exporting bullion to England. 'The Indian traitors dealing in bullion have deliberately impoverished us to enrich the enemy ... The bullion merchants have struck a direct blow at our struggle for independence. Sir Purshotamdas and Mr. Birla have made lakhs from this immoral

---

[27] J. Nehru to T. Prakasam, 18 April 1928; S. Naidu to J. Nehru, 17 April 1928; J. Nehru to S. Naidu, 21 April 1928, *ibid.*

[28] Congress Textile Mills Exemption Committee, Shankerlal Banker, Hon. Secretary, 24 October 1930, AICC D-3/1931.

[29] *Bombay Congress Bulletin*, No. 232, 29 September 1932, Purshotamadas Thakurdas Papers.

traffic.'[30] The *Bulletin* in Bombay and other parts of the country was suppressed from time to time, but managed to carry on the struggle in print in one form or other. In July 1931, after a period of suppression, Sir Phiroze Sethna, Bombay businessman and liberal sympathizer, contacted the Viceroy's private secretary, noting the mischief that had been caused by the *Bulletin* in inciting the masses against the business community. Since Gandhi was to see Lord Irwin that day, Sethna asked Mieville to suggest that the Viceroy press Gandhi to drop the *Bulletin*.[31] The extra-ordinary nature of the particular network which was used to bring Bombay business concerns to Gandhi's attention is only one example of the mixed and changing alliances which came together around particular issues. In this case, it did not have the desired result and the *Bulletin* returned to the struggle. When Thakurdas described picketing of the Cotton Ring, a cotton traders' organization, as un-Gandhian and a danger to trade, the *Bulletin* denounced his remark as 'blasphemy'. It insisted that Thakurdas, a multimillionaire, had no right to use Gandhi's name. 'He is ours,' declared the *Bulletin*, 'not yours.'[32] Swaminath Sada-nand defended Thakurdas' record of service to India, the Congress, and the cotton trade. The *Bulletin* printed his article but remained unrepentant.[33]

The *Congress Bulletin* had been founded by Jawaharlal Nehru in January 1929, and supplied free to all provincial Congress Committees, members of the AICC, and a select list of individuals and organizations. The *Bulletin* appeared at irregular intervals in its first year and was published by the Allahabad Law Journal Press which was regularly used by the Nehrus for their publicity work. When Nehru became President of the Congress in December 1929, direct responsibility was passed on to others. Sixteen issues were published in 1929 and eight in 1930, until 26 May, when the Law Journal Press refused to continue publication in response to a warning from the Government.[34] Space was found in *Young India* to continue publication but efforts continued to resume publication of the full *Bulletin* on a twice-monthly basis. It had become a useful means of circulating resolutions passed by the Working Committee as well as the views of the leaders on important issues and events. It had often included as much as sixteen demi-pages of news and views and in addition to the *Young India* outlet, a reduced cyclostyled version was brought out from

[30] *Ibid.*
[31] P. Sethna to Mieville (PSV), 18 July 1931, Sethna Papers (1931), pp. 218–19.
[32] *Bombay Congress Bulletin*, Vol. II, No. 244, 13 October 1932, P. Thakurdas Papers, 101.
[33] *Bombay Congress Bulletin*, Vol. II, No. 241, 10 October 1932, *ibid.*
[34] Memorandum, AICC G-89/1931.

time to time.[35] As often happened with many similar initiatives, the *Bulletin* published at the centre, meant to be a means for a regular flow of information and instruction to the provinces was, as in the case of the *Bombay Congress Bulletin*, replicated by local workers with their own agenda.

When such sources of information were denied to Congress leaders either by suppression or imprisonment, the press provided a ready alternative. Especially during periods of crisis when a leader was pulled from the struggle in the midst of a battle, news of subsequent events was a high priority in prison. Although newspapers were sometimes denied for a period, generally these 'first-class' prisoners received one or two papers. They were usually Anglo-Indian or moderate Indian publications, but the information was there; and a prisoner could provide his own editorial comment and prepare views for future use and dissemination. Jawaharlal Nehru's correspondence reflects his ability to follow the activities of colleagues during his periods of regular imprisonment or absences from India through announcements and reports in the press. He carefully noted false information that required refutation and meeting dates that were inconvenient.[36] He could sympathize with Abul Kalam Azad when an illness was reported in one paper, and insist that he had said nothing to support the suggestion that Azad intended to resign the Congress presidency when stories appeared in the *Leader* and *Hindustan Standard*. In response to a press report of a speech given by the south Indian nationalist leader, Rajagopalachari, he could respond immediately with a note describing the distress it had caused him.[37]

The Indian press had become so aggressive and determined in its coverage of political affairs that sensitive negotiations which required a measure of privacy could not easily be arranged. Plans for a meeting of Congress leaders with the Viceroy in late December 1929, to avoid the confrontation that was looming at the end of the year, were stymied in the view of the Government of India by premature publication. The Viceroy was concerned that press reports suggesting that he was calling a conference with Gandhi and Motilal Nehru at the eleventh hour before the Congress meeting gave the impression that he was trying to buy off the Congress. T. B. Sapru contacted Motilal Nehru in this regard, noting the

---

[35] *Ibid.* See also J. Nehru to Mohanlal Manganlal Bhatta, Manager, *Young India*, 9 June 1931, and S. H. Thompson, district magistrate, Allahabad to Babu Raja Ram, Secretary, AICC, 26 May 1930, *ibid.*

[36] Memorandum, AICC, *ibid.*

[37] J. Nehru correspondence, J. Nehru Papers, Vol. V; J. Nehru to A. K. Azad, 4 August 1940, 17 October 1940, 20 October 1940, and J. Nehru to Rajaji, 26 January 1942, Jawaharlal Nehru Papers.

need for both to talk without the assumption that either party was giving in. To ensure that the press would not become aware of these preparations, Sapru's message was sent through the Home Department as a cypher telegram to the United Provinces Government and then passed on to Nehru.[38]

The Congress wanted as much press coverage as it could attract, but not necessarily the kind it got. It was important for the public and the larger audience outside India to be aware of the continuing struggle and the leading role of the Congress, but there was also the need for the press to reflect unified support for congress positions and actions. As in the case of senior officials in the Government of India, nationalist leaders often wished they could suppress unhelpful or antagonistic viewpoint, but their support – sometimes grudging – for a free press limited their influence to denial of financial support in those cases where such funding was significant, response and attack – often in the pages of another newspaper, and to patriotic persuasion.

Editorial comment regarding the Rowlatt Acts and the Punjab situation in the spring of 1919, reflected the differences in perspective. The Government responded to the angry editorials of the *Bombay Chronicle* by arresting and deporting its English editor, B. G. Horniman. The opposition of other national papers, however, was more restrained, and there was also support for repressive legislation. The *Hindu* lamented the unrestrained response of the Punjab Government. 'There is a point of persistence beyond which justice degenerates into vindictiveness and any further tales of the exploits of the 'no d—d nonsense' school will only serve to convince the public that that point has been reached and passed.'[39] The *Tribune* described the Rowlatt Acts as 'a colossal blunder'. Like the *Hindu*, the argument was cast in the context of a denial of rights and justice which had been available to Indians in the past. In effect it was argued, the British regime was 'de-legitimizing' itself by acting arbitrarily and outside 'the law'.

The most fundamental of the rights of the people, the right which, in the absence of representative instutitions, is the chief security for all their other rights, the right of open and regular trial by ordinary courts and on the basis of lawful and adequate evidence before a hair of one's head is touched by way of punishment, comes automatically to an end.[40]

The *Leader* was also concerned about the challenge to civil rights in the Rowlatt legislation. But it was concerned as well with violent opposition

[38] T. B. Sapru to M. Nehru, 19 December 1929, Motilal Nehru Papers.
[39] *Hindu*, 8 May 1919, quoted in G. Kasturi, compiler, *The Hindu Speaks*, Bombay: Interpress, 1978, p. 131.
[40] *Tribune*, 21 March 1919.

and anarchy in the Punjab – also in its view, a challenge to law and order. In a lengthy and detailed analysis of the new laws and the current situation, it supported the Government's action. The Rowlatt Acts were 'intended only to cope with anarchical and revolutionary crime', it insisted. 'Peaceful and law abiding citizens will have nothing to fear from it.' It rejected the *Tribune's* argument about the loss of the protection of 'ordinary law', noting that the special court to be established would consist of three high court judges. 'The impartiality and ability of the Tribunal Court cannot therefore be questioned.' The *Leader* concluded that 'peaceful citizens would have nothing to fear from the Act' which was directed 'only against revolutionary criminals'.[41] For Congress leaders who sought to use the Punjab Wrong and the Rowlatt Acts to mobilize support for a nationalist attack on an alien regime, even the supportive editorials were often not very helpful. While Gandhi would attempt to achieve Swaraj in one year by launching the new Non-cooperation campaign, the *Tribune* and *Hindu* sought to rein in a Government which had overstepped legal bounds. And for the *Leader*, Non-cooperation in the following year would be attacked as a far more dangerous challenge to law and civil Government than the means utilized by the British regime in defence.

In October 1929, Jawaharlal Nehru wrote to the editors of the *Bombay Chronicle*, *Swarajya*, *Liberty*, *Basumati*, *Amrita Bazaar Patrika*, *Tribune*, and the *Hindustan Times*. These were all Congress or independent nationalist papers from which the AICC was seeking cooperative support at a strategically sensitive moment in its confrontation with the Government. Nehru noted that an official announcement was anticipated in a few days and that it was not likely to meet Congress demands. It was, therefore, 'desirable that nationalist India should preserve a united front as far as possible'. He called on the editors to oppose 'divide and rule' by limiting their response to critical reporting without commitment. He urged them to wait a few days to enable the country, through Congress, 'to give a dignified and powerful reply' to the Government. His letter concluded by noting that this suggestion was only for consideration and that there was no desire to fetter the editors' discretion.[42]

Most of these papers could be counted on to give a loyal response, but the independents retained their virginity and there were many influential papers which Nehru would assume would not be influenced by even such a gentle suggestion. The alternative of enhancing the in-house ability of

[41] *Leader*, 14 April 1919.
[42] J. Nehru to editors of *Bombay Chronicle*, *Hindu*, *Swarajya*, *Liberty*, *Basumati*, *Amrita Bazaar Patrika*, *Tribune*, *Hindustan Times*, 29 October 1929, AICC G-15.

the Congress to gather information and disseminate appropriate publicity was always under consideration and institutionalized from time to time in the form of specialized committees, commissions of enquiry of departments of a 'Government in waiting'. In 1936, the Political and Economic Information Department of the Indian National Congress was established for the collection of political and economic information bearing on the Indian situation. A great effort was made to gather a comprehensive collection of official and demi-official literature both from India and outside, that might be useful in the nationalist campaign or in the design of programmes. But the effort foundered within two years, pressed aside by other priorities and the inability to attract the continuing interest of Provincial Committees or to establish any effective coordination between central and local Congress workers.[43]

Throughout the 1920s and 1930s there were periods of fundamental difference magnified by the press and propaganda campaigns of competing groups. Non-cooperators struggled with those who sought to 'work the Reforms'. Khilafatists were attacked by those who rejected any communalist campaign as well as Hindu communalists who were offended by the Muslim content of this one. Swarajists, No-Changers, and Responsivists each in turn sought to gain or retain control of mainstream Congress policy. In addition, independence and dominion status were proposed as competing descriptions of the immediate or ultimate goal. As each new viewpoint emerged, attracted support and sought some institutionalized identity as a party within the Congress, or, if necessary, outside; the leaders sought to mobilize support in the press. In the early days of Swarajist attempts to finesse the dogmatic elements in Non-cooperation, their underdog status was apparent in the attacks of the orthodox Congress press, and they sought redress by establishing their own. In Madras. A. Rangaswami Iyengar attempted to defend the new party in his Tamil language *Swadesamitran*, but the effort was clearly insufficient. 'The *Hindu* is continuing to attack our party, its leaders and its programme and though I have been doing my best to counter the same in my vernacular paper the necessity for an English organ for our Party has become so manifest and urgent that ... I have decided to start an English weekly newspaper.'[44] In Bombay Jayakar sought similar press support for the Swarajists, and with the help of Motilal Nehru attempted to gain control of a number of papers. There were similar efforts throughout the country. The same sense of disadvantage was reflected in

[43] K. M. Ashraf to J. Nehru, 2 September 1938, Jawaharlal Nehru Papers.
[44] A. Rangaswami Iyengar, ed., Swadesamitran to M. R. Jayakar, 6 February 1923, Jayakar Papers, 402, Pt 1.

the correspondence of Responsivist leaders a few years later, as they lamented the lack of sufficient press coverage of their speeches and their meetings or the one-sided versions that were going out to the provinces which had a 'depressing effect on our work there'.[45]

In 1928, the Nehru Report and the meeting of the All-Parties Conference stimulated an attempt to popularize the developing unity at the centre and undermine the attacks of those who opposed the proposals with a massive propaganda campaign. Motilal Nehru wrote to leaders in every province seeking support for the All-Parties' Fund that would be used to advocate the scheme. The competition was quick to respond. Jawaharlal Nehru and his more radical supporters advocated independence rather than the limited and confusing formula of dominion status recommended in the Report; and they managed to gain the support of a majority at the Congress meeting convened in Madras. Similarly, communalist Hindu and Muslim groups rejected the compromises that had been made on their behalf in regard to reserved seats and joint electorates by more accommodating co-religionists. The Anglo-Indian *Times of India* noted and emphasized the divisions and compromises that appeared to nullify the work of the All-Parties Conference.[46] In response, Motilal Nehru negotiated with his colleagues at the centre in order to achieve a temporary solution that would allow him 'to ride two horses' as Congress President and principal sponsor of the Report which carried his name. And he contacted those outside the inner circle who might be able to influence resisting Muslim and Hindu Mahasabha leaders.[47] S. N. Banerjee had noted in an 1883 *Bengalee* editorial that 'the voice of a unified nation, backed by a united press would be simply irresistible'. In the years between the wars, however, the nation was still not united and the press represented the parts as well as the whole. The significance of a particular community's possession of its own newspaper is reflected in C. F. Andrew's description of the divided Indian community of Dar es Salaam. He noted that the 'danger of rivalry and recrimination was much greater as each faction possessed its own newspaper'. Through Andrew's intervention, the opposing factions came together as one united community, and the Muslim-edited *African Comrade* and Hindu-edited *Tanganyika Opinion* were amalgamated into one paper.[48]

The competing propaganda campaigns were joined by the major nationalist press. For most, the Report appeared to provide the best

[45] A. R. Iyengar to Vasudeorao Joshi, 20 May 1926, *ibid.*
[46] *Times of India*, 5, 6, 7 November 1928.
[47] M. Nehru to P. Thakurdas, 28 April 1928, Thakurdas Papers, 40–4.
[48] C. F. Andrews to J. B. Petit, secretary, Imperial Indian Citizenship Association, 16 October 1926, copy in Jayakar Papers, 77.

opportunity for a solution to communal differences regarding the franchise. But the continuing problems were obvious and well advertised. The *Hindustan Times* noted its preference for the complete abolition of communal representation in any form; but accepted the need to recognize the situation of distrust which required the maintenance of reserved seats in Muslim-minority provinces for ten years. The *Pioneer* supported the Report and urged Muslims to formulate a constructive critique. The *Tribune* described the Report as a 'wise and statesmanlike treatment of the communal problem'; and the *Hindu* noted its enthusiasm as well. But the *Amrita Bazaar Patrika* was more pointed in its defence of the Hindu interest, noting that Muslims would likely enhance their political strength in a system of joint electorates. And the *Bengalee* perceived 'an excessive leaven of idealism' in the euphoria surrounding the Report. There was a Muslim view, Anglo-Indian view, Non-Brahmin view, and Sikh view, it insisted, and the implicit response in the Report was 'the total rejection of their plea for protection'. It urged its readers to face facts and be sceptical of this 'extremely philosophic treatment of the claims of the minority'. The *Muslim Outlook* spoke for those who believed that the loss of separate electorates condemned Muslims to permanent subordination in a future Hindu Raj. It rejected the general attack on community identity and the use of the word 'communalist' as an epithet; and asked its readers to consider what was so essentially undemocratic in communal representation.

It is clear that the Muslims of India will not, and should not assent to any constitution that is not based on the principle of communal representation, without which 'dominion self-government', will only be a euphemism for Hindu 'Raj' for who can doubt that the joint electorates will everywhere be captured by the Banias and their allies the Brahmin lawyers.[49]

The support given to the independence resolution at the Madras congress compromised the work of the Nehru Committee and weakened the resolve of some leaders who had entered into the negotiations with strong views and had accommodated others on the basis of a delicate balance of interests. But there was no delicacy in the advocacy of viewpoint on the platform and in the press. The *Hindustan Times* publicized the tension and divisions in the mixed messages sent to its readers. The flag-raising ceremony marking the celebration of 'Independence Day' was described, followed by warnings that the leaders would probably be arrested. 'It is reliably understood that the Government had definitely decided on a

---

[49] All of the press comment cited was reproduced in 'What India Thinks', *Indian Daily Mail*, 22 August 1928.

repressive policy.'[50] Gandhi's vivid description of 'the agony of slow and lingering death' of the impoverished masses under this 'rule of spoilation' is presented in detail;[51] but the action of the 'moderates' is also noted in a description of lengthy discussions of Indian legislators in response to Lord Irwin's reference to dominion status as the 'final' and not the 'immediate' goal.[52] Competing images of independence achieved, revolutionary fervour and denunciation, and the 'business as usual' political confrontation and debate were all made available for readers to choose. The compromise accepted by Motilal Nehru which allowed both the dominion status and independence goals to retain a place in the Congress programme led to the establishment of Independence Leagues and a defensive response from Liberals and Independents who perceived an early death to any commitment to All-Party accommodation. Soon after Jamnadas Mehta formed an Independence League in Bombay, M. R. Jayakar became more restive about Motilal Nehru's compromise. When Nehru asked Jayakar to accompany him on a propaganda tour to Madras in support of the All-Party initiative, he noted the difficulty in their preaching from the same platform and reiterated his view of Bombay's concern that the Nehru Report's advocacy of dominion status had been subordinated to the Madras Congress' independence resolution. Jayakar insisted that the All-Parties Conference was 'a bigger thing than the Indian National Congress', but this was never a position that could be sustained for very long. Congress leaders generally insisted that unity had to be achieved under their umbrella. The occasional All-Party initiatives were only a temporary refuge for those who had left the Congress or had always rejected its pre-eminent position.[53]

The 1932 Communal Award promulgated by the British Government reinforced divisions and community identity, now easily described and defended by a loyal press and in a range of propaganda instruments. In August, M. R. Jayakar denounced the Award in a press statement and described the likely impact – further division and challenge to the Hindu interest.

The Lucknow Pact divided India into Hindu and Moslem. This Award will divide it further into Hindu women verses Moslem women, European versus Anglo-Indian, white Christians versus coloured Christians, high caste Hindus versus Depressed Classes, and eventually North India versus South India. Temporarily it will place the majority community under heavy disadvantages; but I have enough

---

[50] *Hindustan Times*, 26 January 1930, p. 1.
[51] *Ibid.*, p. 5.
[52] *Ibid.*, 27 January 1930, p. 1.
[53] M. R. Jayakar to M. Nehru, 4 October and 13 November 1928, Jayakar Papers, 442.

confidence in the recuperative power of that community, and I feel sure that it will soon rise erect against the first effects of this blow.[54]

John Gallagher has described the impact of the Award in Bengal, where the PCC's heightened Hindu communalist identity seemed essential in their struggle against Pandit Malaviya and a Congress Nationalist Party which had made the defence of Hindu interest the core of its programme.[55] Congress leaders at the centre might find this deplorable in principle and a blow to their campaign to maintain Muslim support, but practical realities took precedence in what was perceived as a struggle for survival. In 1934, Birendra Nath Gupta described to Gandhi the armoury of press support available to these protagonists.

Amrita Bazaar Patrika is communal. The vernacular *Basumati* is frankly sanatanist. *Amrita Bazaar Patrika* ... is a vehement supporter of the Hindu Sahba ... and *Advance* is a close ally. These two papers seized the opportunity of the resignations of Panditji [Malaviya] and S. J. Aney ... to make their party strong by damning the Parliamentary Board and the Working Committee as having played into their hands ... *Forward* [*Liberty* under a new name] has no love for the Working Committee or for you either. But it supports because it has to.[56]

As usual, Gandhi chose his own issue and his own means of response to the Communal Award. In August 1932, he wrote to the British Prime Minister, Ramsay MacDonald, to announce a fast that he intended to begin later in the year in opposition to the establishment of separate electorates for untouchables, thus depriving them in Gandhi's view of political identity with mainstream Hinduism. This particular issue would not have been the priority of Congress leaders but Gandhi's initiative took the decision out of their hands. He told MacDonald that the fast would end on his death or if the British Government 'of its own motion or under pressure of public opinion' reversed its position. Gandhi asked that his letter, as well as earlier correspondence with the Secretary of State be published. 'I want, if you make it possible, public opinion to be affected by my letters.'[57] MacDonald agreed and their publication set in motion a chain of events which eventually produced the desired result. The letters appeared in newspapers throughout India and around the world, stimulating a mix of responses which extended Gandhi's initiative in a range of supportive and antagonistic publicity campaigns.

---

[54] Jayakar statement to the press on the Communal Award, 21 August 1932, *ibid.*, 445.
[55] John Gallagher, 'Congress in Decline: Bengal 1930–1938', in J. Gallagher, G. Johnson, and A. Seal, eds. *Locality, Province, Nation 1870–1940*, Cambridge University Press, 1973, p. 305.
[56] *Ibid.*, p. 277.
[57] M. K. Gandhi to Ramsay MacDonald, 18 April 1932, (Home Pol) 31/113/32 and K.W.

The Home Department debated the significance of Gandhi being held in prison and whether it was more likely that he would die in gaol or outside. It noted that his followers were unprepared and that there were significant differences on this issue – leaving the Government an opening for a counter-propaganda campaign.[58] Local Governments were contacted and told to emphasize the point that this was not a struggle between Gandhi and the Government, but between Gandhi and the Depressed Classes. In an 11 August secret note, local publicity agencies were advised to note the generations of mistreatment by caste Hindus, the impossibility of untouchables gaining a legislative seat without special electorates, and the Government's reluctance to move until it was clear there was no alternative. Gandhi was to be depicted as using force rather than rational discussion.[59] In Britain and the United States, and in some of the Indian press, there was support for the Government's viewpoint; but at the same time further publicity for a great national leader who was sacrificing his life and confronting alone the power of the British Empire.

For Gandhi's supporters, the announcement of the fast stimulated a range of initiatives that might influence the Government to meet his demands. Plans were made to have the Hindu Mahasabha declare its support for Gandhi and to arrange untouchable meetings that would pass motions in favour of joint electorates.[60] There were also exchanges about holding Hindu Mahasabha and Depressed Classes Conferences in Bombay near to Gandhi in order to focus public attention and increase the pressure on the Government.[61] G. D. Birla, who was organizing part of the campaign wired Gandhi on 14 September and asked him to delay the start of the fast for ten days, in order to provide more time for his supporters to work.[62] The power of Gandhi's personal act of sacrifice, as a well-publicized public event, required his followers to concentrate on an issue that would not otherwise have attracted such committed attention, and eventually forced the untouchable leader, Dr Ambedkar, and subsequently the Government to accommodate.

Ambedkar's agreement to give up separate electorates in return for guaranteed seats for untouchables was enshrined in the Poona Pact. For some, the Pact reflected a great victory for Gandhi over the British 'divide and rule' weapon. Others concentrated on the nature of the

---

[58] M. G. Hallett note, 21 August 1932, *ibid.*
[59] Home Department secret note for Local Governments, 11 August 1932, *ibid.*
[60] P. Thakurdas to G. D. Birla, 14 September 1932; G. D. Birla to Walchand Hirachand, 14 September 1932, Thakurdas Papers, 129.
[61] W. Hirachand to M. M. Malaviya and G. D. Birla to P. Thakurdas, 15 September 1932, *ibid.*
[62] G. D. Birla to P. Thakurdas, 14 September 1932, *ibid.*

accommodation required to achieve All-Parties and all communities agreement. For many, the price was too high. The *Hindustan Times* and the *Hindu* emphasized the positive achievements. Like all of the 'national press', Gandhi's fast was covered in daily bulletins and the 'ceremony of breaking the fast' in 'solemn scenes in Yerawada Prison' was described in detail as a great national event. The responsibility of caste Hindus to end all social and religious disabilities for untouchables was emphasized in long quotations from Gandhi's remarks and editorial homilies about the lesson for India that had emerged from this confrontation.[63]

The *Hindu* applauded the Pact as both an attack on untouchability and an indication of 'our ability to compose our domestic differences'. It hoped that this success might be a model for further agreements among other communities and noted as well that the Government might now recognize the benefit in cooperating with Gandhi and the Congress.[64] The *Hindustan Times* shared the *Hindu*'s positive reading regarding the ability of Indians 'to learn and practise the lessons of mutual accommodation in lieu of outside direction.'[65] But it also emphasized its caste Hindu perspective which was reflected in a continuing reticence regarding All-Parties compromises. 'What the Minorities Pact could not give them the caste Hindus have, under the inspiring leadership of Mahatma Gandhi, now offered and it hence becomes the charter for their enfranchisement in modern Indian policy.'[66]

The communal issue continued, however, to stimulate the right wing of the Congress to join hands with conservative forces outside in opposition to the leadership of both Gandhi and Nehru, which demanded compromises that seemed increasingly dangerous to the Hindu interest. In April 1934, *Amrita Bazaar Patrika* noted in a lead article the connection between the Congress campaign for communal amity and the next dollop of constitutional reform. It lamented that there was a 'clear indication that the Hindus would allow themselves to be taken in again, this time on the bait of combined Hindu–Moslem opposition to the white paper.'[67] The Hindu Mahasabha leader, B. S. Moonje, described the demoralized state of the Hindus after fourteen years of Gandhi's politics, steeped in the feeling that Swaraj was impossible without the cooperation of the Muslims,[68] and the establishment of the new Democratic Swaraj Party seemed to indicate to some of the anti-Gandhian leaders that the dog-

---

[63] *Hindustan Times*, 27 September 1932, p. 4.
[64] *Hindu*, 26 September 1932.
[65] *Hindustan Times*, 28 September 1932.
[66] *Ibid.*
[67] *Amrita Bazaar Patrika*, 6 April 1934, in Jayakar Papers, 207.
[68] B. S. Moonje to M. R. Jayakar, 7 April 1934, *ibid.*

matic policy of the Congress and the unwillingness of its leaders to consider opposition views had been successfully challenged.

In the meantime, let us enjoy the happiness of having seen the establishment of different Parties in India independently of Mahatma Gandhi. After all, we have given the lead and Congressmen will follow! The face of Congressmen is now definitely turned though the point of difference will remain as to whether Gandhi's wishes and vagaries should be the pivot of our policies. Those who want Gandhi may go after him as they have done so far, and we will stick to our principles as we have done so far.[69]

In August 1932, N. C. Kelkar told Jayakar that it was foolish to waste further energy on the dispute over the Communal Award. The solution lay in their 'securing the maximum share of power in the nature of self-government through a federated constitution with responsibility through the Central Government'. He assumed that any attempt to change the Award would require civil war which was 'unthinkable' and 'can give only doubtful results with Government and Muslims and Europeans and Anglo-Indians all ranged on one side'.[70] Jayakar agreed and noted in addition that the Award should convey a serious warning to the Indian princes 'that the communal poison is not introduced into their territories'.[71] There were differences about who was 'communalizing' the constitutional debate, but these competing viewpoints were staunchly held and defended. As was usual with Jayakar and Kelkar, they turned to the press for support. Kelkar controlled two influential papers and his editorial columns were committed to federation. Jayakar attempted one more time to establish his own paper.

The *Federal Times* project was meant to serve a range of complimentary interests. It would challenge the dominance in Bombay of the *Chronicle* on the left and the *Times of India* on the right. And it would advocate the bringing together at the centre of a federation of conservative, communal, and political interests represented by the princes. It was to be a paper for the states and for British India, and Jayakar with his colleagues T. B. Sapru and Sir Kailas Haksar, a senior Gwalior official, sought the moral support of the Government of India and financial contributions from the princes and Bombay businessmen. It was essential, in their view, to establish a strong federal Government at the centre, but to ensure as well the interests of Maharashtra, of Gwalior, and the range of localities that possessed a distinctive identity and viewpoint. They insisted as well on their commitment to the interests of all religious groups while seeking to

---

[69] N. C. Kelkar to M. R. Jayakar, 17 August 1932, *ibid.*, 445.
[70] *Ibid.*
[71] Jayakar press statement, 21 August 1932, *ibid.*

protect the primacy of the dominant Hindu community. While Nehru and central Congress leaders sought to subsume all local interests within an overarching Congress-controlled and -designed unity at the centre, Jayakar and his colleagues were advocates of the integrity of these parts.

Jayakar attempted to take over the *Bombay Chronicle*, thereby accomplishing the double objective of denying publicity to the enemy by putting the *Chronicle* out of business and giving publicity to interests they supported. In addition, Jayakar planned to establish Gujarati and Marathi dailies in order to bring his views to a larger audience thus far 'left untouched by sober views'. Both Lord Brabourne, the Governor of Bombay, and the Viceroy, Lord Willingdon, were asked to support the enterprise by encouraging princes and businessmen to contribute; but their advocacy lacked sufficient commitment to ensure positive response from a constituency that was usually quite cooperative. There were a range of difficulties to overcome. The *Times of India* mounted a counter-campaign and the elite patrons – both English and Indian – sought by Jayakar's group were still reluctant to offend the *Times*.

The owners of the *Chronicle* who had been considering Jayakar's offer had been encouraged by the demise of the *Free Press Journal* to assess positively the business prospects of their paper. And some potential supporters were reluctant to associate with a Jayakar project because of his presumed communal bias. Sapru himself was reluctant to be a director. 'Frankly, I should have nothing to do with Hindus and Mohammedans who are openly associated with communal bodies. The easiest thing in India is to pose as a nationalist.' Willingdon was pressed to join the campaign in order to have the paper established before he left, but the project remained on the agenda of his successor, Lord Linlithgow, who refused to support a venture that was financially and politically unstable. He wanted a sure winner. Some argued the need to have a Muslim on the Board to placate Hyderabad and Bhopal. In addition it was suggested that support from Muslim rulers depended on the resignation of Jayakar and Haksar. As the scheme approached collapse, Haksar reminded Jayakar of the forces ranged against them. 'Perhaps our anticipations bore no relation to the realities of Indian condition, Indian mentalities, Indian patriotism and Indian promptitude in a national cause.'[72] They were, of course, discussing the lack of support for *their* national cause as it did battle with the alternatives advocated by others in powerful and entrenched positions. In July 1936, Jayakar and his colleagues resigned from the Board, and the project moved in a purely commercial direction.

---

[72] *Federal Standard* Project, July 1935–July 1936, Jayakar Papers, 429–34. In regard to the *Federal Standard* project, see also M. Israel, 'M. R. Jayakar and the Bombay Nationalist

Local struggles which involved distinct communities attracted the attention of both Government officials and Congress leaders who sought to minimize the differences between their centre and this locality and to subsume what they considered to be a parochial interest into their All-India campaigns. In the early 1920s, as Gandhi sought to unify the nationalist movement in support of a particular means and goal, the turmoil in the Punjab was enhanced by the rise of the Akali Movement.

At the turn of the twentieth century, the social and educational revival that had been spreading unevenly across the Indian sub-continent was reflected among the Sikhs in the Singh Sabha Movement and the leadership of the Chief Khalsa Diwan. The recognition and enhancement of distinctive Sikh identity and loyalty to the Raj were the dominant themes, and they remained so until World War One. In the post-war period, however, the emphasis on education was displaced by a new priority for political organization and action. The Central Sikh League was established in December 1919, and began holding annual meetings on the pattern of the Congress and Muslim League. In its second session in October 1920, Baba Kharak Singh was elected President on a nationalist platform. Gandhi and other Congress leaders attended the meeting, and their desire to attract Sikh participation in the Non-cooperation campaign was reflected in a Congress resolution concerning 'the utter disregard shown by the Government for the rights of the Sikh community'.[73] As in the case of Gandhi's enthusiasm for the Muslim Khilafat Movement, it was assumed that the All-India Congress campaign would benefit from the embrace of another 'local' priority.

In July 1921, the League approved a new constitution advocating Swarajya by peaceful means and the promotion of Panthic unity. Loyalty to the British had been displaced by a new commitment to the nationalist campaign, but the parallel emphasis on Sikh interest and identity was retained. In the same year, however, the work of the League was overshadowed by the Shiromani Akali Dal and the Gurdwara reform issue. The Dal was established in December 1920 to spearhead the movement to bring all Sikh temples under the control of the Shiromani Gurdwara Prabandhak Committee (SGPC). In 1919, generations of control of gurdwaras by hereditary *mahants* was challenged by 'Akalis' who traced their lineage and mission back to the band of 'immortals' designated by Guru Gobind Singh at the end of the seventeenth century to be guardians of the

Press: The Struggle for Identity Within a Nationalist Movement', in Wagle, *Images of Maharashtra*.

[73] Cited in Kailash Chander Gulati, *The Akalis Past and Present*, New Delhi, Ashajanak, 'Publications' 1974, pp. 21–2.

Sikh faith. The demand that the gurdwaras be transferred to the SGPC, and by implication, to the Sikh people, produced confrontation with a range of interests including those of the British regime. The general post-war unrest in the Punjab and efforts to undermine the loyalty of Sikh troops informed the decision of the Government to support the hereditary rights of the *mahants*. The Gurdwara struggle lasted for five years, involving the British, the Congress, Sikh princes, and a variety of Sikh leaders and viewpoints. It was at the same time, a 'local' power struggle, a campaign for religious reform, an assertion of ethnic identity, and a fragment of the larger nationalist movement.

The demand for reform of the Gurdwaras was reflected in confront-ation with the British and with those in control of the Gurdwaras whom they patronized. It involved as well internecine struggle within the Sikh community, in particular among the Sikh ruling princes and between them and Akali leaders in the Punjab. The Maharajas of Nabha and Patiala, the former an Akali supporter, the latter an opponent vied with each other in a press and pamphlet war that eventually involved all of the Sikh states as well as a range of interests outside. Typical of the reporting was a 'dialogue' between the Maharaja of Patiala and Dewan Dayan Kishan Kaul, published in the Lahore *Daily Sikh*.

DEWAN DAYAN KISHAN: At present two lakhs would be sufficient. Some money may be distributed as bribes to Sikhs and one Gurumukhi daily newspaper may be started. By spending the above amount the Akali movement would die out, and Your Highness would become Jathedar.

PATIALA: Bravo – This is what I want. The Akali movement must die out, that Government may be pleased with me. There ... should be no interference with my amusements and pleasures and I may become Jathedar.[74]

Stories in the Akali-controlled *Nation* attacking the Government – 'Sikh Soldiers Refuse to Beat Akalis', 'Bureaucracy Sick of the Game' – elicited the usual discussion regarding suppression and eventually the editor of the *Nation* was prosecuted. It was recognized, however, that the Akali Movement was not an ordinary problem and an effort was made to organize a counter-propaganda campaign among cooperative Sikh princes. The Governor of the Punjab, Sir Malcolm Hailey, sought to strengthen publicity organizations in some of the Phulkian states, recog-nizing that any association with a British-patronized group such as the Punjab Provincial Association would weaken the campaign. A conference was convened at Barnes Court, the Governor's residence, in September 1924, including representatives of states with a predominant Sikh popu-lation, and officials of the Punjab and Central Governments. There was

[74] *Daily Sikh*, 25 June 1922 cited in (F & P) Political, R/1/29/157.

consensus about the need to counter Akali propaganda and for close, but indirect, liaison with Punjab publicity bodies. Hailey noted that the Government's priorities included Gurdwara reform as well as opposition to Akali methods and raised some concern among the princes that the states might be pressured to legislate Gurdwara reforms in their own constituencies. But with the strong support of Patiala, there was general agreement to support a united, if separate campaign, and Hailey indicated he would avoid the word 'legislation' in favour of 'constitutional methods'. Hailey sought the establishment of non-official bodies in the Sikh states which would make statements in support of the British Government approach to the Akali and Gurdwara problem, as was the case in the Punjab where Sikh Sudhar committees had been established with official inspiration. But the Viceroy, Lord Reading, was concerned about potential stories of Government collusion and the plan was eventually dropped.[75]

The Congress recognized an interest in the Akali Movement as well. In September 1922, a committee was established under Srinivasa Iyengar to enquire into police excesses. The deposition of the Maharaja of Nabha in July 1932, was assumed to be the result of his pro-Akali, pro-Congress views, and a campaign, well funded by the Maharaja, sought his return to the Nabha throne. In January 1924, the AICC sent A. T. Gidwani to open a 'Congress Embassy' in Amritsar, with Rs 1,000 from the Tilak Fund to support publicity work and help the Akalis. Reflecting the opposition of moderate opinion which had lost its voice at the centre of Congress decision making, C. Y. Chintamani commented on this initiative in his reminiscences of this period.

It is noteworthy and significant that wherever there has been trouble in the land, on any matter and for whatever reason, Congressmen have nearly always been on the spot on the side of the party that caused the trouble provided it was against the Government or capitalists or landlords. Well might they say, 'I bring not peace but the sword.'[76]

Gidwani established an office with a duplicating machine, rented typewriter, and one assistant and made contact with the Akalis in order to supply the nationalist press with as much news and comment as possible. He noted he was also trying to study Sikh writings and traditions in order to provide 'some local touch' in his communiqués, and emphasized the need for more money in order to perform his mission.[77] The Burma PCC

---

[75] Nahba Affairs: re. formation of Sikh Publicity organization in princely states, (F & P) Political, R/1/29/87.

[76] Chiuntamini, *Indian Politics*, p. 151.

[77] A. T. Gidwani to J. Nehru, 23 January 1924, AICC 4 (1) 1924.

sent Rs 3,000 for Sikh families and the *Bombay Chronicle* sent a monthly contribution of Rs 59. *Swarajya* provided an inland press telegraph authorization to send stories to the paper without payment. But these examples were not widely replicated and lack of adequate resources remained a problem.[78]

There were other problems as well. Gidwani noted the 'hardly veiled cynicism regarding Indian National Congress help' of a section of Akali leaders, but internal differences within the SGPC provided the opportunity for his office to strengthen the pro-Congress wing.[79] When Gidwani was arrested, the Working Committee invited George Joseph to go to Amritsar and take charge of the office. Jawaharlal Nehru told him that the publicity work was important, but far more important was the long-term goal of developing ties with Sikh leaders. It was clear to him that no Punjabi was suitable for this work, and therefore the Congress had to rely on outsiders.[80] Joseph was unable to take up the offer, and K. M. Panikkar, the editor of *Swarajya* went in his place. Nehru reiterated his concern that 'the political side of it, and the side which affects the other communities' be given priority.[81] Gidwani had described the Akali attitude toward the Congress as 'more communal than national'. He was also concerned about the hostility toward the Akali Movement of Punjab Hindus 'who do not relish the idea of the Sikhs organizing themselves as a non-Hindu community'.[82] Nehru urged Panikkar to try and induce Hindu and Sikh editors to refrain from publishing material that was antagonistic to the other community. Bringing the two communities together was another element of Panikkar's mandate.[83]

Panikkar arranged for the preparation of articles on the Sikh movement that would be useful in other parts of the country. He also sought out Hindu scholars in the Punjab to write positive stories about the Gurdwara Reform Movement and the unreasonableness of the Government's position.[84] The publication of a critical story in the *Tribune* concerning official policy was considered a great victory. 'I am really proud of being able to do so.'[85] But these small successes did little to alleviate the frustration of seeking to support and attract the loyalty of a reluctant ally. Panikkar told Gandhi that the SGPC was a highly secretive

[78] *Ibid.*
[79] *Ibid.*
[80] J. Nehru to George Joseph, 3 March 1924, *ibid.*
[81] J. Nehru to K. M. Panikkar, 27 March 1924, *ibid.*
[82] A. T. Gidwani to Jai Rasm, 16 March 1924, *ibid.*
[83] J. Nehru to K. M. Panikkar, 27 March 1924, *ibid.*
[84] K. M. Panikkar to D. Chaman Lall, 30 March 1924, AICC 4 (2) 1924.
[85] K. M. Panikkar to Dr Kitchlew, 30 March 1924, *ibid.*

and dilatory body and its propaganda methods were clearly not Gandhian. He enclosed a specimen which he considered to be particularly 'vile', noting that the *Akali* was apparently worse but unavailable to him since he did not read Urdu. He described communal relations in Amritsar as 'mostly narrow vision and fanatical feeling', noting that he had been informed by a number of Hindus that Nehru was unacceptable as an arbitrator because he had stayed in a hotel where the cooks were Muslims.[86] Nehru agreed that the Punjabi Hindu was 'narrow minded' but he insisted that the Sikhs were largely to blame. 'Their movement is largely a separatist movement so far as religion is concerned,' he noted, 'and this has naturally reacted in the social and political sphere.' He considered the Akalis to be arrogant and insensitive to Hindu feelings. 'The bitterness of the Hindus against the Sikh and Muslim is chiefly due to the realization of his utter weakness and humiliation, and being narrow minded and bigotted this bitterness instead of urging him to better himself or make himself stronger turns to hatred and curses.' There were, in Nehru's view, no important Hindu leaders in Amritsar and as a result, the Sikhs had no one to talk to.[87]

By the end of April 1924, the lack of cooperation from the SGPC had led to consideration by the Working Committee of a proposal to close down the Amritsar office and withdraw all financial support for the Akalis;[88] and soon after an agreement between the Government and the Sikhs made any continuation of Congress activity unnecessary. There would be many other attempts to carry the Congress message and mission into provincial situations where local loyalties and priorities seemed to be as much in conflict with the general nationalist campaign as with the Raj regime. The effort to subsume every group's distress – political, social, economic, or religious, under the mandate of the Congress-led nationalist campaign attracted considerable support. But there were many groups and individuals who resented their loss of priority and the designation of their interest as 'parochial' or 'communalist'. These people tended to cling to a single issue or a mix of locality-based priorities, rejecting the compromises that had to be made at the centre if it were to continue to attract the broad-based constituency that allowed it to play an All-India representational role.

The attempt to absorb Sikhs and their interests into the Congress fold in the early 1920s was replicated in the late 1930s in regard to the Muslim community by the Muslim Mass Contact campaign. The emphasis on a

[86] K. M. Panikkar to M. K. Gandhi, 1 April 1924, *ibid.*
[87] J. Nehru to K. M. Panikkar, 2 April 1924, *ibid.*
[88] K. M. Panikkar to J. Nehru, 3 May 1924, *ibid.*

distinctive Muslim identity, as in the case of so many other religious, ethnic, and regional perceptions of self and group, was enhanced and politicized in the context of nationalist struggle in the late nineteenth and twentieth centuries. In response to the post-1857 entrenchment of British power and the increasing success and participation of Hindus in Government service and the professions, the Muslim educational and social reformer Syed Ahmad Khan called on his co-religionists to end their defensive isolation, cooperate with the British and ensure a place and role for themselves in India's future. He established a school at Aligarth in the United Provinces, which educated and trained generations of young Muslims in preparation for full participation in public life, and organizations which sought to focus Muslim viewpoint on the community's distinctive interests and identity. Syed Ahmad worked in parallel with those who founded the Indian National Congress in 1885, but he rejected their invitation to join the Congress which he considered to be Hindu in orientation and control.

The alternative organizations founded by Syed Ahmad were models for the Muslim League which was established in 1906 to represent the Muslim interest in the political 'debate'. The benefits were almost immediate with the agreement by Government to separate electorates and reserved seats for Muslims included in the 1909 Morley–Minto Reforms. From its founding, the Congress had presented itself as an All-India organization, but was always defensive in regard to the 'Muslim issue' – reiterating its general representative role and secular principles, but implicitly accepting the distinctive political identity of Muslims in its desire and need to achieve unity in the campaign against the British. Since the 1916 Lucknow Pact agreement with the Muslim League, the Congress had formally recognized a special Muslim interest in the development of political institutions. Gandhi's commitment to the Khilafat Movement in the early 1920s produced increased Muslim participation in the Congress Non-cooperation campaign; but the decline of both after 1922, led to a parallel decline in any broadly based sense of shared interest and a revival of communal confrontation. Throughout the 1920s, attempts were made to resolve divisive issues at the provincial level (C. R. Das' Bengal Pact, 1923) and at the centre (the Nehru Report, 1928), culminating in the All-Parties conference; but the compromises achieved at the table always failed to include many influential and articulate leaders with large and loyal constituencies. Jinnah produced his fourteen points in March 1929, moving the argument for distinctive Muslim needs and identity another step toward the 1940 'Pakistan Resolution' at the League's meeting in Lahore. The Round Table conferences in the early 1930s and in particular the Communal Award of 1932, supported this thrust, producing a political 'settlement' that institutionalized the solitudes that clearly existed.

In the elections of 1937, the Congress failed to attract substantial support in Muslim constituencies, and in February 1937, the Working Committee under particular pressure from Jawaharlal Nehru, approved a recommendation for the establishment of a Muslim Mass Contact programme. In October the Congress agreed. The thrust of the programme was the carrying of the Congress unity message directly to the Muslim masses who, it was argued, had been misled and betrayed by an elite concerned only with its own interests. It was assumed that a message founded on Marxist class categories would make clear that there was no difference between a poor Muslim and a poor Hindu; and that only the Congress was capable of redressing real economic grievances which had been cunningly represented as communal conflicts. Nehru appointed Dr K. M. Ashraf, the Muslim Secretary of the Congress Political and Economic Information Department to head the special cell established to achieve this goal.

Ashraf contacted the editors of influential Muslim newspapers and toured extensively with his class-conflict–communal-unity message. He was wary of formal conferences which produced recommendations for pacts or negotiations with Muslim organizations. The old methods of dealing with Jinnah and the League in this way, he insisted, had produced further disunity and were 'fraught with dangers'.[89] Ashraf attacked the aggressively communalist section of the Urdu press – 'sometimes one despairs of Hindustani journalism'; and was cautioned by Syed Brelvi, the editor of the *Bombay Chronicle*, 'not to do anything unwittingly that might hurt the sentiments of the Mussalmans, specifically in respect to their language'.[90] There was, Ashraf insisted, no alternative for Muslims to the Congress programme. And within that broad-based movement, only those who perceived the fundamental issues through a Marxist perspective were worthy of attention. But he recognized that 'you Muslims fight shy of that scientific programme'.[91]

In response to the congress message, Ashraf was continually told that Muslim communalism was a product of Hindu communalism. The Punjab *Sunrise* noted that Ashraf was a good example of Muslim support for the Congress cause, although Muslims were often accused of being anti-nationalist. But this apparent support was quickly turned to defensive challenge. 'How many men has Benares contributed?', asked this

[89] K. M. Ashraf to S. A. Brelvi, 23 April 1937, AICC G-68/1937.
[90] S. A. Brelvi to K. M. Ashraf, 26 April 1937, *ibid.*
[91] K. M. Ashraf to Dr Abdul Hami Qasi, 20 May 1937, *ibid.*

writer. Certainly Malaviya was no nationalist. His 'deep Mahasabhite designs' it was argued, reflected the views of 'an ardent Hindu who dreams of the day when India will be secure under Hindu Raj'. The article concluded by noting that congressmen, both Hindu and Muslim, always forgot, that a communal leader could not attract a large following if the mass of the Muslim minority had nothing to fear from the Hindu majority.[92]

Ashraf received a steady flow of correspondence from Muslims throughout the country describing 'the defeat of a Muslim candidate through Hindu communalism'; the confrontation between Congress Muslim and Muslim communalists; Nair Congress leaders' opposition to the accredited Muslim Congress leader of Kerala.[93] And those who perceived themselves to be representatives of the Hindu interest responded as well. Punjab has become a happy hunting ground for Congress propaganda, noted one letter to the editor of the *Eastern Times*. The 'surreptitious propaganda on the part of the Congress to lead astray the Muslim community from the path of well-ordered progress and constitutionalism is not without any sinister import ... what has the Congress done to alleviate the conditions of the Hindu masses let alone the Muslim masses?'[94]

Hindu Congressmen were often no less sceptical of the results of the campaign which appeared to 'flood our Muslim Brethren' with propaganda literature, press stories, Urdu handbills, and Congress meetings specifically for the Muslims.[95] From its inception, this movement to reduce communal tensions and enhance unity produced conflict and a range of responses which tended to enhance the idea of distinctive identity.

In July 1938, Hassan Habib, the editor of the *Agra Citizen*, wrote to Ashraf, noting his respect for the Congress and his faith in the Muslim League as only a temporary measure. But the differences between the two communities were, in his view, significant and undebatable. 'A Musalman is more democratic, more independent, more liberal in his outlook than a hundred Hindus combined.' It was, Habib noted, the Indian Muslim's misfortune to have imbibed 'some of the spirit of submission ... which

---

[92] Cutting from the *Sunrise*, 19 June 1937, AICC 48/1937.
[93] Secretary, District Congress Committee, Mahaba, Hamirpur, to K. M. Ashraf, 3 July 1937, AICC 38/1937; Shams-ul-Huda, Secretary, Barabazar Congress Committee, Calcutta, to K. M. Ashraf, 3 August 1937, AICC 49/1937; President, Congress Propaganda Committee, Parappil Calicut to President, AICC, 5 August 1937, AICC 47/1937.
[94] Letter to editor, *Eastern Times*, 'Sinister Congress Propaganda in Punjab', n.d., AICC 49/1937.
[95] Manzar Rizvi to District Congress Committee, Jubbulpore, 12 December 1937, AICC 54/1937.

characterizes the Hindu', insisting that it was only the British impact on the Hindu pocketbook that had turned them into nationalists. Muslims, however, lacked a nationalistic outlook. It was possible to bring them into the movement, but this would require Congress–League cooperation; and the contact had to be made on terms that reflected respect for distinctive identity rather than seek to absorb them into some imaginative unity. 'It is hypocrisy to sit on the high Congress gaddi and call out to the Musalmans below to come up.'[96]

In his response, Ashraf agreed that there were problems within the Congress which had its share of reactionaries and divisions. But he insisted that the Muslim community could not achieve freedom on its own; a national struggle was required. Implicitly accepting Habib's profile of a Muslim, Ashraf suggested that they should join in order to enhance the progressive forces in the Congress. He concluded with a restatement of the message that he had carried across the United Provinces and the Punjab. 'I do not subscribe to the belief that Muslims can be united on the basis of a common political belief. Politics is essentially dictated by class interests.'[97]

Jawaharlal Nehru had urged the Working Committee to establish the Contact Movement, and he was its most articulate spokesman throughout 1937. His message, like Ashraf's denied legitimacy to any politicized communal identity, insisting that the only pertinent issue was poverty and the need for class struggle to alleviate it. 'The realities of today are poverty and hunger and unemployment ... How are these to be considered communally?'[98] In his position as Congress President, Nehru insisted that he represented innumerable Muslims, particularly the poor. 'I represent the hunger and poverty of the masses, Muslim as well as Hindu; the demand for bread and land and work and relief from innumerable burdens which crush them; the urge to freedom from an intolerable oppression.'[99]

He attacked all those who insisted on Hindu rights and Muslim interests as 'job hunters' who were simply seeking the benefits of office. 'How long are you going to tolerate this nonsense,' he queried, 'this absurdity?'[100] In a Bombay speech, he reminded his audience, as he had

[96] Hassan Habib, ed., *Agra Citizen*, to K. M. Ashraf, 6 July 1938, AICC G-68/1937.
[97] K. M. Ashraf to H. Habib, 15 July 1938, *ibid.*
[98] J. Nehru, 'The Congress and the Muslims', press statement, Purnea, 10 January 1937, published in *Hindustan Times*, 12 January 1937, cited in *Selected Works of Jawaharlal Nehru*, Vol. VIII, New Delhi: Orient Longman, 1975, pp. 119–22.
[99] *Ibid.*
[100] J. Nehru speech, Ambala, 16 January 1937, published in *Hindustan Times*, 18 January 1937, cited in *ibid.*, pp. 7–9.

done throughout his tour, that the primary struggle was with British imperialism. In a sentence, he described the divide and rule technique of their rulers who attacked socialism and posed as sympathizers of both Islam and Hinduism. 'The real fact is that they do not want us to think in political and economic terms for once we grasp these realities we shall no longer submit to imperialist domination.'[101] At a meeting in Ahmedabad, he reiterated his call for unity and his insistence that Muslims had no choice. 'Congress is a force which no one can resist.' It had routed the Hindu Sabha, he declared, and the Muslim League was significant only in a few provinces and remained a party of the upper classes.[102] Nehru's performance was the kind of aggressive demand for unity that had attracted so many and repelled large numbers as well. The Muslim Mass Contact work continued for another year, but with diminishing enthusiasm among workers, increasing concern among conservative Congress leaders, and relatively little impact on the rural Muslim constituency that was being mobilized. In September 1938 Ashraf wrote to Nehru, who was in Europe, noting the formal abolition of the programme and his deeply felt frustration with the current situation in the Congress. 'Socialists should be sure of a majority in the Working Committee', he told Nehru, 'before they put their ideas into definite shape'.[103]

Jawaharlal Nehru's personal campaign

Jawaharlal Nehru deliberately placed himself at the central interchange of the incoming and outgoing messages which linked the Congress with All-India and the world outside. His breadth of experience, a perspective – which tended to isolate him from his colleagues – and the longevity of his participation in the Congress Secretariat, allowed him a virtual free reign over information policy – especially concerning the outside world. And he moved with ease from village to international platform – informing his speeches and writing for one with knowledge and understanding gained from the other. Nehru insisted that he was 'not a literary man', and 'not a historian' – just a 'dabbler in many things'. But words flowed easily and stylishly from his pen and – because he responded emotionally and intellectually to experience and events – his descriptions and arguments often produced a similar response in others, whether one agreed with him or not. He was a 'great communicator'. It could be argued that virtually

[101] J. Nehru speech, Madanpura, Bombay, 11 April 1937, published in *Bombay Chronicle*, 12 August 1937, cited in *ibid.*, pp. 173–5.
[102] J. Nehru, speech at Muslim meeting, Ahmedabad, 17 September 1937, published in *Hindustan Times*, 19 September 1937 cited in *ibid.*, p. 178.
[103] K. M. Ashraf to J. Nehru, 2 September 1938, Jawaharlal Nehru Papers, A 100.

everything Jawaharlal Nehru wrote before 1947 – and in significant measure after – was a form of propaganda, of advocacy of well defined and consistently held principles, ideology, and goals.

In the late 1920s, Nehru had cast himself in the role of mediator of Indian nationalism's relations with the West. He was not the first, but his 'West' subsumed the broad range of continental ideological position and conflict and produced concern, sometimes dismay, among colleagues still content with the nineteenth-century legacy of the British liberal tradition. S. N. Banerjee noted in his autobiography that Mazzini was his guide; but his was a moderate nationalist Mazzini. His 'patriotism' and the 'loftiness of his ideals' were useful, Banerjee noted, but his revolutionary teachings had to be discarded 'as unsuited to the circumstances of India'.[104] Nehru, however, advocated and described with pleasure a leftward blowing 'mental wind', perhaps only 'a gentle breeze' but a reflection of significant change. 'The younger men and women of the Congress, who used to read Bryce on democracies and Morley and Keith and Mazzini', he noted, 'were now reading, when they could get them, books on socialism and communism and Russia.'[105]

Within India, Nehru also cast his net broadly, following Gandhi into the villages and into an All-India perspective which included the peasant masses. Conceptualizing and personalizing this part of the equation was, however, far more difficult for him, and he sought throughout his career an access point for himself and his modernizing message. His description of the 'Indian problem' always reflected ambivalence in perspective and purpose. He criticized Indian marriages as 'wasteful', 'vulgar', and 'extravagant', but felt compelled to note the benefits as well: a little colour in the drab life of the peasant; the ingathering of family for the middle classes. He denounced religion in India. 'Blind belief and reaction, dogma and bigotry, superstition and exploitation, and the preservation of vested interests'. But he was convinced there had to be something else, an Indian essence which 'supplied a deep inner craving of human beings'.[106]

Nehru searched, through his speeches and writing, for a source of easy companionship with Indians and India – something that would allow him to be comfortable in the two worlds he occupied; some indication that the whole of India was capable of modernization and change. But he continued to return to the theme of separation between two worlds, and doubts about his capacity to reach out and lead both to some rational and practical synthesis. He discovered the 'old witchery' everywhere,

---

[104] S. N. Banerjee, *A Nation in Making*, Bombay: Oxford University Press, 1925, p. 40.
[105] J. Nehru, *Toward Freedom*, Boston: Beacon Press, 1967, p. 232.
[106] *Ibid.*, p. 241.

implicitly reflecting well-known British stereotypes, the images of the West's East, and his own fears.

To add to his difficulties, Nehru rejected Marxist orthodoxy offending a range of radical individuals and groups – in Europe and India, who were blessed with ideological certainty. He was a link figure in every case, owned by no group, committed to no absolute creed – on the margin and reaching in or out. He sought deliberately to settle his own ideological identity in a carefully balanced mix of liberal democrat and socialist – one designed as much for him as for India. But his ideology and the 'truth' it was meant to achieve would have to secure and attract a range of constituencies virtually all unaware of or opposed to the mission, if not the missionary. He considered himself to be a pragmatist, but others perceived a major flaw in his commitment to theory and his misunderstanding of the realities of a situation.[107]

His advocacy of land reform attracted both support and concern as he carried the message of social and economic revolution into the villages, and organized Kisan Sabhas as a base for mobilization and pressure from below. Although he attempted to placate more conservative Congress colleagues by emphasizing his nationalist rather than nationalizationist priority – his message was tough and direct and – for many – frightening. Swaraj in India, he insisted in a flow of Hindi leaflets and speeches is 'not of the capitalist but of the poor and the peasants'.[108] Zamindars and taluqdars were 'leeches attacking the body of the Indian peasants'; and he urged them to join the campaign. The key phrase in his speeches to Kisan meetings was always the same – 'Their troubles can be removed when the country attains Swaraj.' And in turn, Swaraj was equated with the removal of the poverty of the masses. For the short term he sought rent remission but he emphasized the goal – when freedom was achieved – of permanent remission of rent and revenue.[109]

When he returned from Europe in 1936, Nehru's socialist commitment had become more intense and this was reflected in his speeches to large peasant gatherings. This time, however, his conservative Working Committee colleagues would not be placated and Rajendra Prasad and a group of seven members resigned in protest against a socialist campaign they viewed as a personal attack on their leadership roles. 'We feel that the preaching and emphasizing of socialism particularly at this stage by

[107] Abul Kalam Azad argued that Nehru's 'weakness for theoretical considerations' affected the outcome of negotiations for a federal constitution. A. K. Azad, *India Wins Freedom*, Bombay: Orient Longmans, 1959, p. 129.

[108] J. Nehru, 'To the Kisans', translation of a Hindi leaflet distributed at the Pushkar Fair, 23 November 1931, *Selected Works of Jawaharlal Nehru*, Vol. V, p. 179.

[109] *Ibid.*

the President ... while the Congress has not adopted it is prejudicial to
the best interests of the country.'[110] Gandhi's intervention led to a truce,
but the confrontation enhanced Nehru's sense of isolation and affected
his confidence in his ability to play the role he had designed for himself.
He was, however, used to life on the margin, to being the outsider, and
such incidents only created a brief pause in his personal campaign.

The debate regarding the substitution of Nehru for Gandhi as Congress
President in 1929, reflected the fundamental ideological differences which
informed the internal struggles of the Congress high command. Typically
for Nehru, it began in compromise. His father had urged Gandhi to pass
the responsibility to the new generation represented by his son, a move
that would not require a complete withdrawal. His analysis of the current
situation indicated 'that the need of [the] hour is the head of Gandhi and
the voice of Jawaharlal'.[111] The younger Nehru was convinced, however,
that he was the wrong choice. 'I represent nobody but myself', he declared
in a letter to Gandhi, urgining him to look elsewhere. 'If I have the
misfortune to be president, you will see that the very people who put me
there ... will be prepared to cast me to the wolves.'[112] Gandhi, however,
had already made up his mind. Although he recognized that Nehru was
'an extremist, thinking far ahead of his surroundings', Gandhi was confident that he was 'humble enough and practical enough not to force the
pace to the breaking point'.[113] It was a safe gamble.

While Nehru insisted that it was 'not possible to ride a number of
horses at the same time',[114] he managed the feat by accepting a largely
symbolic role of 'leader of leaders'. He became, in fact, an expert per-
former of this equestrian feat. In his presidential address to the 1929
Lahore Congress, Nehru made clear his awareness that he was not the
popular choice for the office – blaming fate and Gandhi for conspiring
together and thrusting 'me against your will and mine into the terrible seat
of responsibility'.[115] But, having accepted the job, he pressed his mission,
turning the office into an entrepôt for the great exchange of ideas and
ideology that he considered essential for the vitality of the nationalist
programme. He sought to place the Indian nationalist struggle in an
international context. 'You are not the only people who are faced with

[110] Rajendra Prasad and others to J. Nehru, 29 June 1936, cited in D. Norman, ed., *Nehru:
The First 60 Years*, Vol. I, Bombay: Asia Publishing House, 1965, p. 454.
[111] M. Nehru to M. K. Gandhi, 13 July 1929, *ibid.*, pp.189–90.
[112] J. Nehru to M. K. Gandhi, 9 July 1929, *ibid.*, p. 190.
[113] M. K. Gandhi, 6 July 1929, *ibid.*, p. 191.
[114] J. Nehru to M. K. Gandhi, July 1929, *ibid.*, p. 193.
[115] J. Nehru presidential address, 44th Congress, Lahore, 1929, in *Congress Presidential
Addresses*, Madras: G. A. Natesan, 2nd edition, 1934, p. 885.

problems', he declared, and described a world that was 'one vast question mark' with every country and people 'in the melting pot'.[116] Unlike the selected cultural gifts brought by the British, he noted the West now offered a range of options, opportunities, and dangers because the old verities were no longer safe.

Nehru insisted that nationalism alone was no longer enough. And its sources in the colonially mediated ideology were in the process of fundamental change and challenge. 'We appear to be in a dissolving period of history,' he suggested,'when the world is in labour and out of her travail will give birth to a new order.'[117] India had to be part of it. Whether those to whom he carried his message were aware of it or not, India, he insisted, was already part of a world movement in which China, Turkey, Egypt, Persia, Russia, and the countries of the West were all involved. If India 'ignores the world' he continued, 'we do so at our peril'. India had messages to send out but many that had to be received.[118]

For Nehru, the burden of the incoming traffic was clear as was his role as messenger. 'I must frankly confess that I am a socialist and a republican', he declared, but noted in the next sentence his recognition that the Congress would not adopt a socialistic programme.[119] He insisted, however, that only the pace and method of advance was in doubt. Socialism was in India's and the world's future. From his position at the transition point – on the margin of both the conservative convictions of Congress colleagues and the orthodox creed of communist revolutionaries, he was in turn rejected and embraced by both and from this self-constructed vantage point he mounted his personal campaign – generally defensive, sometimes aggressive, always intermixed with periods of disillusionment and withdrawal.

In a series of speeches and press statements in December 1928, Nehru described anti-Simon Commission demonstrations in Lucknow and Allahabad. What raises the quality of his words to the level of art – both a piece of literature and a piece of effective propaganda – is Nehru's highly personal description of a *lathi* charge and his response to being beaten for the first time. He describes the organization of the procession; the horses of the police bearing down on them; the question that crosses his mind of whether to run; the feel of the blows – and the exultation of courage, having survived a test and achieved a personal victory.

---

[116] *Ibid.*
[117] *Ibid.*
[118] *Ibid.*, p. 886.
[119] *Ibid.*, pp. 894–5.

I am thoroughly pleased at the new experience and at having found out that my back is strong and solid enough not to give way before *lathi* and baton blows.[120]

He declared it a magnificent demonstration: 'Even to see it was enough to make a sick man well.' And then he concludes with the lesson – the truth that this experience has produced.

They have brought the real issue before the people of the country bereft of all sophistries and legal quibbles. That issue is that British rule in India means the policeman's baton and the bayonet and the real problem is how to overcome them. Logic and reason is unhappily lost on the baton and the bayonet.[121]

In his 1937 pre-election tour, Nehru's omnipresence and his sense of status and power as Congress President carry over an inherent sense of 'greatness' to the vast crowds he encounters. It flowed in part from his distance, only passing through, sharing a few minutes sufficient for a *darshan* experience and then moving on – a prophet needing to carry his message to as many as possible. In January and February he toured for thirty days, covering 50,000 miles by rail, road, and air. He visited every province except Gujarat, the North West Frontier and Assam, holding ten to twelve meetings a day and speaking to approximately 10,000,000 people.[122] Nehru presumes in his message a vast personal constituency. Entering Bihar, he addresses everyone, 'Comrades of Bihar ... I come to you after several years.'[123] And at the end of his tour, when leaving the south, he addresses the 'South'. First describing the north's response to the Congress campaign: 'their thundering cry for freedom reverberates through the broad plains and valleys of Hindustan' and then to the south: 'What echo does that find in your hearts? Does not your blood quicken in your veins at the heartening cry of the masses? India awaits your own grave response.'[124]

Nehru rejected and them embraced Gandhi as he rejected and embraced India. He had the option of choosing those messages from the West that seemed the most useful for the solution of India's problems as he perceived them. But the need to meld that choice with an Indian reality which would not be totally displaced was increasingly apparent, if not in his rhetoric, in his willingness to adapt and accommodate. 'Our politics

[120] J. Nehru statement on lathi charge at Lucknow, 1 December 1928, the *Tribune*, 4 December 1928; cited in *Selected Works of Jawaharlal Nehru*, Vol. III, pp. 115–16.
[121] J. Nehru press statement, Allahabad, 1 December 1928, the *Leader*, 3 December 1928, cited in *ibid.*, pp. 108–15.
[122] J. Nehru, pre-election tour, January–February, 1937, cited in *ibid.*, Vol. VIII, pp. 42–3.
[123] J. Nehru press statement, 5 January 1937, *Indian Nation*, 6 January 1937, cited in *ibid.*, p. 4.
[124] J. Nehru, message to South and West India, Belapur, 16 February 1937, published in *Hindu*, 16 February 1937, cited in *ibid.*, pp. 27–8.

must either be those of magic or of science', he insisted, but he knew that the continuing mystery would not be easily solved. Through socialism he thought he had found a way to connect with the traditional group base of Hindu society;[125] but like Banerjee's excision of Mazzini's revolutionary message, this Indian socialism had to be adapted to Indian circumstance. In the context of the commitment to non-violence and national unity, it was an inevitable accommodation, a replication of the standoff between Gandhi's East and Nehru's West, which mandated a second-best solution for both.

The nationalist press: a life of its own

The multiplicity of 'centres' which competed for influence and place in the evolving Indian nation's internecine struggles included the press both on its own terms and as camp followers of others. Below its masthead, the *Hindu* declared itself 'India's National Newspaper', and its editors held court in the old Hindu building on 100 Mount Road with no less confidence in their role and mission than the political princes of the AICC and Working Committee. For Rangaswami Parthasarathy, the day he gave his notice to the Anglo-Indian *Mail* and joined the staff of the *Hindu*, he entered 'the gates of heaven'. For this professional newspaperman, joining the *Hindu* as a 'sub' was no less a signal of commitment to the national struggle than the decision made by others to abandon law practices or Government posts and become full-time Congress workers. Parthasarathy described the 'shame and agony of working in an anti-nationalist newspaper where you mortgaged your conscience and sold your soul'. The move to the *Hindu* had ended that agony, because this national institution provided its staff with the opportunity to 'breathe the free air of nationalism and join the patriotic forces'.[126] But the commander of this army was Kasturi Srinivasan,[127] not Nehru nor Gandhi; and the interests of the paper and the professional traditions of the press informed perspective and sometimes constrained cooperation from the point of view of the 'full-timers'. Such was the context of Sardar Petal's frustration with critical rather than loyal press support; and Jawaharlal Nehru's concern with the illusion of normality that seemed to pervade such places as the large room where Parthasarathy worked in one of the batches of subeditors whose primary goal was the production of an error-free issue of the *Hindu*.

[125] See Francine Frankel, *India's Political Economy, 1947–1977*, Princeton University Press, 1978, Chapter 1, pp. 3–27.
[126] Rangaswami Parthasarathy, *Memoirs of a News Editor*, Calcutta: Naya Prakash, 1980, p. 72.
[127] Kasturi Srinivasan was the proprietor of the *Hindu*.

Ashis Nandy has described the 'secular hierarchies incompatible with the traditional order' which attracted so many Western-educated Indians to a collaborative relationship with the Raj.[128] The result he suggests was a 'second colonialism' which produced a 'shared culture', and a state of mind that allowed one to be at home in it. It was this apparently easy adaptation – not to their profession, but to the perception that they were pursuing it in a context of normality – that so irritated Nehru when significant elements of the Indian national press did not loyally support India's nationalist leaders. In a letter to the editor of the *Amrita Bazaar Patrika*, he responded to an attack on the Congress Working Committee for operating secretly.

People forget sometimes that we are functioning abnormally. They discuss the constitutional issue in terms of normality or they criticise the Congress for its inactivity, forgetting that the Congress has arrived at a certain stage of historical growth. It is not at present a constitutional or legal body and many of the safe and brave deeds that are performed on public platforms are no longer in its line. Constitutionalists naturally dislike this; they cannot function in an illegal atmosphere. But why should those who think in terms of revolutionary change object to this inevitable and desirable development?[129]

M. Chalapathi Rau, one of the muster of young southerners who travelled north with their good English educations to serve the major national press, has described the formidable personalities who dominated these papers and journals in the 1930s, insisting on a life of their own making – a nationalist role of their own choosing. As a student in Madras, he described the *Hindu* as 'our daily bible', and the virtually mythic reputation of that institution and the extraordinary family that owned and edited it was widely endorsed throughout the country. But there was Annie Besant as well, who wrote 'passionate and clear prose' for her *New India*; and A. Ramaswami Mudaliar, who served his own mission in the *Daily Express*, by 'hurling his Disraelian invective on all Brahmins passing by'. In Calcutta, Ramananda Chatterjee's *Modern Review* continually called attention to the cultural and intellectual life of the country which, he insisted, retained its creativity even in the midst of political struggle. Chatterjee argued that nation building required more than a political perspective, but his scholarly, often pedantic style, limited his readership, and as Rau noted, he 'rather scared us with his intimacy with Radindranath Tagore and other grey-beards'. Rau's view of C. Y. Chintamani may well have been influenced by Jawaharlal Nehru's impatient

---

[128] Ashis Nandy, *The Intimate Enemy: Loss and Recovery of Self Under Colonialism*, Delhi: Oxford University Press, 1983, pp. ix-xi, 3.
[129] Jawaharlal Nehru to editor *Amrita Bazar Patrika*, 24 November 1933, Jawaharlal Nehru Papers, E-3 (V).

critique during the years he worked for Nehru's *National Herald*. He joked about Chintamani's 'elephantine syntax' and a technique that was 'archaic even in his life-time'. But he noted as well that 'the Chintamanis had individuality, personality, character', regrettably lacking among most of their successors. Other examples of this genus were the reclusive Kalinath Roy who edited the *Tribune* and delivered his opinions 'somewhere in the north ... logic chopping'; and K. Natarajan, whose editorship of the *Indian Social Reformer* was a widely respected, although generally unsupported mission and who inspired 'awe with his austere pronouncements' among a loyal following and the professional press fraternity.[130]

Professionalism might be placed in the service of nationalism, but for those who were serious about their calling, news tended to be given as high a priority as views, and a range of protagonists found some notice in their columns. Those who argued that official action and pronouncements should not be given space in nationalist papers were no more successful with this group than the defensive civil servants who cautioned information officers about the dangers of enhancing the reputations of nationalist leaders by recognizing their special status in print. And nationalism produced such a range of viewpoint, that loyalty in any case required a particular political judgement. The Congress attempted to provide something for everyone, a synthetic nationalism with which all could identify. But however successful it became in dominating the struggle, it failed to achieve its goal. The Raj was a monolithic target. Nationalism remained eclectic, providing a place for a multiplicity of groups to play out their roles under its overarching umbrella.

Pothan Joseph noted in his memoirs that he had held twenty-six jobs in his career as a newspaperman. All of them had been held 'in honour' and he saw no need to differentiate among those with nationalist or Anglo-Indian papers, or with the Government of India which he served as news editor of the Indian State Broadcasting Service. 'Patriotism in territorial terms', he argued 'to me has not been a substantive virtue as compared with radical humanitarianism.'[131] And there was as much professional satisfaction in breaking the European monopoly on the editorial staff of *Capital* as in the memory of riding to a conference at Anand Bhavan in a railway compartment with Tilak and Kharparde. Joseph interviewed Tilak while his companion G. S. Raghavan took

---

[130] M. Chalapathi Rau, *Journalism and Politics*, New Delhi: Vikas Publishing House, PVT Ltd, 1984.
[131] Joseph, *Glimpses of Yesterday*, p. 8.

down notes.[132] Motilal Ghose had suggested to Gandhi when the Congress adopted Non-cooperation as its policy, that there should be concessions for professionals, lawyers, and the educated classes generally. But Gandhi refused and left them all to deal with their own interests and consciences.[133]

In 1922, fearing that he was near the end of his life, Ghose's principal concern was the future of the *Amrita Bazaar Patrika*. He told M. R. Jayakar that he thought the paper might collapse after his death and urged him to accept a contract to contribute articles on a regular basis. Throughout his life, Ghose had measured achievement in terms of the successes of the *Patrika*. His struggles with S. N. Banerjee and the *Bengalee* were both professional and political. He admitted that Banerjee was a better platform speaker, but insisted that his editorials were far superior.[134] And he strove to be competitive with peers throughout India. Paramananda Dutt has responded to Ramsay MacDonald's comment on Ghose's large, crowded, and crumbling house by noting that in the adjacent printing house, the Linotype machines were at work. MacDonald had neglected to note that 'this queer Bengali had installed them years before they were adopted by his English contemporaries in Calcutta'.[135]

Survival in a competitive professional world while denied an even playing field by an alien imperial regime, required extraordinary and continuing effort. The *Leader*, the *Hindu*, and the *Amrita Bazaar Patrika* were generally profit-making enterprises. All of them tended to dominate a particular provincial market, especially the *Patrika* in Calcutta. And the policies of the *Hindu* and the *Leader* were sufficiently respectful of official interests and sensitivities to allow the regular flow of Government advertisement and a large and mixed readership. But these were anomalies in a profession where struggle for survival was the norm. There were a variety of potential sources for press revenue. Since most of the large basic industries and business houses were British-owned, their advertising generally went to the Anglo-Indian press with only a small portion spread around the larger Indian-owned papers. Among these, the Liberal and independent press benefited far more than nationalist enterprises, and even this meagre revenue source diminished in phase with an editor's enthusiasm for the Indian political struggle.

---

[132] *Ibid.*, pp. 34–5.
[133] Motilal Ghose and M. R. Jayakar exchange of correspondence, 25 February 1922, 10 March 1922, 17 March 1922, Jayakar Papers.
[134] Paramananda Dutt, *Memoirs of Motilal Ghose*, Calcutta: Amrita Bazaar Patrika Office, 1935, pp. 335–6.
[135] *Ibid.*, p. 375.

The reluctance of the business community to advertise in the Indian press was as much a reflection of self-interest as concern for particular interests of the Government of India. When it seemed likely that Indian customers might be attracted to their product, advertisements began to flow to Indian papers. It was a commercial decision, which aided the Anglo-Indian press for a long period, and subsequently would aid the Indian-controlled press. Similarly, official advertising generally went to the standard British press but the flow to selective Indian papers increased dramatically in the late 1920s, and for the same reasons. The change was important as Government departments at all levels of the Raj had advertising budgets, and a relatively small increase in revenue made a difference to the stability of struggling papers. J. N. Sahni has noted that the *Statesman* lost approximately Rs 8 lakhs a year in Government advertising revenue after the transfer of power in 1947. Attempts by the Government of India and Local Governments to purchase the good behaviour of influential newspapers by manipulating their advertising budgets were generally unsuccessful, but once that advertising income began to flow to nationalist papers, there was a desire to keep it and avoid the kind of confrontation that might put it at risk. Most of the vernacular press had no possibility of receiving advertising income from either business or Government, and those committed to extremist positions used another calculation and ran different risks. Many were one issue propaganda sheets and the possibility of their demise was accepted as an ordinary cost of doing business. But for the major national press – both Indian and Anglo-Indian – there was a sense of institutional identity committed to survival.

Aside from ordinary advertising, there were a range of subsidy arrangements that kept small papers alive or provided a bit of gravy for the majors. J. N. Sahni has noted the example of one British firm that paid the *Statesman* Rs 48,000 per year for the publication of a quotation which appeared above the editorial. The company had nothing to advertise.[136] Government provided an implicit subsidy to the Anglo-Indian press by being such a good and stable customer. It was its press; and subscriptions to one or more of these papers were part of the ordinary cost of living in India for every department, service club, and military mess. And every Anglo-Indian family required the *Pioneer* or the *Statesman*, the *Times of India*, or the *Mail* on their tea trays or breakfast tables. These papers with their larger budgets, more professional formats, easy access to the news services and correspondents which provided the latest news and

[136] J. N. Sahni Interview, December 1970. The company was Bommer and Lawry (iron and steel).

viewpoint, greater coverage of British and world events, and intimacy with the Government of India, were bought and read by the Indian educated elite as well.

The nationalist press was patronized by Indian businessmen and companies by the purchase of shares which would never produce an income and by advertising. The latter was also good for their businesses. There was usually a mix of practical interest and patriotic responsibility that attracted Indian businessmen to invest in the press. Swaminath Sadanand and his business patrons used each other to allow the launching of the FPI news service and the *Free Press Journal*. The *Bombay Chronicle* required the interest and support of Indian merchants and bankers, and the *Hindustan Times* was maintained by Birla resources. With the exception of the few profit makers with significant advertising revenue, Indian newspapers were too dependent on circulation for their basic income and there simply were not enough customers.[137] As a result, competition in major centres among a number of papers often required them to ignore the fact that they shared a commitment to the same nationalist struggle. In many cases they were committed to different camps and viewpoints that required confrontation for political reasons. But the ordinary press competition for customers, and, therefore, for survival as a business, was present as well. In a few cases the competition included the Anglo-Indian press. The *Hindu* had no difficulty competing with the *Mail*, which generally considered itself the underdog in Madras by the late 1920s; and the *Times of India* and *Bombay Chronicle* were always conscious of the presence of the other in this period. But there remained little contact and competition between these two groups. The Anglo-Indian press had been reduced to one major paper in each metropolitan centre by an internal competition enforced by a changing market. And the Indian press competed as well with its own kind.

There was substantial public giving to the press, especially to meet the cost of Government-imposed security deposits. The *Hindustan Times* conducted a successful campaign to meet these losses. The *National Herald* at the end of the 1930s like the *Free Press Journal* in an earlier struggle attracted sufficient support to neutralize the impact of official pressure and stimulate the Government to recognize its inability to 'beat them' and the need to find some way to 'join them'. Many of these papers ran at a loss as an accepted cost of doing business; and loyal share- and debenture holders tended to concentrate their energies on limiting the

---

[137] *Ibid.*, balance sheets for the *National Herald* (J. Nehru Papers) and the *Bombay Chronicle*, *Free Press of India*, and *Indian Social Reformer* (M. R. Jayakar Papers) reveal the same problem. See also Sahni, *The Indian Press*.

increase in the annual shortfall rather than reducing their burdens or even considering the possibility of profit. J. B. Petit committed himself and his fortune to the *Indian Daily Mail*, accepting the inevitable losses, while a paper like the *Indian Social Reformer* attracted the patronage of a small number of loyal shareholders who considered the *Reformer* and its editor, K. Natarajan, to be national institutions, and the survival of both to be a patriotic cause. But these wealthy patrons tended to settle for bare survival and Natarajan was required to meet his personal and family expenses by writing for more affluent papers.[138] Major papers like the *Bombay Chronicle* survived because they provided an influential base for propagating viewpoint and attracted the interest of leaders who managed to gather sufficient support to maintain the company. There were those who remained convinced that there was the possibility for an Indian-owned paper to make a profit in a large marketplace like Bombay. The Cama family bought and held on to the *Chronicle* as a business investment.

There was more than one way, however, for a paper to lose its independence. J. N. Sahni has provided a description of the transition of the *Hindustan Times* from its founding mission as a vehicle for Akali propaganda, funded by the Maharaja of Nabha and other Sikh sources to a more broadly based nationalist enterprise, funded by a combination of loans and grants to M. M. Malaviya. The principal investors in this new enterprise were the Birlas, who already owned a number of newspapers in Bengal. From the beginning, the personal agenda of the directors found space in the paper. For Malaviya and his colleagues Lajpat Rai and M. R. Jayakar this generally meant support for Hindu Sanatanist interests, although there was no requirement that editorial policy follow the same line. In the case of G. D. Birla, his financial interests would generally be reflected in a long supportive article, but again with no requirement of editorial support. Throughout the 1920s, it seemed possible to balance this mix of interest and control in support of a nationalist paper loyal to the Congress. By the early 1930s, however, Birla joined the Board and eventually recast its membership to suit a more restrained political and business agenda. The paper remained nationalist, but Sahni, who had resigned in the midst of this 'takeover' decided there was room in Delhi for a committed Congress paper and founded the *National Call*. Its politics were clearly demonstrated in its Board, chaired by Dr Ansari, the President of the Congress, and made up entirely of Congress leaders.[139] It seemed clear that the kind of loyalty sought by Congress leaders at the

---

[138] K. Natarajan to M. R. Jayakar, 24 December 1929, Jayakar Papers, 606.
[139] J. N. Sahni interview, December 1970.

centre required virtual ownership of a paper, with no opportunity for a takeover.

The princes tried not to antagonize the Government of India, but many were convinced that their interests might be protected by influencing nationalist opinion, usually through the medium of the nationalist press. The Maharaja of Nabha supported the Akali *Nation* and his interests, especially after his forced abdication in 1923, received strong support. Similarly, the *Indian National Herald* and the *Indian Daily Mail* in Bombay benefited from the spread of Nabha funds to virtually every major paper and many local vernacular papers in the Punjab, that would advocate his cause. Porbander and other states received support from the *Hindustan Times* and the paper benefited from princely advertising revenue and increased circulation in these states.[140] And J. B. Petit sought princely support for the *Indian Daily Mail* in 1928, when he decided to spread the financial burdens of ownership by converting to a public company. Petit was sufficiently moderate in his politics and concerned about the views of British officials, to make certain that there was no Government of India objection.

He contacted the Governor of Bombay, Sir Leslie Wilson, to seek his endorsement, noting that the Nizam, Bhopal, and the Jamsaheb of Nawanagar had indicated they would provide support if the Government approved. It was generally recognized in official circles that the *Indian Daily Mail* was moderate and well run, and that Petit should be supported. However, when the possibility of Nahba support was introduced, Political Department officials objected. 'If Petit wishes to stand well with the Government, he had better have nothing to do with it.'[141] After discussions with the Viceroy, Lord Irwin, and Wilson at Simla in May 1929, the Government of India indicated there was no objection to Petit seeking support from the princes. In addition Irwin agreed to speak to some of them on his behalf.[142] Substantial princely investment followed.[143]

In April 1928, the Governor of the Punjab, Sir Malcolm Hailey, wrote to the Home Member, enclosing an extract of a letter from Naoroji Dumasia, an employee of the *Times of India*. Dumasia pointed out that the Maharajah of Patiala had virtually saved the *Bombay Chronicle* from collapse by the timely investment of Rs 1 lakh, and that additional purchases of *Chronicle* debentures had been made by the Jamsaheb of

---

[140] *Ibid.*
[141] Telegram, 14 December 1928, (F & P) Political File No. 1-P (secret) 1929, R/1/29/413.
[142] C. C. Watson, Political Secretary to Government of India to J. B. Petit, 11 May 1929, 7 June 1929, *ibid.*
[143] J. B. Petit to C. C. Watson, 22 December 1928, *ibid.*

Nawanagar and the Maharao of Cutch. Dumasia suggested that the movement to boycott the Simon Commission might have died out in Bombay had not the proprietor of the *Chronicle* been such a successful intriguer,[144] and followed up this contact with a letter-writing campaign. He told the Home Member that Patiala was virtually the proprietor of the anti-Government *Chronicle*,[145] and emphasized to Rushbrook Williams that he only sought to help the Government in every possible way. He urged officials to contact Patiala and get him to sever his connections with the *Chronicle*.[146] There were continuing discussions within the Home Department about the financial affairs of the nationalist press and the possibility of inducing industrial and capitalist interests to use their resources 'to bring such papers as the *Forward*, the *Bombay Chronicle*, and so on to a better frame of mind.' But there was recognition of the delicacy of the situation which stimulated various princes to invest in the nationalist press to advance their own causes and prevent hostile criticism. Dumasia's association with the *Chronicle*'s major Anglo-Indian competitor was also noticed.[147]

The establishment of the Butler Committee to report on the relationship between the Government and the Indian states and possible adjustments that might be made in the future stimulated substantial princely propaganda in both India and Britain. A *Chronicle* editorial on 8 February 1928 is an example of the kind of support which they could purchase. 'No responsible Indian publicist contemplates the abolition of the Indian States or has any desire to countenance the violation of the legitimate treaty rights of the Indian Princes. The democratic and monarchic principles can certainly coexist and work together for the common good of India.'[148] The *Hindu* editorial page, however, was clearly not available to the princes, and they were attacked for their efforts 'to seek against a Government composed of their own countrymen, the protection which the coloured races need against their white exploiters'.[149] Dumasia also contacted the Jamsaheb and Patiala directly, emphasizing that the *Chronicle* was really an enemy of the princes and in any case, a losing investment.[150] And he maintained regular contact with the Government

---

[144] Sir Malcolm Hailey to James Crerar, 7 June 1928 (HomePol) 141.
[145] N. Dumasia to C. C. Watson, 12 April 1929 (F & P) Political, File No. 1-P (secret) 1929, R/1/29/413.
[146] Telegram to Rushbrook Williams, 12 April 1929, *ibid.*
[147] J. Coatman note, 4 January 1929, *ibid.*
[148] *Bombay Chronicle*, 8 February 1928.
[149] *Hindu*, 17 August 1929.
[150] N. Dumasia to Jamsaheb of Nawanagar, 13 April 1929; to Maharaja of Patiala, 16 April 1929 (F & P) Political, File No. 1-P (secret) 1929, R/1/29/413.

of India, noting the connection between a story favourable to a particular prince and an investment in the paper.[151]

On 2 May 1930, Lord Irwin wrote to Patiala, Bhopal, and the Jamsaheb noting the 'most unsatisfactory' attitudes of the *Chronicle*. He suggested that the calling up of the debentures currently held by the princes 'might prove so embarrassing to the editor and those responsible for the present policy and attitude of the paper that they might be compelled to modify them'.[152] In response, the Nawab of Bhopal told Irwin that he held no *Bombay Chronicle* debentures. He described a plan that might have led to Bhopal taking control of a number of papers, including the *Chronicle* which would have involved a commitment of 10 lakhs of rupees. To gain a lien on the *Chronicle*, Bhopal agreed to lend Rs 50,000 for three years to N. H. Belgaumwalla, the proprietor, on the security of debentures issued by *Samachar*, which Belgaumwalla also owned. Rs 25,000 were paid. Bhopal noted his willingness to call back the money on the *Samachar* debentures, but was uncertain whether they would comply with his request. He also mentioned his concern that the papers would 'insinuate all sorts of motives. They might go further and attribute my action to Government pressure on me'; and concluded with a pledge of loyalty and devotion to the Crown.[153]

Patiala told Irwin that he had purchased Rs 1 lakh's worth of *Chronicle* debentures on the advice of Nawanagar. He had been trying to pull out of the arrangement and was informed that the *Chronicle* had paid back one-quarter and the balance would come in Rs 2,000 monthly instalments. 'I am now instructing my Agents to put the screw on and press for a complete change of its policy,' he declared, 'and failing this, to demand immediate repayment of the balance.'[154] Jamnagar made the same conciliatory response to the Viceroy. He indicated that his Rs 50,000 investment had been meant to preserve the original moderate policy of the paper. He had recommended Belgaumwalla to Patiala in response to a proposal in the Chamber of Princes to seek newspaper support 'to counteract the deliberate lies and falsehoods, spread by vernacular journals against us and our States generally'. The possibility of attracting the *Chronicle* to the princely cause and to moderate its nationalist views as well was no longer under consideration by 1930. Belgaumwalla told Patiala that the *Chronicle* 'could not "live" unless he was on one side or the other' and his only hope of existence lay 'in going over to the other

---

[151] N. Dumasia to C. C. Watson, 11 May 1929, *ibid.*
[152] Irwin to Patiala, Bhopal, Nawanagar, 2 May 1930 (F & P) Political, File No. 498-P (secret) 1930, R/1/29/638.
[153] Bhopal to Irwin, 7 May 1930, *ibid.*
[154] Patiala to Irwin, 9 May 1930, *ibid.*

side', since it was clear the Government side had many papers. By June, the Foreign and Political Department was able to advise Dumasia, who continued to press his case, that the princes were gradually divesting themselves of their *Chronicle* investments.[155] The desire to keep their papers 'alive' caused numerous editors to accept a range of significant as well as petty missions on behalf of those who provided the life-giving support. Some of these commitments offended Government; others offended the Congress high command. It was clear to men like Belgaum-walla that those who demanded their loyalty generally could not ensure the survival of their papers. To achieve that goal, they made deals and provided support for those who reciprocated.

These newspapers developed over time very individual identities and reputations. On 2 January 1928, A. Rangaswami Iyengar was appointed editor of the *Hindu*. The proprietor, Kasturi Srinivasan, had been con-cerned that Iyengar's active role as a Congress leader and secretary of the Swaraj Party would introduce partisan party politics into a paper which had always emphasized its independence from such influences. Iyengar agreed and resigned his political office. 'I feel bound to say that I shall have to content myself to do my duties in the sphere of journalism more than in the sphere of the various organizations in the Congress to which all of us have a right to belong.'[156] Although there was no question about the *Hindu*'s national credentials, its loyalty to the Congress was never uncritical. Its owners and editors were determined to build an institution that would achieve a national and international reputation for the quality of its production and the independence of its views. The rotary press installed in 1921, was the first of its kind in Asia, and this equipment was replaced at the end of the decade when hand composing had been superceded by new rotary and Linotype machines. The *Hindu* employed correspondents in Britain and contracted a flow of material from China and the United States. In 1927, it began publishing its *Educational and Literary Supplement*. In 1933, it opened an office in London. When the first teleprinter was installed in the Hindu offices in 1939, Srinivasan delighted in this latest evidence of his paper's ability to compete on the world stage.

In the service of the nationalist cause, the *Hindu* was clearly anti-Government, but it was not a lawbreaker. The interests of the paper, which the owners insisted was an asset to the freedom struggle, were never sacrificed to some higher order of commitment suggested by Gandhi or his colleagues at the centre of the movement. When asked to risk a serious

155 C. C. Watson to N. Dumasia, 2 June 1930, *ibid.*
156 Narasimhan, *Kasturi Srinivasan*, pp. 27–8.

threat to the paper, the proprietors and editors said no. The *Hindu*'s reputation allowed it to develop a relationship with both the Government and the Congress largely on its own terms. Its quality was recognized and its independence accepted. The *Hindu* remained an advocate of order and struggle through dialogue throughout the Non-cooperation and Civil disobedience years. Whenever the situation allowed, it focused attention on the possibility for peace and accommodation. In response to the 1931 Gandhi–Irwin Pact, the blame and praise were equally distributed.

That a settlement has been made possible by the fact that these two men in true religious spirit strove with a determination to achieve peace and goodwill between two great peoples where bitterness and mutual distrust had been brought about by policies and incidents of the past is no less significant.[157]

The reluctance of the *Hindu* to follow Gandhi's lead uncritically is reflected in an August 1933 editorial concerning the relationship of the Congress to Gandhi's continuation of the campaign as an individual civil resister. It reviewed the history of Gandhi's leadership role, emphasizing that Congress acceptance of non-violence and Non-cooperation did not mean the adoption of all of Gandhi's views. The Congress was not committed to Civil Disobedience, the *Hindu* insisted, merely because Gandhi was using that means. In an editorial marking the sixtieth anniversary of the paper the *Hindu* restated its well-known principles.

Whatever may be the duty of a political opposition it is not the duty of the Press to oppose any more than it is to support without adequate reasons. In every case it must be guided solely by consideration of the public interest ... The great heart of the public has displayed a constant affection for this journal and acclaimed it as a national institution.[158]

The Government knew it had a guarantee of reasonable coverage in the *Mail* and at minimum the publication of important official information in the *Hindu*. The Congress knew the position of the *Hindu* and sought loyalist commitment from other papers. In 1921, Rajagopalachari, the Gandhian leader in Madras, provided a Rs 10,000 Congress grant to establish *Swarajya*, a paper that would completely identify with the Congress and provide its leaders in Madras with uncritical support. *Swarajya* was not meant to be a business and professionalism was not a priority. Its editor, T. Prakasam, set the standard in a description provided by K. I. Dutt. 'He had not the gifts of a great editor nor even an adequate understanding of the requirements of a modern daily.'[159] Like

157 *Hindu*, 17 April 1929.
158 *Hindu*, 7 December 1939.
159 G. Rudrayya Chowdari, *Prakasam: A Political Study*, New Delhi: Orient Longmans, 1971, p. 122.

Gandhi's papers, there was no advertising to diminish the context of the mission. But even this unconstrained commitment to the Congress cause did not eleminate the possibility of internal controversy. In the No-Change–Pro-Change controversy that succeeded the first Non-cooperation Movement, Prakasam and Rajagopalachari took different sides and throughout the 1920s, their differences evolved into animosity. Eventually Rajaji dissociated himself from *Swarajya* and demanded the return of the Rs 10,000. Prakasam refused and was no more cooperative when Gandhi supported the demand. The paper survived a few more years, but finally succumbed to bankruptcy in 1935.[160] The *Hindu* was unaffected by the struggle until the end when Rajaji established the *Indian Express* in Madras to achieve the purpose left unfulfilled by *Swarajya*. These three nationalist papers struggled for dominance in the province, cutting into *Hindu* sales and driving one of the last nails into *Swarajya*'s coffin.[161]

Like the *Hindu*, the *Tribune* attracted the same reverential respect from those English-educated northerners who perceived the world about them through its pages, and formulated their opinions about the Punjab's place in the nationalist struggle with the views of its editor in mind. 'Punjabis read it aloud,' Prem Bhatia reminisced, 'as if they were reciting the scriptures.'[162] Although Gandhi received a mixed review from its long-time editor, Kalinath Roy, as he did from the *Hindu*, he recognized the quality of the principles which motivated those who formulated the policies of the two papers. In regard to the 1920 Non-cooperation campaign, the *Tribune* noted 'with the greatest respect for Mr. Gandhi', the need to confess its 'utter inability to follow his reasoning in this matter'. For Kalinath Roy, the only alternative to 'so-called cooperation with the Government' was 'something positively worse.'[163] But Gandhi told his secretary, Mahadev Desai, that 'the *Tribune* is the best viewspaper as the *Hindu* is by and large the best newspaper'.[164] In the midst of the Communal Award crisis, Gandhi found an ally in Roy. 'Long live Kalinath Roy. His articles nowadays on the communal problem and on joint electorates for Harijans bear witness to his deep knowledge and wide experience.'[165]

The *Tribune* was an editor's paper throughout the 1920s and 1930s, and its reputation was in large measure a reflection of the talent and distinction of Kalinath Roy. Like so many of the northern press elite, Roy was

---

[160] *Ibid.*, pp. 132–3.
[161] DPI Tour, January 1–21, 1934, note, GOI (HomePol) 16/19/34.
[162] Prem Bhatia, *All My Yesterdays*, Delhi: Vikas Publishing House, PVT Ltd, 1972, p. 29.
[163] *Tribune*, 19 August 1920.
[164] M. Desair, *The Diary of Mahadev Desai*, Vol. I, Ahmedabad, Navajivan Publishing House, d1953, p. 339.
[165] *Ibid.*, p. 35.

an outsider, a Bengali; and the independent reputation of the paper applied as well to a range of local issues and interests which distanced it from any possibility of attracting a popular constituency in the Punjab, even without the language barrier. Roy's lifestyle appeared to complement this distinctive place and role. J. N. Sahni has provided a portrait of an 'unshaven, dreamy-eyed, austere looking' man – short, in his sixties, a woollen cap on his head and wearing a food-stained threadbare tweed coat. He wore thick-lensed glasses and had poor teeth, and it was difficult to understand him. 'He almost babbled.'[166] But his articles, Sahni noted, 'had been perhaps the most important source of whatever knowledge I gained of current politics in India.'[167] Depending on the issue, Roy's editorials might run to three columns and at times it required a number of days to complete an idea. When he came to the *Tribune* in 1917, the first page was devoted to Notes and Comments, and on occasion a four-column editorial took the whole of it.[168] In order to accomplish this daily task, Roy tended to isolate himself from the rest of the staff, spending much of the day shaping his editorial.[169]

The *Tribune* was the 'paper of record' in the Punjab. It perceived itself as representing the best views of the province and its loyal readers generally agreed. In this context it was the northern link in the chain of national papers which provided one of the communication networks joining the various regions together. But its sense of 'national' identity tended to place it on the side of communal amity and unity, and outside of the sectarian debates which informed much of the political struggle in its own province. It spoke for itself and a small educated minority. In the 1930s, its commitment to unity placed it in temporary alliance with Hindu protagonists, attacking separate electorates,[170] the Communal Award,[171] and the White Paper,[172] as Muslim inspired and dangerous to the integrity of the nation. In an April 1932 editorial the Hindu Mahasabha was lauded for attacking these 'preposterous demands'.[173] If this engagement with sectarianism did not increase the long-term influence of the paper in the Punjab, it made it clearly, if temporarily, more representative of the reality of its politics. There were limits of course. In a July 1938 editorial, Roy reasserted his transcendent unity theme. The idea of Hindustan for

---

[166] Sahni, *Indian Press*, p. 8
[167] *Ibid.*
[168] Bhatia, *All My Yesterdays*, p. 6.
[169] Sahni, *Indian Press*, p. 10.
[170] *Tribune*, 16 April 1931.
[171] *Ibid.*, 24 July 1932.
[172] *Ibid.*, 16 October 1933.
[173] *Ibid.*, 24 April 1932.

the Hindus was basically unsound, indefensible in theory and dangerous in practice. India was the motherland of Muslims, Christians, Hindus, and many other groups, he asserted, and those who sided with the nation did not have to prove their credentials by denying or subordinating their individual identity.[174]

The *Tribune* was funded by the income from a trust established by Dyal Singh Majithia, who was interested in reducing the level of parochialism in the province and was not concerned if the paper's leadership role denied it a large constituency. In this liberal environment, Kalinath Roy was able to develop and publicize his independent views without fear of any managerial constraint or pressures from outside. Other editors were less fortunate. In June 1936, the chairman of the Board of the *Sind Observer* wrote to the editor, K. Punniah, objecting to naming Congress politician Bhulabhai Desai in the paper. It was sufficient, Fakirjee Cowasjee insisted, that only 'a few local Congressmen' be mentioned. He also wanted to discuss the coverage of a planned visit to Sind of Jawaharlal Nehru. Cowasjee attacked the socialist policies of both Nehru and the Congress, and noted his intention to deny them any publicity in his paper.

The Congress which is the outcome of level headed brains has been taken possession of by irresponsible and feverish brains and has done more harm to the cause of India than good and as my name is unfortunately connected with the *Sind Observer* it is my duty that the paper does not become the medium of giving publicity to the Congress' wild efforts to upset the civilization and law and order and in which I desire your cooperation and that of others who have to attend to the publication of the paper.[175]

Punniah resisted the pressure from the chairman, noting that he had brought the paper 'through three non-cooperation movements and without a scratch'.[176] He instructed his staff to accept no instructions from anyone other than himself, and entered into a daily exchange of notes with Cowasjee and the managing director of the company. After sixteen years of journalism, he insisted, such pressures were unacceptable and he reiterated his position that he was 'only a professional journalist pure and simple'.[177] On the eve of Nehru's visit to Karachi, Punniah received a note signed by 'an Indian'. It instructed him to provide only minimum reporting with no details and no pictures of the event. He refused and on 20 July he was fired. In a statement to the press, Nehru noted the hard lot of a journalist in India, endangered by both Govern-

---

[174] *Ibid.*, 27 July 1938.
[175] Fakirjee Cowasjee to K. Punniah, 28 June 1936, AICC G-62/1936.
[176] K. Punniah to F. Cowasjee, 15 July 1936, *ibid.*
[177] *Ibid.*

ment action and the biases of reactionary elements in the country who held power over a newspaper. Although neither Punniah nor the *Observer* were pro-Congress and had often criticized his policies, he defended the 'fundamental privileges of journalists', to act according to the standards of their profession.[178]

The denial of coverage was far more significant than a critical review in a circumstance where only a handful of papers, and sometimes only one, reached an influential constituency. An event not mentioned in an important paper virtually meant that it had not taken place in the experience of those who depended on that paper for their news. At minimum, ignoring an event denied it importance. Editors of major papers could be influenced by a politician or stockholders to give their views and interests coverage and positive comment. Punniah's experience was not an isolated event. Sahni's exit from the *Hindustan Times* was less dramatic but clearly the result of confrontation with the new Birla-controlled Board. And Horniman's second term as editor of the *Bombay Chronicle* was short-lived for similar reasons. Sadanand had to take over his own company in order to free himself from Board constraints, and those editors who worked for papers controlled by politicians such as the *Independent* and *National Herald* were continually burdened as well as blessed with advice they recognized could not be refused. The problems encountered by most papers and editors made the 'protected' situation of the *Tribune*, *Hindu*, and *Amrita Bazaar Patrika*, all the more significant.

The increasing influence of Indian-owned papers and the nationalist issues which filled their pages and attracted editorial comment made a slow but deliberate impact on those Anglo-Indian papers which remained in the great urban centres to represent the views and interests of the colonial establishment – official and unofficial. There were two elements to the change. In regard to the substantive issues of the nationalist campaign, absolute rejection gave place over time to debate, recognition of legitimacy, partial support, and eventually acceptance of the inevitable. In parallel with this dialogue with an enemy that was likely to become the dominant political power in the country, was the realization that their sales and, therefore, their survival depended upon their making peace with the 'new India' and finding a place that would allow them to survive successive transfers of power. The *Mail* in Madras under the editorship of A. A. Hayles pressed ahead with a policy of Indianization of its staff and response to political issues on their own merit. Hayles also retained his connection with the Government which was prepared to provide what support was available for the last significant British paper in the south. He

178 J. Nehru, press statement, n.d., *ibid.*

sought advertising revenue not only from official sources but from the more lucrative business interests in England, warning Hugh MacGregor that without it, the only press left would be Indian, most of it 'wholly anti-British'. There was an increase in his advertising business, but not enough to satisfy a continuing need. He noted that the flow into Indian newspaper was also increasing, lamenting 'the stunt to convince British manufacturers that only the Indian Press counts in these days of nationalism having apparently succeeded'.[179]

During a brief period of financial distress in the early 1930s, the Government noticed a change in the policy of the *Times of India* in the direction of greater accommodation with nationalist views. The paper became so 'time-serving', noted the DPI, 'that Government could not rely on the only English-owned journal in Bombay for help'.[180] But business improved and with it a return to reasonable loyalty. In 1936, Frank Moraes became a junior assistant editor at the *Times*, the first Indian in an editorial post. He noted a number of 'imperial hangovers' such as the British-only senior staff canteen and lavatory and his exclusion from the daily morning conference of editors. But he complained about the latter and was invited to participate. 'My British colleagues had a sense of fair play,' he noted, 'which I respected.'[181] The messages that the *Times* was sending to Indians and to the Government in the 1930s, were mixed and sometimes confused. It was clearly partisan, and advocated its British positions aggressively. But it was also a major newspaper with a professional ethos, and a history and tradition of its own.

When the *Times of India* published a story in 1939, about a British Cabinet decision that had not been authorized for public release, the Defence Secretary reiterated a viewpoint that the Raj bureaucracy had slowly but reluctantly accepted. As in the case of Reuters and the *Mail* and the *Statesman*, professional and business interests as well as changing viewpoint, had displaced uncritical loyalty to the Raj. 'The main point is, after all, perfectly clear which is that the *Times of India* is not at present to be trusted.' There was an investigation of the leak which apparently occurred at a party in Bombay, and a letter of complaint was drafted. The Home Department version was considered too mild by the Defence Secretary, but the stronger version was eventually recast again at the urgings of the Home Secretary. In difficult times it was clear that the Government needed all the friends it could attract, and the *Times* remained a powerful and useful ally. 'I feel that it would be inadvisable to

[179] A. A. Hayles to H. MacGregor, 15 September 1932 (IO) L/I/1/345, File 131/15.
[180] DPI Tour, January 1–21 1934, note, GOI (HomePol) 16/19/34.
[181] Moraes, *Witness to an Era*, pp. 44–5.

adopt in correspondence with the Editor of the *Times of India* the line of approach suggested in Defence Secretary's note.'[182]

The *Statesman* had moved more quickly than these other Anglo-Indian papers to respond to the new political realities and the demands of Indian readers. As a result, its left of Anglo-Indian centre reputation attracted a large Indian readership and a highly profitable advertising business.[183] In 1928, it was advocating a 'made in India' solution to India's constitutional problems, arguing that internal problems could be resolved after an appropriate and popularly accepted framework was in place. 'Clearly the first thing is to get a Government in this country which has its origins here, and is not the instrument of London.'[184] Like the *Times of India*, its ties with Britain and the Government of India were clear, but both of these papers wanted to survive and assumed they could continue to do business with whatever successor regime rose to the top and with their increasing number of Indian customers.

The most striking example of the transition in the Anglo-Indian press establishment in this period was the collapse of the *Pioneer* and its restoration as an Indian-owned paper. The *Pioneer* had been the dominant Anglo-Indian paper in north India. The intimate relationship of its editors and correspondents with the Government of India had made it into a virtual official gazette, the paper of the services. But after World War One, its sales and financial position had diminished, and by the late 1920s, it was required to experiment with a radical editor, F. W. Wilson, who changed the tone of the paper and antagonized the Government and its traditional constituency, without solving the fundamental problems. Circulation went up among nationalists but declined among Europeans. More important, there was an additional loss of revenue in the withdrawal of advertising by British firms. Wilson was fired and after some desultory attempts to revitalize the paper, its owners, a European group headed by C. T. Allen, decided in 1931 to dispose of it.

There was concern in the United Provinces Government that Nehru and the Congress would attempt to take over the *Pioneer* and leave them without press support. The *Leader* was Liberal and often anti-Congress, but it was often anti-Government as well. Sir Malcolm Hailey, the Governor, involved in the establishment of a United Provinces constitutionalist party founded on taluqdar opposition to the Congress, helped organize the transfer of the paper to a group of new owners which included landholders, a number of ruling princes, and some of the larger

---

[182] Home Secretary note, 27 July 1939.
[183] Ian Stephens, *Monsoon Morning*, London: Ernest Benn, 1966, pp. 15–16.
[184] *Statesman*, 7 June 1928.

European and Indian firms in Cawnpore. The group was headed by J. P.
Srivastava, the Education Minister in the United Provinces Government.
The transfer was made in the summer of 1932, a new editor, Desmond
Young, arrived in the following year, and in order to gain a strong
foothold in its own market; it was moved from *Leader*-dominated Allahabad to Lucknow.[185] Young pressed the Government for advertisement
revenue and its business supporters for more capital. Circulation
increased and the paper's general situation improved, but it remained
weak and the danger of collapse was apparent.[186] There was some discussion in 1934, about the possibility of amalgamating the *Pioneer*, the *Civil
and Military Gazette*, and the Delhi *Statesman*. Young argued that
without amalgamation all three might fold which would be a disaster
from the point of view of Government publicity.[187] However sympathetic
the Government might be, it was clearly beyond its capacity to do very
much about it. An alternative source of financial support was the states,
and Young began an aggressive campaign to attract the interest of a large
number of princes.

There had been some princely support from the beginning, both Bhopal
and Bikaner having responded to Srivastava's request. They committed
Rs 2 lakhs but sent only Rs 123,000. There were also promises from many
others but the result was usually disappointing. Hyderabad promised Rs
25,000 but gave nothing, and Jind's Rs 10,000 was never received. Travancore promised Rs 10,000 and paid half, while Patiala promised Rs
25,000 and paid 10,000. Udaipur, Jodhpur, and Kapurthala refused.[188]
The negotiations were conducted through K. M. Panikkar, an officer of
the Chamber of Princes, but he remained pessimistic. He pointed out to
Young that the *Pioneer* had promised to make itself into a virtual Princes'
Paper but had done very little in its first two years under new ownership.
'We have done nothing more for them than the *Statesman* does gratis ...
that is to write occasional leaders in support of them when the opportunity arises.'[189] The flow of princely grants continued, but they remained
small and insufficient.

In May 1932, the Jamsaheb of Nawanagar wrote to the Maharaja of
Patiala about the need to propagandize the princely case, and suggested
that the *Pioneer* presented a unique opportunity. It seemed possible to
gain control with half the shares while the other half remained in the
hands of friendly landowning and business interests. The discussion was

[185] I. Stephens note re. *Pioneer*, GOI (HomePol) 65/34.
[186] D. Young to I. Stephens, 12 March 1934, GOI (HomePol) 65/34.
[187] H. W. Haig to H. G. Hallett, 8 December 1934, GOI (HomePol) 146/1934.
[188] D. Young to I. Stephens, 24 December 1934, GOI (HomePol) 33/4/35.
[189] K. M. Panikkar to D. Young, 8 February 1935, GOI (HomePol), *ibid.*

broadened to include Kashmir, Bhopal, and Bikaner, but it was agreed that approval was required from 'higher quarters'. Within the Government there was a willingness to consider any reasonable solution to the *Pioneer*'s problem, but pessimism about success. The paper survived but without the great infusions of resources that was desired from either Government or the states.[190]

While other English-owned newspapers had been displaced by nationalist organs, with both the name and the memory of the predecessor quickly forgotten by the subscribers to the new paper, the *Pioneer* survived as an establishment paper for a different elite. It held onto the memory of its golden days and many of its old readers and it became an Indian paper. But it took a long time to establish a secure hold on a market and a reputation. It was no longer an official paper, neither was it Liberal or Independent. It was owned by a clutch of wealthy and powerful men who strove to survive with their businesses and principalities intact. Nationalists remained sceptical, while Government could provide little more than moral encouragement. In September 1933, Desmond Young asked Nehru for an interview. His response described the problem. Nehru noted that the owners of the *Pioneer* were

a unique combination of autocracy, the feudal order, British capitalism and Indian capitalism. Applying the Mendelian Theory, I wondered of what this very mixed assortment could be the offspring. Or perhaps, in these days of topsy-turveydom, the *Pioneer* has decided to reverse that theory and, starting with the offspring was trying to incubate the parents, whoever and whatever they might be.[191]

While an increasingly defensive Government of India became more cautious and sensitive to the professional and business interests of its surviving Anglo-Indian 'press agents', Congress leaders became more impatient and demanding with the Indian press. These leaders were no less defensive than the official establishment in the Secretariats, but their fundamental concerns were different. While the Raj negotiated its demise, leaders at the centre of the nationalist movement struggled to create and control a unified institution and programme that could sit across the table with confidence. Constitutional advances after the war had provided Indians with greater access to positions of power and influence and produced as well greater awareness among many groups and individuals outside these charmed circles, of the need to secure a place for their own future interests. The national press was absorbed into this internecine

---

[190] Hallett to Sir Bertrand Glancy, 8 January 1935; Glancy note, 12 January 1935, *ibid.*
[191] J. Nehru to D. Young, 1 September 1933, Jawaharlal Nehru Papers, Vol. CIV.

struggle as advocates of one party or another, and on occasion as advocates of its own interest.

In June 1927, the President of the Congress, Srinivasa Iyengar, attacked the press for its criticism of Congress leaders and programmes. He was referring in particular to B. G. Horniman's *Indian National Herald* and T. Prakasam's *Swarajya*, which had terminated a long and loyal commitment to Gandhi's leadership. Iyengar suggested that these politician–editors should give up one or other of their activities and generalized the argument for the whole of the Indian press. In response, the editors of the major national papers rejected the attack on their professional independence and the implicit denial of the important role they were playing in the shared nationalist struggle.

C. Y. Chintamani reminded Iyengar that Gandhi, Lajpat Rai, Tilak, Annie Besant, and Motilal Nehru had felt no need to choose between a political and press career. The Congress President could not have his political–journalists and deny the same right to others not in agreement with current policy. The editor of *Basumati* insisted that the sacrifices of the nationalist press were greater than those of leaders like Iyengar. 'Journalism in India is not the pleasant pastime of prosperous leaders,' he noted, 'who have made their pile at the bar or in the Exchange.' It was 'a struggle in the open arena of danger'. The *Tribune* wondered what would have bcome of public life if Iyengar's suggestion were accepted, and Roy provided a long list of distinguished patriots from Kristodas Pal to the present, and who had contributed to the development of the independence movement as pressmen and politicians. 'Does not India, indeed, owe nine tenths of what she values in the Mahatma's teachings', Roy insisted, 'to his connection with *Young India* and *Navajivan*.'[192]

In 1930, there was another confrontation, with another Congress President. In response to the enactment of the Press Ordinance, Motilal Nehru asked all Indian papers to unite in protest by ceasing publication. The response was mixed and there was some confusion regarding the desires of the Working Committee. Maintaining business as usual and ignoring the Ordinance was the initial position, subsequently replaced with the call to cease publication. What seemed absolutely essential was a united response. But individual papers were making their own decisions and measuring their own interests.

Nehru noted that there were less than a dozen English-edited nationalist Indian papers which mattered and suggested that united action among them would have defeated the Ordinance.[193] But these were the

---

[192] Press survey in the *Indian Daily Mail*, 9 June 1927.
[193] AICC circular No. 43 to Provincial Congress Committees issued by Motilal Nehru, AICC G-143/1930.

papers that were least likely to take instruction. A conference of editors convened in Bombay to consider the issues raised by the actions and demands of both the Government and the Congress high command. But they failed to achieve a consensus.[194] For some of those who rejected the call to cease publication, it seemed far more important to continue in their nationalist role of disseminating news and mobilizing opinion through their editorials.[195] Others were concerned about their business interests, especially in metropolitan centres where the continuing publication of a competitor seemed to require an uninterrupted response.[196]

The Ordinance made relatively little impact on this subset of nationalist papers, which tended to address critical issues with professional restraint. And the call of the Congress President had an equally unobtrusive effect. Each of these centres of identity and position had asserted territorial rights that widely overlapped, and everyone was disappointed with the performance of the other protagonists. In regard to the uncooperative press, Motilal Nehru lamented: 'I must say however that this section is henceforth to be classed among those who take a profession to eke out a living and not to foster the spirit of independent journalism.'[197] Ramananda Chatterjee reiterated the argument of his profession that their role was important and its quality was in large measure dependent on its own tradition of freedom. He also advised nationalist leaders to allow their supporters some independent choice.

No nation, no class of men can consist only of heroes. Nor is it practical to suppress all timid people or cowards. So I would advise accepting from all what ever service they can render. I am not for fighting neutrals or friends.[198]

---

[194] Lala Girdharilal to M. Nehru, 23 May 1930, *ibid.*, pp. 99–111.
[195] R. Chatterjee, 'Notes', *Modern Review*, May 1930. See also R. Chatterjee to M. Nehru, 22 May 1930, 4 June 1930, AICC G-143/1930.
[196] *Ibid.*
[197] M. Nehru to R. Chatterjee, 11 June 1930, *ibid.*
[198] R. Chatterjee to M. Nehru, 4 June 1930, *ibid.* See also M. Israel, 'Ramananda Chatterjee and the *Modern Review*: The Image of Nationality in the National Press', in M. Israel, ed., *National Unity: The South Asian Experience*, New Delhi: Promilla and Co., 1982, pp. 1–46.

4   *The Bombay Chronicle*: a case study

As was the case in every region and locality in the sub-continent, there was a particular Bombay debate and perspective, the product of the concentration of industrial and commercial interests, local communal issues, and the perceived tradition of a Maharashtrian response to challenge, tested by the British since 1818, and more recently by the nationalist movement itself. From its founding in 1907, and particularly in the 1920s, the *Bombay Chronicle* provided a platform on which many of the contending parties fought for influence and support. There were approximately 250 papers published in the Bombay Presidency in 1925, and the *Chronicle* was among the 8 or 10 with a circulation above 10,000. It was also among another elite grouping on an All-India level, read and quoted beyond its metropolitan and provincial borders and a deliberate participant in the work of a nation building as well as nationalist–Raj confrontation. It was, in this context, an important focus for the exchange of information and viewpoints within the Presidency, and between Bombay and the rest of India. The *Chronicle*, like the *Tribune, Hindu, Amrita Bazar Patrika*, and other papers with a national perspective, attempted to play a mediating role by advocating and describing a coalescence of viewpoint and interest between the All-India and provincial leadership, and the constituencies they sought to mobilize.

Throughout the 1920s, the *Chronicle*'s attempt to remain loyal to Gandhi and the mainstream Congress programme made it the principal English-language nationalist paper in the Presidency. It also placed it in competition with other local nationalist papers representing conflicting views and constituencies – such as the Liberal *Indian Daily Mail* and the Responsivist *Kesari*. In the context of the changing pattern and content of nationalist action in this period, the *Chronicle*'s desire to be a national voice tended to deny it a stable base in Bombay, with its range of camps opposing the leadership at the centre. It made it, as well, a continuing candidate for takeover by various groups and individuals, both within the Congress and outside. The *Chronicle* sought to limit its distance from what was perceived as a Maharashtrian perspective, but its position on the margin of the local–national exchange was a continuing source of instability.

Unlike the Lahore *Tribune* which had been endowed with a trust by its founder, or the *Hindu* and the *Amrita Bazar Patrika* with their Iyengar and Ghose owner–editors, or the *Leader* with its own party and resident institution in C. Y. Chintamani, the *Chronicle* had to be concerned about its financial support, and its editors were employed by a Board conscious of the connection between resources and viewpoint. The result was recurrent crises, usually the reflection of political action at the Congress centre or within the Presidency. Viewpoints in the ascendancy would be represented by changes in the Board's membership, and new sources of funding would replace the gifts of disenchanted financiers. Identification with the Congress was no guarantee of security, as the paper was confronted with policy choices which divided Congressmen and precluded the possibility of not offending some large and influential constituency. The Congress might be able to subsume a vast array of differing viewpoints under its spacious umbrella, but an editorial position, daily reiterated in print, tended to antagonize – especially those who found no home at the centre and sought loyalty from opinion makers when they were at home.

The *Chronicle* tried to respond to these different viewpoints and, as a result, was continually attacked for its lack of a 'settled policy';[1] for those whose political views were principled convictions wanted loyalty and propaganda. Over time, the *Chronicle* supported the Moderates, the Extremists, Non-cooperation, Swarajists, No-Changers and Pro-Changers, leaving in its wake anger and disappointment. This was particularly the case in Bombay which had played such a major role in initiating the All-India movement. Its leaders had carried with them viewpoints and strategies evolved out of local experience and tradition, and factional struggle at the centre could often trace its lineage to earlier confrontations within the Presidency.[2] In the early 1920s, however, the Maharashtrian content of the national programme and its advocates lost their privileged position, and the *Chronicle*'s loyalty to the new leadership antagonized old constituencies which had once considered the paper their own.

Gandhi's apparent appropriation and synthesis of Maharashtra's mixed nationalist legacy (calling Gokhale his political *guru* and adopting

---

[1] Vaikunth Mehta to S. A. Brelvi, 21 January 1931, Brelvi Papers. See also *Annual Report on Indian and Anglo-Vernacular Newspapers Published in the Bombay Presidency for 1925*, GOI (HomePol) F-261/1926.

[2] Gordon Johnson, *Provincial Politics and Indian Nationalism: Bombay and the Indian National Congress 1880 to 1915*, Cambridge University Press, 1973.

confrontational techniques more akin to Tilak's methods), did not attract an easy transfer of loyalty and support. Many of these local heirs of the founders of the Congress – Moderate or Extremist – were now described as 'slackers', plotting to regain control from a new generation, whose lineage and political base were alien and distant. Soon after the Congress's adoption of Non-cooperation, N. C. Kelkar, the editor of the *Mahratta*, had insisted that Maharashtra was not opposed to Gandhi's leadership, and that their differences concerned only details of the programme. Over time, however, while asserting his loyalty to Congress, he reiterated his concern about the impracticality of viewing Non-cooperation in terms of principle, rather than as a temporary tactic to achieve a specific, attainable objective, and associated his pragmatic view with a Maharashtrian perspective.[3] In response, the *Chronicle* utilized well-known images of local political identity in order to isolate the opponents of Gandhi's leadership as either collaborationists in the case of Moderates, or disgruntled reactionaries in the case of the leaderless Tilakites.

In a continuing exchange of leader and editorial charges and responses, the *Chronicle*, speaking for the Congress centre, and the *Mahratta*, for the Maharashtra branch, carefully directed their rhetorical armoury at the heart of the opposing programmes. In response to a *Chronicle* suggestion in July 1922, that those who opposed the mainstream Congress programme cherished the ambition of reviving Peshwa rule in Poona, Kelkar insisted that he spoke for 'the real mind of the whole of Maharashtra'. Citing the All-India contributions of Ranade, Gokhale, and Tilak, he insisted that those who shared his views were the descendants of that tradition of 'true Indian nationalism'. The reference to the Peshwas was interpreted as an attack both on this Maharashtra-based national accomplishment, and on the Poona-based Brahmin elite which was its source. In addition, Kelkar reminded his readers that the *Chronicle* was no longer the paper founded by Pherozeshah Mehta, 'a truly cosmopolitan Parsee', financed by many 'catholic Hindus'. It was, he lamented, now run 'more in the interests of pan-Islamism than the *Mahratta* or the *Kesari*, founded by Brahmins, are in the interests of the Peshwa's rule.'[4] Kelkar's vision of a pragmatic, cosmopolitan and enlightened Hindu Maharashtrian nationalism was often recast in *Chronicle* commentary as unprincipled,

---

[3] N. C. Kelkar, 'What is Passive Resistance?', *Sarvajanik Sabha Quarterly Journal*, 1981, reproduced in Kelkar, *A Passing Phase of Politics*, Poona: A. W. Awati, 1925, p. 6. He continually returned to this theme and opposition to the *Chronicle*, insisting that Non-cooperation was a political movement and it was necessary not to overdo the spiritual side. *Mahratta*, 3 December 1923, reproduced in *ibid.*, p. 178.

[4] N. C. Kelkar, 'The Chronicle and Maharashtra' (1922), reproduced in Kelkar, *A Passing Phase*, pp. 86–90.

parochial, and communalist. For him, and M. R. Jayakar, at whom the Peshwa charge was directed, such views confirmed the *Chronicle*'s position as an enemy of Maharashtra.[5]

The Indian Newspaper Company had been established by Mehta in 1907, to provide a voice for another presumed Maharashtrian perspective: the moderate nationalist politics of Bombay's Westernized intelligentsia and business establishment. Mehta considered himself to be the spokesman for a progressive and enlightened viewpoint, threatened by reaction from an aggressive, indigenous revivalism represented by Tilak's *Mahratta* and *Kesari*, and a defensive, alien colonialism supported by the powerful *Times of India*. The *Chronicle*, which first appeared in 1913, was meant to occupy the middle ground. Bombay was a city founded on accommodation with the lifestyle, values, and norms of its alien governors,[6] and the *Chronicle* was a Bombay paper – confidently associating with the centres of power: the Government of India and the Indian National Congress, on its own terms.

If Tilak, and subsequently Kelkar, from their base in Poona were not seeking the restoration of the Peshwas, they did seek a place for their heirs, and a stake at the bargaining table where the new Indian nation was being envisioned, and the campaign designed. While Bombay city had its own distinctive life, reflected in its heterodox mix of British businessmen, Parsee industrialists, and Gujarati traders and shroffs, Poona remained dominated by a Brahmin elite, the self-professed designers, beneficiaries, and representatives of a Maharashtrian viewpoint reflected in the peculiar mix of Ksatriya and Bhakti traditions, and symbolized in the achievements of Shivaji and Ramdas. Tilak's Ganapati and Shivaji Festivals were as much a challenge to Mehta's moderate moderns, who perceived themselves to be the beneficiaries of British rule, as to the British themselves, and he brought his defensive struggle to the heartland of both adversaries – Bombay.[7]

In the period of its ascendancy in nationalist politics, Mehta's Bombay tradition and his Bombay newspaper lived on the margins of Poona's Maharashtra. In 1915, however, both Mehta and Gokhale died, and Tilak, after six years in exile, had managed to integrate his confrontationalist style into a constitutional context in the form of the Home Rule

[5] M. R. Jayakar to S. A. Brelvi, 19 July, 1922, Brelvi Papers.
[6] *Capital*, 4 January 1919. Quoted in Gordon, *Businessmen and Politics*, p. 60.
[7] See R. Cashman, *The Myth of the Lokamanya*, Berkeley: University of California Press, 1975, for an extended discussion of the Bombay–Poona dichotomy. Gordon Johnson has also noted that Gokhale's Moderate career was dependent upon an alliance with Bombay's politicians. His political base was the Bombay Political Association, which provided the money and influence to launch his All-India career.

League. In response, the *Chronicle*'s policy, now controlled by its editor, B. G. Horniman, moved to support home rule and, therefore, away from the orthodox liberal creed of its founder. It was a relatively small change, merely a 'deviational angle', in the view of its associate editor, Pothan Joseph,[8] but it required a choice between the two major Maharashtra factions. In the view of the Tilakites, the paper had finally come home, while Mehta's old colleagues on the Board considered the *Chronicle* to be lost to their party. There were a sufficient number of resignations and replacements to create a new Board, described by M. R. Jayakar as 'now flooded with Mr Horniman's friends and allies'. Jehangir Petit, one of the founders of the Indian Newspaper Company, resigned, lamenting that the *Chronicle*, after ten years of difficulties and hardships, had been 'handed over to a noisy minority'.[9]

This 1917 confrontation and internal reorganization established a pattern for change in the *Chronicle* over the next thirty years, as the paper continually moved to accommodate the dominant forces within the Congress leadership, with a Maharashtrian base. In 1917 it remained a Maharashtrian choice, and only indirectly a choice of national policy as well. Both Maharashtra and the Congress were, however, soon caught up in the transition that would bring Gandhi to power, and with it a reversal of the relationship. Maharashtra, or at least those who believed that they represented its interests and viewpoint, found themselves in the minority, attempting to keep up with and influence a movement that appeared to be going out of control.

B. G. Horniman, the *Chronicle*'s first editor, was brought from the *Statesman* on the recommendation of both Gokhale and S. N. Banerjee, the latter noting that he was 'as good an Indian as myself'.[10] Notwithstanding this spotlessly moderate pedigree, it was Horniman who became associated with the evolving extremism of the Home Rule League, and with the early satyagraha experiments in Kaira and Ahmedabad. He severed the *Chronicle*'s allegiance to the Moderate formula of the Congress founders and likewise destroyed the accommodative relationship with the Government, which Mehta had considered essential for a powerful and influential organ on the pattern of the *Times of India*. For the next year and a half, officials in Bombay and Delhi carefully recorded the increasingly antagonistic editorials and political coverage of the *Chronicle*, filing them away for future use. In April 1919, they finally moved to arrest Horniman.

---

[8] Joseph, *Glimpses of Yesterday*, p. 33.
[9] GOI (HomePol) 47/1918. See also Israel, 'M. R. Jayakar and the Bombay Nationalist Movement', p. 13.
[10] S. N. Banerjee to P. S. Mehta, quoted in S. P. Sen, ed., *Dictionary of National Biography*, Calcutta, 1973, p. 170.

It was no ordinary arrest. A delegation of officials including the Acting Commissioner of Bombay, a CID inspector, and three doctors came to his bungalow at Worli where Horniman was recuperating from recent surgery. The doctors were there to advise on his ability to travel; the Commissioner, to serve an order requiring him to leave British India. He was asked to dress quickly and pack a few necessities, leaving the rest in the care of servants and police orderlies. Within an hour, Horniman was carried down the hill to a shuttered ambulance which transferred him to the dock and the steamship *Takada*, scheduled to sail for England the next day. Throughout the afternoon a squadron of lancers had been kept ready at Worli, while traffic on the road to the harbour was held up until Horniman and his escort had safely passed. While the ship remained in port, a European inspector, two European sergeants, and a force of Indian constables guarded the prisoner. The next day, the Governor of Bombay, Sir George Lloyd, sent a personal message and a parcel of books, and Horniman was allowed to receive one visitor. Soon after, the *Takada* sailed and Lloyd, savouring his success and the release of tension, was able to inform the Viceroy that Horniman was gone and Bombay was quiet.[11]

Officials in Delhi and Bombay believed they had waited an inordinately long time to rid the country of this dangerous man. In 1917, Lord Willingdon had favoured deportation, but no action was taken.[12] In the following year, Rule 3(d) of the Defence of India Rules was framed 'in order to deal with him particularly'.[13] At regular intervals throughout these years, the Home Department in Delhi and the Judicial Department in Bombay would exchange their concerns about Horniman's activities and their plans to put an end to them.[14] The immediate cause which led to a decision to deport was the publication on 5 April 1919, of a lead editorial denouncing the Government for allowing troops to use soft-nosed bullets against rioters in Delhi.[15] The opportunity might have been

---

[11] B. G. Horniman, 'How I was Deported', *Bombay Chronicle*, 5 September 1919. Lloyd to Chelmsford, 30 April 1919 GOI (HomePol) 619–640 and KW, 1919.

[12] H. D. Craik note, 28 April 1919, *ibid*.

[13] *Ibid*.

[14] *Ibid*.

[15] *Bombay Chronicle*, 5 April 1919. For discussions within the Home Department see GOI (HomePol) 192–195/1919. The charge was not correct and the *Chronicle*'s daily correspondent had sent a correction on 17 April which did not arrive until 6 June. In response to Jinnah's cable (Jinnah was chairman of the *Chronicle*'s board), the Home Department ordered a search for the missing message. It was traced to the CID, then to the Deputy-Chief Censor, Delhi, then the Deputy Superintendent, Telegraph Office, Delhi, then to the Deputy-Chief Censor, Simla. It was eventually found and forwarded and the Government decided that the whole business should be dropped, rather than allow a debate regarding censorship. GOI (HomePol) 42/1919. See also *Bombay Chronicle*, 14 June, 25 June, 4 July, 11 July 1919.

allowed to pass again without action, but April 1919 was a difficult month for the Government of India. The Punjab was in turmoil, and allusions to 1857 appeared repeatedly in the reports and telegrams of worried officials. Unrest had spread across north India, stimulated by a variety of causes in temporary but vigorous alliance against British rule. The Khilafat Question, Punjab repression, disillusionment with the Reforms, the excitement of discovering a new leader in M. K. Gandhi, the context of post-war malaise and economic distress – all appeared to give reasonable cause to man the barricades and to defend the Raj from violent revolution. On 13 April, Dyer had ordered his troops to fire on a great crowd of civilians in Jallianwala Bagh. A defensive, if not endangered Government, needed to take advantage of any opportunity to demonstrate that it was being unfairly and often viciously maligned, and that it retained the power to reestablish both order and its reputation, and to govern effectively.

Chelmsford and Lloyd had discussed the possibility of deporting a number of nationalist leaders, including Gandhi and Jinnah, in order to end the rioting and the aggressive propaganda campaign which appeared to be causing its spread. But the situation was quieting down in Bombay by 12 April and there was concern that deportations might cause more trouble.[16] Horniman remained the sole target. In the two years since the 1917 'coup', Horniman and the *Chronicle* had attracted wide support as effective representatives of an evolving partnership between a still-influential Maharashtra left wing represented by the Tilakites and the new left supporters of Gandhi. Horniman's personal reputation as a nationalist leader was considered one of the *Chronicle*'s greatest assets; and a Board still far more conservative than either the paper or the editor accepted his leadership as good for the *Chronicle* and not sufficiently powerful to undermine their own interests. It had been clear for some time, however, that the Government was less willing to accept the rhetorical barrage on its own interests, however much these seemed to be shared with the businessmen who patronized the paper; and officials had difficulty understanding the apparent lack of concern among these men for their own survival.

Throughout the 1920s, senior information officers in the Government of India monitored the *Chronicle*'s vicissitudes of stability and financial distress, occasionally attempting a discreet incursion that might further weaken a paper considered to be irredeemably extremist, but more often merely talking about it. Its perceived pro-communist sympathies at the

---

[16] Secretary to the Government of India, Home Department to Chief Secretary, Government of Bombay, Political Department, 12 April 1919, GOI (HomePol) 619–640 and KW, 1919.

end of the decade seemed totally incongruous with its continued dependence on Bombay capitalists and various princes.[17] But business had
discovered a need for propaganda in support of its interests, and nationalist newspapers like the *Chronicle* provided a useful link with influential
politicians who could support their claims on British promises along with
the more general challenge to alien privilege.

Horniman continued to receive substantial financial support from the
Bombay business community as he moved to the margin of legal constraint and beyond. However dependent that relationship became, he was
able to argue in good conscience that 'I have flirted with big business but I
have kept my virginity.'[18] He offered help to the millowners in the name of
Swadeshi; boosted Indian insurance in the name of nationalism; and
supported Indian shipping as a national enterprise.[19] On their part,
industrialists and merchants, in addition to those like Jamnalal Bajaj and
Vaikunth Mehta who had been converted to Gandhism, provided the
funds for campaigns which were potentially threatening to their long-term
interests. But nationalist political life was no more single minded than the
world of business. If Gandhi seemed difficult, Motilal Nehru was useful,
as they were to him. In 1924, he wrote to Purshotamdas Thakurdas
lamenting the inertia in nationalist life and noting that any substantive
political work was now dependent on the Swarajists.[20] Thakurdas agreed
and helped to organize the Party campaign for funds. Nehru sent the same
message to F. E. Dinshah, the Bombay financier and associate of the
Tatas, urging him to impress his friends with 'a purely business viewpoint',
with the benefits of an alliance with his Party. Protection and currency
legislation, he noted, were important Swarajist priorities and their shared
interests needed public advocacy in papers like the *Chronicle* for which he
requested an Rs 11,000 contribution to pay off an accumulation of debt.[21]

While agreeing that it was impossible to remain aloof from nationalist
politics, businessmen continued to debate the terms of their participation.
Dorabji Tata became convinced that Indian politicians had failed to
protect essential economic interests of the country, and in particular to
stand up to the menace of communism. He urged his colleagues in industry
and commerce to establish their own party and propaganda organization.[22] In response, Thakurdas spoke for an increasing majority. 'Indian

[17] Note by John Coatman on the tone of certain sections of the press and the policy to be
adopted towards it, GOI (HomePol) file 178/29/129 and KW, 1 January 1929.
[18] Sahni, *The Indian Press*, p. 121.
[19] *Ibid.*
[20] Motilal Nehru to Purshotamdas Thakurdas, 8 October 1924, Thakurdas Papers, 40–1.
[21] M. Nehru to F. E. Dinshaw, 18 October 1924, Thakurdas Papers, 40–2.
[22] N. M. Mazumdar (Tata) Ltd to P. Thakurdas, 22 May 1929, Thakurdas Papers, 42 (III).

commerce and industry', he insisted,'are only an integral phase of Indian nationalism and that deprived of its inspiration in Indian nationalism, Indian commerce and industry stand reduced to mere exploitation.'[23] G. D. Birla agreed. The Tata proposal would fail because there was no possibility of such an association influencing the masses or the middle class. 'There was no solution for us', he argued, 'in joining hands with a reactionary element.'[24] Businessmen pursued the interests of their own community within the mainstream political debate – always spacious enough to accommodate a range of viewpoints. In 1932, Thakurdas responded sympathetically to Chintamani's lament that the interests of Hindus had been sacrificed in the Communal Award in order to cater to the Muslims. An even worse result from his point of view was that thirty-six of the forty-four Commerce seats had been given to European Commerce. It was unfortunate, he argued, that undue importance had been given to the Muslim question while 'treating the extravagant gains of the Europeans with indifference.'[25]

When the decision to deport Horniman was made, Lloyd had hoped that it would be viewed as an opportunity by the *Chronicle*'s Board to hire a more amenable editor and reduce the level of confrontation to acceptable limits. Horniman had been removed, at least out of the jurisdiction of the Governor of Bombay. But the *Chronicle* remained, and Lloyd's attempts to get the paper into 'respectable hands,' was a far more difficult undertaking. On the day of Horniman's arrest, the Bombay Government issued an order to the directors of the India Newspaper Company to submit for pre-censorship all material prepared for publication in the *Chronicle*. Three days later the paper suspended publication.[26] 'The nation will certainly feel hurt', noted Gandhi in a special manifesto, 'to find that the one who presented it with a daily drought of liberty is no more in its midst'; and he urged his followers to practice satyagraha, without public demonstrations, to illustrate the superiority of India's ancient civilization over modern civilization in its nakedness.[27]

The pre-censorship order was withdrawn on 17 June,[28] and publication was resumed. Although Horniman was supposed to be safely back in England, and no longer able to participate in Indian politics, his presence seemed hardly diminished. Over the next seven years he was the editor across the water – filing stories regularly, acting as the *Chronicle*'s London

[23] P. Thakurdas to N. M. Mazumdar, 7 June 1929, *ibid.*
[24] G. D. Birla to P. Thakurdas, 30 July 1929, Thakurdas Papers, 42 (V).
[25] P. Thakurdas to C. Y. Chintamani, 19 August 1932, Thakurdas Papers, 129.
[26] J. Crerar to the directors, Indian Newspaper Co. Ltd, 26 April 1919, Jayakar Papers, 364.
[27] M. K. Gandhi, 'To Brothers and Sisters', GOI (HomePol) 619–640 and KW 1919.
[28] J. Crerar to M. R. Jayakar and other directors, 17 June 1919, Jayakar Papers, 364.

correspondent, publishing articles in *India*, the journal of the British Committee of the Congress, and in the *Catholic Herald*, for subsequent reprinting in the *Chronicle*. As president of the Indian Press Association in London, his speeches and writings on the repression of press freedom in India attracted large audiences, and he was generally included in any Congress delegation in London. Throughout the last half of 1919, stories about Horniman – his services to India, his arrest and deportation, rebuttals concerning the soft-nosed bullet charge – and descriptions of his London-based activities appeared regularly. In subsequent years the stories diminished, but no regular reader of the *Chronicle* was allowed to forget that Horniman languished in exile in Britain and wished to return. The campaign was carefully orchestrated from London, and Horniman corresponded with his former colleagues in the *Chronicle* regarding issues that required greater coverage.[29] The paper seemed always willing to give as much space as necessary. In large type, and often with a portrait of 'the King across the Kala Pani',[30] the anniversaries of his deportation were noted with special messages;[31] his inability to obtain a passport was attacked and his return demanded,[32] and his absence was regularly associated with the general denial of fundamental rights in India: in short, Horniman's return was a matter of 'national self-respect'.[33]

While Horniman was carrying on his personal struggle in London, and committing himself as well to Gandhi, Non-cooperation and the struggle against the Reforms, his old responsibilities were shared briefly by Syed Hossain and S. A. Brelvi. Both recognized that they were only tempo-rarily filling in for their exiled master, and neither had the experience and influence that allowed for strong, independent control of the *Chronicle*'s editorial policy. In any case, the paper remained in danger of closure for some time, and the Board was committed to re-establishing a working relationship with the Government that would at least allow for un-censored publication. Both M. A. Jinnah and M. R. Jayakar, who alter-nated in the chairmanship in 1919–21, were critics of Non-cooperation and it appeared that the paper might return at least in the direction of the Moderate camp, from which Horniman carried it away in 1917. Jayakar was able to congratulate Brelvi on the 'courageous yet gentlemanly tone' of the *Chronicle*'s editorial comment on a speech by the Governor;[34] and

[29] *Bombay Chronicle*, 13 May 1920 (Horniman wrote to the *Chronicle*'s manager, Umar Sobhani regarding his passport difficulties).
[30] *Ibid.*, 26 April 1920.
[31] *Ibid.*, 28 April 1921.
[32] *Ibid.*, 6 March 1920.
[33] *Ibid.*, 17 March 1924.
[34] M. R. Jayakar to S. A. Brelvi, 22 August 1919, Jayakar Papers, 364.

the Board meeting under Jinnah's chairmanship, decided unanimously that the *Chronicle* would remain neutral in regard to Non-cooperation.[35] Even an editorial lamenting Tilak's death noted that although he was a great leader of the people of Maharashtra, Tilak 'shared some of their distinctive failings as well as all of their characteristic virtues'. In regard to his 'sometime reactionary views on social reform,' it appeared that 'he succumbed to the constant temptation of a popular leader to give the people what they want'.[36] As was often the case, however, it remained difficult to assign the *Chronicle* to a specific camp, since its messages were always mixed. The continuing flow of Horniman's colourful prose shared space with Brelvi's more measured political comment, and neither reflected the conservative priorities of the Board.

In 1920, however, any confusion regarding the policy of the *Chronicle* was resolved with the appointment of Marmaduke Pickthall as the new editor. Pickthall was a novelist and religious writer, particularly well known for his interest in the Middle East, his conversion to Islam, and his pro-Turk position on the post-war treaty concerning the remnants of the Ottoman Empire. He took the job because he needed the money, and because his political views denied him the opportunity of using his expertise in London.[37] In Bombay, he was quickly recognized as a Khilafatist leader, and, in that context, a staunch Non-cooperator as well.

The *Chronicle* had taken a strong pro-Turk position under Horniman, who insisted that the question could only be regarded from a Muslim point of view, and that it was 'absurd and perverse' for non-Muslims to quarrel with Muslim views. The history of the conflict was rehearsed in a flow of editorials associating the issue with the Muslims of Bombay, and all India.[38] Pickthall now carried on the campaign with the fervour of a true believer. Although initially reluctant to accept the appointment, he discovered an ideal opportunity for using his writing talents in support of his religious and political convictions. During the first year of his appointment, however, Pickthall's acclaim in the Khilafat Committee was not reflected in the *Chronicle*'s Board, where concern with the paper's un-

[35] *Bombay Chronicle*, 18 April 1921.
[36] 'The Lokamanya', *Bombay Chronicle*, 2 August 1920.
[37] A. Fremantle, *Loyal Enemy*, London: Hutchinson and Co., 1938, p. 322.
[38] 'The Moslem Demand', *Bombay Chronicle*, 21 March 1919. Horniman was committed to pan-Islamic nationalism. In 1917, in response to a request from Jinnah to prepare remarks for the Raja of Mahmudabad's speech as the presiding officer of the Muslim League meeting of December 1917 in Calcutta, he 'drafted a speech, instinct with the spirit of Islam, which contained references to the Khilafat in terms very objectionable to the Government'. The Raja of Mahmudabad refused to read the speech. See P. C. Bamford, *Histories of the Non-cooperation and Khilafat Movements*, Delhi: Deep Publications, 1974.

restrained support for the whole of Gandhi's programme led to resignations and reorganization. Jinnah resigned in April 1921 and Jayakar,
who seemed to enter and withdraw at regular intervals, resigned again
from the chairmanship and the Board at the end of the year. On this
occasion, he was angered by Pickthall's appointment as chief leader writer
in addition to his editorship without consultation with the Board. He
considered his position to be 'very anomalous if not humiliating' and
decided not to continue as a 'rubber stamp' for the actions and views he
could not support.[39]

The changes in the Board were greeted enthusiastically by Pickthall,
who felt that he had been forced to be guarded in his views. He now
looked forward to 'boldly uttering the Gandhian sentiments and views,
insh'allah'.[40] Any constraint had been more evident to Pickthall than to
his critics, who had already concluded that the *Chronicle* had been lost
again. The hoped-for rapprochement with Government was stillborn. In
his first interview with Sir George Lloyd, the Governor rejected a constructive relationship with a 'vile rag' and the Pickthalls experienced an
almost total European social boycott.[41] Within the Board, Jamnadas
Dwarkadas, a Gujarati dye-importer, home ruler and, by 1921, anti-
Gandhian, spoke for the 'Loyal Opposition'. He dissociated himself
entirely from the editorial policy of the *Chronicle*, noting that it was in
conflict with the agreed policy of the directors. The paper was not meant
to be an active protagonist of Non-cooperation and Dwarkadas was
particularly angered by implied attacks on his patriotism for retaining his
membership in the Legislative Council. He further lamented that Pickthall had 'allowed his pro-Muslim leanings to convert the paper into
practically an Islamic organ'.[42]

Gandhi, Non-cooperation, and Khilafat arrived in Maharashtra as a
single package, concentrating a range of concerns and grievances, defined
as Maharashtra's response;[43] and the *Chronicle*, the declared voice of the
Congress in the Presidency, helped to entrench the communal focus of the
new politics. The inordinate emphasis on Khilafat was particularly
offensive in Poona, where Tilak's heirs perceived a combined attack on
their cultural heritage. Among the major national newspapers published

---

[39] Jayakar to Hon. Secretary, Board of directors, Indian Newspaper Co., 19 December
1921, Jayakar Papers, p. 364.
[40] Fremantle, *Loyal Enemy*, p. 339.
[41] *Ibid.*, pp. 322, 331.
[42] 'Mr Jamnadas' Grievance', *Bombay Chronicle*, 18 April 1921.
[43] Richard Gordon, 'The Hindu Mahasabha and the Indian National Congress', *Modern
Asian Studies*, 9, 2 (1975), 162, has noted that Bombay was the treasury of the Khilafat
Movement, but that Maharashtra was never reconciled to Gandhi.

by Indians, the *Chronicle* was virtually alone in its uncompromising stand on the Turkish Question. Britain's policy was variously described as 'mad and idiotic',[44] 'a crusade against Islam',[45] and an 'insult to the Muslims of India and to the Indian people'.[46] The Khilafat and Punjab Wrongs were twinned as inseparable grievances which had to be jointly redressed.[47] While the campaign continued throughout the early 1920s in the *Chronicle*, others attempted to put the issue into perspective and distance it from the mainstream of Indian nationalism. By the spring of 1920, the *Hindu* asked 'What can Musalmans of India do?', and suggested that Montagu and Chelmsford had sincerely tried to help, while Gandhi's use of Non-cooperation on their behalf would lead to bloodshed and rioting and 'innocent people, who have nothing to do with the Treaty, would be the only sufferers'.[48] The *Leader* agreed. While recognizing the pain caused to Mohamedans in India and throughout the Islamic world, there seemed no alternative but to 'swallow the hard pill'.[49] The *Bengalee* suggested 'philosophic patience and calmness' to its Muslim readers,[50] and even the loyal *Independent*, while supporting the Khilafat cause, noted ominously that it was not possible to 'control the forces created by this movement by any sudden change of its temper or ideals'.[51]

The *Chronicle*'s perspective was reflected in regular editorial and leader writing. The Moplah riots were ascribed to the 'passions of a most excitable people ... whose religion was above all most sacred'. It was argued that the situation was brought under control by Khilafat workers who had convinced the Moplahs that non-violent Non-cooperation would rid the country and all Islamic countries containing holy places of Islam of foreign domination, and would eventually lead to the restoration of the Turkish Khalifa.[52] In a February 1922 editorial titled 'Allah-o-Akbar' Pickthall provided a new definition of *jehad* in non-violent Gandhian terms.[53] His preoccupation with casting the nationalist struggle in Muslim terms is reflected in an article titled 'Azad' in which a Muslim boy who lived in Benares, became a Non-cooperator and was caught and whipped by the police. He refused to apologize, insisting he

[44] *Bombay Chronicle*, 9 October 1922.
[45] *Ibid.*, 10 October 1922.
[46] *Ibid.*, 18 March 1922.
[47] *Ibid.*, 3 October 1921.
[48] *Hindu* quoted in the *Bombay Chronicle*, 22 May 1920.
[49] *Leader*, cited in *ibid.*
[50] *Bengalee*, cited in *ibid.*
[51] *Independent*, cited in *ibid.*
[52] *Bombay Chronicle*, 31 August 1921.
[53] *Bombay Chronicle*, 7 February 1922.

had done his duty as an Indian; and shouted *swatantra Bharat ki jai* (Victory to Free India) as the whip was landing on his back.[54]

The criticism of its apparent Muslim bias poured into the *Chronicle*'s office and much of it was published. Pickthall met his opponents directly in a December 1922 editorial noting concerns about his emphasis on the Turkish Question. In response to the argument that the *Chronicle* ought to be a national organ and not concern itself with such issues, Pickthall insisted that what was being asked for was a 'provincial organ concerned with the opinions of Mr This and Mr That of local fame, rather than with those of India in relationship to the world at large'.[55] There was no lack of support. At a Khilafat conference in the following week, the delegates noted their appreciation of the work of Pickthall, and the *Chronicle* and appealed to all Muslims to help the paper. A Bombay participant, Seth Khatri, noted that the *Chronicle* had brought a 'message of hope' and 'sustained the faith of Muslim India'. It was, he insisted, the duty of all Muslims to 'stand by the *Chronicle* under all circumstances'.[56] As in the case of his critics, Pickthall shared such applause with his readers.

His enthusiasm for Gandhi's leadership and programme was no less fervent than his commitment to righting the Khilafat Wrong, and he surely tested his command of laudatory adjectives to describe him. In one 1922 editorial, Gandhi was styled 'the greatest leader in the East', 'the national leader', the 'strategic chief', 'the leader', the 'absent general', 'Mahatma', 'the great commander', and 'Mahatmaji'.[57] He delighted in the opportunity to share a platform with Gandhi, always dressed on such occasions in *khaddar* and Gandhi cap. To his correspondents in England he described Gandhi as a saint and his movement as a form of 'self-purification',[58] and the religious nature of his enthusiasm was always evident in his *Chronicle* stories. 'Our weapon, thank God is a clean one', he noted in applauding the Bardoli decision to abandon Non-cooperation in 1922.[59]

It was in this context that Kelkar had rebutted the charge that Gandhi's opponents in Maharashtra were reactionary dreamers, seeking to retain power, symbolized in the restoration of Peshwa rule. In retrospect,

[54] 'Azad', *Bombay Chronicle*, 7 August 1922.
[55] 'The Chronicle and Some Critics', *Bombay Chronicle*, 21 December 1922.
[56] *Bombay Chronicle*, 1 January 1923. Pickthall wrote to a friend about his attendance at the Nagpur Congress as the guest of the Central Khilafat Committee. 'We travelled up in the Khilafat Special Train, bedecked with Muslim flags, and full of what the ordinary onlooking Englishman would doubtless have mistaken for a crowd of wild fanatics.' Fremantle, *Loyal Enemy*, p. 332.
[57] *Bombay Chronicle*, 31 May 1922.
[58] Fremantle, *Loyal Enemy*, p. 322.
[59] *Bombay Chronicle*, 14 February 1922.

Jayakar described in his autobiography the viewpoint of the defenders of Maharashtra who had experienced injustice, a situation which in his view had continued throughout the balance of the nationalist period.[60] The fault, Jayakar lamented, was largely their own because Poona had not openly attacked Gandhi but settled instead for 'halting and disingenuous conversion'.[61] Jayakar had noted in 1922 the 'marked dislike of Maharashtra and its politics' evinced by the editor of the *Chronicle*,[62] and he continued throughout his life to reiterate the same defensive theme: 'the non-receptivity of the Maratha mind to Gandhian fancy and asceticism', 'the essential incompatibility between the Maratha mind as moulded by Tilka's doctrines and Gandhi's teachings', 'the practical Maratha genius'.[63]

In 1921, V. D. Savarkar secretly sent out his *Hindutva* (Hinduness) manuscript from his Ratnagiri gaol cell, having arranged for its publication under the pen-name of 'Mahratta'. It sought to establish the basis for a Hindu nationalist movement in reaction to Gandhi and his apparent anti-national Muslim demands. After his release in 1924, he continued to attack what seemed to be Gandhi's obsession with Hindu–Muslim unity. And in his *Hindu Pad-padshahi: or A Review of the Hindu Empire of Maharashtra*, he recalled for his countrymen the achievements of Shivaji and Ramdas and the need to continue 'the same mission of winning back the political independence of the Hindu Race and defending the Hindu Dharma from the alien and barbarous foe'.[64] Kelkar and Jayakar might deny any plan to revive Peshwa rule but Savarkar retained the dream. 'Hope, with frankincense and offerings even as Mary did in loving solitude', he urged. 'For who knows when the Resurrection comes!!'[65]

Richard Tucker has described the defensive nature of nationalism in Maharashtra founded on the cultural priorities of its high-caste elites.[66] The elaboration of a competitive and powerful alternative vision forcefully introduced into their own country, appeared to threaten their cultural survival; and the politicized nature of the conflict suggested the possible imposition of a new form of alien control. For Jayakar, who operated as emissary between Brahminical Poona and Westernized Bombay, such concerns as consolidating 'the Hindus against Mahomedan

[60] M. R. Jayakar, *The Story of My Life*, Vol. I, Bombay: Asia Publishing House, 1958, p. x.
[61] *Ibid.*, p. 377.
[62] *Ibid.*, Vol. II, p. 16.
[63] *Ibid.*, Vol. I, pp. 378–9.
[64] V. D. Savarkar, *Hindu Pad-padshahi: Or A Review of the Hindu Empire in Maharashtra*, New Delhi: Bharatiya Sahitya Sadan, 1925, p. 43.
[65] *Ibid.*, p. 241.
[66] R. Tucker, 'Hindu Traditionalism and Nationalist Ideologies in Nineteenth Century Maharashtra', *Modern Asian Studies*, 10, 3 (1976), 322, 330.

aggression was particularly problematical'. A message that elicited an easy response in Poona appeared to be useless in cosmopolitan Bombay, where it was difficult 'to appeal to the communal sentiments of those who are politically minded'.[67] Gandhi could temporarily unite in opposition the two Maharashtrian camps, but not erase the fundamental differences in viewpoint on which their initial conflict had been founded. The collapse of the Non-cooperation campaign, however, provided an opportunity for the reassertion of Maharashtrian leadership,[68] and the *Chronicle*, although reluctantly, responded to the change.

In 1924, a series of legal disputes and substantial financial losses led to the *Chronicle*'s takeover by a group considered to be more sympathetic to Maharashtra. As had been the case after the 1917 Horniman coup, and again in 1921 when additional Gandhian supporters removed any constraint on the *Chronicle*'s advocacy of Non-cooperation and the Khilafat Movement; Pickthall resigned along with three other Gandhi loyalists on the Board: L. R. Tairsee,[69] Shankerlal Banker,[70] and N. H. Belgaumwalla.[71] In their place Jayakar returned again with Swarajist Party leader Motilal Nehru, and V. D. Govindji.[72] It appeared that the Swarajists were about to gain control of a Bombay paper that would support and advocate their views.

It had been a slow transition. In January 1922, commenting on the desire of Swaraj Party leaders, Motilal Nehru and C. R. Das to enter the Councils for the purpose of obstruction, the *Chronicle* called on 'our friends of Maharashtra' to explain their position. Did those who advocated Responsive Cooperation accept this goal, or were they likely to cooperate with the bureaucracy when a 'beneficial measure is brought forward'.[73] Throughout the year the *Chronicle* attacked Council entry in general, and the Maharashtra PCC in particular, for apparently more traitorous plans. In response, Kelkar challenged the *Chronicle* for attempting to make him and the Maharashtra Party the 'scapegoat for NCO fire eaters', noting that he reserved the right to be a critical Congressman under the orthodox Non-cooperators, just as he had been

---

[67] M. R. Jayakar to B. C. Moonje, 14 June 1925, Jayakar Papers, 405.
[68] M. R. Jayakar to C. R. Das, 6 January 1923, in M. R. Jayakar, *The Story of my Life*, Vol. II, London: Asia Publishing House, 1959, p. 75.
[69] Laxmidas R. Tairsee was a social worker, landlord, shroff, and merchant. He was an active home ruler and a radical member of the Indian Merchants' Chamber.
[70] Shankerlal Banker was a home ruler and active Congress politician throughout the 1920s.
[71] N. H. Belgaumwalla was a Parsee businessman and speculator. During most of the decade he was either a director or the owner of the *Chronicle*. He sold it to the Cama family at the end of the decade.
[72] Director's report, the Indian Newspapers Co., 28 November 1922, Jayakar Papers, 365.
[73] *Bombay Chronicle*, 'A Poona Explanation', 11 January 1922.

at one time under the orthodox Moderates. In contrast to the *Chronicle*'s uncompromising attack, he noted the 'mild and genial fire of *Young India*' that had been directed against the Maharashtra Party during the last two years.[74]

In January 1923, the *Chronicle* began its slow migration by noting that the new Party was at least within the Congress,[75] but the Maharashtra participants remained less trustworthy. They were again pressed to state, formally and publicly, their allegiance to, or deviation from, Das' obstructionist priority. Kelkar responded by noting his rejection of both 'the blind chelas of the Mahatma' and the 'selfish group of moderate politicians'.[76] Throughout the year the growing accommodation within the Congress of the reality of Swarajist Party success was reflected in reticent enthusiasm in the *Chronicle* 'At least Swarajists have gotten rid of the moderates.'[77] By January 1924, in a lead editorial entitled 'Forward to Work', the *Chronicle* formally withdrew from the battle, adopting along with the Congress a policy of benevolent neutrality.[78] The desire of the Swarajists for advocacy awaited the takeover in July.

The new Board met on July 30, under the chairmanship of Motilal Nehru. He recognized that the Swarajists still lacked a loyal majority and, therefore, declined the permanent chairmanship. He also warned his Bombay Swarajist colleagues that there would be no Party money for the *Chronicle* until their control was solid. In regard to the editorship, there was still a preference for Horniman if he were allowed back into the country. It was agreed, however, that his editorial skill would have to be complemented by a commitment to the Swarajists after Nehru reminded them that Horniman's contributions had been 'in support of the orthodox Gandhian doctrines'. K. M. Panikkar was proposed but he refused to keep the seat warm for Horniman. The Board finally agreed to turn to S. A. Brelvi.[79] He had been introduced to Pherozeshah Mehta by Lallubhai Samaldas and appointed assistant editor in 1915. Throughout all the subsequent crises and changes Brelvi was available to fill in: acting editor after Horniman's deportation, joint editor under Pickthall, acting editor again after Pickthall's resignation, and, finally, editor, but only until 'the King across the Kala Pani' returned.

Although there was concern about his ability to conduct effective Swarajist propaganda through the medium of the *Chronicle*, Nehru

[74] N. C. Kelkar, 'A Statement of Personal Explanation', *Mahratta*, 3 February 1923.
[75] *Bombay Chronicle*, 26 November 1923.
[76] 'Walk into my parlour, eh?', *Mahratta*, 4 February 1923.
[77] *Bombay Chronicle*, 26 November 1923.
[78] *Ibid.*, 2 January 1924.
[79] Motilal Nehru to M. R. Jayakar, 30 July 1924, Jayakar Papers, 365.

assured Brelvi that he had agreed to join the Board only because he relied on him to serve the Party.[80] He then went back to the United Provinces charging Jayakar with the responsibility of organizing the campaign for funds among the industrialists and merchants of Bombay. Both the party's programme and the future of the *Chronicle* as its major voice in the West were dependent on attracting such support. Nehru relied on F. E. Dinshah's money and Tata connections[81] to seal an alliance between Bombay industry and his Party, but their donations always disappointed him. Lalji Naranji[82] was also generally willing to support the *Chronicle*, but he tended to be politically vacillating and, therefore, not trustworthy to the orthodox of any party.[83]

While the struggle for secure funding and party loyalty continued within the Board and in the offices of selected Bombay business moguls, Brelvi eased the paper back from the confrontational style of his predecessor. He shared, however, Pickthall's loyalty to Gandhi as well as his concern for Muslim issues, and his *Chronicle* never satisfied those in the Swaraj Party who wanted their own paper like Das' *Forward*. Brelvi's solution to the problem of competition and conflict within the Congress was to provide a forum for all positions. He noted with concern that the *Chronicle* had been criticized for reproducing in whole Jayakar's Bombay Council speeches and suggested that an article about Party activities might be more appropriate than unbalancing the news columns.[84] Although he assured Jayakar that he was always prepared to take up any point editorially, this kind of evenhandedness and latent professionalism seemed inappropriate to Jayakar who thought the *Chronicle* was supposed to be a Swarajist paper. The struggle for purity – party and press – continued throughout 1924. When Swaminath Sadanand's FPI messages became too blatantly Swarajist, Brelvi told him to stop sending them to the *Chronicle*. He pointed out that there were other groups in the Council that deserved notice and insisted on an 'impartial attitude.'[85]

In January 1925, the partial support the Swarajists had been receiving from the *Chronicle* was threatened by the company's continuing insolvency and another takeover bid. Nehru and Jayakar attempted to rally support from F. E. Dinshah, Lalji Naranji, Purshotamdas Thakurdas, and other members of the Bombay business establishment, to prevent the

[80] Motilal Nehru to S. A. Brelvi, 4 August 1924, Brelvi Papers.
[81] Motilal Nehru to M. R. Jayakar, 30 July 1924, Jayakar Papers, 365.
[82] Lalji Naranji was proprietor of Mulji Jetha and Co.
[83] Gordon, *Businessmen and Politics*, p. 247.
[84] S. A. Brelvi to M. R. Jayakar, 20 October 1924; Brelvi to Jayakar, 20 October; Jayakar to Brelvi, 22 October 1924; Jayakar to Brelvi, 28 October 1924; Jayakar Papers, 404, Pt 1.
[85] S. A. Brelvi to S. Sadanand, 17 October 1924, *ibid*.

paper from 'being acquired by people who will not run it on independent, progressive, nationalist lines'.[86] Discussions were held in R. D. Tata's home and a financing package to allow for a competitive bid was tentatively arranged.[87] The anticipated support did not materialize, however, and N. H. Belgaumwalla, with the support of a group of investors that included Lalji Naranji, took control. Belgaumwalla had been a director with Pickthall, and had left the Board with him; and Jayakar was convinced that the Swarajists and Maharashtra had lost again, and the *Chronicle* would become 'the organ of Mr Gandhi's devoted followers'.[88]

Like its possession of the previous five months, the loss was not complete. Belgaumwalla offered a directorship to Jayakar and some control over the paper's editorial policy. The *Chronicle* would not be a Swarajist paper as proposed in the losing takeover bid of Jayakar's group,[89] but it would not be orthodox Gandhian either. Formal terms of agreement were prepared by Jayakar, providing for support of Swarajist Council activities, without precluding other forms of political agitation. It was also noted that should Swarajists decide to accept office in the unreformed Government, the *Chronicle* was at liberty to be critical, provided that its criticism was 'dignified and decorous' and did not 'ascribe motives to persons or indulge in any unbecoming abuse of individuals'. Belgaumwalla and Jayakar also agreed to meet regularly and Jayakar was given the right of approval of any future directors.[90]

These measures for the interests of the Party should have been adequate, but the resulting performance of the paper clearly did not measure up to Jayakar's expectations. There was too much of Gandhi, too many Muslim stories, too much evenhandedness and too little loyalty to the Swaraj Party. By March, Jayakar returned to his old theme of the need for a Party paper in Bombay.[91] The need was becoming even more compelling, as Jayakar's wing slowly moved towards full Responsive Cooperation and office, likely bringing renewed isolation for Maharashtra.[92] Relations with Belgaumwalla soured, and it seemed that the paper would finally make its return to the orthodox Gandhian camp.[93] But he remained ambivalent, never willing to part completely from the *Chron-*

[86] M. R. Jayakar to F. E. Dinshah, 14 January 1925, *ibid.*, 404, Pt 1.
[87] Jayakar to Umar Sobhani, 16 January 1925, *ibid.*, 365.
[88] Jayakar to G. S. Raghavan, *Hindustan Times*, 16 January 1925, *ibid.*, 404, Pt 2.
[89] Memorandum of January 1925, *ibid.*, 365.
[90] Jayakar memorandum, *ibid.*
[91] Jayakar to J. K. Mehta (secretary, Indian Merchants' Chamber), 9 March 1925, *ibid.*, 404, Pt 2. Also, Jayakar to Jairamdas Doulatram, editor, *Hindustan Times*, 30 August 1925, *ibid.*, 405.
[92] Jayakar to Motilal Nehru, 10 March 1925 and 16 March 1925, *ibid.*, 404, Pt 1.
[93] Jayakar, *Story of My Life*, Vol. II, pp. 595–6.

icle's affairs. It had become in micrososm his battleground for the control of India's national programme and future. He assured Brelvi that 'in spite of its indifferent and languid support', he was still a friend and would remain so 'until it becomes impossible'.[94] But he lamented his inability to gain control or even an effective partnership.[95]

In July 1925, Jayakar complained to Lajpat Rai that the Swaraj Party was languishing in the 'backwaters of the Non-cooperation movement' by denying itself the power and prestige of office which could be utilized to beat down sectional opposition like that from the Non-Brahmins.[96] B. V. Jadhav, the Non-Brahmin Education Minister, had consistently managed to steer the Non-Brahmin Members into the Bombay's Government's lobby on close votes, and Jayakar was convinced that a Swarajist Minister could attract the same response 'by being of use to them in their limited ambitions ...'[97] On 15 October, Jayakar was quoted in the *Indian Daily Mail* as an advocate of office and power in order to better serve Swaraj,[98] followed by an angry response from Motilal Nehru published in the *Chronicle*.[99] For the balance of the year, Jayakar and Kelkar were engaged in reasserting the practical priorities of the Maharashtra ideal, recalling that it was their opposition to Gandhian orthodoxy in 1921 that had paved the way for the establishment of the Swaraj Party. In 1925, the need seemed no less critical to challenge orthodox Swaraj policy.[100]

Kelkar pressed the argument in the *Mahratta*, noting that there had already been some compromise in Nehru's acceptance of a place on the Skeen Committee and Vithalbhai Patel's appointment as President of the Legislative Assembly.[101] It was assumed that the *Chronicle*, only grudgingly Swarajist would become the Party's champion against the rebels. In November, Jayakar wrote to Kelkar, noting that 'the Pandit was on the war path', and warned him that Nehru was building his strength for a struggle with the Responsivists. It appeared that he had secured control of the *Chronicle* and the *Advocate of India* by promising both a subsidy in return for loyalty for his views.[102] In fact, the *Chronicle*'s absolute loyalty remained as elusive as ever, but it was always a political barometer for

---

[94] M. R. Jayakar to S. A. Brelvi, 31 July 1925; Jayakar Papers, 365.

[95] M. R. Jayakar, *Story of My Life*, Vol. II, p. 495.

[96] M. R. Jayakar to L. L. Rai, 28 July 1925, Jayakar Papers, 365.

[97] *Ibid.*

[98] M. R. Jayakar to the Ordinary and Associated Members of the Bombay Legislative Council Swaraj Party, 21 October 1925, Jayakar Papers, 488 (II).

[99] *Bombay Chronicle*, 18 October 1925.

[100] M. R. Jayakar to the President of the Executive Committee of the All India Swaraj Party, 27 October 1925, Jayakar Papers, 496.

[101] *Ibid.*

[102] M. R. Jayakar to N. C. Kelkar, 8 November 1925, Jayakar Papers, 496.

Jayakar which he assumed would forecast rain whenever he planned a parade.

In January 1926, however, the *Chronicle* supported the new Responsivist Party. Gandhi's willingness to accommodate deviationist views had reduced the ranks of the orthodox, and the mixed signals emanating from the centre made it easier to remain pure, while experimenting at the same time. Belgaumwalla, who returned to control the paper in 1925, after his resignation in the previous year with the rout of the Gandhians, had become more flexible. He also could not antagonize potential backers. And Brelvi's view of Congress loyalty had already demonstrated a measure of tolerance for a range of tactics and viewpoints. An important element in this change in the *Chronicle*'s policy was the sudden re-appearance of B. G. Horniman.

The India Office had cabled the Home Department in December 1925 that Horniman had left Paris and was believed to be heading for India, although his passport was valid only for France and Italy. The Government of India was advised to prevent him from landing or to arrest him under the Passport Act and send him back to England. There was, however, an important loophole in the lack of passport restrictions between India and Ceylon. Horniman arrived in Colombo on 7 January, and despite an attempt instantly to amend the Indian passport rules by executive order, he sailed into Madras harbour on the 8th. Frustrated officials produced the 'Horniman Amendment' to prevent a similar incident in the future, but he was back and no law had been broken that would allow his deportation.[103]

The Indian press throughout the country celebrated his return, the *Chronicle* noting that there had been no event 'since the release of Gandhiji to give the people of India greater cause for rejoicing and thankfulness and greater encouragement in their struggle for freedom'.[104] Among the old adversaries who greeted him was M. R. Jayakar, who hoped that the new situation in India would attract Horniman away from the Gandhian orthodoxy of his last years in India.[105] On 12 January, he returned to Bombay, moving from the train station to the Congress House and then to the *Chronicle* office where he reassumed the editorship of the paper. 'I am not changed. I am not aged', he declared,[106] and told his readers in his first editorial that total editorial control had been given to him by the Board and that the *Chronicle* would remain the 'voice of the

[103] GOI (HomePol) 34/29 (1927) and KW.
[104] *Bombay Chronicle*, 12 January 1926.
[105] B. G. Horniman to M. R. Jayakar, 14 January 1926, Jayakar Papers, 365.
[106] *Bombay Chronicle*, 12 January 1926.

National Spirit of India'.[107] Horniman plunged into an active political role, making clear in the meetings he attended that there was no substance to Responsive Cooperation since there was nothing that called for a response, nothing worthy of cooperation.[108]

At a Bombay Provincial Congress district meeting, he insisted that the lack of unity in the Congress was the primary reason that India's demands had not been met. Arguing that there should be no compromise in the Cawnpore Resolutions, calling for a boycott of Assemblies if Swaraj Party demands had not been met;[109] Horniman declared that he would be there when Civil Disobedience returned.[110] Clearly the Jayakar-hoped-for change in Horniman's views had not occurred. He had remained true to the orthodox creed, enjoying the struggle vicariously from his English exile. But the years after the cessation of mass Non-cooperation had been frustrating and disillusioning except for the lucky few who shared Gandhi's convictions and patience. Within Maharashtra, the imported strategy and goal of Non-cooperation and Khilafat restoration had produced unsolicited alliances now coming apart in fratricidal collision. Defensive organizations to protect Hindus, Muslims, Non-Brahmins, Capitalists, and Maharashtra itself were the response to the call for united action against the shared alien enemy.

The Swaraj Party had appeared to provide a partial solution to the stalemate, and the newly independent Responsivists were satisfied that they had restored Maharashtra's practical good sense to the nationalist strategy rooms and provided, as well, an opportunity to voice their concern about the danger to their Hindu heritage. Horniman's suggestion that it was lack of unity which had created the problems seemed totally wrong to men like Jayakar and Kelkar, who found the source in the intolerant attitude towards conflicting views created by a strategy of confrontation founded on spiritual conviction. The *Chronicle*'s Board although willing to use Horniman's editorial talents, refused to admit him to Board membership and the possibility of another coup.

On 2 March, Horniman resigned from the editorship in a flurry of charges and counter-charges, proclaimed in public meetings and published in the press.[111] Subsequently he founded and edited the *Indian National Herald*, from which he continued his attack on Non-cooperation heretics including Gandhi himself, and after losing control of that paper in another celebrated contest, ended his career with the *Bombay Sentinel*.

[107] *Bombay Chronicle*, 19 January 1926.
[108] *Bombay Chronicle*, 25 January 1926.
[109] *Ibid.*
[110] *Ibid.*
[111] *Bombay Chronicle*, 3 and 4 March 1926.

The commitment to support the Responsivists, given by Belgaumwalla in January was restored, and Responsivist Party workers continued their efforts to collect funds for the *Chronicle*'s support.[112] In April the paper's precarious financing required another reorganization and another flurry of correspondence and meetings to gather support for its current policy.[113] In October the paper was sold, again to Belgaumwalla who was now associated with a group of investors including L. R. Tairsee who had sat on Pickthall's Board and had been moving away from confrontational politics.[114] Jayakar was able to assure Pandit Malaviya that the *Chronicle* promised to be 'the bulwark of the old world nationalism as we understand it',[115] and received a pledge of support to stabilize its finances in regard to the new threat from Horniman's *Indian National Herald.*

Brelvi used the announcement of the sale of the *Chronicle* as an opportunity to reiterate the paper's commitment to the national cause and to Congress. After thirteen years of advocating a particular viewpoint – Moderate and anti-Extremist, Extremist and anti-Moderate, Orthodox Gandhian, marginal Swarajist, and so on – the *Chronicle* declared a unilateral peace. Brelvi noted his commitment to 'the old, undiluted, creed of Mahatma Gandhi', and his aversion to councils and office, 'those playthings of designing bureaucracy'. But he recognized that the growth of national consciousness had produced 'a richness and variety of views regarding new ways and means'. In this context, he argued, the Congress ought to be sufficiently broadly based 'to welcome and absorb every shade of nationalist opinion'. There was room enough for all mainstream views, Brelvi suggested, and the *Chronicle* would find room to deal with them fairly and critically.[116]

By the end of the year, the *Chronicle* was urging Swarajists to modify their policies regarding working the Government of India Act rather than moving in a disorganized way – and through the backdoor – towards cooperation. It suggested that 'the shrewd Swarajists may be well advised to request the Gauhati Congress (meeting at the end of the month) to frame a practical programme of such coordinated action as may enable them to cooperate with all independent parties for the good of the people'.[117] As if to certify the rapprochement between Bombay and

---

[112] Jayakar's general letter to Kelkar (Poona), Dr B. S. Moonje (Nagpur), M. S. Aney (Yeotmal), R. C. Pradhan (Nasik), Mr Ketkar (Nasik), and N. B. Patankar (Nasik) on 5 January 1926, Jayakar Papers, 365.
[113] Belgaumwalla to Jayakar, 12 April 1926; Jayakar to Lalji Naranji, 29 September 1926, *ibid.*
[114] Auction of the *Bombay Chronicle*, 1 October 1926, *ibid.*
[115] Jayakar to Malaviya, 5 October 1926, *ibid.*
[116] *Bombay Chronicle*, 12 October 1926.
[117] *Ibid.*

Poona, Jayakar spoke to Kelkar about the paper's continuing financial problems, and it was agreed that the *Kesari* would recommend the *Chronicle* to its readers.[118]

The dominant theme of Brelvi's editorship, like the dominant theme of the decade, was the search for unity, its achievement and loss, its friends and enemies. As he settled back into the editor's chair, which would never be denied him again until his death in 1949, he lamented the lost opportunities and the obvious difficulties ahead.

If a modern Diogenes were to hunt out for Indians with his lantern in these days, he would be sure to come across fervid Hindus, bigoted Muslims and fanatical souls deeply engrossed with the problem of tirelessly finding out how unjustly their own particular community was being treated, and he would have to ask in sorrow: 'Where are the Indians!'[119]

As the only Muslim editor of a major, national, English-language paper, Brelvi was especially sensitive to the communalist context of the political debate. He tried to keep the *Chronicle*'s commentary on the high ground, but unlike Chintamani, Iyengar, and Kalinath Roy, he did not have absolute control of his paper. Deeply felt divisions, violent confrontation, and emotional reaction surrounded him in the *Chronicle*'s office, and were evident in its pages. Often Brelvi's impatient and defensive idealism on the editorial page debated with an article in the same issue. And Jayakar was always there to render judgement. In a 1927 Diwali review of the previous year, he described the current communal conflict as only superficially religious in nature. The cow and music questions, he insisted, were far less significant than the political aspirations of the Mahomedans whose leaders, 'in their desire to have the loaves and fishes of office as also larger power, did not scruple to make use of the religious fanaticism of their less educated compatriots, but make it as a pawn in the game'.[120]

B. G. Horniman was an outsider, however committed to the cause of India's freedom, and was, therefore, able to operate on the surface of community and tradition. Similarly, Marmaduke Pickthall's Islamic zeal was neither informed nor constrained by a lifetime's experience of India. It was, in fact, to avoid such constraints that he took up the *Chronicle*'s offer. But Brelvi's was an Indian life, and contacts and experiences as a young man continued to make an impact on his views throughout his career. Vaikunth Mehta was a classmate at Elphinstone College, and

---

[118] Jayakar to D. V. Gokhale (editor, *Mahratta*), 9 December 1926, Jayakar Papers.
[119] *Bombay Chronicle*, 20 May 1926. Belgaumwalla did offer Jayakar the editorship in December 1926, but he refused.
[120] *Bombay Chronicle*, 12 October 1927. Jayakar wrote the review.

Brelvi was treated as a family member in the home of Lallubhai Samaldas (Mehta's father). His friendship with Mehta was the most important of his life, and in an extraordinarily intimate correspondence he shared his most personal feelings and views.

Long before I knew you, I believed in Hindu–Muslim unity. But it has been the contact with you all that has saved me many a time from the danger of losing my balance in moments of crisis which test one's nationalism, and I can now sincerely claim that I am able to rise above communal consideration spontaneously and without any effort in every crisis.

Brelvi noted that he was studying Sanskrit but had not as yet been able to form a definite opinion regarding the theory of transmigration of souls, though he felt 'it offered the only adequate solution of the riddle of life'. He planned to write a book on the teaching of the Prophet and its similarity to that of the Gita.[121]

Just after the announcement of Gokhale's death in 1915, Brelvi had visited the Servants of India Society and shared his sense of 'calamity' and new purpose with Mehta. Before Gokhale, there were workers for social, educational, and political reform, he noted, but 'there was nothing like a public life'. There was nothing like a selfless public career. 'Mr Gokhale's was the first public career.'[122] Brelvi hoped that Gokhale's death would bring differing groups together and suggested that if this did not happen, 'then we deserve no political, no real progress'. At the beginning of his own public career, he committed himself to Gokhale's model of service and to the goal of unity.[123]

Brelvi's idealism and lack of personal, political ambition were obvious to a range of contacts who called on him to deal with sensitive issues in *Chronicle* stories. Another Elphinstone classmate, Mahadev Desai, Gandhi's secretary, noted his preference for dealing directly with Brelvi during the Kaira Satyagraha in 1918, rather than with Horniman whose lack of 'moderation and perspective' was endangering the movement.[124] Desai read Brelvi's letters to Gandhi in order to 'convince him that there is at least one level-headed man on the staff of the *Chronicle*'.[125] Throughout their careers, Desai provided Brelvi with a direct link to Gandhi and suggestions for stories or commentary received immediate response in the pages of his paper.[126]

---

[121] S. A. Brelvi to Vaikunth Mehta, 21 January 1931, Brelvi Papers.
[122] S. A. Brelvi to Vaikunth Mehta, 21 February 1915, Brelvi Papers.
[123] S. A. Brelvi to Vaikunth Mehta, 26 February 1915, Brelvi Papers.
[124] Mahadev Desai to S. A. Brelvi, 9 April 1918, Brelvi Papers.
[125] Mahadev Desai to S. A. Brelvi, 14 April 1918, Brelvi Papers.
[126] Mahadev Desai to S. A. Brelvi, 28 August 1927; 4 January 1927; 29 October 1930; 19 August 1934, Brelvi Papers.

Hindu–Muslim amity and socialism were the two essential elements in Brelvi's unity mandate. But however idealistic his personal commitment, in the editorials of an influential newspaper they invariably attracted and helped to entrench divisiveness. His designation of Muslim participation and agreement as essential for any significant political progress or change of strategy tended to overshadow his commitment to political tolerance in the minds of defensive Maharashtra leaders. Jayakar and Kelkar were quick to respond to any nuance that suggested criticism of the Responsivists.[127] But he continued to argue for the 'utter inevitability of united action'.[128] No responsible party, he insisted, would pledge itself to cooperation with Government at any cost, and none would accept the practicality of total Non-cooperation. Any useful programme had to have a composite character. The lesson as applied to the communal issue was always read – Muslims feared arbitrary Hindu action that would weaken their political influence.[129]

Brelvi assured readers that Shivaji had no quarrel with Muslim rule in the north, but was solely – and quite properly – concerned with incursions into Maharashtra. He pressed his Hindu readers to reject the communalization of their history, and that of all of India, whose heroes were Ashoka, Akbar, and Shivaji.[130] Brelvi attempted to redirect the debate among Indians to the confrontation with the British – 'they will try to divide us in regard to the Simon Commission';[131] the bureaucracy would be the greatest loser if separate electorates were abolished[132] – but there was clearly no united front to carry on the fight. He was particularly derisive about the apparent fanaticism of some No-changers,who pressed for a return to Non-cooperation but ignored its essential component, 'complete cooperation between Hindus and Muslims'. Without it, and, in addition, the cooperation of peasants and workers, the Congress would remain, he lamented, 'a paper organization'. In a conclusion that might have been written by Kelkar eight years before, Brelvi insisted that Congress desired 'no more spectacular fireworks which end in smoke'.[133]

The focal point in Bombay for his unity struggle in the period 1926–9, was the *Chronicle*'s conflict with Horniman's *Indian National Herald*. The latter's policy reflected its editor's uncompromising radicalism as it lashed out at everyone who appeared to constrain an immediate return to

---

[127] M. R. Jayakar to S. A. Brelvi, 22 November 1927, Jayakar Papers, 365.
[128] *Bombay Chronicle*, 28 October 1926.
[129] *Ibid.*
[130] *Ibid.*, 3 May, 1927.
[131] *Ibid.*, 27 April 1927.
[132] *Ibid.*, 16 May 1927.
[133] *Ibid.*, 25 April 1927.

Non-cooperation. Horniman called on the Indian people to 'hold down the small oligarchy that was the ruling Congress', and advocated the non-payment of taxes. He rejected Gandhi's argument that the country was not ready for mass Civil Disobedience, and toured north India with his message. In response, Brelvi reiterated the need for Muslim co-operation, reminding his readers of the 'glorious days of 1921', when Hindu–Muslim unity had allowed the country to confront the British successfully. Muslims were now opposed to Non-cooperation, he argued, and the first task was to deal with the reasons for their reticence.[134]

Brelvi attacked the leaders of both communities who suggested that Islam or Hinduism was in danger;[135] and blamed the problem on swamis and maulanas who had no place in politics.[136] He applauded the establishment of a League Against Mullaism, arguing that nothing should be accepted as true religion which was repugnant to the dictates of reason.[137] Brelvi was particularly concerned that Jawaharlal Nehru gave too little attention to the communal question as a fundamental constraint on further progress.[138] Nehru agreed; in the context of the political lull of 1933, following two years of active confrontation, he admitted that the diversion of public attention to the positive economic and political side of the struggle had not made any impact on the problem. He was now ready to speak out forcefully and noted that he was accused of using unnecessarily strong language. 'I think the right line to take', he suggested, 'is that communalism is merely a cover for political reaction.'[139] Brelvi was pleased with Nehru's change of perspective, but believed that his diagnosis was far too simple. Throughout the late 1920s Brelvi had attempted to deal with communal identity on its own terms, understandable if not laudable. During the extended negotiations concerning separate electorates and the Nehru Report, he agreed that there was disagreement among Muslims and that Hindus were reticent about making a deal. But, he insisted, there was no possibility of making any progress unless the risk that the Muslims have taken was matched by the Hindus. 'Complete unity and trust do not exist', he declared; and India had to accept this reality.[140] But, however much he tried to be balanced in his arguments on this issue, the *Chronicle* remained for many a Muslim paper, and a permanent candidate for takeover. In February 1930, Jayakar heard a rumour, which

---

[134] *Bombay Chronicle*, 23 May 1927; 8 June 1927; 10 June 1927; 15 June 1927.
[135] *Bombay Chronicle*, 18 April 1927.
[136] *Bombay Chronicle*, 9 July 1927.
[137] *Bombay Chronicle*, 10 October 1927.
[138] Brelvi to J. Nehru, 29 November 1933, Jawaharlal Nehru Papers, Vol. X.
[139] Nehru to Brelvi, 3 December 1933, *ibid*.
[140] *Bombay Chronicle*, 14 April 1927.

turned out to be incorrect, that the *Chronicle* was likely to be auctioned off at a reasonable price. He immediately contacted a potential buyer in Bombay, who might be interested in 'acquiring the paper for the Hindu Cause'.[141]

While other socialists recognized an enemy in M. K. Gandhi, Brelvi found the source for his beliefs. He noted his hatred for the capitalist system in a 1922 letter to Mehta, and his new awareness of the greatness of Gandhi, who had placed before the Indian people and the British the ideal of righteousness and non-violence in preference to economic exploitation camouflaged as civilizing mission.[142] While retaining a sensitivity to legitimate Muslim concerns and the reality of distinctive Muslim identity, Brelvi came to associate his commitment to Hindu–Muslim unity with his socialist convictions. He insisted that the June 1932 communal riots in Bombay were largely crimes against 'helpless and suffering victims, the poor Hindus and the poor Muslims'.[143] Brelvi considered both his socialist and communal missions to be in the service of Indian unity, but there was no easy satisfaction or achievement. Animosity between the League and Hindu Sabha was paralleled by the confrontation between the left and right wings of the Congress.

He told Nehru that the Congress socialists had done good work, but they were using 'wrong tactics' in denouncing Congress policy and abusing its leaders. He noted that attacks on Gandhi had antagonized rank-and-file members, and his particular concern about the apparent campaign in Bombay against conservative leaders like Vallabhbhai Patel and Bhulabhai Desai. It was in response to such challenges that Jayakar, Tej Bahadur Sapru, and representatives of some princely states had established a syndicate in 1935, with the help of the manager of the *Times of India* to start a new paper for propaganda in favour of working the new constitution. In Brelvi's view the scheme was designed to kill two birds with one stone: suppressing the *Chronicle* and starting their own paper. Jayakar had first attempted to buy the *Chronicle* but the price was too high. Now the paper was on the market, and since the Congress could not afford to buy it, Brelvi considered the possibility of starting another. His concern about socialist attacks on Patel and Desai were associated with the *Chronicle*'s problem, since they would play a major role in the establishment of any new paper in Bombay. He reminded Nehru that the socialists had been given a lot of publicity in the *Chronicle* and, as a result,

[141] Jayakar to Raja Narain Lal Bansi Lal, 26 February 1930, Jayakar Papers, 365.
[142] S. A. Brelvi to Vaikunth Mehta, 24 June 1922, Brelvi Papers.
[143] S. A. Brelvi to Vaikunth Mehta, 27 June 1932, Brelvi Papers.

both Brelvi and his paper had offended these prominent Congress leaders who dubbed the *Chronicle* a socialist paper.[144]

Brelvi contacted Gandhi, and asked him to intercede with Patel and Desai, and Gandhi duly urged them to support the establishment of a Congress paper in Bombay, which should, if possible, be 'ready on the very day the *Chronicle* changes hands'. In regard to Brelvi's future, Gandhi advised that if he were otherwise eligible, his 'socialistic inclinations ought not to be regarded as a bar' to his selection as editor.[145] This was not the unreserved support he had sought and anticipated, but he was doubtless used to his idealism being categorized as someone else's enemy. In a subsequent conversation with Patel and Desai, they agreed that a Congress paper should be started, but they denounced the *Chronicle*'s support for the socialist programme. They insisted that their paper would be a party paper, 'giving publicity and support only to the majority view of the Congress and suppressing the minority view altogether'.[146]

Brelvi had argued with Patel and Desai that the function of a newspaper was to publish all views in its news columns while reserving the editorial for its dominant policy. But in response to his query whether they would allow him even to report a Congress socialist meeting, they said no. He was astounded by their 'narrow-minded and reactionary views about the function of a newspaper', and did not think it would be possible to work under their control. Happily, the sale of the *Chronicle* fell through and he was able to finish his life and career in its editor's chair. But the interview was 'an eye-opener' for him, demonstrating yet again the particular difficulties for a Congress newspaperman.[147]

There was a complex mix of assumed and envisaged unity subsumed in the words 'Indian Nationalist Movement'. In this context, nationalism for many was part of the problem as well as the solution. In the case of Maharashtra, the *Bombay Chronicle* was one locus of the internal struggle for control of means and ends – an expropriated voice of one party or another fending off opposition, or a professional institution attempting to assert a margin of independence. At exchange points like the *Chronicle*, choices had to be made to represent 'Poona' or 'Bombay' or 'Delhi'. Although the overlap was, in fact, substantial, a mix of fear, defensiveness, and intolerance produced demands for loyalty and concern for any accommodation.

While Horniman and Pickthall were willing representatives of Gandhi-

---

[144] Brelvi to Nehru, 14 November 1935, Jawaharlal Nehru Papers, Vol. X.
[145] Mahadev Desai to Brelvi, 26 October 1935, Brelvi Papers.
[146] Brelvi to Nehru, 14 November 1935, Jawaharlal Nehru Papers, Vol. X.
[147] *Ibid.*

an orthodoxy, as reflected in the Khilafat Movement and Non-cooperation, Brelvi's idealism and Muslim identity moved him and his paper to seek an accommodation of viewpoint with the reality and presumed legitimacy of division. This was not, however, reflected in support for a Maharashtrian reluctance to become a fragment of an aggressively asserted All-India entity. Brelvi's concerns concentrated on nationwide categories: Muslims and the poor. As a result, he antagonized those who chose to speak for Maharashtra, and denied the *Chronicle* an easy relationship with all the orthodoxies: Gandhian, socialist, capitalist, communalist. His paper came to be categorized as 'socialist' by the Congress right, 'Islamic' by defensive Hindus and anti-communalists, and 'undependable' by all who measured loyalty in terms of absolute acceptance of their position. By the early 1930s, the *Chronicle* had become more like the *Tribune* and the *Hindu*, a Congress supporter with a mind and life of its own – a good representative of the mix of pragmatism and passion of heterodox Bombay.

5   The struggle overseas

The founders of the Indian National Congress assumed that the struggle for self-government in the form of petition, propaganda, and mobilization of support, would have to be carried out in both Britain and India. A British Committee of the Congress was established in 1889, and its maintenance and staffing were given the same priority as administration in India. The Congress paid the salary of William Digby, the Committee's secretary and editor of its journal, *India*; and the perceived significance of its work was reflected in regular votes of substantial funding. In 1902, *India* was given a measure of stability by the allocation of quotas of subscribers to the provinces, and the decision to require a special delegation fee of Rs 10 for this purpose.[1] In subsequent years, the flow of money, petitions, and delegations of leaders continued to denote Congress confidence in British goodwill, or at minimum the lack of any apparent alternative locus for the achievement of their goal.

But divisions over strategy and tactics, and the definition of the goal also made the 6,000-mile sea journey; and the representation of the nationalist struggle became a subject for debate in Whitehall offices, Parliamentary Committees, and gatherings of the Labour Party. In 1919, in addition to the official delegation of the Congress which travelled to London to meet the Joint Parliamentary Committee considering the Reforms, there were also deputations representing the Moderates, the Justice Party, the Home Rule League, and a minority branch carved out by Annie Besant, the National Home Rule League.[2]

There was as well a range of resident activists in addition to the British Committee. When Har Dayal reached Britain in 1908, he dismissed *India* as a useless propaganda vehicle, and deputations to London as a waste of time.[3] Shyamji Krishnavarma's *Indian Sociologist* advocated confront-

---

[1] B. Pattabhi Sitaramayya, *History of the Indian National Congress*, Vol. I (1885–1935), Delhi: S. Chand and Co., 1969, p. 54.

[2] *Ibid.*, p. 174.

[3] Emily Brown, *Har Dayal, Hindu Revolutionary and Rationalist*, Tuscon: University of Arizona Press, 1975, p. 54.

ation and demands rather than accommodation and petition; and when he left for Paris in 1907, the control of India House, the central gathering place for expatriate Indian students in London, passed into the control of V. D. Savarkar and his extreme Hindu nationalism. An early convert to Savarkar's India House revolutionary group was Virendranath Chattopadhyaya (Chatto), one of the founders of organized Indian nationalist propaganda in Europe. Savarkar, Chatto, and Dayal, with the support of radical patrons like Mme Bhikhaiji Rustom K. R. Cama, were willing to work with the Congress; but only on their own terms. Their bases in Britain, Europe, and eventually the United States allowed them a measure of freedom from both Government of India repression and the self-imposed constraints many nationalist leaders in India accepted as the price for unity. 'Exile has its privileges', Dayal noted in his Geneva-based journal, *Bande Mataram*. 'It is the price paid for the right of preaching the truth as it appears to us.'[4]

The British Committee's founding President, William Wedderburn, was also President of the Congress in 1889; and he left no doubt about the significance of the London branch and work in England for the success of the movement. 'Our hopes depend entirely', Wedderburn noted with axiomatic conviction, 'upon the degree to which the British people can be induced to exert their power with reference to India.'[5] Since freedom was to be won in England, the Committee was perceived as the 'real centre of work'[6] and Committee members were confident that whatever the vicissitudes of activities in India, in the end they would play the essential mediating role in working out an accommodation acceptable to both parties. They perceived themselves as members of the Congress – some were in fact employees of the Congress – and also as committed, informed, and influential friends – guardians of the Freedom Movement rather than the Raj.

The mixed response to the announcement of the Montagu–Chelmsford Reforms in 1918, appeared to British Committee members as another opportunity to mediate among rival Indian groups and between them and the British Government. H. S. L. Polak noted his concern to G. A. Natesan that the Congress might reject the Reforms and their best chance for a significant advance of their cause. Although there was clearly strong support for the Reforms in Britain from both Liberals and Conservatives closely associated with India, Polak assumed that the influence of Curzon

---

[4] *Ibid.*, p. 74.
[5] Presidential address, Indian National Congress, Bombay, 1889, *Speeches and Writings of Sir W. W. Wedderburn*, Madras: G. A. Natesan and Co., 1918, p. 3.
[6] H. S. L. Polak to G. A. Natesan, 1 August 1918, Natesan Papers.

and Milner would likely support a less generous commitment, and Lord Sydenham and his supporters on the far right would probably reject it all. In addition, Polak reminded Natesan that the British public had little interest in Indian affairs at the best of times, and five years of war had concentrated their attention on local issues of far greater immediate importance to them. In this context, it seemed essential to the British Committee that a Congress delegation come to England to participate in the final determination of the Reforms and to assess and influence public opinion. He described the efforts of the Committee to offset the poor press received by Congress, noting that the situation was the result of years of failure to cultivate the British public, in spite of the urgings of Wedderburn and others, 'save in a ludicrously inadequate degree'. Polak outlined a scenario of increasing isolation for the Congress, with the dominions, now favourable to the Reforms, becoming absorbed in their own reconstruction, and Parliament refusing to move beyond Montagu's scheme. And if the Congress were captured by those who would reject the Reforms, the British Committee would also be lost, becoming the representative 'of what will generally be regarded here as the sober element in Indian public life'.[7]

In a subsequent letter, Polak defensively described a British Committee that could remain in the struggle, but only on its own terms. He asked for £2,000 for *India*, noting that the 1917 commitment had not been met and nothing had been provided as yet for 1918.[8] In response to the Annie Besant–Tilak ascendancy in the Congress and the decline of moderate control, Polak insisted that the British Committee was not only the representative of Congress in Britain, but retained the right to take an independent line if necessary. In particular he warned Natesan that there should be no attempt to tamper with the independence of *India* and its editorship.[9]

In April 1919, the Congress finally sent its delegation to London, along with the representatives of rival groups and the British Committee sought a consensus for the Reforms by suggesting that each delegation send a representative to a meeting of the Committee where an agreed strategy and viewpoint would be achieved.[10] The response of V. J. Patel, the leader

---

[7] British Committee critique of Congress policies had apparently led to a hold back of support. Sitaramayya, *History*, Vol. 5, p. 204.

[8] H. S. L. Polak to G. A. Natesan, 15 August 1918; 2 October 1918, Natesan Papers.

[9] Polak to Natesan, telegram, 26 November 1918: 'Confidential, Tilakites endeavouring capture Committee newspaper suicidal, consult friends, endeavour prevent Congress with drawing support or interfering policy'. *Ibid.*

[10] In December 1918 at Delhi the Congress had called for self-determination and full responsible Government in opposition to the more limited Montagu scheme; apparently

of the Congress group, finally clarified the changed situation which had somehow eluded his British colleagues. The Committee, Patel insisted, was created and funded by the Congress. It existed to represent the Congress view in Britain and any member who could not accept that situation was invited to resign. For the future, the Committee was asked to draw up a new constitution that made this relationship explicit and to submit it to the Congress for confirmation.[11]

The transfer of the internal struggle among nationalists to Britain and eventually other countries, enhanced the scepticism of Congress leaders who had little enthusiasm for foreign activity. It was business as usual, but in an environment even less amenable to their control. Patel and his delegation confronted a double fight in England, noted Congress historian, Pattabhi Sitaramayya. 'On the one hand they had to settle with the British Committee of the Congress, and on the other with Mrs. Besant who was indefatigable in her energies and in her opposition to the Congress.'[12] They were determined that any future arbitration would take place in India.

The need for foreign propaganda and publicity for the Congress viewpoint, however, retained a prominent place in the resolutions of the Amritsar Congress in December 1919. Lajpat Rai was thanked for his work in the United States. He had recently made clear his commitment to publicity abroad in an open letter to the Indian leaders in London, arguing that ignorance rather than prejudice was responsible for the general lack of support for India's cause. 'People held very peculiar views about us', he informed his Congress colleagues, and their ignorance about all things Indian – history, culture, politics, and economics – was 'simply colossal'. What was required was a well-organized propaganda campaign both within and outside India, and certainly not limited to Britain.[13] The British Committee was also formally thanked for its efforts, especially in regard to the 'Amritsar Massacre' propaganda; and Tilak was apparently responsible for suggesting the establishment of a 'permanent mission' in England and elsewhere to organize Congress propaganda.[14]

After months of press censorship, a high priority was given by the AICC to publicizing the events in Amritsar; and the Congress Punjab

---

reversing the position taken at the special Bombay session in September which accepted limited provincial autonomy as prescribed in the Government paper.

[11] Sitaramayya, *History*, Vol. I, pp. 175–75.
[12] *Ibid.*, p. 175.
[13] 'Need for Publicity Abroad', an open letter to Indian leaders in London, 25 July 1919, published in the *Tribune*, 4 September 1919, and reprinted in V. C. Joshi, *Lala Lajpat Rai, Writings and Speeches*, Vol. I, 1888–1919; Delhi: University Publisher, 1966, pp. 317–23.
[14] Sitaramayya, *History*, Vol. I, p. 181.

Inquiry Report caused the Government of India particular concern in Britain where it was assumed that press comment before the publication of the official Hunter Committee Report would stimulate renewed confrontation. In an effort to compete and contain what would become a constant element in their relationship, the Home Department asked the India Office to hold up publication of any press summary of the Congress Report, or at least influence the press 'to suspend judgement or moderate its comments' until their side had been heard.[15]

It is most important that home press should not comment without restraint on non-official reports because success of such comments will be repeated to India and will as happened in December last revive and accentuate anti-Government agitation which will not only threaten public tranquillity but also prevent the Hunter Report from receiving fair hearing.[16]

Quick action by the India Office allowed the Secretary of State to inform the Viceroy on 8 April, that the press summary of the Report had not been published by the *Times* and the *Daily News* had published it without comment.[17] Reuters provided a brief summary the following day which was published in the *Times* and the *Morning Post*, but longer summaries and abstracts of the Report were published in other papers, again without comment.[18] *India*, however, remained unsusceptible to India Office influence, and the AICC was able to congratulate the editor for her efforts: 'The special atrocity number was really grand.'[19]

The reconciliation between the British Committee and the Congress was brief. In the spring of 1920, Motilal Nehru contracted the services of R. C. R. Nevill, a London solicitor, for propaganda work concerning the Punjab troubles. A payment of £1,000 was provided for the preparation and distribution of a pamphlet analysing and commenting on the three Punjab Reports: the Majority and Minority Hunter Reports and the Congress Report. Nevill hired St Nihal Singh, an experienced Indian journalist, to prepare the pamphlet and the work was well under way when the British Committee heard about it. The Committee had requested a Congress special grant of £1,000 for its own Punjab work and

---

[15] Viceroy (Home Department) to India Office, 6 April 1920, IO L/P5/6/1678.
[16] *Ibid.*
[17] Secretary of State to Viceroy, 8 April 1920, *ibid.*
[18] *Ibid.*, 9 April 1920.
[19] Gokaran Nath Mistra, Joint General Secretary, AICC, to Miss H. Normantan, editor, *India*, 3 March 1920, AICC 10/1920, Pt 1. Throughout 1920, the Assistant Secretary, AICC, Raja Rao, sent articles to *India* for publication 'as editor sees fit without signature', B. G. Horniman, the exiled editor of the *Bombay Chronicle* was a major contributor to the campaign in Britain. See B. G. Horniman, *Amritsar and Our Duty to India*, London: T. Fisher Unwin Ltd, 1920.

was informed that the funds had already been sent to Nevill to be spent in consultation with them.[20]

G. P. Blizard, the Committee Secretary, responded with a contentious letter to the AICC Secretariat copied to C. R. Das, Kasturi Iyengar, and B. G. Tilak. He insisted that the Committee was 'the only body authorized and competent to conduct propaganda in England', and urged the AICC to instruct Nevill to hand over the funds and responsibility to them. V. J. Patel supported their claim this time and there was an immediate response from the AICC. Nevill was asked to comply and after a brief exchange with Committee officials the draft pamphlet and unspent funds were forwarded to them.[21] In a contest among Englishmen, AICC officers were willing to accept without comment Blizard's assertion that the British Committee should have 'supreme control' over propaganda in Britain,[22] and a small amount of additional funding and India-produced propaganda material were sent during the following five months. The next confrontation, however, concerned Indian participation in the London campaign and the issue of the final authority of the AICC first raised by Patel in 1919.

In the Committee's new constitution approved by the AICC, it was agreed that an Indian, chosen by the Congress, would be appointed to the Committee's staff. Before a selection was made in India, however, an election was held in London and Syed Hossain was appointed secretary and joint editor of *India*. Hossain had come to London as a member of a Khilafat delegation and decided to remain in order to carry on publicity work there, and eventually in the United States. He had been a member of the *Bombay Chronicle* staff under B. G. Horniman, and when Motilal Nehru sought Horniman's advice regarding an editor for his new paper, the *Independent*, he suggested Hossain. It was a brief and unhappy tenure. Hossain seemed willing, in Nehru's view, 'to risk everything just for the sake of a strong adjective', and they parted company before the end of the first year.[23] Far more important in this case, was the Congress determination to assert its right to that appointment, and V. J. Patel informed the Committee that Hossain had to go. If he wanted the job, it would be necessary for him to apply directly to the AICC.[24] The ensuing

---

[20] *Ibid.*
[21] Notes on correspondence and interviews with reference and interviews with reference to £1,000 remitted to Mr Nevill, AICC 10/1920, Pt 2, pp. 199–205.
[22] G. P. Blizard, Secretary British Committee, INC, to the General Secretary, INC, 3 May 1920, *ibid.*
[23] Motilal Nehru to Jawaharlal Nehru, 3 April 1922, Jawaharlal Papers. See also memorandum dated 22 October 1921, Motilal Nehru Papers, 52 (1–5).
[24] V. J. Patel to British Committee, 7 October 1920, AICC 10/1920, Pt 2.

controversy continued until the end of the year when Gandhi delivered the *coup de grâce*.

In a speech at the Nagpur Congress in December, 1920, Gandhi insisted that it was necessary 'to revolutionize the country's ideas about foreign propaganda'.[25] Motilal Nehru had noted earlier, especially in regard to the Punjab, the need to communicate to the Indian people the national significance of these events, and the far less significant role for propaganda outside. Nehru was willing to allow the British Committee to do the work in England, but he did not anticipate significant benefit for India. It was apparent to him that Britain or the United States, or any of the states of Europe would sympathize with India's cause 'only so far as is conducive to its own well-being'; and in his view, nationalist leaders should concentrate on building their strength and only then their case 'for presentation to the civilized world'.[26]

Gandhi was less accommodating. 'The Congress has deliberately burnt its boats', he insisted. 'It has decided to become self-reliant.' In this circumstance, it was inappropriate to continue to subsidize a foreign agency and the British Committee had to be abolished 'as a matter of principle'. In response to a *Bombay Chronicle* critique regarding this decision, Gandhi voiced concern that any Congress funds should be allocated for foreign propaganda. The Rs 45,000 that had been committed for this purpose by the AICC could be better used, in his view, for the purchase of spinning wheels or the building of schools. The apparent good work being done by the British Committee and in particular by *India*, was, he suggested, part of the problem; for 'it raised in us false hopes'. The programme of Non-cooperation to which the Congress had committed itself required 'new methods for combating the evils of sensational and untruthful journalism in public life'. The Congress had now led the way, he asserted, by the abolition of the Committee and *India*.[27]

It was in fact the Committee's own memorandum on the constitutional issue which prepared the way for its abolition. J. M. Parikh, the vice-chairman, reminded the AICC that the founders of the Committee were themselves the leaders of the Congress and there was no question of misunderstandings in the relationship. The Committee was independent and self-constituted, carefully changing and increasing its membership with colleagues who shared the founders' view and commitment. Under the new constitution drafted in 1918, however, membership was obtained

[25] M. K. Gandhi, speech on foreign policy, Nagpur, 29 December 1920, *The Collected Works of Mahatma Gandhi*, Vol. XIX (November 1920–April 1921), Publications Division, Ministry of Information and Broadcasting, Government of India, 1966, pp. 235–37.

[26] Motilal Nehru to Lala Girdharilal, 11 March 1920, Motilal Nehru Papers, 162–73.

[27] Gandhi, *Collected Works*, Vol. XIX, pp. 235–7.

through election. The result, lamented Parikh, was the introduction of political competition by the formation of an interest group which continued to nominate and elect members who supported their views. Because the Committee was small, a few members had the opportunity to pack the Committee, and in subsequent elections, pack the executive as well. Parikh noted in particular the role of B. G. Horniman, the exiled former editor of the *Bombay Chronicle*, who had contrived to bring 'Besantists' into the Committee. It was also the Horniman group which had nominated Syed Hossain for the editorship. When the vote was deadlocked between Hossain and Fenner Brockway, the candidate of the old mainstream, it had been agreed to appoint both as joint editors of *India*.

Parikh concluded that the present constitution was unworkable, in effect providing for an executive of the Congress in Britain totally outside the control of officers in India except through the denial of supplies and funding. He recommended abolition of the Committee as presently constituted and its replacement by a Congress agency, its control dependent on Congress appointment. He suggested, however, that the AICC would do well to invite the current Committee chairman, Ben Spoor, a Labour MP, to form a Committee of MPs willing to work for India. It would be this Committee, financed by the Congress agency and using the rooms and staff of the agency, that would promote the Indian cause.[28] Parikh had prepared his memorandum and a confidential note for the use of Ben Spoor, who planned to travel to India to attend the 1920 Congress session and represent the Committee's case to concerned AICC officials. He was also proposing a constitutional coup that would allow the inheritors of the Wedderburn tradition, led by Spoor, to regain control of the mission in Britain, under the patronage of the Congress.

By 1920, the Congress leadership were experienced arbitrators and manipulators of Provincial Committee management crises. The only difference in this case was consideration of the question whether a London committee was necessary. There had been an angry exchange between Patel and the Committee concerning Hossain and the lack of adequate funding, concluding with a pyrrhic victory for the Committee on 17 November. Patel sent a draft for £1,000 with a note indicating that none of the funds were to be used for payment to Hossain, 'whose appointment was made in defiance of the Congress Executive'.[29] Spoor and two of his Committee colleagues, Holford Knight and Colonel

---

[28] J. M. Parikh, 'Observation on the Present Constitution of the British Committee', 18 November 1920, AICC 10/1920, Pt 2, 1920, pp. 281–96.
[29] V. J. Patel to Ben Spoor, 17 November 1920, *ibid.*

Wedgwood, attended the Calcutta Special Congress in September, and the Nagpur Congress at the end of the year. At Nagpur, Wedgwood warned the members of the Subjects Committee that Non-cooperation would make it difficult for their friends and supporters in England to support their cause. They were 'going into the wilderness', he lamented, and they would have to travel alone.[30] It was clear that Wedgwood spoke as a friend of the Congress, but there was no delay in taking up his challenge. 'We have no friends outside of India', declared the next speaker. 'Our salvation lies in our own hands.'[31] But the connection was not easily broken.

The Subjects Committee appointed a Sub-Committee chaired by Motilal Nehru to consider the British Committee memorandum and the Committee's future. All of Parikh's recommendations were accepted. The Committee was abolished, *India* discontinued, and a Congress agency was established and granted an initial £3,000 funding. The formation of an Advisory Committee was left to Spoor and those colleagues who attended the Congress session. In spite of Gandhi's reservations, the Sub-Committee committed the Congress to continue and expand its propaganda activities in foreign countries. In addition to the renewed support for the work in England, a recommendation was made for recognition of the Indian Information Bureau of New York as the official agency of the Congress in America with an annual grant of $3,000 to support its work. It was further recommended that additional agencies be established in Paris and Tokyo as funding became available.[32]

Although some Congress supporters envisioned an international communications network connecting press bureaus in London, New York, Tokyo, and Paris with an Indian National Congress press bureau in India; sufficient funding, manpower, and a measure of consensus regarding the nature of the messages eluded the grand planners. The handful of leaders in India who perceived some benefits in a foreign campaign were too busy launching or opposing the Non-cooperation Movement at home. They were concerned about publicity but getting a good press in India, communicating with colleagues throughout the country, and mobilizing mass understanding and support at home was sufficiently difficult to keep them fully occupied. They would make news, but others with the leisure to concentrate their energies on publicity and propaganda alone, would have to carry the message overseas.

[30] Quoted in Sitaramayya, *History*, Vol. I, p. 208.
[31] *Ibid.*
[32] Motilal Nehru, Report of the Sub-Committee appointed by the Subjects Committee to consider the question of foreign propaganda on behalf of the Congress, 28 December 1920, AICC 9/1922, pp. 83–5.

Rather than a well-organized, centrally controlled publicity network, Indian nationalism was represented in Britain, Europe, and the United States by a range of individuals and organizations, often self-appointed, who worked for the cause according to their own views and desires for India's future. Some sought official recognition and funding from the Congress and accepted without question the policy positions of the AICC. Others took the money, but like the old British Committee asserted their independence in advocating positions they considered to be in India's best interests. It was virtually impossible for Congress officials in India to control the situation. There was never sufficient funding to guarantee that denial of further support would end an undesirable campaign; and disaffiliation was only useful if the action itself could be given wide publicity. Since control of these 'foreign agents' depended on the interest and time available to the few leaders who gave them any continuing attention, there were long delays in responding to problems and misrepresentation. From the Government of India's perspective, however, the Congress appeared to have established some form of international network of support; and throughout the 1920s and 1930s, they sought to compete.

When official influence, ordinary law, and professional interest failed to attract a sufficient collaborative response, the power to censor and ban was available to the protectors of the Raj. Much of this activity concerned the effort to contain the international traffic in news and views that appeared to endanger imperial interests throughout the world. Books, letters, newspapers, and pamphlets were scrutinized for any support they might offer to presumed revolutionaries within India, or to critics of the Government outside. A roster of dangerous men and dangerous journals was established and a corps of censors and customs officials to deny them entry or exit. In the years after World War One the challenge to Britain's imperial hegemony was clearly not limited to India. The export of revolution by the Bolshevik regime in Moscow and the emergence of the United States as a world power had to be taken into consideration in any plan for the preservation of their world-wide interests. The audience for propaganda – theirs and their enemy's – was increasingly cosmopolitan.[33]

The Home Department was convinced that persistent efforts were being made to 'flood India with communist literature', and every example that turned up was added to the file, such as a cutting from the *Indian Social Reformer* which referred to the regular receipt of *Vanguard*, a communist journal that had been banned by the Government.[34] The banned list in

[33] See Barrier, *Banned.*
[34] S. P. O'Donnell, Secretary, Home Department, 2 August 1922, GOI (HomePol) 955/1922.

1921 included 115 items. Shyamji Krishnavarma's *Indian Sociologist*, a monthly now published in Paris, had been banned since 1907, and the New York based *Gaelic American* suffered a similar fate in 1909. H. M. Hyndman's *Justice* carried on the struggle in London and Har Dayal's *Bande Mataram* in Geneva – but both were denied easy access to Indian readers. The list was continually updated by officials who generally recognized the futility of their attempt to deny India an ordinary communications relationship with the rest of the world, but strengthened the barriers with the powers available to them.[35]

An elaborate system of informants in India, Britain, North America, and Europe helped to stop the gaps in the coastal walls. In April 1921, sixteen members of the crew of SS *Kandahar* were arrested and prosecuted at Singapore for bringing in seditious literature. The material had originated in the United States and both the India Office and the Home Department were concerned that Indian lascars hired in New York might become regular couriers for expatriate revolutionary societies. It was suggested that the British Consul in New York check such seamen and notify officials in India regarding known agitators. But the Foreign Office refused to take on the responsibility and the India Office refused to pay for it. Information officials in India were content to rely, as in this case, on the cooperation of the masters of these ships.[36]

Nehru, Chatto and the League Against Imperialism

After his initiation as a nationalist propagandist in London, Virendranath Chattopadhyaya moved on to Paris and then Berlin, where he edited *Talwar* (Dagger) and with a small group of expatriates established the Indian Committee of National Independence in 1915. Their radical views were clearly out of touch with current Congress policies, and no attempt was made to associate the Committee with the mainstream movement in India. In 1921, however, the Gandhian revolution within the Congress appeared to provide a basis for associating the activities of the Berlin group with their compatriots at home. A new organization, the Indian News Service and Information Bureau, was established and Chatto wrote to the AICC to describe its mandate and seek support. The Bureau would supply European news to the nationalist press and Indian news to the press of Europe. It would also look after Indian students and travellers. The work was begun with a weekly news sheet to India, but the whole effort, he insisted, depended on the Congress response.

[35] Memorandum re. newspapers prohibited from entering India under Section 10 of Sea Customs Act and Sections 25 and 26, Indian Post Office Act, GOI (HomePol) 159/1921.
[36] H. D. Craik inter-office note, 15 October 1921, GOI (HomePol) 234/1921.

It seemed apparent to Chatto and his colleagues that the Congress had now come of age and should take on the responsibility of supporting Indian work outside. In this context, those responsible for these activities in Germany, France, England, America, and Japan 'should be regarded as representatives of the foreign policy of India'. Their specific requests were recognition of the Berlin Bureau, a grant of Rs 5,000 for the coming year, and the deputation of a few able men to come out from India to help with the propaganda effort.[37] A similar request was made by Fenner Brockway who wanted to establish a London press bureau in the old British Committee offices, and sought a £3,000 annual grant.[38] Another request had come from the United States and the AICC attempted to dole out its limited funds on the basis of personal knowledge of the people involved. Lajpat Rai and N. C. Kelkar recommended the work of D. V. S. Rao in America, and his Home Rule League received $1,000.[39] Brockway had established his credentials as a useful supporter and his expenses were reimbursed.[40] The Berliners received support as well, but not at the level their ambitious plans required.

A continuing measure of the success of these initiatives was the efforts of the Government of India to respond to the challenge and neutralize the perceived damage. An attempt was made to improve the sale of official publications in England and proposals were considered for facilitating visits of American newspapermen to India. The Home Member doubted that it was worth spending money on trying to influence Labour MPs, but a publicity agent in England for the Government of India was appointed as an officer in the India Office.[41] The Home Department was particularly concerned about the activities of the Berlin Bureau, but it was assumed there was nothing to gain from issuing a warning communiqué regarding the Bureau because of 'the stigma attached to such Government documents'.[42] The India Office had been given detailed information regarding the Bureau's activities by Sir Ashutosh Chaudhri after a visit to Berlin. He described its work with Indian students who were both assisted in settling into their studies and attracted to Chatto's political views.[43] The India

[37] Pandurang Khankhoje, Vivendranath Chattopadhyaya, Bhupendranath Datta to AICC, 29 November 1921, AICC 4/1921.
[38] A. Fenner Brockway note re. setting up a London Press Bureau for the INC, AICC 9/1922.
[39] Sitaramayya, *History*, VOl. I, p. 213.
[40] General Secretary, INC, to Ben Spoor, 3 February 1922, AICC 9/1922.
[41] Home Department memorandum, 30 September 1920. Lloyd Evans was appointed Publicity Officer in the India Office, GOI (HomePol) 771/1992.
[42] Sir F. W. Duke, Under-Secretary of State, IO to W. Vincent, Home Member, GOI, 18 October 1922, GOI (HomePol) 259/1924.
[43] *Ibid.*

Office considered setting up a similar service through some unofficial agency, 'which would be supported by the Government as unobtrusively as possible', since the large number of Indian students attracted to Germany for technical training by the fall in the value of the mark appeared to constitute both a problem and an opportunity. But the Government of India did not consider the issue pressing and was reluctant to commit the required funds.[44]

The establishment of the Tilak Swaraj Fund in 1921, provided a measure of stability for Congress activities in India and some support for the work outside. The campaign goal was Rs 1 crore and it was oversubscribed by approximately Rs 15 lakhs.[45] Foreign propaganda was frequently discussed in the AICC and Working Committee but it remained on the margin of interest and expenditure. In 1925, the AICC authorized the establishment of a Foreign Department to look after the interests of Indians abroad,[46] but foreign propaganda did not receive a specific allocation until a Rs 5,000 fund was established in March 1926.[47] The level of funding reflected the mixed reception the proposal received and the concern of conservative leaders that the Congress mandate not be unduly informed with the rhetoric and content of continental radicalism. But it was an important victory for Jawaharlal Nehru, who was the leading advocate of an international connection for India's freedom fighters.

Nehru travelled to Switzerland in 1926 to arrange medical care for his wife. From Germany he wrote enthusiastically to his father about the League Against Oppression in the Colonies which would hold a congress at Brussels in January 1927. Even Mexico would attend, he pointed out to Motilal Nehru, 'because of its fear of the USA'. It was obvious to him that India should be represented 'for after all the most menacing imperialism of the day is British imperialism in India'.[48] Nehru attended the Brussels meetings as the official Congress delegate and went on to attend the meeting of the Executive Committee of the League Against Imperialism, in Amsterdam.

---

[44] *Ibid.*

[45] Sitaramayya, *History*, Vol. I, p. 297.

[46] *Ibid.* AICC accountants were kept busy keeping Foreign Department records in order. They chased Sarojini Naidu for four months concerning Rs 897 spent in connection with South African propaganda work. Between 30 March 1926 and 30 September 1927, Rs 5082 were allocated to the Propaganda and Publicity in Foreign Countries Account. In addition to funds raised within India, donations came from expatriate groups. In 1931, the INC of Japan gave Rs 2615; the Indian Association, Gulu (Uganda) East Africa gave Rs 405; the Indian Association, Tanganyika Territory gave Rs 2088; and the Welfare of India Association, California gave Rs 1,000, AICC 25, F–43, 8/1931.

[47] Jawaharlal Nehru to Motilal Nehru, 16 November 1926, AICC G–21/1926–7.

[48] Jawaharlal Nehru to Rangaswami Iyengar, 7 March 1927, AICC G–29/1927, Pt 2.

Nehru discovered in Europe an array of countries which shared India's burdens, and colleagues who had joined the struggle against colonial oppression. They also shared and stimulated his broad intellectual concerns about the state of the world and India's place in its changing power structure; and he pressed the new lessons on his less cosmopolitan associates at home. In March, he wrote to the Working Committee, not only to keep them in touch with European developments, but to 'divert the attention of the members for a while at least from Hindu–Muslim riots and murders'. He also carefully emphasized for the benefit of his more conservative colleagues, that he had been described as 'the tame bourgeois representative of the Indian National Congress', a description he accepted as correct. He noted as well that the Brussels meeting was socialist–labour and not communist, although communists were present and welcome.[49]

Nehru had committed himself to associate the masses of peasants and workers with both the nationalist struggle and the national goal. But he recognized that it remained unclear how far the Congress would identify with socialism. In the cosmopolitan and intensely competitive ideological environment of the European conferences, he was also made aware of a potential conflict between individual national interests and those shared by all the world's underclass. Shapurji Saklatvala, a radical expatriate in London, had opposed the boycott of Lancashire goods in India because they damaged workers in Britain. Whatever the concerns, however, Nehru urged the Congress to join the League and contribute to its funding. Membership would provide the opportunity to associate with others in a similar position in Asia, and the means of carrying on a propaganda campaign on a vast scale. There was a possibility of communist domination of both the organization and the message, but it seemed unlikely to Nehru that Russia would gain control of Indian nationalism through the intervention of the League. 'We can cope', he insisted. 'Soviet Russia opposes British imperialism and so do we.'[50]

During the next three years the League, and particularly the personal contacts he made at its meetings and through correspondence, provided Nehru with an ongoing association with radical movements in the West and support for trade union and *Kisan Sabha* development in India. That support generally was little more than moral; but the League's international contacts could be mobilized to participate in orchestrated letter-writing campaigns to change views among Congressmen as well as outsiders in the direction of a further radicalization of the movement.[51]

[49] Jawaharlal Nehru to Working Committee, INC, February 1927, AICC G–29/1927.
[50] *Ibid.*
[51] V. Chatto to J. Nehru, 5 December 1928, AICC (FD)1 (ii), Pt 3, 1929, pp. 166–8.

The major link figure in this enterprise was Virendranath Chattopadhyaya and in this period there was a regular exchange of letters and memoranda between him and Nehru. In the context of the new internationalism which had been injected into the proceedings of the AICC, the Congress joined the League and reiterated its support for the establishment of a Foreign Department.. The initial commitment made in 1925 had resulted in more expenditure on foreign activities but no stable institutional base. In 1929, however, Nehru took on the responsibility and he pressed Chatto for names and addresses of pertinent foreign organizations with which he should correspond.[52]

Chatto left Berlin in January to carry on League work, but arranged for Congress support for the Berlin Indian Students' Information Bureau now administered by A. C. N. Nambiar.[53] In addition to his role in the Bureau, Nambiar was employed as the Berlin correspondent for a number of Indian papers.[54] When Swaminath Sadanand established a London office for his FPI news service, Nambiar became his Berlin correspondent, providing the FPI with German material in addition to his weekly notices to the Indian press.[55] As was the case with all such organizations, stable funding remained elusive and patriotic commitment had to fill the gap. The AICC provided £30 per month for the Berlin office, but the funds often arrived late and a small increase in October 1929, left the Bureau still dependent on Nambiar's income as a journalist.[56] Political workers like Nambiar laboured in Europe as loyal Congressmen, ready to respond to the instructions of AICC officials and flexible enough to accept a strategy of confrontation or collaboration as the situation in India appeared to demand. Chatto, however, represented a different group – firmly equipped with ideological certainty and unwilling to accommodate any significant change in either method or goal.

Chatto returned to Berlin in March 1929, after being expelled from Belgium. He assumed the British Government had told the Belgians that he was living in Brussels, and they certainly kept a detailed log of his movements. Like Nambiar, he had to scramble for a living, depending on a mix of stipends from the League for his work as Secretary, donations

[52] J. Nehru to V. Chatto, January 1929, *ibid.*, p. 173. Nehru wrote to the editors of major nationalist papers in India urging them to send complimentary subscriptions to Berlin, AICC G–15.

[53] Secretary, AICC, to V. Chatto, 10 January 1929, AICC (FD) 20/1/1929, Pt 1.

[54] A. C. N. Nambiar to J. Nehru, 4 January 1929, *ibid.*

[55] J. Nehru to A. C. N. Nambiar, 22 February 1929; Nambiar to Nehru, 6 March 1929, *ibid.*

[56] A. C. N. Nambiar to J. Nehru, 12 August 1929, *ibid.*, Pt 3, J. Nehru to Nambiar, 1 October 1929, *ibid.*, Pt 2.

from Nehru's Foreign Department fund, and earnings from translation work.[57] Nehru's description of the situation in India did not lessen his burdens. Affiliation with the League had always been a divisive issue, not only in the Congress, but generally among radical groups. As the result of a massive anti-communist campaign by the Government, a large number of arrests had been made and Nehru informed Chatto that the All-India Trade Union Congress might be left in the hands of an anti-League moderate majority. He also noted that the Government had given the League prominence at the Meerut Conspiracy Trial which he assumed 'frightens away the timid folk in the TUC'.[58]

The Meerut case was carefully managed by the Government of India to obtain maximum propaganda advantage for its anti-communist, anti-terrorist campaign. R. S. Bajpai, the Deputy Director of the Information Bureau, was sent down from Simla to Meerut to supervise publicity arrangements, and as usual with such major events, API and Reuters sent out a full subsidized report.[59] The analysis of the information sent to Chatto, reflected the increasing tensions and ambivalence in their relationship. Nehru assumed this 'pure propaganda effort' designed to 'prejudice the accused in the eyes of the nationalists', would achieve considerable success, because the far left, with Chatto's enthusiastic support, seemed to attack nationalists and Government with equal vigour.[60]

Nehru sought the help of the League in publicizing the Meerut defence position, not merely as a case that should concern radical groups, but all labour organizations. He urged Reginald Bridgeman, the Secretary of the British Section of the League, to attract British labour support to the plight of Indian labour, and in a memorandum copied to Saklatwala and Chatto and widely circulated by the League, he notes a connection between the Meerut trial, the Trade Disputes Act, and the Public Safety Ordinance which had recently been certified by the Viceroy after being denied Assembly support. Taken together, he insisted, they indicated a concerted attack on the trade-union movement in India, and therefore on trade unionism everywhere.[61] But Nehru's easy association of nationalist and radical socialist argument continued to concern some of his colleagues in the AICC. Chatto in Berlin, however, was concerned that Nehru's resolve and that of the Indian nationalist movement would weaken.

---

[57] V. Chatto to J. Nehru, 20 March 1929, AICC (FD) 1.
[58] J. Nehru to V. Chatto, 20 June 1929, *ibid.*
[59] *Ibid.*
[60] *Ibid.*
[61] J. Nehru to Reginald Bridgeman, 25 October 1928; 25 April 1929; 7 May 1929, AICC (FD) 23/1929.

Throughout the last half of 1929, Chatto and Nehru corresponded regularly and with increasing intensity. While Nehru's conservative colleagues, moderates outside the Congress, and the Government of India built separate but complementary images of a left-wing, radical, communist, revolutionary leader, Chatto challenged Nehru's credentials as a true freedom fighter and his determination to reject accommodation with imperialism. In August, Chatto stated his concern that Nehru might accept the presidency of the Congress and compromise his radical principles in order to maintain unity. Their subsequent exchange reflected the increasing distance in viewpoint that would make it difficult for them to work together in the future. Chatto insisted that Nehru had to be prepared to split the Congress and lead the country 'with a fully revolutionary programme'.[62] In October, when Nehru's selection was confirmed, Chatto lamented the 'false step' in Nehru's career, noting that his nomination by the 'cunning Mahatmaji' was an obvious attempt to 'kill you and the opposition'.[63]

The struggle within the Congress in India was reiterated in a struggle within the League on the continent. While Chatto attempted to retain Nehru's loyalty to the 'militant' cause being challenged by 'reformists' and 'reactionaries',[64] others reported 'a wild heresy hunt' by the dominant left-wing section of the Communist International 'against everyone who was not absolutely trustworthy from their point of view'.[65] The continental ideological struggle had been replicated in regard to the Indian nationalist campaign – the militants at their accustomed place on the margin, and a mix of pragmatists and idealists at the centre of the movement. In January 1930, the two met in India with a circular letter addressed by the League to all anti-imperialist organizations. Largely inspired by Chatto's concerns, it was an indictment of the Congress leadership and policy and a call for left-wing rebellion. In his response, Nehru lamented their willingness to attack and subvert without any accurate knowledge of the actual conditions in India and the advances in the political and social views of the Congress. He noted their willingness to cooperate with communists in a common task, but emphasized that most Indian nationalists and certainly the Congress were not communists.[66] It was clear that this branch of their 'foreign service' was no longer working for them. In April, addressing Chatto as 'Dear Sir', Nehru

[62] V. Chatto to J. Nehru, 28 August 1929, AICC (FD)1 (ii) Pt 2, 1929.
[63] V. Chatto to J. Nehru, 6 October 1929, *ibid.*, Pt. 3.
[64] *Ibid.*, pp. 125–7.
[65] Edo Fizmen to J. Nehru, 12 November 1929, AICC (FD) 23/1929, pp. 21–3.
[66] J. Nehru to Secretaries, League Against Imperialism, 30 January 1930, AICC (FD) 1/1929–30, pp. 47–60.

resigned from the League's Executive Committee and Congress disaffiliation soon followed.[67]

Competing messengers and messages

While the League tended to dominate Nehru's and the Congress' activities in Europe in the last half of the 1920s, the centre of the external
campaign remained in London where decisions were being made about
the pace and content of reform. Motilal Nehru had sent Iswar Saran to
London in 1929, to describe and attract support for the Nehru Report.
Saran encountered considerable difficulty in getting his letters published
in *The Times* and other major papers; but he kept up his efforts
throughout the summer, distributing a thousand brochures entitled *The
National Demand*, which Nehru had sent him. Nehru provided detailed
instructions regarding the need to emphasize the inter-communal and
all-party support for the Report and the threat of a return to Non-cooperation if India's demands were not met.[68] The less confrontational style of
this kind of propaganda work attracted the Congress's traditional constituency of liberal and radical English supporters who continued to write
and speak on their behalf.

In 1929, Fenner Brockway was editor of the *New Leader* and a newly
elected MP. He had maintained the connection with India established
during the final years of the British Committee, and more recently had
corresponded regularly with Jawaharlal Nehru. Responding to developments on the continent, he warned Nehru not to rely on the communists
in Britain since they had no influence and would likely hinder any
effective work.[69] Nehru, already in the process of withdrawing from the
League, assured him that he retained his independence. But he noted that
repression continued in India and a Labour Government in power did not
appear to make any difference.[70] Police brutality, press censorship, and
the general environment of repression in India became Brockway's subjects for House of Commons' speeches, and the AICC provided the
evidence in provincial reports, press clippings, and copies of speeches and
publications which had resulted in prosecutions.[71] In response to questions raised by Brockway in the House of Commons, the India Office
sought information from the Government of India, which it shared, in

[67] J. Nehru to V. Chatto, *ibid.*, p. 3.
[68] Iswar Saran to Motilal Nehru, 13 June 1929; Motilal Nehru to Iswar Saran, 1 August
1929, Motilal Nehru Papers, I–3, 216–20.
[69] A. Fenner Brockway to J. Nehru, 2 July 1929, AICC (FD) 33.
[70] J. Nehru to A. F. Brockway, 1 August 1929, *ibid.*
[71] Under-Secretary, AICC, to A. F. Brockway, 4 December 1929, *ibid.*

part, with Brockway. The result, noted the Secretary of State to Lord
Irwin, was a considerably more moderate opponent. Brockway was
apparently convinced that maintenance of order required many arrests
and the subsequent debate in the House turned out to be 'intensely dull'.
The House was not full, and 'Brockway played up splendidly.'[72]

A new organization, the Friends of India Society, was established in
London in 1930, after Reginald Reynolds returned from India and a
meeting with Gandhi. Reynolds sought to bring together a number of
India activists to influence public opinion in favour of self-determination
and in particular to popularize the significance of Gandhi's non-violent
movement as a moral alternative to war. Pamphlets by Reynolds, Horace
Alexander, H. N. Brailsford, and V. J. Patel were published and distributed. Weekly meetings and lectures in London attracted an increasing
constituency, and a touring motor van, the 'Indian Caravan', provided an
opportunity for propaganda work throughout the country. In February
and March 1931, thirty-four meetings were held in eighteen towns. The
Society also issued a fortnightly bulletin, *India Events*, and regularly
distributed, 2,000 free copies.[73] As was the case with all such groups, the
Home Department monitored its activities, appraised its impact, and
sought out the sources of its funding. Apparently only one member, Mrs
Jane Fetherstonhaugh, associated with Indians with communist leanings,
and the Society was considered relatively moderate – certainly well within
the bounds of criticism that had to be accepted in 1931. Although its
initial funding may have been substantial – possibly through the patronage of R. B. Lotwala, by the end of 1931, the Society needed funds and
received some support from Pandit Malaviya. The Government of India
decided that its bulletin did not constitute a threat and it was allowed
ordinary entry into India.[74]

Whenever possible, the Government of India attempted to use the
passport system to prevent entry of people considered undesirables,
especially known communists; and to prevent as well the outward travel
of 'undesirable British Indians'. All Russian visa applications were automatically referred for review and rejected unless there was assurance the
applicant was not a communist.[75] Part of the early warning system was a
fortnightly passenger list supplied to the India Office by the P&O shipping
line home office.[76] There were, however, some 'undesirable' travellers

[72] Secretary of State to Viceroy, 24 December 1930) GOI (HomePol) 11/19/1930.
[73] Note, the Friends of India Society, 11 November 1931, GOI (HomePol) 35/32/1932.
[74] *Ibid.*
[75] Note re. prevention of entry of communists, etc., into India, GOI (HomePol) 325/1930.
[76] Memorandum re. supply of publications, posters and other published materials, Edwin
Haward (IO) to F. H. Grosvenor, Manager, P & O House, 11 March 1929, IO (InfoDept)
L/I/1/1 and 2, File 27/1.

who could not easily be denied entry. In the autumn of 1930, H. W. Brailsford, a Labour journalist, arrived with a litany of charges of police brutality in the best 'Paget, MP' tradition. When he travelled to a meeting with the district magistrate in Surat 'in a car flying the nationalist flag and full of white caps', the Bombay Government's view that his purpose was anti-Government propaganda seemed confirmed.[77] J. D. Garrett, the commissioner, Northern Division, decided to accompany Brailsford on his tour through his territory in order to 'wrest him from the Congress', but the third passenger was Mahadev Desai who filled him with 'inflated tales' carefully taken down by Brailsford and incorporated in a long note to Government on police violence.[78]

Garrett's report was the first of many sought by the Home Department in order to prepare advice for the Secretary of State who would have to deal with Brailsford's views in print when he returned to Britain. A warning was sent out to Bengal, the United Provinces, the Punjab, and the North West Frontier Province that Brailsford was coming and detailed reports were required of what he saw and heard.[79] Since his articles appeared in the British and American press, censorship was impractical. Local Governments' were urged to provide Brailsford with the official point of view,[80] while the Governor of Bombay asked the Viceroy to consider what would do more harm – accepting such visits or preventing them. Irwin agreed to ask the Secretary of State to prevent such visits in the future, but he recognized the political difficulties in Britain. He was also concerned about the Indian police and noted the need to ensure that 'the actual details of our administration – as carried out by subordinates – expose us to no flank attacks with the Brailsford sort'.[81]

The Viceroy's reference to the possible reality of police brutality – aside from the 'inflated tales' manufactured by Congress propagandists – rippled through the system and produced a defensive response. The Bombay Chief Secretary noted that there were some instances of overzealous police, although he insisted that generally the situation was normal and quiet. Where there had been problems, the Government appeared to have its own communications problem in obtaining hard evidence.[82] The

---

[77] District magistrate Surat to Government of Bombay, 23 October 1930, GOI (HomePol) 5/35/1931.
[78] J. D. Garrett, Northern Division to Government of Bombay, 28 October 1930, *ibid.*
[79] H. W. Emerson, Secretary, Home Department to G. F. S. Collins, Chief Secretary Bombay Government, 12 November 1930, *ibid.*
[80] H. W. Emerson to C. W. Cotton, Chief Secretary, Madras, 18 November 1930, *ibid.*
[81] Irwin to F. H. Sykes, Governor of Bombay, 18 November 1930, *ibid.*
[82] G. F. S. Collins, Chief Secretary, Bombay to H. W. Emerson, 25 November 1930, *ibid.*

Home Department informed the India Office that the Congress campaign to arouse public feeling in India and abroad was, with the exception of some slips, totally unfounded. The defensive nature of the Government's position was noted, as were its efforts to collect information and draft statements that could be used competitively in response. The India Office welcomed the material, but suggested that the Congress had the advantage of getting their charges into print in India and England long before the Government at home had sufficient information to launch a convincing defence. Although cost was always an issue, the Home Department was urged to use Reuters' services in especially significant cases.[83]

The publication of Brailsford's *Rebel India* sent officials in India and Britain to the barricades. He faithfully reported the stories of beatings and police violence, assuring his readers that he had not been 'misled by subtle Indians'. His witness had been the local commissioner (who no doubt regretted the decision to accompany him), 'who saw the wounds and bruises, and his cross-questioning did not shake the peasantry'.[84] Like V. D. Savarkar's *The Indian War of Independence of 1857*, the pamphlets of H. M. Hyndman: *Oh Martyrs, Infamies of Liberal Rule in India*, and a speech by Éamon de Valera, 'India and Ireland', delivered at a Friends of Freedom for India meeting in New York, *Rebel India* was banned, but was none the less well known in India.[85] The damage could be partially controlled – at least among professional publicists in India, by holding their presses and livelihoods hostage. In this situation, self-censorship achieved a goal shared by both protagonists – survival with principle largely intact, reflecting as well an inability to do very much more.

Brailsfords' book did get to India, and was reviewed in the *Modern Review* by no less a luminary than Rabindranath Tagore. Tagore was delighted with both the author and his message. 'Reading it, I feel encouraged to hope that individual Englishmen in our land will emulate his attitude of sober judgement and, no matter how inconvenient it may be to do so, dare face facts as they really are to-day in India.'[86] But some of Tagore's words seemed a bit too forceful for Ramananda Chatterjee, the editor of the *Modern Review*, whose nationalist credentials were widely respected. Chatterjee returned it to Tagore and sought some changes in

[83] Sir Findlater Stewart, Under-Secretary of State, India, to H. W. Emerson, 15 December 1930, *ibid*.

[84] H. J. Brailsford, *Rebel India*, 1930, cited in H. J. Brailsford, *Subject India*, London: Victor Gollancz Ltd, 1943, p. 195.

[85] Note re. newspapers prohibited from entering India under Section 19 of Sea Customs Act and Sections 25 and 26, Indian Post Office Act, GOI (HomePol) 159/1921.

[86] Rabindranath Tagore reproduced in *Modern Review*, June 1965, pp. 81–2.

order to comply with the prevailing legal ban on 'legitimate criticism of Government'.[87] 'The humility flowing from my inability to publish what I know to be wholly true', lamented Chatterjee, 'has been robbing me of my sleep.'[88] But in the published review, the loss of 'moral probity' became 'honesty', 'ruthless' power became 'military' power, 'enormities' became 'unsympathetic treatment', 'smothered' became 'neglected', and 'most brutally inhuman' became 'the impersonal'.[89] There were many who attacked Chatterjee's unwillingness to risk imprisonment (he was briefly imprisoned for publishing J. D. Sunderland's *India Under Bondage*) and the loss of his journals, but he had a clear conscience. He was in the nationalist struggle, but unlike 'full-time' nationalists who might call Gandhi 'dictator', Chatterjee chose to fight on his own terms and with the professional skills he thought would be useful. For that, he needed his journals and the freedom to publish them.

The *Times*, like Parliament and the Crown, was both a British institution and an elite symbol of superiority and power. It was also a communicator which amplified, reiterated and distributed that message of place and achievement throughout the world. The paper's views on foreign and imperial affairs were assumed to influence decision making in Whitehall, and Government of India officials read it for trustworthy information and signals of change in perspective and policy which would eventually affect their working lives.

The *Times* was also read by editors of the Anglo-Indian and Indian 'national press' – one of the countless country constituencies of this aspect of the imperial metropole. In its pages they measured the quality of their own style and format, and discovered the apt quotations that reflected shared or antagonistic viewpoint. Quoting the *Times* to support an argument or as a foil to make a case against the colonial regime was a standard device of the press in India.

The propaganda campaign launched against the Ilbert Bill in 1883, demonstrated both the influence of the *Times* and the extraordinary international routing of powerful opinion. The new law provided for a significant expansion of the jurisdiction of Indian judges over British residents in the *mofussil*, the countryside beyond the major urban centres where the European population was concentrated. The *Times* published the first press response, written by its Calcutta correspondent, R. C. Macgregor, described by the Viceroy, Lord Ripon, as 'a small Calcutta

---

[87] Ramananda Chatterjee to Rabindranath Tagore, 12 December 1932, reproduced in *ibid.*, p. 81.
[88] *Ibid.*
[89] *Ibid.*

barrister'.[90] In MacGregor's weekly telegram, he emphasized the sudden nature of the change and the new danger to the British engaged in business in the country. The Bill, he warned, would make it 'unsafe for any Englishman to reside outside the limits of the three Presidency Towns'.[91] Raymond Renford has noted the impact of the *Times* editorial regarding that 'mischievous Bill' when read in India. The Calcutta *Englishman* published a similar comment the following day, and the opposition argument was subsequently picked up by most of the Anglo-Indian press.[92] In Renford's view, the *Times* article and editorial were the catalyst for the extreme opposition response, overwhelming more moderate viewpoint initially expressed in the Calcutta *Statesman* and *Bombay Gazette*.[93]

In 1918, the *Hindu* noted the 'commendation of the *Times* and of the Anglo-Indian press' for the Congress split and the establishment of the moderate Liberal Federation as 'sufficient condemnation of the seceders'.[94] But in 1940, it referred to the *Times* in a positive context noting its criticism of Jinnah's demands for a virtual Muslim veto on any proposed constitutional change.[95] In its lengthy discussion of the 1935 Government of India Act, the *Hindustan Times* noted that the Act was 'not what India wanted but what Britain was prepared to concede'. The transfer of power was 'in form only', the paper insisted, since the two parties involved were the British Government and the Governor-General and Governors – not the representatives of the Indian people.[96] On the following day, however, the viewpoints of the *Times* and the major British papers were extensively quoted. The India Act, exulted the *Times*, was 'the highest expression of political courage and wisdom of this generation … a true and characteristic facet of tradition.'[97] But the *Hindustan Times* editorial page made clear that it was not a wholly shared 'tradition', and reiterated its opposition and the differences between 'us' and 'them'.

For a generation of *Times* readers, their 'Indian voice' was Valentine Chirol. As head of the foreign department of the paper, his views were particularly influential and regularly reflected in *Times* editorials. In 1910, Chirol published a collection of his Indian articles in a book titled *Indian*

[90] *The Times*, 5 February 1883, cited in Raymond K. Renford, *The Non-Official British in India to 1920*, Delhi: Oxford University Press, 1987. All of the subsequent discussion of the Ilbert Bill controversy has been taken from Renford's book.

[91] *Ibid.*

[92] Renford, *Non-Official British*.

[93] *Ibid.*

[94] *Hindu*, 30 August 1918, cited in Kasturi, *The Hindu Speaks*, p. 127.

[95] *Ibid.*, 22 January 1940, p. 204.

[96] *Hindustan Times*, 4 August 1935, p. 10.

[97] *Ibid.*, 5 August 1935, p. 1.

Unrest. Ten years later a second book, *India Old And New*, included letters from a recent visit to India published in the *Times*. Two major themes inform both books: the significance of Britain's progressive role in India and the confrontation of two civilizations which would determine the success of that mission.

In the early *Times* articles published in *Indian Unrest*, Chirol noted the importance of English education and his concern that those who had moved into professions and the civil service, were in the first decade of the twentieth century, advocating revolt. For Chirol this constituted 'the most ominous feature of Indian unrest'.[98] He cited the Calcutta *Yugantar*'s view that 'sedition has no meaning from the Indian standpoint',[99] insisting that a significant source of the problem was a 'Hindu Revival' and reassertion of 'Brahman power'. Since in British India, the 'brahmanical and reactionary character of Indian unrest' could be 'disguised under the "patriotic" aspects of revolt against alien rule', Chirol directed his readers' attention to Kolhapur, a native state in the Deccan, whose ruler claimed descent from Shivaji, the primary symbol of Tilak's resurgent Hindu nationalism.[100]

In Chirol's view Western education had largely failed in India because it was founded on conceptions entirely unrelated to Indian culture and Indian situation. As a result, the Western-educated elite who dominated the Congress could not be perceived as representatives of the Indian people and members of some kind of proto-parliament.[101] If India were to progress, he argued, continued and long-term cooperation with the British was essential. In addition to the enemies of progress and British rule, Chirol also noted their allies – not surprisingly among the most conservative elements of Indian society: Muslims, 'a great conservative force', the quiet and conservative south, the princes and potentially the vast depressed classes. 'From the political point of view the conversion of so many millions of the population of India to the faith of their rulers would open up prospects of such moment that I need not expatiate upon them'.[102]

As evidence for the significance and possibility of this prospect Chirol cited the 'extremist' newspaperman B. C. Pal's concern regarding British efforts to 'captivate the mind of the teeming masses', and the revolutionary propaganda of *Yugantar*'s writers which sought to undermine the

---

[98] Valentine Chirol, *Indian Unrest*, London: Macmillan and Co. Ltd, 1910, p. 7.
[99] *Ibid.*, p. 16.
[100] *Ibid.*, p. 64.
[101] *Ibid.*, p. 154.
[102] *Ibid.*, p. 184.

confidence of the Indian people in their alien rulers.[103] Chirol insisted, however, that cooperative association with educated Indians was required to suppress the resilient and regressive forces of indigenous tradition. 'We want the Western educated Indian', he concluded. 'We have made him and we cannot unmake him if we would'.[104]

This theme of civilization struggle is central to Chirol's second book as well. 'It would be folly to underrate the forces of resistance which are by no means altogether ignoble.'[105] These forces, he argued, were the source of 'the strange Non-cooperation Movement' against British rule and against 'the progressive forces which contact with Western Civilization has slowly brought into existence ...'[106] Gandhi represented for Chirol the ultimate danger of a politicized Hinduism which could destroy the 'great Constitutional experiment'.[107] In 1921, Chirol could report initial success in resisting 'the first onslaught of a singular combination of malignant forces', but the long-term result of the struggle remained unclear.[108]

On 23 March 1937, the *Times* published an 'India Number' to commemorate the implementation of the 1935 Government of India Act. The old princely allies noted by Chirol in 1910 were all represented in full and half page descriptions of the relationship between progressive policy and British experience. The Maharaja of Indore's Oxford education and European travel had produced the 'firm foundations of character which were to prove an invaluable asset in later years'. Mysore was a 'Model State' reflecting the influence of British institutions. Baroda, Gwalior, Travancore were all British success stories. The princes had paid for their sections in the 'India Number' which were identified as advertisements by the *Times*. In 1937, both the princes and the Government of India needed to propagate their success stories.

In a range of articles by scholars, old India hands and officials in London and India, the Reforms were described in the context of 'A New Era Opened'. The history of Britain in India and British achievements in social development, health, industry, agriculture, and enhanced standard of living were described. The continuing opposition of the Congress was also noted, but the *Times* India correspondent reassured readers that the reputation of the Congress was greater than its accomplishments. 'The claim that it speaks for all the social and political elements in the land is

---

[103] *Ibid.*, p. 295.
[104] *Ibid.*, p. 326.
[105] Valentine Chirol, *India Old and New*, London: Macmillan and Co. Ltd, 1921, p. vi.
[106] *Ibid.*
[107] *Ibid.*, p. 299.
[108] *Ibid.*

strongly repudiated by liberals, Moderates and by most Moslems'. The problem remained, however, that Congress advocacy of nationalism was hard to attack. In 1937, the assertion of progressive British mission in confrontation with Indian reactionary challenge was muted; but the Chirol themes remained as a leitmotif – almost submerged in the descriptions of beautiful landscape, travel opportunities, sports, village life, and progress all around, but still apparent as an argument for a mission not yet fully realized. The 1935 Act was another step and the prognosis was quite positive; but the grand association in a federation which included all the major constituencies identified by the British and constitutionally enpowered by them, remained in an experimental state.[109]

Nehru's confrontation with Virendranath Chattopadhyaya on the continent was replicated in England with Shapurji Saklatwala. This scion of a wealthy Parsee family arrived in London in 1905, and almost immediately became involved with a number of labour and social organizations. By 1910, he was an active member of the Independent Labour Party and eventually became a member of the Communist Party. He was twice elected to the House of Commons and in 1929, was in the last year of his second term when he wrote to Nehru about Congress foreign propaganda. Like so many other self-appointed representatives of Indian nationalist interests, Saklatwala complained about being ignored and unappreciated. In a litany of apparent lost opportunities, the Congress was criticized for cutting back their foreign propaganda activities just at the time they needed more. Citing Catherine Mayo's *Mother India*, the subsidized Reuters service, the Red Scare, and over-dramatic coverage of communal confrontation as evidence of a well-organized campaign by the British, he lamented the spare and inadequate Indian response.

Worse than no response was allowing the wrong people to speak for the Congress and send the wrong message. It was widely assumed in Britain, he noted, that Annie Besant still represented the Congress – or at least the sensible elements who would likely regain control. Unlike, Chatto, Saklatwala was willing to work in support of a constitutional advance short of absolute independence; but he insisted that dominion status would only be defined generously if Congress demands were taken directly to the British people.[110] The argument he and his colleagues were making would have been supported by the old British Committee, but Saklatwala had another agenda more in keeping with his radical political views. He intended to play a leadership role in steering an appropriate Indian

---

[109] *The Times*, 'India Number', 23 March 1937.
[110] S. Saklatwala, K. M. Pandhy, G. B. Vakil, Tarini P. Sinha to J. Nehru, 9 April 1929, AICC (FD) 23/1929.

response and argument to the British people and their leaders. As a beginning, he sought to consolidate the organization of propaganda in London in an 'authoritative committee', a small group of independent people who would be unsusceptible to Government pressure and police spies. There were, in Saklatwala's view, very few people who could be trusted, since the majority of Indians in London were either students who were too weak and dependent to risk challenging the authorities or wealthy retired countrymen who had settled in England as a refuge from the struggle. He asked Nehru to provide a £600 annual grant for the new Committee's work, insisting that the need was urgent if the struggle were not to be lost by default.[111]

Nehru welcomed the support but resisted the proposal and the additional drain on meagre funds. Within a few months, however, Saklatwala's unwillingness to subordinate his views to AICC control was apparent. The London branch of the Congress had been formally granted affiliation in December 1928, and Saklatwala and his supporters immediately sought to take control. After a brief period of cooperation with more moderate colleagues, he asserted his independence and began attacking the Congress leadership. He condemned Gandhi and Motilal Nehru and any suggestion of accommodation with the Irwin initiatives, and received in response warnings from the Congress that the branch risked disaffiliation. The confrontation continued throughout 1930 and 1931. In June, Vithalbhai Patel presided over a conference in London which had to be adjourned because of a demonstration initiated by Saklatwala and other branch members. The major propaganda leaflets published by the branch in this period were Saklatwala's 'The Treachery of the Indian National Congress Leaders at Karachi under the Arch-Hypocrite, Gandhi', 'The Congress Coward', 'Betrayal of Liberty', and 'Forces of Exploitation and Profiteering'. Although none of these publications appear to have been reprinted by the India Office, clearly no attempt was made to repress them. After the proposal of a plan to launch a black-flag demonstration against Gandhi when he appeared for the Round Table Conference, and the forced resignation of the branch president who disagreed, Nehru decided to act.

At the August meeting of the AICC in Bombay, he presented a Working Committee resolution for the disaffiliation of the London branch; but its approval was delayed by a demand for proper parliamentary form which probably would have been appreciated by their Home Department protagonists. S. Satyamurthi rose to a point of order concerning the Working Committee's power to make the decision. He

111 *Ibid.*

insisted that the AICC had to act as the 'future Swaraj Government' and that formal charges had to be 'placed before the House, so that the members may be in a position to vote for or against the resolution'. Nehru reviewed the branch's activities in the previous two years and the warnings that had been issued, but Satyamurthi insisted that he circulate a memorandum. The issue was deferred but in a subsequent debate in which Sardar Patel denounced all foreign branches since they could not be effectively controlled, the London branch was disaffiliated. The New York branch had been disaffiliated early in 1930, for similar reasons; and the Kabul branch was apparently no longer functioning.[112] Soon after the Bombay meeting, responding to a suggestion from Fenner Brockway and others that another organization in London be recognized by the Congress, Nehru noted that the AICC had too many bitter experiences and was now opposed to foreign commitments. He urged Brockway to find other ways to work with them.[113]

Cutting its ties with officially representative agencies overseas did not leave the Congress or Indian nationalism generally without foreign support. The messages may not have been framed in the Working Committee or the AICC, but they continued to be sent out. Quite apart from the work done by old friends of the movement and old enemies of British imperial power, Gandhi and Nehru were newsmakers and there was an increasing constituency for information about the struggle they led. Taken together, the press coverage, pamphlet literature, books and journal articles, lecture tours and parliamentary debates gave the appearance of a well-orchestrated international campaign. The response of the Government of India was defensive, concentrating on putting out fires that had been lit by a radical speech or a strong editorial. Within India, their powers, though increasingly constrained, were well defined. They could proscribe an offending newspaper and imprison those who advocated violence or incited communal confrontation. And the borders could be defended, however inadequately. But in Britain and Europe, and especially the United States, the task was far more difficult. There, except for occasional support from local intelligence agencies, they had to convince.

Rather than inhibit the work of London representatives of nationalist papers, the India Office began to supply them with useful material for their letters[114] and facilitate their access to the House of Commons press

---

[112] *Free Press Journal*, 8, 9, 10 August 1931.

[113] J. Nehru to A. F. Brockway, 20 August 1931, AICC (FD) 30.

[114] E. Haward to D. T. Monteath, 23 January 1930 re. cooperation with F. J. Grubb, London correspondent for the *Hindu* and *Tribune*, and Leonard W. Matters, London correspondent for the *Hindu*, IO L/I/1/344, File 131/14.

gallery. When MacGregor was able to secure ten extra special press tickets for the India debates in July 1931, he considered it quite a victory over the sergeant at arms.[115] A fortnightly confidential *Appreciation* of the political situation in India was prepared for the dominions, and eventually the list of receivers was extended to a range of diplomatic posts and individuals. The *Appreciation* attempted to describe events in a useful context: Gandhi's attendance at the Round Table Conference was a victory for the Government, but his ignorance of constitutional issues would inhibit his usefulness. The 1931 Press Bill was passed by a substantial majority in the Assembly and unanimously in the Council of State.[116] In addition, Ian Stephens began to issue a weekly, eventually fortnightly, letter to a much larger constituency, and bulk packages were sent to Local Governments and to London for distribution to the major British Press, London correspondents of foreign newspapers, the India Office, and selected private individuals. There was also a package for the British Library of Information in New York.[117] The India Office emphasized the need for a 'purely objective line', but R. T. Peel clarified the situation in a subsequent letter noting that it was 'not intended that too rigid an interpretation should be placed on the request'.[118] The Home Department's concern was that the Information Bureau be safeguarded from Assembly attack by avoiding any direct quotation.[119]

In the autumn of 1931, the Information Bureau attempted to negotiate a contract with K. C. Roy for a special service of telegrams to foreign countries, but the cost and concern for Assembly opposition prevented agreement.[120] As an alternative, arrangements were made to use British consular facilities. Rather than limit these contacts to centres of strategic importance and influence, virtually every receptive target was utilized. The *Baghdad Times*, the *Tanganyika Herald*, the *Bangkok Daily Mail*, five Japanese papers, and newspapers in Fiji, Mauritius, and Palestine began publishing selected India messages distributed through local British Missions. Attitudes toward Britain and British India were also surveyed as well as the availability of useful news. The responses were mixed, but gave little reason for optimism. Japan could 'not be said to be rabidly anti-British', while the press in China had a 'strongly anti-British tone'. Fiji was 'on the whole anti-British', while Mauritius was 'in no way anti-

---

[115] H. MacGregor to H. S. C. Polak, 6 May 1931, IO L/I/1/342, File 131/12.
[116] Viceroy to Secretary of State, 6 September 1931, re. Appreciation 25; 8 October 1931, re. Appreciation 26, GOI (HomePol) 1551/I/1931.
[117] Stephens note, 3 August 1932, GOI (HomePol) 39/4 2KW.
[118] R. T. Peel (IO) to M. G. Hallett, 1 October, 1932, *ibid.*
[119] R. T. Peel to M. G. Hallett, 5 April 1934; 23 May 1934, *ibid.*
[120] E. P. Howell Note, 11 September 1930, F & P Department 119–X (secret).

British'. The Tanganyika press ranged from 'innocuous' to 'anti-British', while the presses of Iran and Palestine were unfriendly. The press in the Straits Settlements was safely in the hands of British management and Sourabaya in the Dutch East Indies was happily 'free from anti-British bias'.[121] Information officers were clearly moving well beyond their immediate mandate, but the Foreign Office was increasingly concerned with Britain's general reputation around the empire and the world, and a measure of cooperation often denied earlier was now available.

Wherever a new target group or individual came to the attention of Information officials, a contact was made and material flowed. When it was discovered that some Scottish missionaries had 'wrong views' about Government of India policy, Mr Justice Sir Stewart Macpherson of the Patna High Court agreed to contact leaders of the Church of Scotland and arrange for them to receive the fortnightly review.[122] The visit to India of Señor Aurelio Miro Quesada was considered a valuable opportunity to provide a 'true picture of the political situation' for a member of an influential Lima family which owned the most widely read paper in Peru. Although it frequently published stories on Gandhi and the nationalist movement, it was dependent on the American United Press and Associated Press services for its information. Arrangements were made for Quesada to receive the fortnightly reviews through the British legation in Lima, including six months of back issues.[123] Although chastened by a generation of challenge, the 'man on the spot' continued to insist that the truth was revealed only from his highly specialized perspective.

In 1933, the German Government's general attack on subversive communist organizations and propaganda took into its net many Indian students and political activists. A. C. N. Nambiar was arrested along with M. J. S. Naidu, Sarojini Naidu's son, and eventually deported. Various other arrests and releases followed, including one Indian suspect in an assassination plot against Hitler.[124] Clearly Germany was no longer a safe base for radical expatriate Indians, and Vienna became an increasingly important meeting place. There was a small permament Indian community in Vienna, and a steady flow of others who came to the city for medical attention. A rise in anti-British propaganda now signalled the

[121] R. S. Bajpai Note, 28 January 1931, *ibid.*
[122] Home Department note re. supply of DPI's fortnightly reviews and other material to certain leaders of the Church of Scotland for publicity work in that country, 3 April 1933, GOI (HomePol) 39/6/1933.
[123] British Legation, Lima to Foreign Secretary, F & P Department (GOI) 19 July 1933, GOI (HomePol) 39/51/34.
[124] Home Department Memorandum: S. N. Tagore was arrested as a suspect in the assassination plot but released and allowed to leave Germany, n.d., GOI (HomePol) 6/3/1933.

arrival of the new element which challenged the business-as-usual environment. The British Legation responded quickly. It recognized that statements with an obvious official source were now discounted or considered biased, especially by students who had been exposed to an intensive propaganda campaign. The Hindu Academical Association which had been considered innocuous was now becoming another India House; and the Foreign Office was urged to co-opt high-profile Indians to issue statements to the press, speak to students' organizations, and meet members of the Austrian Press Association when they came to Vienna. It was clear to British officials that the local press was easily impressed by people like the Nawabs of Rampur and Bhopal – both in Vienna in 1934 for medical treatment, and the Legation proposed to arrange the meetings.[125] The proposals flowed from the Foreign Office to the India Office, and then to India where Home Department officials noted that the problem was similar to the Geneva situation and arranged for DPI material to be sent to Vienna. Finding Indian lecturers 'of the right type' was not easy, however, since there were no funds to send someone, and it was difficult to know who was planning a visit.[126]

Frustration and a heightened sense of distance and marginality were shared by the 'foreign service' of both camps. After his deportation from Germany, Nambiar eventually settled in Prague and attempted to continue his work as a journalist and Congress activist. Nehru sent him money from time to time, but never enough to provide a stable base for a major propaganda campaign. Nambiar continued to write for the Indian press but received little encouragement and financial return.[127] In the autumn of 1937, he was still considering the possibility of establishing an Indian information bureau in Prague, but Nehru could only respond with regret that the Congress could provide no help. He noted that acceptance of office in the provinces had produced a range of complications which prevented him from even broaching the subject.[128] But those provincial majorities provided opportunities as well. In the autumn of 1936, Nehru sought and received permission from the United Provinces Government to publish foreign newsletters and a survey of foreign affairs. Their content eventually became sufficiently offensive to cause Home Department officials to consider banning their export, but the new constraints on

---

[125] R. H. Hadon, HM Representative at Vienna to Foreign Office, 14 September 1934. CID note, 9 September 1934, GOI (HomePol) 39/1934.
[126] Home Department to India Office, 29 September 1934, GOI (HomePol) 39/1934.
[127] A. C. N. Nambiar to J. Nehru, 22 March 1937. Jawaharlal Nehru Papers, Vol. LXXX (AICC and Foreign).
[128] A. C. N. Nambiar to J. Nehru, 6 August 1937; J. Nehru to A. C. N. Nambiar, 11 November 1937, ibid.

the Government's power severely constrained its response. Prohibiting the export of the newsletter would have left the AICC free to publish within India, with the inevitable flow of material to the Indian press and then to foreign countries. The power to apply the provisions of the 1931 Indian Press Act lay entirely with Provincial Governments. In this case, the Congress majority in the United Provinces legislature had limited the Government's options; and the 'cleverly prepared' newsletters, although clearly full of false material in the view of officials, could not be described as seditious. Like so many of his predecessors, the Home Member brooded on the suitability of 'applying British standards in unsuitable circumstances' which in the present case appeared to tie the Government's hands and allow full freedom to its opponents.[129]

The campaign in America

In February 1945, the *Hindustan Times* published an editorial on the 'astounding revelations' revealed in a series of articles by Chaman Lal on British propaganda in America. Comparing their talents in this area to those of Dr Goebbels, a lengthy list of false allegations and false friends was presented – all part of the campaign against the Congress and Mahatma Gandhi.[130] By 1945, no journalist should have been astounded by the content of the propagandist's message, but the existence of an American debate and an American branch of the Indian nationalist struggle seemed extraordinary to those who had not participated in it.

The need for the right kind of Indian publicity in the United States was noted by Sir Stanley Reed in 1918, in an exchange of letters with Arthur Willert, the chief correspondent of the *Times* in Washington. Reed was engaged in the dismantling of the central and provincial publicity boards and in discussions concerning the continuing need for Government publicity in the post-war era. The apparent success in the United States of Annie Besant and her Theosophical Society adherents in spreading anti-Government of India propaganda produced the 'true facts' response in Reed, who organized the despatch of official material to Washington. Willert agreed to help contact influential American journalists and public men.[131] Among the new constraints arising from World War One was a more widely spread awareness of British action and interest, producing audiences that appeared to be watching them in such previously

---

129 Measures to counteract anti-British propaganda by the Congress in India and abroad. Home Department memorandum 291/37, 6 July 1937, GOI (HomePol) 4/17/37.
130 'A Mendacious Campaign', *Hindustan Times*, 17 February 1945, reprinted in Chaman Lal, *British Propaganda in America*, Allahabad: Kitab Mahal, 1945.
131 Sir Stanley Reid to Arthur Willert, 22 August 1918, IO L/P & J/6/1581.

privileged corners of their imperial enterprise as India. Although reluctantly, they accepted the need to describe and explain. Unlike the effort in Britain and Europe, in the case of the Americans, the Government of India attracted the support of the Foreign Office which was firmly committed to steer any post-war American interest in world affairs in an unchallenging direction.

Like so much of the campaign in India and Britain, the effort in America would remain largely *ad hoc*, responding to challenges and opportunities with minimal planning and resources. Much depended on individual interest and initiative within Government and unsolicited offers to participate from outside. For the enthusiasts the work was all to do, since they agreed with Lajpat Rai that American ignorance of all things Indian was 'simply colossal'. But the question of balance was always a consideration – sufficient understanding to produce sympathetic understanding, but not interference. American participation in Irish affairs had not yet been played out and there was no desire to add an Indian dimension to that role. At the core of any campaign, however, was control of the flow of messages, and it was agreed to continue the special cable service which provided Indian material for America via London.[132]

American contact with India was initiated by traders in the late eighteenth century, and with the exception of some missionary activity, remained only commercial until the end of the nineteenth. Between 1898 and 1914, approximately 6,000 Indian labourers migrated to the United States, but the relationship remained distant as prejudice and fear replaced the geographical barrier. The nationalist struggle also made the sea journey in this period. Taraknath Das arrived in 1906, and within two years had brought out his *Free Hindustan* in association with a group of Irish–American publicists. Har Dayal moved to California in 1911, organized the Pacific Coast Hindustan Association, and established *Ghadr* in 1913 as the revolutionary voice of a new party. But the intervention of the British Embassy had led to the suppression of *Free Hindustan* in 1911, and a similar fate for *Ghadr* after its involvement in a scheme to send arms to India with the support of the German Foreign Office. With information provided by British agents, a 'Hindu Conspiracy' to violate American neutrality laws led to arrests and convictions, and the targeting of Indians as enemy agents after the United States entered the war.[133]

These small efforts, carefully watched and quickly suppressed, involved

---

[132] Rushbrook Williams memorandum, 1 October 1921, GOI (HomePol) 405/1921.

[133] The information in this paragraph has been taken from the introductory chapter, Gary Hess, *America Encounters India, 1941–1947*, Baltimore: The Johns Hopkins Press, 1971.

very few people and tended to entrench stereotypical views. But the arrival in 1914 of Lala Lajpat Rai in New York rather than San Francisco, and with the purpose of seeking support rather than advocating and abetting revolution, initiated the establishment of a small but committed constituency for India. Rai's response to the 'Hindu–German plot' was 'contempt mixed with pity', insisting that India's salvation would have to be won in India by Indians. But he was convinced that support for Indian aspirations in America would strengthen the freedom struggle and his five years' residence was commited to that goal.[134] The India Home Rule League of America, its journal, *Young India*, and a steady flow of pamphlets attracted liberal support. Roger Baldwin and Norman Thomas added an Indian dimension to their reform mandate, and J. T. Sunderland, who had already added the Indian struggle to his New York ministry, became Rai's co-worker and the editor of *Young India* when he returned to India in 1919. This collaborative beachhead created a more difficult and potentially dangerous challenge for the protectors of British interests in America.

Official Indian publicity had been coordinated by an ICS officer, Colonel Faunthorpe, until he left the United States in 1920, and passed on the responsibility to Robert Wilberforce, the head of the British Library of Information in New York. The Library remained the base for Government of India propaganda operations in North America until World War Two. The loss of Faunthorpe's services, together with continuing debate within the Government of India regarding its own publicity organization and policy, stimulated a discussion about the special nature of the American situation and the kind of expertise required for the bearer of their messages. The key characteristic was 'elasticity'.

With elasticity go tact and patience and the power of cheerful but non-committal acquiescence, imperceptibly spiced by the gentlest of argumentative protestation, in the face of statements that America won the war, that the Philippine Government is better than the Indian, that prohibition is God's blessing ... that the American Indian is a higher civilization than anything India can produce.

The ideal candidate was thought to be an Indian civilian with some experience in publicity and intelligence work, but with a liberal viewpoint concerning Indian affairs in order to complement the American tendency – demonstrated in the past in regard to Ireland, to support nationalism and the greatest measure of self-government.[135]

---

[134] Lala Lajpat Rai, 'A Call to Young India', *Indian Home Rule League*, New York, 1919, quoted in V. C. Joshi, ed. *Lala Lajpat Rai, Writings and Speeches*, Vol. I, 1888–1919, Delhi: University Publisher, 1966, p. 319.

[135] Sir Arthur Willert (FO) to J. W. Hose (IO), 22 May 1922; J. W. Hose to S. P. O'Donnell (GOI), 24 May 1922; Willert memorandum re. Indian publicity in the United States (urgent), 16 May 1922, GOI (HomePol) 30/III/1922.

Both the need for such an appointment and the source of funding engaged the attention of officials in New York, Washington, London, and New Delhi for five months before it was determined that an appointment was too expensive and it would be necessary to rely on a Government of India subsidy for an enlargement of Wilberforce's office staff. The Library was the responsibility of the News Department of the Foreign Office, but its enthusiasm for the India work was not reflected in any investment of its own resources. Since Indian officials were convinced that the Imperial Government benefited from the Indian propaganda in the United States which it was required to fund, the issue remained contentious for more than a decade.[136] In 1922, however, there was no choice. Wilberforce informed the Foreign Office that the Library already spent one-quarter of its time on Indian propaganda and any more work would require more means since only $26 remained from their Indian funds.[137]

There was a range of 'agents' involved in publicity work in the United States, but as in the case of the Congress, initiative and control was not always the result of selection and planning. Rustom Rustomjee emigrated to the United States in 1912, and actively promoted a positive image of Britain's role in India for eight years before he was offered a contract by the Home Department through the British Library. For a monthly salary of $200, with an additional $200 for rent and travel, he carried his message to universities and colleges throughout the country. In 1922, it was agreed to send Rustomjee back to India since his ten-year absence had clearly left him out of touch with the current situation. Although officials in India were convinced of his usefulness and accepted their obligation to one who had served the cause for many years without remuneration or recognition, the usual debate about funding occurred and his straying from duty while in India suggested to the Home Secretary that 'he seems to have enjoyed a pleasant vacation at Government expense'.[138]

Rustomjee returned to the United States and continued his propaganda work but, by the spring of 1924, he was regarded as an indiscreet ally who had allowed his official connections to become known.[139] V. J. Patel questioned the Government in the Legislative Assembly about the remuneration for Rustomjee's lectures and demanded a list of any others

[136] J. W. Hose, to Rushbrook Williams, 2 March 1922; J. W. Hose to S. P. O'Donnell, 4 September 1922, *ibid.*
[137] Robert Wilberforce to P. A. Koppel (FO), 1 April 1922, *ibid.*
[138] S. P. O'Donnell to J. W. Hose, 10 August 1922; Home Department discussion re. R. Rustomjee: R. S. Bajpai to DCBI, 23 March 1922; Gwynne note, 27 March 1922; R. S. Bajpai note, 25 July 1922; correspondence between India Office and Home Department (GOI), 19 July 1922–5 September 1922, GOI (HomePol) 30/I/1922.
[139] Deputy Secretary, Home Department note, 10 November 1924, GOI (HomePol) 417/1924.

engaged in similar work. Although Rustomjee's salary had been paid from secret service funds through a non-votable grant in the Director of the Information Bureau's budget, the Government could not deny the opportunity to members of the Assembly to seek information they knew would not be given. To the Home Member's response that the expenditure was included in Secret Service Contingencies and outside the Assembly's jurisdiction, the ritual repartee followed: 'What are Secret Services?' 'Secret, Sir.' 'Will the Hon. the Home Member satisfy?' 'I am amply satisfied.'[140] But clearly he was not. Rustomjee's contract was cancelled in June, but he remained a target for nationalist opposition to the American campaign. In an editorial entitled 'Mendacious Propaganda' which cited Rustomjee's role, the *Bombay Chronicle* lamented the fate of India, condemned 'to pay for her own enslavement'.[141]

The significance which the Home Department assigned to Rustomjee's work in 1922, reflected in the provision of an additional Rs 10,000 allocation to the British Library,[142] seemed to reflect as well, the lack of any more productive alternatives. There was consensus within the Government of India that something had to be done in America, and Rustomjee was a beginning – already operating in the field and only needing to be officially co-opted. The initial concentration on students and universities was a response to a perceived nationalist campaign to organize the same target groups, particularly Indian students; and an exchange programme for professors was proposed in order to provide an academic chaperone who might protect them from anti-British propaganda. In regard to the University of California, it was hoped that a suitable professor might also have some controling influence over Indian farmers and merchants in the area.[143]

The Government of India sought to limit its role to the selection of the Indian professor, leaving the public arrangement as a simple exchange between two universities. After almost two years of discussions concerning the right candidate and the problems of getting the funding through the Standing Finance Committee, it was noted that the number of Indian students attending the University of California had sufficiently decreased to eliminate the need for that particular exchange, and a broad-based programme was substituted for general exchanges between India and the United States.[144] But the responsibility for exchanges was

140 Home Department note concerning R. Rustomjee, n.d., GOI (HomePol) 60/24.
141 'Mendacious Propaganda', *Bombay Chronicle*, 6 December 1924.
142 S. P. O'Donnell, Home Secretary, note, 27 April 1922, GOI (HomePol) 225/V/1922.
143 G. W. Gwynne note, 15 November 1923, GOI (HomePol) 242/25.
144 Home Department correspondence and inter-department memoranda, 1 December 1923–4 May 1925, *ibid.*

eventually devolved on individual universities before the Home Department's political agenda could be served and information officers lost interest in the project.[145]

There was always more initiative from outside than within the system: challenges that required response, offers of help from loyal subjects or those with an anti-Indian bias or grievance, or simply opportunistic entrepreneurs and professionals with a service to sell. Each received a respectful hearing within the Home Department, often resulting in an extended correspondence and the despatch of materials to support the individual effort. Some opportunities, however, seemed worth a substantial investment. When Lowell Thomas, an influential American journalist, requested assistance in obtaining material 'which would be useful for placing favourable accounts of India before his American audiences', India Office officials pressed their colleagues in India to provide whatever help he required.[146] It was generally agreed that there was a need for Indian films for American propaganda that dealt with the working life of the people, irrigation projects, railways, and those Indians with a stake in the country and in stable institutions.[147]

The new emphasis was meant to suggest constructive partnership under British rule, and de-emphasize both the glorification of the British and the negative images of Indian life and culture. In addition to the Thomas project, the Government of India agreed to advance Rs 25,000 to be repaid out of the proceeds of five films on contemporary India. The model for this undertaking was *Nanook of the North*, a good story which had attracted large audiences, and an evocation of happy people living on the bounty of the constructive work of British rule. This was the message they wanted sent from India, 'a general impression produced by the pictures of a people living normally among picturesque surroundings'.[148] Angus Fletcher, the new director of the British Library, contacted the Burton Holmes organization regarding the preparation of the films. They were interested but insisted that the Rs 25,000 should be a non-returnable subsidy. Fletcher noted that it was difficult for people to dissociate the Government of India from vast riches and that Rs 25,000 appeared to be a paltry gesture.[149] Discussions continued, but the cost was too great for

[145] Home Department note, 6 December 1928, 6 January 1929, *ibid.*
[146] J. W. Hose to S. P. O'Donnell, 18 May 1922, IO L/P & J/6/1816.
[147] *Ibid.*
[148] S. P. O'Donnell to J. W. Hose, 29 June 1922; Angus Fletcher (BLI) to Arthur Willert (FO), 15 September 1922, *ibid.*
[149] Angus Fletcher to Sir Arthur Willert, 5 January 1923, *ibid.*

Government, and the presumed inadequate demand in the United States for Indian materials made the project too risky for the film makers.[150]

Thomas came to India to make his film, and was provided with facilities and advice which officials hoped would guarantee the product they sought. He received railway courtesy, copies of the official film of the Prince of Wales' tour, and an army officer was placed at his disposal. Rushbrook Williams rehearsed the story of India's progress under British rule and Thomas agreed to direct his lens toward the practical benefits of that boon.[151] After seven months, Thomas contacted the India Office and asked for a loan of £2,000 to complete the film. He emphasized that the funds should not be considered a subsidy for propaganda work and they agreed to a one-year arrangement at 6 per cent.[152] Neither the film nor the loan repayment materialized during the next twelve months, and in response to India Office queries in the following year, Thomas insisted he was broke and offered to exchange the India rights of the film he had now produced, *Romantic India*, for the £2,000. He noted also that he was currently touring the United States with a film on the first circumnavigation of the world by air and that a considerable amount of time had been devoted to India. 'This has given me an opportunity to tell tens of thousands of Americans', he insisted, 'of the great work you people have done in India.' Although he continued to reject the suggestion that the outstanding debt was an official subsidy, he made it clear that he felt he had given them what they wanted. 'I hope it is off-setting some of the pernicious propaganda that has been scattered far and wide over here by Indian agitators.'[153]

Romantic India was considered useless in India and, therefore, the Indian rights were of no value; and it lost money in North America and Europe where the Burton Holmes' impression of the likely market appeared to be correct. In a desultory correspondence over the next five years, the India Office continued to pursue Thomas and debated the possibility of legal action. In April 1930, Thomas wrote to the British Consul-General in New York. He described himself as the only person in the United States who was presenting a picture of India that offset the anti-British campaign. Insisting that his work was not propaganda but simply the truth as he saw it, he hoped the India Office would 'ultimately

[150] Angus Fletcher to Sir Arthur Willert, 2 February 1923; J. Crerar to Secretary, P & J (IO), 22 March 1923, *ibid.*
[151] Rushbrook Williams note, 3 May 1922, GOI (HomePol) 30/III/1922.
[152] Lowell Thomas to J. G. Blaithwaite (IO), 1 January 1923; C. W. Gwynne to Secretary, P & J (IO), 29 March 1923, IO L/P & J/6/1842.
[153] Secretary, P & J Department (IO) to Secretary, Home Department (GOI), 10 January 1924, *ibid.*

decide that I have long ago given them far more than their 2000 pounds worth'. Whatever their judgement, the debt was written off the following month.[154]

Throughout the 1920s, the Government of India provided the British Library with an annual $2,200 secret service grant to cover the cost of one typist and the rent for one room. It was clearly an unsatisfactory operations room for a great propaganda effort, but it reflected well the reticent nature of the enterprise. The issues were complex and their explanation in film or print designed for an audience with no experience of India and no sympathy for Britain was a daunting task for those with burdens enough in Delhi. The constraining context for every proposal was the assumed belligerence of the Finance Member and the unofficial members of the Assembly. There was no long-term sense or plan of what was necessary or possible, beyond the distribution of Government of India paper in America and the despatch of some useful information and advice in the return mail.

The Indian student and immigrant community were obvious targets for positive propaganda and intelligence gathering; but the American people, and even their elite opinion makers were difficult to assess in this regard. It was assumed there was a wider audience for anti-British propaganda and therefore the need to respond; but there does not appear to have been a very substantial audience for either. Officials remained convinced, however, as did those Congress leaders who were concerned about the world outside India, that Americans were watching and developing a viewpoint about Indian nationalism and the British Empire. Their experience with Ireland suggested the difficulties that might lie ahead, particularly if Americans started taking their new world power status seriously.

There was a continuing flow of informal intelligence from British travellers which was passed on to the India Office and then to Delhi. One Cambridge don returned from the United States in January 1922, and informed Edwin Montagu that the Irish Question appeared to be less prominent but there had been a marked increase in the amount of attention paid to India, 'almost entirely of an unfriendly nature'.[155] Another contacted J. W. Hose with a detailed description of anti-British propaganda activities in America sent to him by a friend. He noted that S. K. Ratcliffe had been lecturing for the League of Political Education and using the 'Amritsar incident' when speaking about Ireland. It appeared to this obviously incredulous correspondent, that Ratcliffe was

[154] *Ibid.*
[155] Geoffrey Butler to E. S. Montagu, 25 January 1922, GOI (HomePol) 30/III/1922.

advocating freedom for both Ireland and India. In regard to the American Commission to Promote Self-Government in India, it was noted that Jews had apparently taken control. Although insisting he was not anti-Semitic, the writer was concerned that 'the number of alien Jews in this society seems to constitute a menace'. He concluded with a call for action before this anti-British movement produced serious results.[156] Such information was filed away, to be brought out as needed to support their own propaganda effort. Much of it was redundant since an Indian Intelligence organization was maintained in the United States and Canada. But this too was in jeopardy in 1923.

As part of the continuing search for budget cutting opportunities, the India Office suggested the abolition of official intelligence work in America. The value of the material seemed questionable and its gathering was expensive. Newspaper clippings were available, and most important, the situation was generally quiet in the United States and Canada. Since the long term could not be easily divined, and funding allowed for little more than emergency firefighting, such opportunities were not allowed to pass. The responsibility for maintaining a watch on returning Indian extremists to India was transferred to British consular offices, and it was agreed that some of the saved funds could be utilized for propaganda work.[157] In the following year, the Canadian Government abolished the office of special immigration officer at Vancouver. This office had collected intelligence regarding seditious movements among Indians in Canada, and in North America generally. It had also kept a watch on remittances of funds to India collected among disaffected Sikhs in California and British Columbia. Here again, the Government of India would have to rely on the use of regular consular personnel and keep a tighter check on the mails in India.[158]

The loss of an official establishment in the United States increased their dependence on volunteers, and Home Department officers seemed to pocket their concern for secrecy by agreeing to informal relationships with no apparent attempt to check the credentials of their correspondents. Since no salaries were being paid, they assumed disinterest in the Assembly and clearly there was none in the Finance Department. Voluntary help replaced any regular systematic campaign which they could not afford financially, or afford to ask for constitutionally. In November 1921, A. H. Doherty, an American engineer, was killed in Bombay during

156 F. W. Buckler to J. W. Hose, 7 April 1922, *ibid.*
157 J. W. Hose to J. Crerar, 10 May 1922, GOI (HomePol) 211/1923.
158 Secretary, J & P Department (IO) to Secretary, Home Department (GOI), 10 January 1924, *ibid.*

a riot associated with the visit of the Prince of Wales. The Government of India provided his widow with a grant of Rs 1 lakh which three years later turned out to be an unexpectedly good investment.

Mrs Doherty wrote to the Viceroy in September 1924 as vice-president of the European Travel and Lecture Bureau in Los Angeles, and offered to lecture on behalf of the Government of India. She asked for slides, pictures, and statistics, and described her plan to 'enlighten some of the foolish people who pity the *Poor Indian*, of which they know so little'. She particularly asked for 'some scenes of the uprisings of the mobs'. While rejecting the request for 'mob scenes', Crerar responded enthusiastically, and Mrs Doherty was supplied with materials through the British Information Library.[159] She proved to be an aggressive adversary for the most determined advocates of the nationalist cause. In a speech to the Women's City Club in Los Angeles which received detailed coverage in the *Los Angeles Times*, she insisted that only 1 per cent of India's 325 million people supported Gandhi and that emissaries from Gandhi had attempted to bribe her to keep quiet. He was the 'greatest political schemer that the world has ever known', she declared, 'only seeking to create hatred for Britain in the United States as well as India. It was clear that India had never been 'so prosperous, never so happy and never so well cared for as now during the British rule'; and she concluded with the view that the people were totally unfit for self-government.[160] British Embassy officials in Washington were delighted with her performance.[161]

There were many reasons for such offers of support. Mrs Doherty's anger and desire for revenge had been channeled into the service of the Indian Government. Another American traveller, Mr Fairchild, a sugar exported from Philadelphia, contacted Rushbrook Williams after a visit to India. He noted that a foreigner crossing from Bombay to Calcutta carries away an impression that the methods of cultivation currently in use seemed unchanged since biblical times and it appeared that the British did little to help the peasant. Fairchild apparently assumed that this could not be the case, and suggested that an attractive pamphlet be prepared for the information of tourists. He clearly had some insight into the propagandist's art, suggesting that in the context of a general narrative, they might 'inconspicuously feature' British achievements in agriculture, railways, and other areas of progress. Fairchild, in advocating his solution, noted the 'effect of the propaganda which is being carried on by your

[159] Mrs A. H. Doherty to Viceroy, 18 September 1924; J. Crerar note, 27 October 1924; Rushbrook Williams note, 5 November 1924, GOI (HomePol) 13/1/25.
[160] *Los Angeles Times*, 9 December 1934, *ibid*.
[161] Esme Howard, British Embassy, Washington, to Austin Chamberlain, 26 February 1925, *ibid*.

enemies'. The proposal was well received in the Home Department, and Rushbrook Williams wrote to the United States for some sample material. But it was eventually agreed that other publications were available and there were no funds for this one.[162]

Mrs Millicent MacKinnon wrote to the India Office from Toronto, and her letter was passed on to the Home Department. The reaction of Information officials to her proposal to carry on counter-propaganda for British India was the despatch of the standard set of materials, but the Home Secretary insisted that this was inadequate and people like Mac-Kinnon had to be encouraged. Additional memoranda, speeches, statements, and photos were added to the package, and the covering letter redrafted to include warm appreciation of her work and an offer of all possible assistance. He asked the Information Bureau to treat the case as urgent, and discounted Bajpai's concern about sending some material marked confidential 'to a lady whom we did not know'. Mrs MacKinnon was asked to use the facts and avoid quotation from unpublished material and was put in contact with Angus Fletcher at the British Library of Information.[163]

Like Mrs Doherty, she became an effective 'agent' as both an advocate and source of useful local information. She noted that religious bodies in Toronto were generally pro-Gandhi and that the public libraries were filled with pro-Gandhi material. In response, eighteen copies of *India 1929–1930* were forwarded to her and placed in libraries around the city. She also noted similar failings in the libraries of Victoria College at the University of Toronto and the YMCA, and additional materials were sent from New York for these institutions. Small victories seemed to enhance her enthusiasm for her work, however insignificant their impact on the larger cause. In a speech at a Kiwanis Club luncheon she was delighted to be able to dissuade her audience from making Gandhi a life member by providing the true facts. 'They were sorry to learn it but glad to know the truth.'[164]

In 1919, Rushbrook Williams had noted the need for someone attached to the British Library of Information to do expert Indian work, and the proposal had been reiterated by Wilberforce in 1922. The issue reappeared on a regular basis in exchanges among the Government of India, the India Office, and the Library in New York. It seemed clear that

[162] Mr Fairchild to Rushbrook Williams, 8 May 1925; Home Department note, 12 June 1926, GOI (HomePol) 2 March 1926.
[163] Home Department memorandum re. supply of materials to Mrs MacKinnon: Mac-Kinnon letter, 11 November 1931; response, 3 March 1932; Emerson note, 10 March 1932; Bajpai note, 16 March 1932; Home Department, 21 March 1932, GOI (HomePol) 35/2/1932.
[164] Mrs MacKinnon to I. M. Stephens, 4 October 1932, *ibid.*

the tone of the American press in regard to India and the British Empire generally had deteriorated in the decade of the 1920s as a result of the activities of Indian agitators and the sensational reports of apparently anti-British American correspondents. There seemed to be a solid section of the American press that published constant misrepresentation, and the meager efforts of the British Library were clearly insufficient. There had been an effort to send a fuller service of Indian news to the United States, but Reuters could not increase the flow without demand and the Indian Government was unable to provide a subsidy on an adequate scale. It was also assumed that such subsidized messages would be suspect in both countries.[165]

In 1930, the need for additional coverage of the constitutional discussions and the preparations for the Round Table Conference were reflected in a request by the Secretary of State for an increase in the Indian Government's subsidy for the British Library to $5,500.[166] From Delhi's point of view, the political and constitutional constraints, quite aside from the financial burden that prevented the establishment of a professional organization in America, placed the responsibility in London. In any case, it had always been the opinion of the Government of India that the Imperial Government should pay for the campaign against anti-British propaganda in the United States, since this propaganda was widely targeted. India has often associated with Ireland, and good relations with the United States was not the responsibility of the Indian Government. The argument was not rejected in London but no additional funds were provided.[167]

Angus Fletcher added his voice to the call for funds in 1930 with a grand plan that required an additional annual outlay of Rs 25,500, and a backup proposal for Rs 9,350. It was finally agreed that the Home Department would provide an additional $3,000 but only for one year, and these funds were used to hire Lieutenant-Colonel A. V. Gabriel (ICS ret.) to be employed in London as a special correspondent of the British Library for three months. Gabriel had spent considerable time in the United States and had helped the Library voluntarily in the past. In Fletcher's grand plan, he and Robert Wilberforce were to act as a special Indian team, one in London and one in New York. They would alternate every six months and thereby insure continual updating of experience and well-informed advice for the India Office and the Indian Government.[168]

---

[165] R. S. Bajpai note re. propaganda in the United States, 2 March 1932, GOI (HomePol) 35/15/1932.
[166] Secretary of State note, 1 November 1930, GOI (HomePol) 88/1931.
[167] Bajpai note, 2 March 1932, GOI (HomePol) 35/15.
[168] Arthur Fletcher note, 23 September 1930, GOI (HomePol) 88/1931.

But neither grand plan, nor backup, nor any long-term planning was affordable or, for some, even appropriate: 'I would further add that in view of the impending constitutional changes, it would be undesirable to make a permanent arrangement which, whether it becomes unnecessary after a change in the political conditions or not, is almost certain to be turned down by a Minister responsible to the Indian Legislature.'[169]

There was general agreement about the usefulness of America's good opinion of their acts and policies. Reprinted in the Indian press, it would demonstrate the futility and failure of nationalist anti-British exports, and perhaps chasten the extremists who thought American pressure might speed up the process of power sharing and transfer. For the most optimistic, it seemed to reflect a more sensible and pragmatic response to having power in the world, and a willingness to restrain the emotional idealism which appeared to be a permanent invitation to the freedom fighter. Interest in the American response was especially noted when the Government of India considered one of its acts to be a dramatic vindication of its principles, as in the case of Lord Irwin's promise of dominion status in October 1929.[170]

The lack of extensive coverage of Irwin's initiative was disappointing, and the editorial comment produced was generally not useful in India. The *Herald Tribune* considered the commitment to be a triumph for MacDonald's Government since it seemed to promise 'practically nothing', but had created a 'cordial atmosphere'. The *New York World* found 'nothing new' in the speech, and the Hearst press, usually critical on political issues, allowed its concern for Indian social backwardness to damn the British with their support. It was dangerous for a nation of 40,000,000, it noted, to give any sort of ruling power to 300,000,000 Asiatics. But it was confident that 'the wise British can be trusted to make voting or other self-governing powers of Hindus as unreal a phantom as the ruling powers of Rajas'.[171] The usually cooperative London *Times* correspondent in Delhi could occasionally help with articles sent to the *New York Times*;[172] but direct contact with the correspondents of American papers was preferred. This was more difficult than anticipated. The Americans seemed less willing than others to respond to the invitations of Information officials and the achievement of a cooperative relationship with one of them was not considered an insignificant victory. The *Christian Science Monitor*'s enthusiastic approval of Irwin's

---

169 Bajpai note, re. additional funds for the BLI, 20 October 1930, *ibid.*
170 Viceroy to Secretary of State (telegram) 8 November 1929, GOI (HomePol) 342/1930.
171 US press views re. Viceroy's announcement, 7 November 1929, *ibid.*
172 Viceroy to Secretary of State, 21 May 1930, GOI (HomePol) 39/17/33.

announcement appeared to be directly related to the work of its correspondent in India, who had helped the Government of India send 'true
reports' to the United States.[173] The *Herald Tribune* recognized Gandhi's
sincerity but noted that he now spoke as a high-caste Hindu in his
opposition to special status for untouchables.[174]

There was clearly an effort by the DPI to rush this material to the
Indian press, but there were few takers other than the Anglo-Indian
newspapers where it would make the least impact. As an alternative, the
India Office was asked to arrange for similar comments to be cabled to
India by news agencies, always considered less tainted than official
sources. But there were problems with the agencies too. Reuters had been
sending out numerous telegrams regarding resolutions adopted and fasts
undertaken in England in support of Gandhi's action. The company was
duly requested to give the Government of India more of what it wanted
and less of what it considered undesirable. As was usual in such situations, Reuters responded positively without giving total satisfaction.[175]

Getting material into the American press, either in response to a
particular story or editorial, or as part of the general-information campaign was the more difficult part of the British Library's responsibilities.
Generally Fletcher asked for information or memoranda on particular
subjects and the response was prepared either in the CBI or by a Local
Government when appropriate. In order to deal with the continuing
interest in the Punjab, the Home Secretary, H. W. Emerson, suggested
that a compilation of information 'showing the good that had been
achieved' in the various departments of the Government of the Punjab
under British rule be prepared for publicity officers.[176] This request was
subsequently broadened to include all provinces with the Home Department vetting the material for American consumption.[177]

The critique of the Punjab Publicity Department's effort reflected the
Government of India's concern to avoid overstatement and generalization that might provide material for the critical pens of American
pressmen and nationalist propagandists in the United States. While
Punjab officials described the growth of village enterprise, the initiation

---

[173] R. S. Bajpai note re. propaganda in the United States, 2 March 1932, GOI (HomePol)
3J/1J/1932. Bajpai note re. US correspondents, 6 December 1930, GOI (HomePol)
39/17/33.
[174] Secretary of State to Viceroy, 30 April 1930, GOI (HomePol) 39/17/33.
[175] Secretary of State to Viceroy, 15, 17, 20 September 1932, GOI (HomePol) 35/25/1932.
Viceroy to Secretary of State, 23 September 1932; Secretary of State to Viceroy, 24
September 1932, *ibid.*
[176] H. W. Emerson to D. J. Boyd, Chief Secretary, Punjab Government, 21 November 1930,
GOI (HomePol) 35/2/1931.
[177] H. W. Emerson to Chief Secretaries to all Local Governments, 21 November 1930, *ibid.*

of new cottage industries by Government, the increase in all kinds of manufactured articles, the rise in car and bus travel, and India's high position among the trading nations of the world, Home Department editors modified this success story. There was uncertainty whether village industries were growing, and it was clear that Government provided some help to new cottage enterprises but did not initiate them. The detail was eliminated in favour of a general reference: 'handwork yields to machine work'. The Punjab Government paper's suggestion that the detailed data might not be easily understood 'by the ordinary man's intelligence' was struck out by the Home Secretary who wondered 'why we should decry the ordinary man's intelligence when we are appealing to it as against the misrepresentation put forward by the other side'.[178] The size and complexity of the audience for Government of India productions had enhanced the significance of the information officer's task while making it virtually impossible to carry out. Material for Indian consumption, British consumption, and American consumption – aside from information it was hoped could be kept secret from all of them – was prepared with increasing care; but there were always others, particularly the news services, who did not recognize these political pigeonholes and made much of the Government's effort a waste of time.

The ability of the nationalist camp to generate a flow of effective speakers to carry their anti-British messages across America left Fletcher continually lamenting his dependence on volunteers and amateurs. That the opposition was in the same position was no doubt apparent to him, but the presentation of the situation to his masters in London and Delhi seemed to suggest a well-organized and professional campaign that might itself turn the United States into a dangerous enemy. Their own efforts in this regard had made no lasting impact. Rustomjee had been available and at a price they were willing to pay. Mr Horne, the principal of Patna College, had been effective at Harvard and surrounding colleges during his year's posting in America, but the Assembly refused to fund a second tour. A permanent exchange arrangement was rejected in order to avoid a debate they were unlikely to win. Edward Thompson had willingly offered his services, but his style was pedantic and he produced little press coverage. A speech by the Maharaja of Burdwan might bring out a large audience, but was unlikely to influence the opinion makers they needed to contact.

In 1930, as yet another component of his grand plan, Fletcher suggested that Rushbrook Williams be sent to the United States, to meet

---

[178] Home Department discussion re. two notes prepared in the Punjab Publicity Department, n.d. (notes received 26 November 1930), *ibid.*

what was in his view, the urgent need to make the British case regarding India.[179] He appeared to be the ideal spokesman for British India – articulate, informed, experienced in publicity work, and now in the service of the Maharaja of Patiala, no longer an official in the Indian Government. Fletcher suggested that his association with 'the third party in the triangle' made him in a sense detached, and this might be reflected in a greater willingness to accept his information and viewpoint.[180] Others saw no benefit in detachment from a cause which required loyal service, and feared he might be merely a 'propagandist for the Princes'. It seemed essential that Rushbrook Williams agree not to repeat a line of argument reflected in some of his British publications which tended toward the 'exaltation of Indian States Government at the expense of the administration of British India'.[181] It was finally agreed that he would make the tour, primarily under the sponsorship of the English Speaking Union, since the mission was of a kind, Fletcher noted, with 'which for well-known reasons, it is not desirable that the Library should be connected'.[182]

Rushbrook Williams' month-long tour in May 1930 brought him in touch with the kind of audiences and individuals whose support or simply acquiescence, it was assumed, would dampen the ardour of policy makers in Washington for any significant attack on British interests in India. He was determined to 'bring home to America the true facts of the Indian situation', and in a continual cycle of speeches, radio broadcasts, informal question periods, and individual meetings, he emphasized the complexities of the problems, Gandhi's opposition to all Western civilization, the differences between the Indian and Irish situations, and the special significance of the princely states. In New York, the Foreign Policy Association, which had recently welcomed two nationalist speakers, S. N. Ghose and T. H. K. Rezmie, received Rushbrook Williams as well and he came away with the feeling that he had done some good. Fletcher had thought it particularly important for him to make this speech of response, although he remained puzzled by the attitude of the Association for allowing Ghose and Rezmie to speak at all. 'This is an illustration of those differences between American and British conduct of public affairs', he noted, 'which are so difficult to explain.'[183]

A flow of press reports began almost immediately after his arrival. The *New York Times* merely reported his statement that unrest in India would

---

[179] A. S. Fletcher to Sir Arthur Willert (News Director, FO), 13 February 1930, IO L/P & J/6/1989.
[180] *Ibid.*
[181] E. Howard to V. Dawson (IO), 27 March 1930, *ibid.*
[182] A. S. Fletcher to Sir Arthur Willert, 13 February 1930, *ibid.*
[183] A. S. Fletcher to Ronald Campbell, British Embassy, Washington, 12 March 1930, *ibid.*

end soon and there should be general concern about Soviet involvement on the North West Frontier.[184] But a subsequent lunch meeting with the editorial staff of the *Times* was considered to be quite successful, although there was some concern that their sources of information were so largely British.[185] The *Herald Tribune* reported his view that Gandhi was 'a political failure', but here too there was no editorial comment.[186] Regrettably, editors who sympathized with the nationalist cause did respond. The *New Republic* noted the timeliness of his visit.

Mr Williams is travelling privately, and it is of course sheer coincidence which causes him to bob up in New York at the moment when the British case so badly needs stating. It reminds us of the similar coincidence by which Sir Gilbert Parker arrived to tell us, during the War, how sweet and pure were the Allies and how dastardly the Germans.[187]

The *Nation*, described by Fletcher as 'evil minded',[188] noted that Rushbrook Williams was the representative of the Chamber of Princes, 'probably the most reactionary body in India', and cautioned its readers to 'carefully scrutinize' his statements.[189]

His meetings with students and professors in New Haven, New York, Ann Arbor, and Madison were surprisingly tranquil, even with the presence of a large number of Indians; and his eight-city tour for the English Speaking Union produced large meetings of interested people, and no evidence of either strong anti-British or pro-Gandhi points of view. In general, Rushbrook Williams clung to his carefully scripted tour and avoided any direct confrontation with those who carried a different message about India. He was pressed by the British Consul-General in Chicago to meet Syed Hossain in a debate before the combined Irish Societies, but he insisted he could not amend his programme. There was a tendency in the United States, he noted, to view the situation 'as a conflict between a people desirous of freedom, and a grasping Imperialist power'. The need to act defensively in such 'dog-fighting in public' would diminish the impact of his message, since he was convinced that Americans were wary of propaganda.[190] Quite aside from Syed Hossain, the combined Irish Societies would have no doubt been a daunting audience for any British speaker, but this was the kind of meeting that produced press

---

184 *New York Times*, 10 May 1930, IO L/P & J/6/198.
185 Rushbrook Williams, 'American Bulletin', May 1930, p. 3. Report of lunch meeting with editorial staff of *New York Times*, 14 May 1930, *ibid.*
186 *Herald Tribune*, 10 May 1930, *ibid.*
187 *The New Republic*, 21 May 1930, *ibid.*
188 A. S. Fletcher to Sir Arthur Willert, 23 May 1930, *ibid.*
189 *Nation*, 18 May 1930, *ibid.*
190 Rushbrook Williams, 'American Bulletin', May 1930, pp. 4, 10, *ibid.*

coverage and tested the ability of the official viewpoint to meet the enemy. Rushbrook Williams appeared to be convinced that he was received as an independent speaker and therefore avoided the American tendency to be suspicious of official British argument as well as the extremist nationalist campaign.[191] Anyone who read his press clippings, however, would have had difficulty accepting this view. He did manage one such victory although still without a personal confrontation. In Chicago, he met 'one typical specimen of the sentimental type of American lady who had been captured by Syed Hossain's "sex appeal"'. He was pleased to report that as a result of his talk, she was 'a little disturbed in her idealism'.[192]

He did find time to meet 'the famous Miss Mayo' who he found shared his concern about American sympathy for Gandhi and Indian independence. She promised to help inform her countrymen about the particular complexities associated with the princely states, and he was able to provide her with some notes for a talk on the Indian situation which she was preparing for Fox Movietone News.[193]

When Rushbrook Williams boarded the *Olympic* on 30 May, for the return trip to England, he was convinced that the tour had achieved its goal and influential Americans were now better equipped with the facts concerning the Indian situation. That it remained unclear which side Americans would take in the continuing contest ahead is reflected in an article entitled 'Our Stake in India', written by Henry Cabot Lodge for the *Herald Tribune*.

Our political and economic interests, for instance, show that we should favor continued British rule, but what are these things if some dusky-skinned patriot with a melodious voice exercises his oratorical charms among us? What do bread and butter matter when the magic word 'freedom' is being heard, even if that freedom is nearly impossible to discern? For though they might be free from British rule there are other and worse tyrannies which would surely await them. But it has been well said that Americans are never deaf to an appeal from a people engaged in overthrowing its existing form of Government. Nevertheless, before we rush in headlong it would do no harm to realize that we have powerful reasons for being sympathetic to the British in their attempt to maintain order.[194]

In a London speech describing his American tour, Rushbrook Williams attempted an analysis of the context and quality of American public opinion on India which generated more evidence of the delicacy and ambivalence of the situation there. In response to his view that the East coast was pro-British and the West, with its large German and Irish

---

[191] *Ibid.*, pp. 3–4.
[192] *Ibid.*, p. 12.
[193] *Ibid.*, pp. 1, 4.
[194] H. C. Lodge, 'Our Stake in India', *Herald Tribune*, 1 June 1930, quoted in *ibid.*

communities, pro-Gandhi, the *New York Times* insisted that the only difference was the Middle West commitment to India's right to be free, and the East's commitment to freedom but achieved at a slower pace. In a *Herald Tribune* editorial titled 'A Hint to the Special Pleaders', Rushbrook Williams was described as an 'effective propagandist' who was better advised to keep some of his views unpublished.

Whatever their truth, it is certainly a cardinal rule that when one is asking for another person's good opinion one should not accuse him of an imbecility which would render his opinion worthless. The experienced advertiser never makes a mistake of implying that his reader is anything less than a paragon of intelligence and judgement. The experienced propagandist should never make it, either.[195]

Fletcher rushed copies of the editorials to the Foreign Office and cautioned Rushbrook Williams to avoid such comment in the future. 'These people are so sensitive and so self-conscious', he noted, 'that it is impossible to speak of them publicly without giving somebody offence.'[196] British publicists, of course, encountered the same problem in India. It appeared to be necessary in 1930, for Britain to deal with much of the world – both inside and outside her Empire, with greater deliberation and sensitivity.

The Congress response to challenges and opportunities in America was similar to that of the British. While the new post-war significance of the United States as a world power was recognized, there was no consensus about the likely nature of the role and the extent to which it would impinge on their primary interests. In the early 1920s, there was still no interest and concern in either the Viceroy's Council or the AICC. Those who did give some attention to an American propaganda campaign attempted to send the kind of messages that complemented the American self-image most useful to their cause. For the British, there were the responsibility and practical interests associated with the possession of great power; for the Indian nationalist, the democratic idealism and revolutionary tradition of the American people. While Jawaharlal Nehru's encounter with Latin American radicals at the League Against Imperialism Congress in 1927, suggested the British message might elicit the stronger response, the United States remained a distant but potent source for the design of nationalist goals and potential practical support.

Both the British and Indians had reputations to live down in America. 'Twisting the Lion's Tail' had its source in the American Revolution itself, and the migration of the Irish in the nineteenth century had reminded another generation that the British Empire still represented a

---

[195] *New York Times*, 21 June 1930; *Herald Tribune*, 21 June 1930, *ibid.*
[196] A. S. Fletcher to Sir Arthur Willert, 25 June 1930, *ibid.*

political system alien to American principles. 'India is a striking example of the hypocritical bunk so often put out by a conquering nation', noted the *Sacramento Bee*, 'in order to justify its unjustifiable treatment of the conquered.'[197] For the Indian publicist there was the more fundamental task of convincing Americans that a modern nation in India was conceivable without the presence of the British; that Indians were capable of moving along the same path taken by the founders of their own country; that Indians were like themselves. From the *Hindoo Fakir* in 1902, the first motion picture with an Indian theme, to *Mother India* in 1927, Catherine Mayo's determined exposé of Indian poverty and social distress, the images were romantic, mysterious, frightening, repulsive, and always alien. Nationalist propagandists had to attract a sympathetic response to the Indian struggle against an alien colonial regime, and at the same time instil a new image of modern, progressive Indian leadership. While Nehru's articulate essays in defence of the Congress case in *Foreign Affairs* and the *Atlantic Monthly*[198] confirmed its presence for the elite readers of those journals, it was Gandhi who attracted popular press coverage, often entrenching rather than eroding traditional stereotypes.

The *Chicago Journal of Commerce* found Gandhi's views to be 'out of harmony with the established principles of advanced peoples'. The *Boston Transcript* found the source of his leadership in the 'spiritual forces still at work in the civilization of India'. It was clear that he would play a major role in India's future, but 'how his country's resources are to be developed without machinery is a problem for which even his most ardent admirers can find no solution'. Even H. W. Brailsford, whose writings had been banned in India, expressed his concern about Gandhi's apparent opposition to economic progress; and British officials in the United States were convinced that, despite the prestige of his saintly personality, his reactionary views remained 'a great obstacle in the way of his recognition in America as a statesman'.[199]

Although British officials in New York and Washington tended to discover signs of a united and coordinated anti-Raj campaign in America, as in Europe, individual expatriates led the way and continued to play the major role. The significance of this activity from the point of view of Congress leaders at home remained unclear and always debatable, and it was necessary to plead one's case each time support was required. For most, the American effort held little interest and it fell eventually, with the

[197] Press-USA, 18 January–7 February 1930, BLI, India, No. 28, 14 February 1930, IO L/P & J/6/1989.
[198] J. Nehru, 'Unity of India', *Foreign Affairs*, 1938; 'India's Demand and England's Answer', Atlantic Monthly, 1940, cited in Hess, *America Encounters India*.
[199] Press-USA, IO L/P & J/6/1989.

rest of the world, into Jawaharlal Nehru's mixed portfolio. In 1920, it seemed clear to some that work in America was far more important than the continuing effort in England. Money spent attempting to enlighten the British public seemed a waste of limited resources, better used to educate the American public, who were potentially a real friend of India. 'American opinion in favour of India', it was argued, 'will be of great value in moulding the English method of Indian Government.'[200]

When he returned to India in 1920, Lajpat Rai left behind a group of talented publicists to continue the work of the India Home Rule League of America. In addition to *Young India*, a flow of circulars, tracts, and pamphlets carried the nationalist message. An Indian Information Bureau with branches in major American cities facilitated access to the press, regular contact with Indian students, and occasional lobbying of Congressmen. Between 1917 and 1920, $18,000 in contributions had been collected, including $6,000 sent by Tilak.[201] All of this activity, reported to the Congress President, Motilal Nehru, with the optimism of a supplicant, depended upon the efforts of a handful of people – Indian and American. N. S. Hardiker, the League's General Secretary in 1920, told Nehru that they could raise only $6,000 a year in America to fund an annual budget of $12,000, and the balance would have to come from India.[202] It was assumed that Lajpat Rai's succession to the Congress presidency would insure a sympathetic hearing, and it was noted that Tilak had promised to provide $250 per month from Indian Home Rule League funds.[203] But Hardiker's request had to join a list of supplicants pressing against a door partially closed by Gandhi. Those who were sympathetic did not yet have access to the Tilak Memorial Fund, which would later provide an opportunity for some contribution to overseas activity.

In the following year, J. T. Sunderland, a member of the League's Advisory Board and editor of *Young India*, again reported on its activities, especially the circulation of the Report of the Congress Committee on the Punjab Disturbances. Thousands of circulars had been sent out in the United States and to Canada as well but 'the Canadian authorities, deeming this literature undesirable, confiscated it'. The League purchased a substantial number of copies of Ellen La Motte's book, *The Opium Monopoly*, and offered it at a reduced price; and, after their extensive lobbying effort, Representative Mason asked the United States

---

[200] Ranchoddas to V. J. Patel, 1 October 1920, AICC 17/1920.
[201] N. S. Hardiker to Motilal Nehru, 12 July 1920, *ibid.*
[202] *Ibid.*
[203] Ranchoddas to V. J. Patel, 2 October 1920, *ibid.*

Government, in a speech in the House of Representatives, to recognize India's freedom struggle.[204] In 1921, the League changed its name to the India Information Bureau of America, and it did receive some funding from the AICC. But insufficient support compelled it to drop most of its propaganda work.[205]

If it had been possible to measure the benefit in terms of increased British defensiveness and concern about the internationalization of their freedom struggle, there might have been more enthusiasm in India for such overseas activity. In October 1921, Hardiker published an article entitled 'Rum Follows the Flag in India' in the *Statesman*, a Montreal weekly newspaper. The British Government was accused of encouraging drinking to increase its excise income and, as a result, India was in danger of complete ruin, 'physical, mental and moral'.[206] A cutting of the article was sent to London, and then on to India. It was considered essential within the Indian Government to answer each such attack with a paper prepared on the same subject and published 'as a purely private contribution, no official channels being used'.[207] The liquor charge was considered particularly offensive to officials who detected enthusiasm for drinking and licensing under the Mauryan Dynasty.[208] It was also assumed that there was a large constituency in North America for anti-drinking propaganda and they sought to deny their nationalist antagonists this part of the market. The official response, 'India and the Drink Problem' was too long and pedantic for a popular journal, but a story eventually made its way into the *Philadelphia Public Ledger*, which had a news service circulated to several Canadian papers including the *Toronto Globe*.[209] However insignificant the impact might be, the publication of a rebuttal seemed to set the record straight, and allow a file to begin again its circuitous journey and likely return when a similar incident recurred. The issue remained a sensitive one throughout the 1920s and 1930s, generating regular press coverage and Government of India response.[210]

[204] J. T. Sunderland to Lala Lajpat Rai, 30 November 1921, AICC 4/1921.
[205] *Ibid.*
[206] N. S. Hardiker, 'Rum Follows the Flat in India', *The Statesman*, 19 October 1921, cutting in Propaganda in Canada, IO L/P & J/6/1778.
[207] P. J. O'Donnell to Sir William Duke, 23 March 1922, *ibid.*
[208] 'India and the Drink Problem', *ibid.*
[209] P & J Department note, 5 December 1921, *ibid.*
[210] 'Dry and Free India is Gandhi's Demand', The *Philadelphia Public Ledger*, cited in Press-USA, 18 January–7 February 1930, India, NO. 28, BLI, 14 February 1930, IO L/P & J/6/1989. In response to Fletcher's concern about the proliferation of publications about 'opium and drink forced on people', I. M. Stephens sent a set of GOI materials stressing that 'excise, including opium is in all provinces controlled by ministers elected by or representatives of the educated classes' I. M. Stephens to A. S. Fletcher, 17 December 1930, GOI (HomePol) 35/21/1931.

Hardiker continued to press for support after he returned to India and, after a conversation with Gandhi, he was asked to draw up a scheme for publicity work in the United States. Gandhi agreed to take the scheme to the Working Committee. A master plan was proposed, dividing the United States into six sections to be organized by tuition scholars sent by the Congress, perhaps on the basis of a competition among Indians living in the United States. A plan for central and local organization, a series of publications, and a foreign news service was included with a required annual subsidy of Rs 25,000 or $7,000.[211] As would be the case with Fletcher's grand plan in 1930, this 1922 proposal would attract some interest and no funding, and Hardiker turned to organizational work in India.

By the end of the 1920s, there was a range of organizations in the United States representing Indian interests and seeking some form of association with the Congress. The order of the agenda had, however, become more sensitive to the problems of Indians living in America, and support for the nationalist cause was often cast in the form of a request for Congress action on their behalf. Gopal Singh Khalsa, the General Secretary of the Hindu National Party of America, contacted Jawaharlal Nehru in 1929, concerning the 'more and more unbearable' situation of Indians in California. He was not certain whether the burden of prejudice and hatred was the result of British activity or 'simple anti-oriental feeling'; but those for whom he spoke were convinced that it was time 'that the case of the Indians in the United States, like that of the Indians in South Africa, is formally taken up by the Indian National Congress'.[212]

Nehru received very different advice from officers of the American branch of the Indian National Congress, which had been formally affiliated in January 1929. He was urged to use his influence with the nationalist press in India to stop the publication of any material depicting the 'dark side of American life'. Not only was it not timely to criticize the United States for its treatment of Indian immigrants, but it was not in India's interests to attack the American Government as imperialistic or materialistic. 'America does not care what India thinks of her. But the time is coming when we must have America's support in achieving our goal.'[213] While noting his inability or desire to control the Indian press,

[211] N. S. Hardiker to V. J. Patel, 7 January 1922, AICC 9/1922.
[212] Gopal Singh Khalsa, General Secretary, Hindu National Party of America to J. Nehru, 17 May 1929, AICC (FO) 16. A similar letter was sent by G. R. Channsa, General Secretary, The India–American Association, to Ramsay MacDonald and copied to Nehru, 12 October 1929.
[213] S. N. Ghose and R. L. Bajpai to Nationalist Press of India (via. J. Nehru), 23 January 1929, AICC A–3/1929–30.

Nehru agreed to consult the American branch regarding India's relations with the United States.[214] He began to doubt, however, the decision to grant affiliation and therefore Congress membership to Sailendra Nath Ghose and Ramlal Bajpai, who guided the affairs of the American branch.

Nehru encountered an America of the left, through letters from radical expatriates and the reports of visiting Congress colleagues. His direct contacts with Americans included Roger Baldwin, a social-reform crusader at home and a colleague in the League Against Imperialism. It was this association in particular that concerned Ghose and Bajpai and would eventually lead to confrontation and the disaffiliation of their branch. Within weeks of their formal affiliation, Motilal Nehru received a rambling letter referring to intrigues and competition among the various groups and individuals who were supposed to be working in India's interests. Ghose cautioned Nehru not to act without referring all such enquiries to them, 'because we know who is what in this country much better than it will be possible for you'.[215] Nehru referred the letter to his son. 'Can you do anything about this matter? Is it worth it?'[216] In March, Ghose and Bajpai wrote to Jawaharlal Nehru, reiterating the concerns referred to in January and noting a British attempt to undermine their branch by using Indian nationals as agents.[217]

Although Nehru was not in a position to assess the accuracy of these concerns, Ghose and Bajpai were clearly involved in propagandizing the nationalist cause. In April they informed Nehru that an 'Indian Legation' was being established in Washington and sought $2,500 for its maintenance.[218] While Nehru approved of the action, the Working Committee did not and no support was forthcoming.[219] In a subsequent letter, Ghose and Bajpai repeated their concern that the struggle was against British imperialism only, and not American. 'Until we are free,' they insisted, 'this is a luxury we cannot afford.'[220] Nehru simply noted that on that subject 'we do not quite agree'.[221]

On 15 May Ghose and Bajpai laid claim to the sort of independence of action which had led to Congress confrontations with the British Committee and the London branch. They wrote to the League Against

[214] J. Nehru to American branch, INC, 6 March 1929, *ibid.*
[215] American branch, INC to Motilal Nehru, 24 January 1929, *ibid.*
[216] M. Nehru to J. Nehru, n.d., *ibid.*
[217] S. N. Ghose and R. L. Bajpai to J. Nehru, 26 March 1929, *ibid.*
[218] *Ibid.*, 5 April 1929. The 'legation' was never established.
[219] J. Nehru to R. C. Bajpai, 7 May 1929, *ibid.*
[220] S. N. Ghose and R. C. Bajpai to J. Nehru, 10 April 1929, *ibid.*
[221] J. Nehru to R. C. Bajpai, 7 May 1929, *ibid.*

Imperialism, noting their view that the Indian National Congress should not affiliate with it. Chatto immediately advised Nehru to part with such reactionary support, and Nehru was clearly offended by this open opposition to a decision of the AICC in which he had played the major role. A similar attack would be launched by Chatto at the end of the year; but now he rejected any challenge to the decision to join the League, and any such assertion of branch independence. 'That policy may be right or may be wrong but it is the policy of the Congress so far and it is not open to any of its subordinate Committees to challenge it.'[222]

Ghose insisted that it was Nehru in his personal capacity and not the Congress who had associated with the League, and suggested that he was taking advantage of the 'passive acquiescence' of national workers who would resent the taking of advice from an alien non-Indian institution. The gist of his argument was that the Congress was a nationalist institution and 'certainly and most emphatically not an anti-Imperialistic Institution'. Support and cooperation, he insisted, was available to India from 'other Imperialistic Nations of the world', and Nehru risked its loss by making this commitment to the League's more spacious agenda. In regard to the functions and duties appropriate to a branch of the Congress, Ghose pointed out that they had never received any instructions. In this context, 'we have accepted the natural functions and duties of a representative of a nation of a foreign country'. Abstaining from criticism of a nation to which you were accredited seemed good practical sense to Ghose but, he lamented, the Congress' lack of a fixed foreign policy and understanding of the nature of foreign work had denied its servants in America the cooperation and support they had a right to expect.[223]

On her return from her American tour, Sarojini Naidu told Nehru that the American branch had only a handful of members and was not representative of Indian residents there. He sought advice from others and Roger Baldwin, his American colleague in the League Against Imperialism, added his voice in support of disaffiliation.[224] In August he wrote again to Ghose requesting a membership list and the affiliation fee which had never been paid. He noted Sarojini Naidu's concerns and reiterated the Congress' commitment to association with the League. In regard to the apparent secrecy of Ghose's operations, Nehru insisted that the open model established by the Congress organization in India was meant to apply to all its branches including those located outside of India.

[222] J. Nehru to S. N. Ghose and R. C. Bajpai, 20 June 1929, *ibid.*
[223] S. N. Ghose, to J. Nehru, 15 July 1929, *ibid.*
[224] J. Nehru to R. Baldwin, 11 August 1929, *ibid.* See also Nehru to Dhan Gopal Mukherji, 16 July 1929, *ibid.*

The lack of special instructions which Ghose had noted in an earlier letter, was a reflection of this view.[225] In effect, Ghose was told to play by the rules or risk disaffiliation.

Bajpai responded with a long letter describing the work of their branch, noting it would not be advisable to disclose the names of its 214 members because of the danger of deportation under new immigration laws. He agreed that a number of groups had boycotted the branch but insisted that the fault lay in India and not New York. It was essential that the Congress make a declaration of independence from all forms of British governance in order to attract those in America who refused to accept any compromise. It had also been difficult to maintain a cooperative relationship with Muslims – again Bajpai noted, reflecting the situation at home. And finally there were a few 'suspicious characters' who were apparently imported into the United States in order to create dissention; and Bajpai regretted to note that some of these were personal friends of Mrs Naidu. Bajpai insisted they had the support of 'practically every bonafide Indian organization of this country', listing a number whose overlapping directorates guaranteed a good report.[226] After noting the continuing coverage of their efforts in the press and on radio, he returned once more to the League and concluded with an ultimatum. If the Congress refused to reconsider its membership, 'then we may part with you and carry on our work in our way as we did in the past'.[227]

The pattern that had been set in 1918, when H. S. L. Polak asserted that the British Committee retained the right to take an independent line, and replicated in 1928 when Shapurji Saklatwala attacked Congress leaders in the name of the London branch, was to be repeated once again. Nehru delayed action for almost six months and then moved to gain Working Committee approval of a disaffiliation recommendation. He argued that the prestige of the Congress had been exploited by Ghose and Bajpai, and that their branch did not represent any substantial number of Indians in America. Most important, they remained critical of Congress decisions and openly advocated violent methods to achieve independence. Their propaganda was in effect anti-Congress since it opposed Congress principles. With Gandhi's support, the recommendation was approved by the Working Committee and subsequently endorsed by the AICC.[228]

[225] J. Nehru to S. N. Ghose, 22 August, 1929, *ibid.*

[226] India Freedom Forum, Friends of Freedom for India Association, India Academy of America, Indian National Congress of America. A 1929–30 Report by the India Information Service, BLI, USA noted the close alliance and overlapping control and membership of these groups, GOI (HomePol) 761/1931.

[227] R. L. Bajpai to J. Nehru, 15 September 1929, AICC A–3/1929–31.

[228] J. Nehru note, 16 March 1930, *ibid.*

Ghose's argument that it was Nehru and not the Congress who had created the link with the League Against Imperialism could be generalized to include the Foreign Department and whatever priority was now given to foreign ties, other nationalist struggles, or events in the west which might have some bearing on India's future. The parochial limits of his colleagues' interests were a continuing concern for Nehru who was convinced of the need of the Congress to explain its position and attract support, but also to participate as an independent entity on its own terms. This meant becoming involved in issues beyond the problems of Indians in East or South Africa, or in the United States. It meant opposition to colonialism and concern for the poor whether in or outside India. Nehru would not have accepted the generalization that my enemy's enemy is my friend, but there was no hesitation in his opposition to the evils of British imperialism wherever it was replicated.

Ghose's challenge to the Congress association with the League was also one he could oppose. Although Nehru argued that overseas branches were the same as those in India, they clearly were not. Such branches were not the creation of the Congress but of individual initiative, and were required to scratch out a living with minimal help from the AICC. In New York and London there was little possibility of the sudden appearance of a leader from the centre and, more important, no local base of traditional power that required accommodation or generated its own representatives. For men like Ghose and Bajpai, working alone, or with the support of a small group of colleagues was the only possibility in the context of the rag-tag constituency of migrants who were generally uninterested in an active political role. For Nehru, it allowed the luxury of being personally offended on behalf of the Congress and his principles. The accommodations required to maintain unity in India could be easily denied to those who had chosen to leave.

Nehru appears to have shared with British officials in America a particular aversion to Ghose's aggressive style, carelessness with facts, and advocacy of violence; but, unlike the British, he gave Ghose less credit than he deserved as an effective propagandist who attracted press coverage for the nationalist cause. In February 1930, Ghose was the guest speaker at a luncheon meeting of the Foreign Policy Association in New York. Among the guests was Eamon de Valera who sat with several prominent Indians. The British Consul-General reported that Ghose 'made the usual irresponsible, wild statements, which are characteristic of him', but the reply by Dr Edward Thompson, although good on facts, lacked fire and apparently failed to make an impression. 'As a rule', the consul-general noted, 'gatherings of Americans are more or less emotional.' In a second response, T. H. K. Rezmie, the founder and

Director of the Indian Independence League, insisted that dominion status was the necessary first step to independence.[229] Although Rezmie and Ghose disagreed on the same fundamental issues as had concerned Nehru, their joint appearance produced useful press coverage.

Angus Fletcher noted in February 1930 that they were 'rapidly acquiring a special position as the spokesmen of India in America'. They had

carried on such an assiduous propaganda in the United States that an entirely false and exaggerated atmosphere has been created, which has led the public and the press to accept the Indian political situation at its face value and to assume in reading the reports that a united India of over three hundred millions, all obedient to Gandhi, is really in serious crisis and on the verge of a bloodless, or more probably a violent revolution.[230]

In February and March, Edward Thompson was visiting the United States to promote his new book on the Indian situation. The result was a series of meetings sponsored by the Foreign Policy Association and university and college appearances, often in the form of a debate with S. N. Ghose.

Clearly neither the style of their presentations nor the particular messages they delivered were considered ideal by those they had chosen to represent. Their performances reflected well the reliance of both British officials and the Congress Foreign Department on opportunity and 'second best' to carry out a programme which as an investment in the future had to give way to compelling immediate tasks. Until World War Two, America remained the great power-in-waiting for those whose attention was concentrated on India's future; and the effort to convince Americans that first, they should be interested in India, and secondly, should be asserting that interest in support of one of the protagonists remained the task of men with more leisure and money than available to either the Congress or the Indian Government. So they depended on patriotism and luck – essential elements in the struggle at home as well.

Thompson had to admit that he was careless enough to let Ghose get away with some 'ghastly things' in New York concerning the opium question, but unlike the British Consul-General, he remained convinced that Ghose had done 'his cause no good on the whole'. Ghose managed to keep opium and alcohol as the central issues of their meeting in Baltimore; but in Boston, Thompson was satisfied that he was the clear winner.

---

[229] T. K. Rezmie, the founder of the Indian Independence League of America shared many platforms with Ghose but opposed his apparent commitment to violent action. British Consul-General in New York to HBM's Ambassador in Washington, 26 February 1930 (copied to FO, IO, GOI), GOI (HomePol) 303/1930.

[230] Press-USA, 18 January–7 February 1930, India, No. 28, BLI, 14 February 1930, IO L/P & J/16/1989.

When the issue of widow-burning was raised in the question period, Ghose lost his temper and declared that 'in 1818 you were still burning witches on Boston Common'. Thompson then took the opportunity to relate the 'salient facts' of the widow-burning at Bahr, in Bihar in November 1927. 'I did not mean to horrify the audience,' he noted, 'but that is what I did do.'[231]

Thompson was convinced that 'chasing Ghose up and down has been worth doing.' He noted that Indians in the audience had been giving Ghose a hard time, and that in general his effectiveness was declining.[232] In May, when Rushbrook Williams toured the United States, he was pleased to report that both Ghose and Rezmie were apparently very hard up for funds and living quite poorly.[233] Like so many others, they had managed to offend the dominant conveners of both sides of the struggle.

As Bajpai had noted in his September 1929 letter to Nehru, they were prepared to work on their own, and Ghose remained a regular source of press cuttings for the files of the British Library of Information. In October 1930, the British Consulate in New York described the efforts of Linn Gale to secure the mailing list of the old Clan na Gael organization for Ghose's fundraising efforts. It was also noted that Ghose was now associated with Judge Cohalan, 'more or less the brains of the Irish movement in this country for many years.' Cohalan now accepted the Irish Free State Scheme, but his firm anti-British views had made him a supporter of the Indian cause.[234]

In February 1934, Ghose wrote to the British Ambassador in Washington, seeking permission to return to India. After seventeen years of political activity in the United States, he was tired and suffering from tuberculosis. He asked for an amnesty and pledged to abstain from any association with extreme politics in India. The issue was considered in London and Delhi. In New York, however, Angus Fletcher noted a recent radio broadcast which was 'poisonous'. It did not appear in his view to suggest that Ghose was 'in good training for the new life'.[235] 'We can only suggest that Ghose wishes to return to India because times are bad for Indian revolutionaries in the United States and show signs of getting worse, while the opening up of opportunities in India for a

---

[231] E. Thompson to Lieutenant-Colonel A. V. Gabriel (special correspondent for BLI in London), 4 March 1930, IO L/P & J/6/1989.
[232] *Ibid.*
[233] Rushbrook Williams, American Bulletin, May 1930, GOI (HomePol) 39/17/33.
[234] British Consul-General New York to British Embassy, Washington (to FO, IO, GOI), 6 October 1930, GOI (HomePol) 29/19/34.
[235] S. N. Ghose to Sir Ronald Lindsay, British Ambassador, USA, 16 February 1934, GOI (HomePol) 29/19/34.

practised professional "politician" under the proposed constitution are definitely attractive.' Fletcher saw the possibility of Ghose returning to India briefly and then coming back to the United States when American liberals would respond to his 'enhanced prestige as one fresh from the scene of trouble'.[236] The Government of India apparently agreed and Ghose's application was rejected. A subsequent debate in the Legislative Council left the situation unchanged.

In a 1928 sample poll of American opinion concerning knowledge of the peoples of forty countries, India was at the bottom. Although a realistic and positive image of Indians was to be presented in the film *The Rains Came* in 1939, *Gunga Din* in the same year attracted larger audiences for its traditional images of dependence and loyalty to the Raj. Success for the nationalist campaigners in America seemed to come in very small, almost insignificant incidents: a Christmas greeting to the Indian National Congress in 1921, signed by thirty-eight Americans including a few Congressmen, or the appearance of the American clergyman, John Haynes Holmes, at the 1925 Congress meeting.[237]

There were, however, important changes which reflected the work of expatriate publicists and political activists. A base of interest and often goodwill was created by the personal contacts in America of a generation of nationalist workers who were neither 'Hindoo Fakirs' nor 'Gunga Dins'. They began the process of demythologizing the image of India. Its replacement was not always attractive to American audiences, but at least it was closer to reality. And it was the reality of colonial oppression and nationalist struggle that they sought to introduce into the American consciousness. Success is probably best measured in the increase in American participation in the debate. Catherine Mayo's best-selling *Mother India* was as important as a target for attack and rebuttal, as it was a selective and damaging narrative of India's continued social backwardness. Rejoinders like J. T. Sunderland's *India in Bondage* insisted that 'a great, historic nation, struggling for freedom, demands a voice'. And in his study 'from the side of the Indian people', he attacked the positive image of British rule and narrated a litany of crimes and abuses which required Americans to sympathize with India's struggle.[238] Similar support came from the pens of William James Durant, *The Case for India*, and Gertrude Emerson, *Voiceless India*.[239]

---

[236] Angus Fletcher to A. F. H. Wiggin (British Embassy, Washington), 19 May 1934, *ibid.*
[237] These examples are taken from the introductory chapter to Hess, *American Encounters India*.
[238] J. T. Sunderland, *India in Bondage*, New York: Lewis Copeland Co., 1932 (originally published in 1929).
[239] Cited in Hess, *American Encounters India*, p. 14.

But it was the press and news services that provided the linkage between Indian events and personalities and Americans; whether through direct coverage by correspondents in India, or through staged events and propagandist publications in the United States. Angus Fletcher noted in 1930 the special significance in America of the terms 'Independence Day', 'National Congress', and 'National Flag', noting that 'it would almost appear as if a particular bid were being made to obtain American support'. He noted especially Gandhi's commitment to prohibition and the effective anti-alcohol and anti-opium propaganda of political workers in America, and their wide coverage in the press.[240]

Press response to the 26 January declaration of independence reflected the typical American reaction to such an event. *The World* printed an article by Nehru quoting the Congress resolution in full and noting the enthusiastic response across the country. Its editorial comment described 'nation-wide demonstrations for freedom from British rule'. In the same paper, Rezmie declared that the 'long-looked-for battle for freedom in India has at last begun'. The *Review of Reviews* carried an article by C. F. Andrews, 'India demands Freedom'; and the British Library's clipping file was filled with 'alarmist headlines': 'India Seething as Crisis Nears', 'India Wild at Independence Celebration – Violence Accompanies Demonstrations as Flag of Freedom is Unfurled', 'Flag of Revolt flies over India'. In New York, the India Independence League of America organized a dinner under the chairmanship of J. T. Sunderland to synchronize with the demonstrations in India.[241] But the 'complexity of the situation', always referred to by British spokesmen, was also observed and described, providing some balance in the batch of clippings despatched to London and Delhi:

The Nationalists had announced that the demonstrations would be used as an experiment to determine what further steps could be taken in the development of the new policy, and presumably they will be encouraged by the results. But the policy itself has already taken on something of that mystical flavour which seems to be inseparable from Indian affairs ... they now announce that the independence demonstrations do not mean declaration of independence immediately, but merely expresses the determination of the Congress to work for ultimate complete freedom of India by way of a campaign of civil disobedience. So things are still much where they were ... Their real power is unknown – parades may be an

---

[240] Press-USA, 18 January–7 February 1930, India, No. 28, BLI, 14 February 1930, IO L/P & J/6/1989, p. 2.

[241] *Ibid.*, p. 4. The Hindustan Association of America organized a meeting in Detroit. The speakers included Robert Monteith, leader of the Devalerists in Michigan. British Consulate, Detroit, to HBM's Ambassador, Washington, 28 January 1930. A similar report came from the British Consulate in Chicago. The speakers in Chicago included Roger Baldwin, director of American Civil Liberties Union, GOI (HomePol) 30/4/1930.

indication of it, but cannot be a final proof ... the Nationalists, whatever their historic role, have made themselves a stumbling block in the way of any gradual constitutional advance ... The Indian problem is immensely more complicated than the Irish problem.[242]

Reuters, the Associated Press of India, and the 'American démarche' in India

In June 1930, only a few days after Rushbrook Williams left the United States, Fletcher telegraphed Willert that American correspondents were sending stories that stressed the gravity of the situation in India, 'thus contradicting the impression which Rushbrook Williams has left behind him'.[243] In addition to *New York Times* and *Chicago Daily News* representatives, special articles on India had been sent to the *New York Evening Post*, the *San Francisco Chronicle*, and the *New York World*. It appeared that Reuters' correspondents were probably acting for the Associated Press of America (APA), and the *Baltimore Sun* was 'aggressively hostile' aside from a rather 'colourless' contribution from Francis Low of the *Times of India*.[244]

There was special concern regarding the apparent antagonism of Webb Miller, the European news manager for the United Press of America (UPA) who had spent eight weeks in India, sending back reports of censorship and general news suppression. The Government of India responded with an invitation to Miller for an interview with the Viceroy or other senior official,[245] but this appeared to make little impact on his stories. On 12 August, the *Des Moines Register* reiterated the charge, quoting Miller's claim that the British did not want the world to know what was happening in India. 'The British butchery of unarmed citizens at Peshawar on April 23 promises, when fully reported, to rival some of the most horrible slaughters of human history.'[246] In the *Chicago Tribune*, Charles Daly's stories added to the context of explosive revelations, prefaced by an editorial note which claimed 'a leak in the British censor's office at Bombay, India, had revealed the complete suppression of a despatch to the *Tribune* giving a vivid eyewitness account of one of the largest civil disobedience demonstrations staged by Gandhi's followers.'[247]

---

[242] Press-USA, IO L/P & J/6/1989, pp. 5–6.
[243] Angus Fletcher to Sir Arthur Willert, 4 June 1930, IO L/P & J/6/2004.
[244] *Ibid.*
[245] Sir Arthur Willert to V. Dawson (News Department, IO), 6 June 1930, *ibid.*
[246] *Des Moines Register*, 12 August 1930, *ibid.*
[247] Angus Fletcher to Sir Arthur Willert, 29 August 1930 (enclosure), *ibid.*

Fletcher was plowing his loyal furrow with as much enthusiasm as he could muster, but the American charges were sufficiently compelling to cause him to seek some reassurance. 'It would be interesting to know whether the stories told by these despatches are mere journalistic exaggerations or whether they approximate to the facts. We are inclined to treat most American correspondents as incapable of a reasonable regard for facts, but we should like to be reassured in regard to the Indian situation.'[248] The stated policy of the Government of India, in June 1930, was that messages to reputable press agencies or newspapers outside India were exempted from censorship, with the exception of material concerning the north-west provinces. The charges produced much correspondence and a question in the House of Commons, but no easy consensus regarding the nature of individual censorship decisions. In 1932, Hugh MacGregor was still reminding the Government of India that censorship was more trouble than it was worth, and particularly bad for its relations with the APA and UPA news agencies.[249] He returned to the same themes in 1934, arguing that editors had to be reassured that there was no authorized censorship of their messages from India. Otherwise, in the event of some new political crisis, they would 'show their former inclination to pay more attention to the opposition version'.[250]

The Government of India's attitude toward the presence of American correspondents in India was always ambivalent. They wanted the coverage but resented the criticism. Officials increasingly believed in the power of 'true facts' to describe and support their continuing mission; but insisted that outsiders tended to take shortcuts in unravelling the complex web of old relationship and responsibility. The presence and apparent power of these outsiders required the attempt to guide and influence them, but perspective was not easily shared. Their small numbers in the 1920s and the lack of interest of most Americans in Indian news suggested a containable problem. But, as the size of the international press corps increased, especially the American component, in the years before the war, additional loss of control became apparent. This was particularly the case in regard to the representatives of the major American news agencies, which threatened the API–Reuters monopoly on which the Government however reluctantly, had come to depend.

By the mid-1930s, American correspondents were becoming familiar participants in the Indian news community and in the years before the war influenced the reshaping of press techniques as the news conference and

---

[248] *Ibid.*
[249] H. MacGregor note, 7 January 1923, *ibid.*
[250] H. MacGregor to R. T. Peel, 22 May 1934, *ibid.*

more informal interviewing became part of the normal relationship of officials, politicians and the press.[251] Nationalist leaders took advantage of this opportunity to reach out directly to the American people, although this would sometimes irritate Indian journalists who begrudged the loss of a good story to a foreigner as they once did with the API.[252] 'I have every right to expect America to throw her full weight on the side of justice', Gandhi told Preston Grover of the APA, 'if she is convinced of the justice of the Indian cause.'[253] A. S. Iyengar has noted that a press conference in the early 1940s without Americans was 'considered to be like *Hamlet* without the Prince of Denmark'; and he described a conference held in New Delhi in 1943, at the office of the *Hindustan Times*. Rajagopalachari waited forty-five minutes before one American correspondent made an appearance and he allowed the meeting to begin.[254]

The challenge to the Reuters monopoly was not limited to India. Kent Cooper had mobilized his APA troops to challenge the agreements which had protected Havas, Wolff, and Reuters for over half a century. The old baronies were confronted in South America, Europe and the Far East with a crusading commitment founded on Cooper's belief that unbiased news was 'the highest original moral concept ever developed in America and given the world'.[255] The concern noted in London in the early 1920s, that the news of the empire not be contaminated by passing through 'foreign pipes', was now reiterated on behalf of America and the APA. Referring to Reuters and Havas, Cooper noted that 'the Associated Press would like, if possible, to secure its news from all sources direct and free from that contamination and association'.[256] In a 1930 speech before the Institute of Journalists in London, Roderick Jones described sixty years of Reuters' service in the Far East, which he believed had contributed more than any other factor to the enhancement of British prestige and influence in the region.[257] Cooper agreed, and fought for the contract which Reuters finally accepted in 1934, ending its monopoly control.[258]

Throughout the last half of the 1930s, and into the war years, concerns about Reuters' loyalty increased with the subsidies, and an appreciation of the need for Reuters to serve an increasingly mixed constituency. In 1937, a meeting was held in Gorton Castle, Simla, to discuss the circula-

---

[251] Iyengar, *Gandhian Era*, p. 105.
[252] Bhattacharyya, *Mahatma Gandhi*, p. 61.
[253] *Ibid.*
[254] Iyengar, *Gandhian Era*, p. 105.
[255] Cooper, *Barriers Down*, p. 9.
[256] *Ibid.*, p. 141.
[257] R. Jones, Institute of Journalists, London, October 1930. Cited in *ibid.*, p. 31.
[258] *Ibid.*, p. 31.

tion of political propaganda by the API. It was agreed that the interests of the Government of India had to be balanced against those of the Provincial Governments and the various political parties, but 'pure propaganda' had to be eliminated from the service.[259] Reuters agreed and a letter from the head office in London cautioned its staff to differentiate between a statement by Gandhi and the 'virulent propaganda of the "Foreign Committee"'.[260] But the circulation of 'undesirable messages' increased and the Government was forced to recognize that in addition to its other Indian customers, Reuters now had serious competitors in the APA and UPA news services.

Joyce was concerned that any attempt to severely restrict Reuters' ability to send out criticism of Government policy would encourage the Indian press to look to the Americans;[261] while Sir Arthur Puckle insisted that the Government had carried 'impartiality' regarding Reuters' service too far. He was convinced that the company was generally ready to cooperate, but it was looking to the future and hoping to preserve its monopoly. In his view, they would not succeed, since 'nothing would keep American Agencies out', but Reuters had the right to defend its business interests.[262] He lamented, however, that Reuters had now joined the dozen American correspondents 'all inclined to take the sentimental view of Indian nationalism'.[263]

As the war progressed, the Government became concerned that Reuters was playing up American intervention in India and wondered if the company was trying to demonstrate its ability to serve American interests in competition with the UPA.[264] The question of Reuters' future began to be considered more seriously in London and New Delhi. It was no longer a question of official versus business interests; but the possibility of the loss of both control of and significant participation in the communications system that linked the various parts of India, and India with the rest of the world. Noting the 'American diplomatic démarche on behalf of the United Press of America', the India Office now made clear

[259] Memorandum, Gorton Castle meeting, 25 September 1937, GOI (HomePol) 39/34/1937.
[260] Reuters Head Office memorandum, cited in John Turner to A. H. Joyce, 8 November 1937, *ibid.*
[261] Joyce memorandum, 9 February 1942, IO L/I/663, File 462/19.
[262] Sir Frederick Puckle, Department of Information and Broadcasting (GOI), 3 March 1942, *ibid.* 'To make our service so comprehensive that there is no room for the American services which are being so vigorously canvassed by newspapers.' (Reuters) John Turner to G. S. Bozman, (GOI), 14 November 1944.
[263] Secretary of State to GOI War Department, 1943 (n.d.), IO L/I/664, File 462/9.
[264] A. F. Morley (IO) to Mr Patrick and General Molesworth in India, 25 September 1943, *ibid.*

that it was 'a major political interest of HMG to see that the business of Reuters is maintained in India'.[265]

In the view of India Office officials, the UPA was

an agency which is at once irresponsible and in no way concerned with British interests or amenable to British official pressure. Our job in the India Office as the Information Department sees it, and that of the Department of Information and Broadcasting in India and others concerned is, on the one hand, to protect Reuters against dangerous rivals and, on the other hand, while allowing them a reasonable amount of rope and sometimes taking a fairly broad view of particular official grievances, to keep constantly before them their general obligations as a concern enjoying the indirect support of HMG.[266]

Reuters was never allowed to forget its increasing obligation to the Government, now a partner in its battle against the United Press of America (UPA), in addition to the subsidies and special relationship.[267] John Turner advised the Government that the most useful way it could support Reuters would be the denial of wireless frequencies to the Americans, for internal news traffic. He noted his concern that the Government's desire to spread war news in India combined with US Government pressure in support of the UPA might deny Reuters this advantage. He reminded Joyce that while the US Government was neutral, its news services sold news from both sides, to Reuters' disadvantage, and also attached a letter from M. N. Cama, the owner of the *Bombay Chronicle*, which noted the possibility of an American competitor gaining advantages because of Reuters' conservative policy regarding foreign news.[268] UPA was denied internal wireless facilities until the end of the war.[269]

While arbitrary Government action in India could protect Reuters from any serious challenge during the war, significant changes concerning control of the company were being negotiated in London. In October 1941, Arthur Moore, president of the Indian and Eastern Newspaper Society (IENS), telegraphed the Minister of Information, Brendan Bracken, urging a postponement in the transfer of Press Association interest in Reuters to the Newspaper Proprietors' Association until the empire's interests had been considered.[270] While the Press Association had represented a mixed grouping of provincial British papers and some of the London press, control of the Newspaper Proprietors' Association,

[265] *Ibid.*
[266] A. F. Morley to William Moloney, 16 October 1943, *Ibid.*
[267] *Ibid.*
[268] John Turner to A. H. Joyce, 20 October 1943; M. N. Cama to John Turner, 16 September 1943, *ibid.*
[269] A. H. Joyce to Sir Frederick Puckle, 23 October 1943, *ibid.* Also B. L. Kircher, Office of Chief Press Adviser, to A. H. Joyce, 8 January 1944, *ibid.*
[270] Arthur Moore to Brendan Bracken, 23 October 1941, IO L/I/1/263, FIle 99A.

which had just purchased half of the capital of Reuters, was concentrated in the hands of the large London papers. The chairman of Reuters Limited, S. Storey, had just resigned because of his concern that too much influence would lie with a few London press bosses; and Moore reiterated that concern on behalf of his own constituency.

In the House of Commons, Sir Stanley Reed attacked this 'great and sinister step', and urged the Government to delay the transfer of control and investigate 'how best there can be preserved in the national and imperial interests the complete impartiality and objectivity of our main news service'.[271] Negotiations began immediately which would eventually lead to the establishment of the Reuters Trust and its general ownership by the whole of the British press. In October 1941, however, Bracken thought there was little for Government to do other than keep a 'fatherly eye' on a deal that had already gone through and on a company they did not own. 'We must face up to the fact', he told the Commons, 'that it is not a Canterbury Cathedral or an ancient British institution. It is a commercial business and a highly competitive commercial business.'[272]

The problem for Bracken was that a great many people in Britain, the empire, and an array of foreign countries did consider Reuters to be 'a Canterbury Cathedral', and did take a 'proprietorial' interest in its control. L. S. Amery, the Secretary of State for India, thought a British trust would be possible, but the problem of including some form of controlling representation from outside, he told Bracken, 'passes my powers of imagination'.[273] In November, Reed contacted Bracken again on behalf of the IENS and described the special situation in India. While in Britain and other countries, Reuters was only a service supplementary to the work of local correspondents, in India, Reuters was the main service and, in addition, owned the major internal news agency in the country, API. It was clearly unacceptable that a small number of London press barons, or even the whole of the British press, should control the main foreign and internal news service in India. At the very least, the Indian press had to be allowed to acquire control of the API.[274]

The issue of control of the API had been raised with Reuters by the IENS in 1940, when the company agreed to consider changes, but set aside until after the war. The proposals now presented by Moore and Reed were discussed by the new Reuters trustees and by officials in the India Office. Joyce assumed that there would be no change in the

---

271 Sir S. Reed in House of Commons debate on news dissemination, 22 October 1941, *Hansard*, pp. 1868–9, *ibid*.
272 B. Bracken, 22 October 1941, *Hansard*, pp. 1870–3, *ibid*.
273 L. S. Amery to B. Bracken, 24 October 1941, *ibid*.
274 Stanley Reed, L. S. Matters, L. W. Mackie to B. Bracken, 5 November 1941, *ibid*.

company's position, and although sympathetic to the proposal from the IENS, he was content to wait as long as possible. For the duration of the war, and 'perhaps so long as British responsibility for the Government of India remains', it seemed essential that the API as the locus of the Indian distribution network – sending Reuters' news and interpretation of events to the Indian press, gathering and distributing news within India, and supplying Reuters with material for its outward service – had to remain under British control.[275] Amery, Bracken, and the company agreed.[276] In response to the decision of the Reuters' trustees to delay any further discussion until the end of the war, the IENS gave 'friendly notice' of termination of their contract with Reuters and their desire to negotiate another on the lines of that between the company and the British press.[277]

In December 1943, Reuters agreed to some alterations in its contract with the Indian press, allowing certain subscribers to take a second service with the *quid pro quo* that Reuters would be allowed the freedom to respond to competition with variation of wordage and charges. But there was no final agreement. There was clearly a desire for an alternative foreign service, but the enthusiasm for the American news coverage of world and Indian events had diminished. In addition, it had become clear that the UPA would have to charge more than most of the Indian papers could afford in order to establish a worthwhile service. It seemed clear that they could only be a supplementary service rather than a full alternative. In any case, it would not be possible to compete with Reuters without teleprinter or wireless distribution facilities in India, and the Government of India had ruled this out until the end of the war. The UPA urged the American State Department to intervene, and encouraged a number of Indian editors to wait before they signed another Reuters agreement,[278] but the officially sponsored stalemate continued until the end of the war.

The Government of India was determined to build up an internal agency which could be regarded as Indian and become so well established that it would be impossible for any foreign agency to operate economically. It was also essential to prevent the API from passing into the hands of the Congress Party or a small group of big industrialists who were in the process of building large newspaper chains. Swaminath Sadanand had submitted a proposal for a national service which might

---

[275] A. H. Joyce to Patrick and Turnbull, IO (confidential memorandum), 4 December 1941, *ibid.*

[276] L. S. Amery to B. Bracken, 5 December 1941 (incl. Joyce note), *ibid.*

[277] IENS cable, 20 July 1941, *ibid.*

[278] B. J. Kircher, Office of Chief Press Adviser to A. H. Joyce, 8 January 1944, IO L/I/1/664, File 462/9.

have met these objectives, but it seemed clear to Information Department officials that it would 'almost inevitably exclude the British angle on news altogether.'[279]

In response to Government of India encouragement and the continuing pressure from the IENS, John Turner developed a proposal for converting API into an Indian rupee company and offering 35 per cent of the shares to the IENS. He assumed that the Anglo-Indian and larger Indian-owned press would agree, but he was concerned that the company at home might not appreciate the seriousness of the situation.[280] In August 1945, however, Joyce proposed to give up a grudging approach to Indian control – and hand over ownership of API to a trust controlled by the Indian press. Reuters would not seek compensation but the management of the agency would remain with Reuters. In addition, the Indian press would agree to subscribe to Reuters' foreign service for a minimum of twenty years, although other foreign services could be added.[281] The Americans were apparently still trying to establish a place in the Indian market by increasing their anti-British messages and 'pandering to nationalism'. In response the API had begun to provide its service free in a number of centres, although it was clearly losing money each month.[282]

In October 1946, the Press Trust of India (PTI) was established and negotiations with Reuters continued regarding its place in India after API passed into the Trust's control. There was tentative agreement that both Reuters and the PTI would operate jointly the teleprinter circuits for six years. Reuters' lease of telegraph channels was due to expire on 30 June, 1949. It was also agreed that the PTI would apply for a lease of telegraph channels in its own name. After June 1949, Reuters would share the PTI circuit. Sardar Patel, representing the Interim Government, however, made it clear that any final decision would be political and national, and rejected the granting of any teleprinter lines to a foreign agency or an indigenous concern linked to such an agency.[283]

In December 1947, a delegation from the IENS travelled to London for a last negotiating meeting with Reuters. Among the five delegates, Kasturi Srinivasan, and C. R. Srinivasan were committed to some arrangement with Reuters; and they were criticized by their colleagues Ramnath Goenka and Swaminath Sadanand as pro-British. Goenka and Sadanand wanted an arrangement with an American news agency. The

[279] G. S. Bozman to A. H. Joyce, 14 March 1945, *ibid.* A. H. Joyce to G. S. Bozman, 16 August 1946, IO L/I/1/343, File 131/13.
[280] Included in IO L/I/1/664, File 462/9.
[281] A. H. Joyce memorandum, 30 August 1945, *ibid.*
[282] W. A. Cole to A. H. Joyce, 14 September 1945, *ibid.*
[283] India Office memorandum, n.d. IO L/I/1/343, File 131/13.

fifth member, Devadas Gandhi, wavered between the two sides. He was not opposed to Reuters, but felt he had made a prior commitment to the APA. On their return, however, the two Srinivasans and Gandhi produced a majority report recommending an agreement with Reuters, with Goenka and Sadanand dissenting; and with Patel's support, the majority report was accepted. The Americans had been finally routed and Reuters had survived, for the time being, the transfer of an important element of power. The agreement, Nehru asserted, was 'another step in our liberation'.[284]

The Reuters contract reflected both the new context of freedom and the continuing significance of the British legacy. The same relationship informed the Indian Government's policy on press legislation. Official attitude in regard to the ideal of 'freedom of the press' continued to be mediated by the need to maintain order. In 1947, the new Government inherited the Central Press (Special Powers) Act and nine Provincial Acts. In the context of continuing communal confrontation and violence, there was little opposition from the press to these laws. In 1948, however, the Government established a Press Law Inquiry Commission with a mandate to review the legacy of colonial press legislation. In its report the Committee recommended the abolition of all laws specifically concerning the press and incorporating whatever constraints were required into 'ordinary law'. This was, of course, not the first time such a recommendation had been made. Macaulay had argued for greater dependence on 'ordinary law' in 1835, and his views were reflected in the Metcalf Press Law. In 1921, the Sapru Press Laws Committee had been given the same mandate and it produced a similar recommendation. The 1910 Press Law was abolished and not replaced. Both the 1835 and 1921 liberal initiatives were eventually displaced by constraining press legislation passed by colonial Governments which considered press laws to be essential weapons in their defensive arsenals.

In 1948, the independent Government of India was unwilling to give up its inherited press control powers and no action was taken in regard to the Press Committee recommendations until 1951. When the matter was taken up again, the Constitution was amended to provide for restrictions on the right of freedom of expression and a new law, the Press (Objectionable Matter) Act was passed. While much of the old legislation was repealed and a major role for judicial review was incorporated into the law, the new Indian Government like the old colonial one for much of its time in power, was unprepared to accept the proposition that the press was an ordinary institution. Its power to influence and excite was extraordinary and an extraordinary law was required to keep its 'extremist' elements under control.

---

[284] Quoted in Narasimhan, *Kasturi Srinivasan*, p. 103.

Conclusion

The British Raj was built by men who were convinced of the superiority of their culture and institutions, and appropriated the responsibility of spokesmen for an Indian mass they assumed would follow them if it could only be made to understand the high quality of their message. They created a range of safe and serviceable pulpits in the Government and the Anglo-Indian papers, and invited an educated Indian elite to participate. But they remained critical of these Indian messengers, particularly when they presumed to take over the spokesman's platform. By the 1920s, the Congress insistence on speaking for all the people of India produced a rejoinder from Raj officials about their own continuing role, cast in the context of protector of a range of economic, regional, ethnic, and communal groups. Although the British were attacked for their policy of 'divide and rule', the pluralism was real. And the Congress effort to establish a single 'voice' that spoke for 'All-India' was continually challenged by competing identities reflected in a complex multi-level exchange of viewpoint and defence of particular interest.

The All-India Movement and its monopoly assertions provided a base for a united campaign. It stimulated as well, the creation of separatist challenges always enhanced in reputation and influence by a parallel campaign in print. As the centrally envisaged India took on more detail and precise definition, counter images, described in more recognizable ethno-historical terms were produced by 'local' 'regional', and 'communal' leaders. For many, their bases were 'centres' too, and their large constituencies were generally unaware of the 'parochial' nature of their participation. Congress message makers never had the luxury of united and committed support that would allow them to concentrate on their British target. Their own imagery owed much to the British, and individual cultural legacy informed an internal competition before the messages could be sent. Congress leaders had to adapt their views and the description of their goals to the sensitivities of many who felt threatened by the increasing likelihood that power would soon be transferred, and not to them. There was a dialogue in the press, in pamphlets, bulletins, mobilization campaigns, and endless speeches. The language could be violent or simply utilize words and phrases that were meaningful to a local constituency and signalled their separation from the rest. There was plenty of apparent accommodation, but no fundamental change in the complex political culture. Multiple solitudes co-existed, often nourished by a continuing British campaign which propagated its own messages: India was not ready for freedom, Non-cooperation would produce anarchy, working the Reforms would achieve the desired goal, communists endangered the stability of business interests and the state, neither Gandhian deconstuction nor Nehruvian revolution was in the interest of the Indian people.

The changed situation in the inter-war years made an extraordinary impact on the communications network that connected all of these messengers with the constituencies they sought throughout India and the rest of the world. The combination of the 1919 Reforms and the abolition of the 1910 Press Act created a requirement for the Government to rely on 'ordinary law'. The illusion of normality was further enhanced by the decline in the size of the Anglo-India press establishment, the complementary rise in numbers and influence of the major national Indian-owned papers, and the partial Indianization of API–Reuters. Financing, technological changes, competition, and independence were priorities for these papers and news services, in addition to their participation in the freedom struggle dialogue.

Among this elite 'national' press corps, a professional life – separate from the nationalist struggle and the Raj regime – was considered to be the product of a tradition which provided continuity with a distinctive past. All Indians had the right to demand their freedom, but in its absence, it seemed possible for the press to have a fragment of independence. For Ram Mohan Roy, freedom of the press was the 'most precious of their privileges'.[1] And Raj officials appeared to agree. Although the British legislated against the press, they continually returned to a liberal policy which was assumed to be an essential reflection of the enlightened nature of their mission. In 1888, the Viceroy, Lord Dufferin, suggested that a free press was a useful alternative to general freedom.[2] While the editors of these papers and news services would have rejected such a proposition, they implicitly adapted themselves to it. Ashis Nandy has described this behaviour of the professional classes generally as a natural

---

[1] Ram Mohan Roy, 'Appeal to the Privy Council on Freedom of the Press', quoted in Sophia Dobson Collett, *The Life and Letters of Raja Ram Mohan Roy*, Calcutta: Sadharan Brahmo Samaj, 1962, Appendix I, p. 488.

[2] Kalpana Bishni, 'Lord Dufferin and the Indian Press', *Bengal Past and Present*, 84, January–June 1965, Pt 1, serial no. 157, p. 42.

response to 'inescapable dominance' which allowed men to 'preserve a minimum of self-esteem'.[3] Others would describe them as freedom fighters in that all inclusive Gramschian 'war of position' prescribed by the hegemonic nature of British power in India. But many of these men savoured their fourth-estate status and role which required an accommodative and 'ordinary' relationship with an extraordinary regime. In time, Raj officials accepted a situation they could no longer control and attempt to gain whatever benefits might flow from news reports of their achievements and the internal struggles of their nationalist opponents.

The need to develop and utilize propaganda materials and settings that appeared to enhance the status and influence of the various message senders produced curious anomalies. The Government of India and Local Governments continued to utilise 'oriental' symbols of authority, which they assumed would impress a mass constituency that was far more 'traditional' than its self-appointed national leaders. Durbars, caparisoned elephants, royal visits, and tours of officers to remind old soldiers of their duty were meant to complement a parallel campaign in print emphasizing the responsibilities of constitutional Government. The nationalist campaign was also a mix of old and new images called up by the obvious opportunities and imagined dangers of the present situation. The demand for freedom reflected both British influence in the design as well as their role as the enemy of its fulfilment. But it was flawed and weakened by competing concerns for: 'Hinduism in danger', 'The Panth in danger', 'Islam in danger', even a cry for 'Anglo-India for the Anglo-Indians'. There was no doubt that these various 'India of my dreams' – or nightmares – were influenced by a British occupation that had penetrated minds as well as markets. They were also informed by the range of ethnic, communal, regional, and cultural identity which had been both marginalized and politicized by the colonial experience, and now influenced the competition for a piece of the succession.

Words and ideas became the weapons of choice in the context of the non-violent struggle which strategy and reality required. And the control of these weapons was no less essential than primacy in ordinary armaments in more conventional confrontations. Words and ideas under control versus words and ideas out of control was often the primary issue on the extraordinary stage on which the national struggle was played out. A careless speech, an emotionally charged editorial or a misdirected campaign could call up a violent response and undermine a carefully laid plan for negotiated settlement. 'The newspaperman has become a walking

---

[3] Ashis Nandy, *The Intimate Enemy: Loss and Recovery of Self Under Colonialism*, Delhi: Oxford University Press, 1983, p. 10–11.

plague', Gandhi declared, in a statement on the assassination of the Hindu religious leader, Swami Shraddhanand.

He speaks the contagion of lies and calumnies. He exhausts the foul vocabulary of his dialect and injects his virus into the unsuspecting, and often receptive minds of his readers. Leaders, intoxicated with the exuberance of their own language, have not known to put a curb upon their tongues or persons.[4]

Of primary concern were other leaders' messages and the possibility of losing a constituency to a 'narrow' and 'parochial' mission, or to a 'national' vision which seemed to endanger one's future place and interest. The stakes were high since they were not merely concerned with an immediate confrontation. The last act of this very long play was yet to be written.

The propagandists and journalists who fed the presses were generally loyal camp followers of a particular leader or party. They were used by officials, politicians, princes, and businessmen, and sometimes received benefits that might ensure the vitality of their particular paper. There were some, however, who considered themselves to be independent actors and resisted any loyalty pledge. Men like Ramananda Chatterjee, Kalinath Roy, and Pothan Joseph were nationalists and also independent professionals. Like so many others, they were required to utilize a range of individual strategies to achieve a sense of personal independence and success under the colonial regime. Editing a major national newspaper provided a unique opportunity. For British professionals as well, particularly in the era of post-World War One competition, an Indian press career required independence, and William Moloney, Arthur Moore, and even an information official like A. H. Joyce, cast their loyalty to the Raj in terms of the ideal of press freedom. Together these men – Indians and Britons, helped to reduce official control of the printed word and facilitate this aspect of the transfer of power. They played an important role as well in determining the transfer of the legacy of the freedom-of-the-press tradition, which in their hands tended to support the liberal secular state which the Congress under Jawaharlal Nehru's leadership envisioned and propagated as India's future.

[4] Quoted in Iyengar, *Gandhian Era*, p. 91.

Bibliography

GOVERNMENT DOCUMENTS

Annual Report on Indian and Anglo-Vernacular Newspapers published in the Bombay Presidency for 1925, 30 April 1926
Annual Report on Indian and Anglo-Vernacular Newspapers published in the Bombay Presidency for 1932, 31 May 1933
Annual Statement of Newspapers and periodicals published in India during 1932
Guide to Prominent English and Vernacular Newspapers published in British India and Indian States, December 1937
Guide to Prominent Newspapers and Periodicals in English and Indian Languages published in British India and Indian States, New Delhi, January 1940
The Press Law Commission Report and Evidence, New Delhi, 14 July 1921
Government of India, Home Political Papers, National Archives of India, New Delhi
Government of India, Foreign and Political Papers, India Office Library and Records, London
Information Department, Political and Judicial Papers, India Office Library and Records
AICC Papers, Jawaharlal Nehru Collection, Nehru Memorial Museum and Library

PRIVATE PAPERS

The collections noted below are housed in the Nehru Memorial Museum and Library, New Delhi, with the exception of the Jayakar Papers which are housed in the National Archives, New Delhi.
Syed Abdullah Brelvi Papers
C. Y. Chintamani Papers
Nagendra Nath Gupta Papers
Sreenivasa Iyengar Papers
M. R. Jayakar Papers
G. A. Natesan Papers
B. Shiva Rao Papers
T. B. Sapru Papers
Pheroze Sethna Papers
Purshotamdas Thakurdas Papers

INTERVIEWS

J. N. Sahni, interview, December 1970
Durga Das, interview, December 1970

NEWSPAPERS AND JOURNALS

In addition to the collections of newspaper files utilized in the Nehru Library and
the Centre for South Asian Studies (Cambridge) Library, substantial clipping files
were available in collections of Government documents and private papers.

Amrita Bazar Patrika (Calcutta), daily, 1920–30
Bombay Chronicle (Bombay), daily, 1918–40
Free Press Journal (Bombay), daily, 1930–35, 1937–40
Hindu (Madras), daily, 1920–40
Hindustan Times (Delhi), daily, 1930–40
Indian Daily Mail (Bombay), daily, 1923–31
Leader (Allahabad), daily, 1920–40
Modern Review (Calcutta), monthly, 1920–40
National Herald (Lucknow), daily, 1938–40
Times of India (Bombay), daily, 1918–40
Tribune (Lahore), daily, 1920–40

SECONDARY WORKS

This list is not meant to be an exhaustive review of the literature concerning the
history of the Indian press. It includes all works cited and others that were
especially useful in the writing of this book.

Agrawal, Sushila, *Press: Public Opinion and Government in India*, Jaipur: Asha
    Publishing House, 1970.
Anderson, Benedict, *Imagined Communities: Reflections on the Origins and Spread
    of Nationalism*, London: Verso, 1983.
Arnold, David, *The Congress in Tamilnadu: Nationalist Politics in South India,
    1919–1937*, New Delhi: Manohar, 1977.
Azad, A. K., *India Wins Freedom*, Bombay: Orient Longmans, 1959.
Bamford, P. C., *Histories of the Non-cooperation and Khilafat Movement*, Delhi,
    Deep Publications, 1974.
Banerjee, Sir Surendranath, *A Nation in Making*, Calcutta: Oxford University
    Press, 1925.
Barrier, N. Gerald, *Banned: Controversial Literature and Political Control in
    British India 1907–1947*, Columbia: University of Missouri Press, 1974.
    'South Asia in Vernacular Publications: Modern Indian Language Collections
    in the British Museum and the India Office Library, London' *Journal of
    Asian Studies*, 28, 4 August 1969, 803–10.
Barrier, N. Gerald and Wallace, Paul, *The Punjab Press 1880–1905*, Asian Studies
    Centre, South Asia Series Occasional Papers No. 14, Michigan State Univer-
    sity, 1970.
Berger, Peter, et al., *The Homeless Mind: Modernization and Consciousness*, New
    York: Vintage Books, 1974.

Bhargava, Moti Lal, *Role of the Press in the Freedom Movement*, New Delhi: Reliance Publishing House, 1987.

Bhatia Prem, *All My Yesterdays*, Delhi: Vikas Publishing House, PVT Ltd., 1972.

Bhattacharyya, S. N. *Mahatma Gandhi: The Journalist*, London: Asia Publishing House, 1965.

Bhattacharya, S. and Thapar, R., eds., *Situating Indian History*, Delhi: Oxford University Press, 1986.

Bishni, Kalpana, 'Lord Dufferin and the Indian Press', *Bengal Past and Present*, 84, January–June 1965, Pt 1, serial no. 157.

Bolton, Glorney, 'Freedom of the Press in India', *Great Britain and the East*, Indian Section, 3 February 1938.

Boorstin, Daniel, *The Image*, New York: Harper Colophon Books, 1964.

Bose, P. N. and Moreno, H. W. B., *A Hundred Years of the Bengali Press*, Calcutta: H. W. B. Moreno, 1920.

Brailsford, H. J. *Subject India*, London: Victor Gollancz Ltd, 1943.

Bright, Charles, *Imperial Telegraphic Communication*, London: P. S. King and Son, 1911.

Brown, Emily, *Har Dayal, Hindu Revolutionary and Rationalist*, Tucson: University of Arizona Press, 1975.

Brown, F. J., *The Cable and Wireless Communications of the World*, London: Sir Isaac Pitman and Sons, Ltd, 1930.

Brown, Judith M., *Gandhi: Prisoner of Hope*, New Haven: Yale University Press, 1989.

Modern India: The Origins of an Asian Democracy, Delhi: Oxford University Press, 1985.

Buck, Sir Edward J., *Simla Past and Present*, Bombay: The Times Press, 1925.

Cashman, R., *The Myth of the Lokamanya*, Berkeley: University of California Press, 1975.

Casty, Alan, *Mass Media and Mass Man*, New York: Holt Reinhart and Winston, Inc., 1968.

Chandra, B., Thapar, R., and Mukhia, H., *Communalism in the Writing of Indian History*, New Delhi: People's Press, 1969.

Chandra, Sudhir, *The Oppressive Present: Literature and Social Consciousness in Colonial India*, Delhi: Oxford University Press, 1992.

Chatterjee, Partha, *Nationalist Thought and the Colonial World: A Derivative Discourse*, London: Zed Books Ltd, 1986.

Chatterjee, Ramananda, *Rammonhum Roy and Modern India*, Allahabad: Panini Press, 1906.

Chintamani, C. Y., *Indian Politics Since the Mutiny*, Waltair: Andhra University, 1937.

'A Plea for Unity', *Modern Review*, January 1908.

Chirol, Valentine, *Indian Unrest*, London: Macmillan and Co. Ltd, 1910.

India Old and New, London: Macmillan and Co. Ltd, 1921.

Chowdari, G. Rudrayya, *Prakasam: A Political Study*, New Delhi: Orient Longmans, 1971.

Collett, Sophia Dobson, *The Life and Letters of Raja Ram Mohan Roy*, Calcutta: Sadharan Brahmo Samaj, 1962.

Collins, Henry, *From Pidgeon Post to Wireless*, London: Hodder and Stoughton Ltd, 1925.

Congress Presidential Addresses, Madras: G. A. Natesan, 2nd edition, 1934.

Cooper, Kent, *Barriers Down*, New York: Farrar and Rinehart Inc., 1942.

Cotes, Everard, 'The Newspapers Press of India', *Asiatic Review*, n.s. 19, July 1923.

Dalton, Dennis, 'The Dandi March' in B. R. Nanda, ed., *Essays in Modern Indian History*, Delhi: Oxford University Press, 1980.

Desai, M., *The Diary of Mahadev Desai*, Vol. 1, Ahmedabad: Navajivan Publishing House, 1953.

Das, Durga, 'Indian Press and its Influence in India', in M. B. Nanavati and C. N. Vakil, *Group Prejudices in India*, Bombay: Vera and Co., 1951.

Deutsch, Karl W., *The Nerves of Government: Models of Political Communication and Control*, New York: The Free Press, 1966.

Donald, Robert, *The Imperial Press Conference in Canada*, London: Hodder and Stoughton, 1920.

Dutt, Paramananda, *Memoirs of Motilal Ghose*, Calcutta; Amrita Bazar Patrika Office, 1935.

Fielden, L., 'Muddled Muzzling: Journalism in India', *New Statesman and Nation*, Vol. 25, 16 January 1943.

Frankel, Francine, *India's Political Economy, 1947–1977*, Princeton University Press, 1978.

Frazer, Lovat, *India Under Curzon and After*, London: William Heinemann, 1911.

Fremantle, A., *Loyal Enemy*, London: Hutchinson and Co., 1938.

Gallagher, John, 'Congress in Decline: Bengal 1930–1938', in J. Gallagher, G. Johnson and A. Seal, eds., *Locality, Province and Nation 1870–1940*, Cambridge University Press, 1973.

Gandhi, M. K., *The Collected Works*, Vol. XIX (November 1920–April 1921), Publications Division, Ministry of Information and Broadcasting, Government of India.

George, T. J. S., *Pothan Joseph's India: A Biography*, New Delhi: Sanchar Publishing House, 1992.

Gokhale, D. V., *The Contempt Case Against Mr. N. C. Kelkar, Editor of the Kesari*, Poona: K. R. Gondhalekar at the Jagadhitechu Press, 1924.

Gole, R. M., *N. C. Kelkar*, New Delhi: Sahitya Akademi, 1976.

Gordon, A. D. D., *Businessmen and Politics: Rising Nationalism and a Modernizing Economy in Bombay 1918–1933*, Columbia: South Asia Books, 1978.

Gordon, Richard, 'The Hindu Mahasabha and the Indian National Congress, 1915 to 1926', *Modern Asian Studies*, 9, 2 (1975), 145–203.

Greenough, Paul R., 'Political Mobilization and the Underground Literature of the Quit India Movement, 1942–44', *Modern Asian Studies*, 17, 3 (1983), 353–86.

Gulati, Kailash Chander, *The Akalis Past and Present*, New Delhi: Asajanak Publications, 1974.

Gupta, Uma Das, 'The Indian Press 1870–1880: A Small World of Journalism', *Modern Asian Studies*, 11, 2 (1977), 213–35.

Hardiman, David, 'The Crisis of the Lesser Patidars: Peasant Agitation in Kheda District, Gujarat, 1917–1934', in D. A. Low, ed., *Congress and the Raj*, London: Heinemann, 1977.

Hardman, Thomas H., *A Parliament of the Press: The First Imperial Press Conference*, London: Horace Marshall and Son, 1909.

Hartz, Louis et al., *The Founding of New Societies*, New York: Harcourt, Brace and World Inc., 1964.

Hasan, Mushirul, *Nationalism and Communal Politics in India*, Delhi: Manohar, 1979.

Hess, Gary, *America Encounters India, 1941–1947*, Baltimore: The Johns Hopkins Press, 1971.

Hirschman, Edwin, 'Using South Asian Newspapers for Historical Research', *Journal of Asian Studies*, 31, no. 1, November 1971, 143–50.

Hobsbawm, Eric and Ranger, T., eds., *The Invention of Tradition*, Cambridge University Press, 1984.

Horniman, B. G., *Amritsar and Our Duty to India*, London: T. Fisher Unwin, Ltd, 1920.

Israel, Milton, 'M. R. Jayakar and the Bombay Nationalist Press: The Struggle for Identity within a Nationalist Movement', in N. K. Wagle, ed., *Images of Maharashtra*, London: Curzon Press, 1980, pp. 9–28.

'Ramananda Chatterjee and the *Modern Review*: The Image of Nationality in the National Press', in M. Israel, ed., *National Unity: The South Asian Experience*, New Delhi: Promilla and Co., 1983, pp. 1–46.

'The Congress and the Press: The Case of the National Herald', in John Hill, ed., *The Congress and Indian Nationalism: Historical Perspectives*, London: Curzon Press, 1991.

Iyengar, A. S., *All Through the Gandhian Era*, Bombay: Hind Kitab Ltd, 1950.

Jayakar, M. R., *The Story of My Life*, Vol. I, Bombay: Asia Publishing House, 1958.

The Story of My Life, Vol. II, London: Asia Publishing House, 1959.

Johnson, Gordon, *Provincial Politics and Indian Nationalism: Bombay and the Indian National Congress 1880 to 1915*, Cambridge University Press, 1973.

Jones, Sir Roderick, *A Life in Reuters*, London: Hodder and Stoughton, 1951.

Joseph, Pothan, *Glimpses of Yesterday*, Madras: The Madras Premier Co., 1959.

Joshi, V. C., ed., *Lala Lajpat Rai, Writings and Speeches*, Vol. 1, 1888–1919, Delhi: University Publishers, 1966.

Kasturi, G., compiler, *The Hindu Speaks*, Bombay: Interpress, 1978.

Kelkar, N. C., *A Passing Phase of Politics*, Poona: A. W. Awati, 1925.

The Case of Home Rule, Poona: Arvabhushan Press, 1917.

Kopf, David, 'Hermeneutics versus History', *Journal of Asian Studies*, 39, 3, May 1980, 495–506.

'Rammohun Roy and the Bengal Renaissance', in V. C. Joshi, ed., *Rammohun Roy and the Process of Modernization in India*, Delhi: Vikas Publishing House PVT Ltd, 1975.

Koss, Stephen, *The Rise and Fall of the Political Press in Britain*, Vol. 1: *The Nineteenth Century*, London: Hamish Hamilton, 1981.

The Rise and Fall of the Political Press in Britain, Vol. II: *The Twentieth Century*, London: Hamish Hamilton, 1984.

Krishna, G., 'The Development of the Indian National Congress as a Mass Organization, 1918–1923', *Journal of Asian Studies*, 35, May 1966.

Kumar, Ravinder, 'From Swaraj to Purna Swaraj: Nationalist Politics in the City of Bombay, 1920–1932', in D. A. Low, ed., *Congress and The Raj*, London: Heinemann, 1977.

Lal, Chaman, *British Propaganda in America*, Allahabad: Kitab Mahal, 1945.

Lippman, Walter, *Public Opinion*, New York: Harcourt Brace and Co., 1922.

Lovett, Pat, *Journalism in India*, Calcutta: The Banna Publishing Co., 1928.

Low, D. A., 'Civil Martial Law: The Government of India and the Civil Disobedience Movements, 1930–34', in D. A. Low, ed., *Congress and The Raj*, London: Heinemann, 1977.

MacKenzie, T. W., *The Fifth Imperial Press Conference (South Africa) 1935*, London: The Empire Press Union, 1936.

MacKinder, H. J., *Seven Lectures on the United Kingdom for Use in India*, London: Waterlow and Sons Ltd, 1909.

Mankekar, D. R., *One-Way Free Flow: Neo-Colonialism Via News Media*, New Delhi: Clarion Books, 1978.

Mannheim, Karl, *Ideology and Utopia*, New York: Harcourt, Brace and World, Inc., 1936.

Marcel, Gabriel, *Man Against Humanity*, London: The Hawill Press, Ltd, 1952.

McLuhan, Marshall, *The Gutenberg Galaxy*, Toronto: The New American Library of Canada, 1969.

McCully, B. T., *English Education and the Origin of Indian Nationalism*, New York: Columbia University Press, 1940.

Mayo, Katherine, *Mother India*, New York: Blue Ribbon Books, 1927.

Mills, J. Saxon, *The Press and Communications of the Empire*, London: W. Collins and Co. Ltd, 1924.

Mody, Homi, *Sir Pherozeshah Mehta*, London: Asia Publishing House, 1921.

Moitra, Mohit, *A History of Indian Journalism*, Calcutta: National Book Agency Private Ltd, 1969.

Moraes, Frank, *Witness To An Era*, London: Weidenfeld and Nicolson, 1973.

Sir Purshotamdas Thakurdas, Bombay: Asia Publishing House, 1957.

Nair, L. R., ed., *Motilal Nehru Birth Centenary Souvenir*, Motilal Nehru Centenary Committee, 1961.

Nandy, Ashis, *At the Edge of Psychology: Essays in Politics and Culture*, Delhi: Oxford University Press, 1980.

The Intimate Enemy: Loss and Recovery of Self Under Colonialism, Delhi: Oxford University Press, 1983.

Narasimhan, V. K., *Kasturi Srinivasan*, Bombay: Popular Prakasan, 1969.

Kasturi Ranga Iyengar, New Delhi: Publishing Division, Ministry of Information and Broadcasting, Government of India, 1963.

Natarajan, J., *History of Indian Journalism*, Publications Division, Ministry of Information and Broadcasting, Government of India, 1955.

Natarajan, S., *A History of the Press in India*, Bombay: Asia Publishing House, 1962.

Nehru, Jawaharlal, *Toward Freedom*, Boston: Beacon Press, 1967

Selected Works, Vols. II–IX, new Delhi: Orient Longman, 1972–6.

Norman, D., ed., *Nehru: The First 60 Years*, Vol. 1, Bombay: Asia Publishing House, 1965.

O'Dwyer, Sir Michael, 'Remarks', East Asia Association Meeting, Caxton Hall, 9 April 1923, in *Asiatic Review*, n.s., July 1923, 436–7.

Orwell, George, 'The Freedom of the Press', unpublished introduction to *Animal Farm*, published in *The New York Times Magazine*, 8 October 1972.

Talking to India: Selection of English Language Broadcasts to India, London: George Allen and Unwin Ltd, 1943.

Pandey, G., 'Mobilization in a Mass Movement: Congress "Propaganda" in the United Provices (India) 1930–34', *Modern Asian Studies*, 9, 2 (1975).

Panikkar, K. M., *An Autobiography*, Bombay: Oxford University Press, 1974.

Parthasarathy, Rangaswami, *Memoirs of a News Editor*, Calcutta: Naya Prakash, 1980.

'Party Journalism in India', *The Near East and India*, India Affairs, 3 September 1925.

Parvate, T. V., *Bal Gangadhar Tilak*, Ahmedabad: Navajivan Publishing House, 1958.

Plamenatz, John, *On Alien Rule and Self-Government*, London: Longman Green and Co. Ltd, 1960.

Ratcliffe, S. K. 'An Indian Editor', *New Statesmen*, 20, 7 October 1922, pp. 9–10.

Rau, M. Chalapathi, *Journalism and Politics*, New Delhi: Vikas Publishing House, PVT Ltd, 1984.

Ray, G. K., *A Handbook of the Laws Relating to the Press in India*, Calcutta: Eastern Law House, 1932.

Reed, Sir Stanley, *The India I Knew 1897–1947*, London: Odhams Press Ltd, 1952.

India: The New Phase, London: Philip Allan and Co. Ltd, 1928.

Reeves, Peter D., 'The Politics of Order, "Anti-Non-Cooperation; in the United Provinces, 1921', *Journal of Asian Studies*, 25, 2, February 1966.

Renford, Raymond K., *The Non-Official British in India to 1920*, Delhi: Oxford University Press, 1987.

Ronaldshay, Lord, *The Life of Lord Curzon*, Vol. II, London: Ernest Benn Ltd, 1928.

Rothermund, Dietmar, 'Traditionalism and National Solidarity in India', in R. J. Moore, ed., *Tradition and Politics in South Asia*, New Delhi: Vikas Publishing House PVT Ltd, 1979.

Roy, K. C., 'Simla vs Whitehall: A Conflict in Angle of Vision', *Leader*, 23 September 1922, p. 7.

Sahni, J. N. *The Truth About the Indian Press*, New Delhi: Allied Publishers, 1974.

Samath, Anil, *Shivaji and the Indian National Movement*, Bombay: Samaiya Publications, PVT Ltd, 1975.

Sandbrook, J. A., 'A Hundred Years of Journalism in India', *The Asiatic Review*, n.s., October 1921, 275–83; July 1922, 312–16, 448–53.

Sarkar Chanchal, 'India's First News Agency', *Vidura*, August 1966.

Sarkar, Sumit, *Modern India 1885–1947*, Delhi: Macmillan India, 1983.

Savarkar, V. D., *Hindu Pad-padshahi: Or A Review of the Indian Empire in Maharashtra*, New Delhi: Bharatiya Sahitya Sadan, 1925.

Scott-James, R. A., *The Influence of the Press*, London: S. W. Partridge and Co. Ltd., n.d.

Seal, Anil, 'Imperialism and Nationalism in India, *Modern Asian Studies*, 7, 3 (1973), 321–47.

The Emergence of Indian Nationalism: Competition and Collaboration in the Late Nineteenth Century, Cambridge University Press, 1971.

Sen, S. P., *The Indian Press*, Calcuatta: Institute of Historical Studies, 1967.

Sitaramayya, B. Pattabhi, *History of the Indian National Congress*, Vol. I (1885–1935), Delhi: S. Chand and Co., 1969.

Speeches and Writing of Sir W. W. Wedderburn, Madras: G. A. Natesan & Co., 1918.

Spengler, Oswald, *The Decline of the West*, New York: Alfred Knopf, 1955.

Stephens, Ian, *Monsoon Morning*, London: Ernest Benn, 1966.

Storey, Graham, *Reuters' Century*, London: Max Parish, 1951.

Sunderland, J. T., *India in Bondage*, New York: Lewis Copeland Co., 1932.

Sykes, Percy, *Mortimer Durand: A Biography*, London: Cassell, 1926.

The Times, 'India Number', 23 March 1937.

The Times of India Centenary Supplement, 7 June 1938.

Tomlinson, B. R., *The Indian National Congress and the Raj*, 1929–1942, Toronto: The Macmillan Company of Canada, 1976.

The Tribune: An Anthology, Chandigarh: The Tribune, 1981.

Tucker, Richard, 'Hindu Traditionalism and Nationalist Ideologies in Nineteenth Century Maharashtra', *Modern Asian Studies*, 10, 3 (1976), 321–48.

Turner, H. E., *The Fourth Imperial Press Conference (Britain) 1930)*, London: The Empire Press Union, 1931.

The Imperial Press Conference (Australia) 1925, London: Hodder and Stoughton Ltd, 1925.

The Sixth Imperial Press Conference (Britain) 1946, London: The Empire Press Union, 1947.

Umrigar, K. D., *Lest I Forget*, Bombay: The Popular Book Depot, 1949.

Wagle, N. K., *Images of Maharashtra*, London, Curzon Press, 1980.

Watson, Sir Alfred, 'Journalism in India', *The Asiatic Review*, n.s., April 1933, 254–75.

Young, Morgan, 'The Press in India and Japan, *East and West*, Vol. 14, No. 162, April 1915, 341–9.

Index

Abhyankar, M. V. 162
Adam Regulations 3–4, 16
Advance 174
Advocate of India 132–3, 235
African Comrade 171
Agra Citizen 186
Aiyar, G. H. Vasudeva 47
Akali 183
Akali Movement 179, 180–2, 200, 201
Alexander, Horace 264
Aligarh Mail 66
Ali, Mohammed 8
Allahabad Law Journal Press 166
Allen, C. T. 211
All-India Trade Union Congress 261
All-Parties Conference 72, 171, 173, 263
All-Parties Fund 171
Aman Sabha 41–3, 74
Ambedkar, B. R. 175
Amery, L. S. 313–14
American Commission to Promote
    Self-Government in India 285
Amrita Bazar Patrika 5, 8, 17, 23, 44–5, 60,
    62–3, 89–90, 94–5, 113, 152, 169, 172,
    174, 176, 195, 197, 209, 217
Amritsar Massacre 10–11, 18, 54, 127, 169,
    222, 228, 249
Andhra Patrika 134
Andrews, C. F. 171, 307
Aney, S. J. 174
Ansari, Dr M. A. 200
Ashraf, K. M. 185, 187
Associated Press of America (APA)
    309–10, 316
Associated Press of India (APA) 53, 82,
    113–26 passim, 137–8, 261, 309–11,
    313–15, 318; founding 113–14; and
    Anglo-Indian Press 119–20, 122; and
    Congress 116–17, 120; and Hindu
    communalism 117, 123–4, 153; and
    Government of India 121–2
Association of Chambers of Commerce of
    India and Ceylon 130

Atlantic Monthly 296
Australian Cable Service 141
Azad, Abul Kalam 167

Bajaj, Jamnalal 223
Bajpai, R. S. 47, 59, 102, 261, 287
Bajpai, Ramlal 300, 302–3
Baldwin, Roger 279, 300–1
Baltimore Sun 308
Bande Mataram 132
Bande Matatam (Geneva) 247, 256
Banerjee, S. N. 171, 189, 194, 197, 220
Banker, Shankerlal 231
Bardoli Programme 159, 229
Barns, Mary 154
Basumati 44, 90, 169, 174, 214
Belgaumwalla, N. H. 203–4, 231, 234, 237–8
Bengal Gazette 2
Bengalee 5, 23, 132, 171–2, 197
Bengal National Chamber of Commerce
    148
Besant, Annie 195, 214, 246, 248–9, 271,
    277
Bhopal, Nawab of 201, 203, 276
Birla, G. D. 36, 94, 130–1, 135, 138–40,
    144, 148–9, 165, 175, 199–200, 224
Blackett, Sir Basil 39
Boehm, Sir Edgar 26–7
Bombay Chronicle 17, 23, 27, 44, 55, 58, 60,
    89, 94, 128, 154, 163, 168–69, 177–8, 185,
    199–204, 209, 216–45 passim, 251–2, 281,
    312
Bombay Gazette 268
Bombay Press Service 95
Bombay Sentinel 237
Bose, Subhas 93
Boston Transcript 296
Brabourne, Lord 178
Brailsford, H. N. 264–6, 296
Blizard, G. P. 251
Bracken, Brendan 312–14
Brelvi, S. A. 185, 225, 232–3, 235–6,
    238–40, 242–5

329

Bridgeman, Reginald 261
British Committee, INC 246, 248, 250–2, 255, 271, 300, 302
British Library of Information (New York) 274, 279–80, 284, 287–8, 290, 305
British Official Wireless (BOW) 145–8
British United Press 140–1, 151
Brockway, Fenner 253, 257, 263–4, 273
Buchan, John 105–6
Buck, Sir Edward J. 12, 102, 128, 140–1
Buckingham, James Silk 2
Burdwan, Maharaja of 291

Cable and Wireless Ltd 145
Cama, Bhikhaiji Rustom K. R. 247
Cama, M. N. 312
Canning Press Act 4, 6
Capital 29, 196
Catholic Herald 225
Central Bureau of Information (CBI) 29, 30–3, 35, 37–8, 40, 48, 54, 58–9, 62–4, 68, 77–8, 87, 95–7, 290
Central Intelligence Department (CID) 43, 163
Central Legislative Elections (1934) 90
Central News 151
Central Sikh League 179
Chakravarty, B. 135
Chatfield Committee 49
Chatterjee, Ramananda 9, 22, 215, 266–7, 320
Chattopadhyaya (Chatto), Virendranath 247, 256, 261–2, 271, 301
Chaudhri, Sir Ashutosh 257
Chaudhury, B. B. R. 126
Chauri Chaura 159
Chelmsford, Lord 222, 228
Chicago Daily News 308
Chicago Journal of Commerce 296
Chicago Tribune 308
Chief Khalsa Diwan 179
Chintamani, C. Y. 16, 24, 42, 156–7, 181, 195, 217, 224, 239
Chiplunkar, Vishnu Krishna 24–5
Chirol, Valentine 268–71
Christian Science Monitor 289
Civil and Military Gazette 48, 212
Civil Disobedience Movement (CDM) 15–16, 27, 82, 85–7, 90–1, 205, 237, 242
Clan na Gael 305
Clark, Sir Reginald 87
Coatman, John 74–5, 92, 140–2, 144
Cohalan, Judge 305
Collins, Henry 99
Communal Award (1932) 89, 173–4, 177, 184, 206–7, 224

communalism 13, 21, 68, 70, 72, 170–2, 176–8, 183, 186–7, 207, 228, 241–2
communism 10, 72–3, 91, 190, 255, 259, 262, 264, 271
Comrade 8
Congress Bulletin 83, 165–7
Congress Textile Mills Exemption Committee 165
Cooper, Kent 310
Cotes, Everard 12, 114, 127
Cowasjee, Fakirjee 208
Craik, Sir Henry D. 28, 57, 67
Crerar, Sir James 63, 286
Criminal Law Amendment Act 93, 150
Criminal Law Procedures Code 71
Curzon, Lord 9, 247
Cust, R. N. 27, 29

Daily Express 195
Daily Herald 109
Daily News 250
Daily Sikh 180
Daily Sun 155
Daly, Charles 308
Dandi Salt March 15, 17–18, 24, 78–9, 82
Das, C. R. 160, 231–3, 251
Das, Durga 116–18, 122–5, 127
Das, Taraknath 278
Daunt, Major C. O'B. 76
Dawson, Geoffrey 121
Dayal, Har 246, 256, 278
Deane, William 2
Defence of India Act 94
Delhi Pact (1931) 15, 17, 18, 24, 78–9, 82, 84
Democratic Swaraj Party 176
deportation 2, 221
Desai, Bhulabhai 208, 243–4
Desai, Mahadev 206, 240, 265
Des Moines Register 308
de Valera, Eamon 266, 303
Digby, William 246
Dinamani 152
Dinshah, F. E. 223, 233
Doherty, Mrs A. R. 285
Dufferin, Lord 318
Duke, Sir William 106–7
Dumasia, Naoroji 201–4
Durand, Mortimer 45
Durant, William James 306
Dutt, K. I. 205
Dwarkadas, Jamnadas 227
Dyer, Brig, R. E. H. 127, 222

Eastern and Associated Companies 145
Eastern Economist 95

Eastern News Agency (ENA), 114, 143
Eastern Times 48, 186
Emerson, Gertrude 306
Emerson, H. W. 63, 290
Empire 16
English language 3, 5, 21–2, 48, 88
Englishman 5, 16, 68
English Speaking Union (New York) 292
Evans, Lloyd 104
Exchange Telegraph 151

Faunthorpe, Colonel 279
Federal Times 177–8
Federation of Indian Chambers of
    Commerce 36
Fetherstonhaugh, Jane 264
film 282–3, 294, 306
Fletcher, Angus 282, 287–8, 291, 295, 299,
    304–7, 309
Foreign Affairs 296
Foreign Policy Association (New York)
    292, 304
Forward 66, 134, 160, 174, 202, 233
Freedom and Fellowship 67
Free Hindustan 278
Free India 152
Free Press Bulletin 133–4, 149
Free Press of India 94, 110, 122, 124,
    126–55 passim, 199; and API/Reuters
    140–2, 146, 152, 154; and BOW 145–8;
    and business community 129–31, 140,
    147; and Congress 128, 130–1, 140, 147;
    foreign service 141; founding 128–9; and
    Indian press 134, 136, 152, 154; and
    Responsivists 134–6; World News
    Service 151
Free Press Journal 149–52, 154–5, 178, 199
Friends of Freedom for India 266
Friends of India Society 264

Gabriel, A. V. 288
Gaelic American 256
Ganapati Festival 219
Gandhi, Devadas 316
Gandhi, M. K. 12–14, 18, 20–1, 28, 46, 48,
    75, 89, 108, 117, 121, 128, 130, 157–9,
    162, 167, 173–7, 179, 184, 189, 191, 197,
    204–6, 214, 217, 220, 222–5, 229–31, 234,
    236–8, 243–5, 252, 254, 256, 262, 270,
    272, 275, 277, 286–7, 290, 299, 307, 311,
    320
Garrett, J. D. 265
General Staff 43, 75
Ghadr 278
Ghose, Aurobindo 37
Ghose, Barendra Kumar 37

Ghose, Motilal, 45, 197
Ghose, Mrinal Kanti 62–3
Ghose, S. N. 292, 300–6
Gidwani, A. T. 181–2
Goenka, Ramnath 315–16
Gokhale, G. K. 24, 217–19, 240
Government of India Act (1919) 11, 14, 16,
    30–1, 52–3, 55, 57, 70, 86, 107, 111, 119,
    238, 248, 318
Government of India Act (1935) 94–5, 268,
    270
Government of India *Appreciation* (of
    political situation in India) 274;
    information and propaganda
    administration 6, 9, 18, 20, 29, 32–5, 51,
    73, 77, 96; Muslim propaganda 69–70;
    oral propaganda 41, 43, 69, 75–6;
    relations with Indian press 7, 44, 47, 49,
    51; and Retrenchment (financial) 11, 33,
    38–9, 112
Govindji, V. D. 231
Gowan, Hyde 89, 126
Guardian 46
Gupta, Birendra Nath 174
Gupta, B. Sen 152
Gurdwara Reform Movement 182
Gwynne, C. W. 39–40, 59

Habib, Hassan 186–7
Haig, H. G. 140–2, 144, 146–9
Hailey, Sir Malcolm 28, 35–6, 39, 90–1,
    180, 201, 211
Haksar, Sir Kailas 177–8
Hallett, M. G. 57, 158
Haq 64–5
Hardiker, N. S. 297–9
Hastings Regulations 3
Havas 99, 310
Haward, Edwin 108, 11
Hayles, A. A. 209
Hennessy, Josslyn 64
Herald Tribune 289–90, 293–5
Hicky, James 2
Hindu 5, 17, 32, 44, 46–9, 58, 60, 88, 94,
    107, 113, 125, 130, 134, 152, 159, 168–70,
    172, 176, 194, 197, 199, 202, 204, 206,
    209, 216–17, 228, 245, 268
Hindu Academical Association (Vienna)
    276
Hindu (Educational and Literary
    Supplement) 204
Hindu Mahasabha 89, 175–6, 186, 188,
    207, 243
Hindu National Party of America 299
Hindu Patriot 6
Hindustan Association of America 307

Hindustan Standard 167
Hindustan Times 23, 46–7, 58, 63, 94–5,
   113, 142, 169, 172, 176, 199, 201, 209,
   268, 277, 310
Hirachand, Walchand 131, 148
Hirtzel, Sir Arthur 27
Hoare, Samuel 120, 153
Holmes, John Haynes 306
Holsinger, F. E. 61, 129
Holwell Monument 28
Home Rule League 246
Horniman, B. G. 147, 168, 209, 214, 220–2,
   224–6, 231–2, 236–9, 241–2, 244, 351,
   353
Hose, J. W. 29, 104, 111, 284
Hossain, Syed 251, 253, 293–4
Hussain, Sir Fazl-i- 74
Hunter Committee Report 54, 250
Hyndman, H. M. 256, 266

Ilbert Bill (1883) 267
Imperial and International
   Communications Ltd 145
'Independence Day' 17, 72, 173, 177, 307
Independent 1, 22, 41, 47, 60, 160–2, 209,
   228, 251
India 246, 248, 250–2, 254
India Events 264
India Gazette 2
India Home Rule League of America 257,
   279
India House 247
India Information Bureau of America 298
Indian and Eastern Newspaper Society
   (IENS) 312–15
Indian Caravan 264
Indian Committee of National
   Independence 256
Indian Councils Act (1851) 5–6
Indian Currency League 131
Indian Daily Mail 23, 61, 129, 141, 200–1,
   216
Indian Daily News 16
Indian Express 94
Indian Independence League 304
Indian Information Bureau of New York
   254
Indian Merchants' Chamber, Bombay 143,
   147–8
Indian Mirror 66
Indian National Congress 2, 6–7, 11,
   13–15, 18, 20, 46, 75–6, 85–7, 92, 94,
   108–9, 158, 160–2, 164–5, 170, 191,
   266–3, 295, 297–304, 314; American
   Branch 299–300, 302; Foreign
   Department 258, 304, 311; London

Branch 272–3, 300, 302; and Muslim
   Press 186–7; Political and Economic
   Information Department 170, 185
Indian nationalism (divisions and
   competition) 7–8, 14–15, 20–1, 71,
   156–7, 159–60, 164, 168, 171–2, 207–9,
   237
Indian National Herald 147, 214, 237–8,
   241
Indian News Agency (INA) 114, 119, 126
Indian Newspaper Company 219
Indian News Service and Information
   Bureau (Berlin) 256–7
Indian press, relations with Indian business
   199, 223–4; relations with Congress
   214–15, and princes 201–4, 212–13
Indian Press Association 225
Indian Social Reformer 196, 200, 255
Indian Sociologist 246, 256
Indian Spectator 8
Indore, Maharaja of 270
Information Bureau 274, see Central
   Bureau of Information
Ireland 284, 292–3, 295
Irwin, Lord 15, 74, 82, 92, 166, 201, 203,
   264–5, 288, 289
Iyengar, A. Rangaswami 46, 132–3, 135,
   170, 204, 239
Iyengar, A. S. 116–17, 122, 124–5, 310
Iyengar, Kasturi 251
Iyengar, Srinivasa 117, 214

Jadhav, B. V. 235
Jallianwala Bagh, see Amritsar Massacre
Jayakar, M. R. 129, 131–6, 139, 141, 149,
   157, 164, 170, 173, 177–8, 197, 200,
   219–20, 225, 227, 230–1, 233–9, 241–2
Jinnah, Mohammed Ali 111, 125, 164, 184,
   222, 225, 227
John Bull in the East 3
Joint Select Committee Report 87–9,
   120–1, 125
Jones, Roderick 102, 122–4, 126, 128, 153,
   310
Joseph, George 182
Joseph, Pothan 22, 48, 118, 196, 220, 320
Joyce, A. H. 95–7, 113, 124–5, 311, 313,
   315, 320
Justice 163
Justice Party 246

Kaira Satyagraha 240
Keane, M. 91
Kelkar, N. C. 17, 56, 135, 139, 177, 218–19,
   229–32, 235, 237, 239, 241, 257
Kesari 5, 8, 17, 56, 218–19, 239

Khalsa, Gopal Singh 299
Khan, Nawab Muzaffar 69
Khan, Syed Ahmed 184
Khare, Dr 94–5
Khilafat Movement 10–11, 18, 43, 163,
  170, 179, 184, 222, 226–9, 231, 237, 245,
  251
Khimji, Mathradas 152, 154
Kisan Sabha 41, 93, 190, 259
Knight, Holford 253
Krishnamachari, R. 95
Krishnavarma, Shyamji 246, 256

Lahiri, B. K. 135
Lal, Chaman 277
La Motte, Ellen 297
Lawrence, John 26–8
Leader 22–3, 42, 44, 58, 66, 94, 113, 152,
  167–9, 197, 211–12, 217, 228
League Against Imperialism 258–9, 262–3,
  295, 300–1, 303
League Against Oppression 258
League of Political Education 284
Legislative Councils (publicity committees)
  37
Liberty 169, see *Forward*
Linlithgow, Lord 49, 93, 178
Lloyd, Sir George 221–2, 224, 227
Lodge, Henry Cabot 294
Lotwala, R. B. 264
Lovett, Pat 16–17, 29, 118
Low, Francis 308
Lucknow Pact (1916) 184

Macaulay, T. B. 3, 316
MacDonald, Ramsay 174, 197
MacGregor, Hugh 111–12, 120–1, 123–5,
  151, 210, 274, 309
MacGregor, R. C. 267–8
MacKinnon, Millicent 287
Macpherson, Sir Stewart 275
Madras Mail 4, 16, 32, 93, 129, 194, 198–9,
  209–10
Madras Times 114
Mahratta 5, 8, 17, 60, 218–19
Majithia, Dyal Singh 208
Malabari, B. M. 8
Malaviya, M. M. 23, 46, 74, 89, 91, 135,
  164, 174, 200, 238, 264
Marconi Company 145
Maxwell, R. M. 93
Mayo, Catherine 271, 294, 296, 306
Meerut Conspiracy Trial 261
Mehta, Jamnadas 173
Mehta, Pherozeshah 12, 129, 218–19, 232
Mehta, Vaikunth 223, 239–40, 243

Menon, V. P. 95
Metcalfe, Charles 3, 16
Metcalfe Press law 4, 6, 316
Miller, Webb 308
Millowners Association of Bombay 131
Milner, Alfred 248
Modern Review 9, 195, 266
Modern Student 67–8
Moloney, William J. 113, 117, 148, 320
Montagu, Edwin 11, 35–6, 64, 248, 284
Moonje, B. S. 176
Moore, Arthur 312–13, 320
Moplah riots 53, 228
Morais, Frank 210
Moral and Material Progress of India 33–4
Morley–Minto Reforms (1909) 184
Morning Post 250
Mudaliar, A. Ramaswami 195
Munro, Thomas 3, 54
Muslim League 10, 88, 243
Muslim Mass Contact 183–5, 188
Muslim Outlook 69, 172

Nabha, Maharaja of 180–1, 200–1
Naidu, M. J. S. 275
Naidu, Sarojini 108, 275, 301
Nambiar, A. C. N. 275–6
Napier, Mark 102
Naranji, Lalji 233–4
Natarajan, K. 196, 200
Natesan, G. A. 247–8
Nation 180, 201
Nation (USA) 293
National Call 200
National Herald 22–3, 94, 162, 196, 199,
  209
National Home Rule League 246
Navajivan 192
Nav Bharat 150–1
Nawanagar, Jamsaheb of 201–3, 212
Nehru, Jawaharlal 12, 14–15, 20, 27, 73,
  93–4, 137, 156–7, 162, 164, 166, 169, 171,
  176, 178, 183, 185, 187–94 passim, 196,
  208, 211, 213, 242–3, 258–63, 272–3, 276,
  295–7, 299–304, 307, 316, 320
Nehru, Motilal 1, 15, 24, 41, 46, 72, 117,
  130–1, 160–2, 164, 167, 170–1, 173, 191,
  214–15, 223, 231–2, 235
Nehru Report 15, 72, 171–3, 184, 242, 263
Nevill, R. C. R. 250–1
New India 195
New Leader 263
New Republic 293
Newspaper Proprietors' Association 312
Newspapers (Incitement to Offences) Act
  (1908) 9, 52

New York Evening Post 308
New York Times 289, 292, 295, 308
New York World 289, 307–8
Non-Cooperation (NCO) 12–15, 41–4, 54,
   60, 65, 70, 84, 130, 156, 158–9, 170, 184,
   197, 205–6, 218, 225, 227, 231, 235, 237,
   241–2, 252, 254, 263, 270, 318

O'Donnell, S. P. 65
O'Dwyer, Sir Michael 52–3
Olivier, Lord 28
'ordinary law' 4, 50–1, 54–5, 84
Oriental Languages (Vernacular) Press Act
   6

Pacific Coast Hindustan Association 278
Pakistan Resolution (1940) 184
Pal, B. C. 67, 269
Pal, Kristo Das 6, 214
Panikkar, K. M. 182, 212, 232
Parikh, J. M. 252–4
Parthasarathy, Rangaswami 194
Patel, Vallabhbhai 79, 93–4, 244, 273,
   315–16
Patel, Vithalbhai 235, 248–9, 251, 253, 264,
   272, 280
Patiala, Maharaja of 180–1, 201–3, 212,
   292
Peel, R. T. 274
Petit, J. B. 129, 200–1, 220
Philadelphia Public Register 298
Pickthall, Marmaduke 226–9, 231–3,
   238–9, 244
Pioneer 4, 23, 41, 127, 142–3, 148, 172,
   211–13
Polak, H. S. L. 247–8, 302
Poona Pact 175
Prabasi 9
Prajamitra 146
Prakasam, T. 164, 205–6, 214
Prasad, Rajendra 190
press, the, advertising 58–9, 61–2, 64, 198;
   Anglo-Indian 4–5, 40, 136, 160, 199;
   blacklisting 60–3; British 6, 312–13;
   censorship and banning 94, 255–6,
   276–7; freedom of 6, 45, 50, 53, 118, 318;
   historical review 2–9; Muslim 69, 186,
   187; national voice 2, 4–5; and Indian
   newsworthy events and personalities
   12–13, 107, 273; official subsidy 37, 58–9,
   66–8, 144; and party politics 7, 51;
   professionalism 22, 45, 48, 51–2, 115,
   118–19, 159, 169, 194–7, 204; regulations
   and legislation 2–4, 6, 9, 16, 30, 49, 55,
   68, 70–1, 82–4, 90, 92; repression 58, 72,
   86; symbolic images and messages 1, 5,

8, 13, 17, 19, 27, 29, 108; technology 7,
   99–100, 107
Press Act (1910) 9, 30, 50, 55, 68, 82, 316
Press Act (1931) 16, 82–4, 274, 277
Press Association 312
Press Bureau 113
Press Law (Sapru) Commission (1921)
   49–50, 52, 316
Press Law Inquiry Commission 316
Press (Objectionable Matter) Act 316
Press Ordinance (1930) 16, 110, 149, 214–15
Press (Special Powers) Act 316
Press Trust of India (PTI) 315
Public Safety Ordinance 261
Puckle, Sir Arthur 311
Punjab Inquiry Report (INC) 249–50
Punjab Sunrise 185
'Punjab Wrong' see Amritsar Massacre
Punniah, K. 208–9

Qadir, Sufi Abdul 69–70
Quesada, Aurelio Miro 275

Raghavan, G. S. 196
Rai, Lala Lajpat 67, 132, 164, 200, 214,
   235, 249, 257, 278–9, 297
Rajagopalachari, C. R. 49, 93–4, 167, 205,
   310
Ranade, M. G. 218
Rao, B. Shiva 49
Rao, D. V. S. 257
Rao, Raghavendra 89
Ratcliffe, S. K. 284–95
Rau, M. Chalapathi 195
Reading, Lord 35, 66, 181
Reed, Sir Stanley 30, 120, 277, 313
'Reforms, the' see Government of India
   Act, 1919
Responsivist Party 92, 129, 134–7, 170–1,
   216, 234, 237–8, 241
Reuters 12, 20, 40, 53, 82, 97, 99–155
   passim, 261, 266, 271, 288, 290, 309–11,
   313–16, 318; establishment in India
   99–100; professional and business
   priorities 103–4, 106, 111, 113; special
   relationship 100–1, 105–6; subsidy 101,
   104, 109–13, 119
Reuters Trust 313
Reynolds, Reginald 264
Rezmie, T. H. K. 292, 303–5, 307
Ripon, Lord 6, 45, 267
Round Table Conference 16, 72, 82, 84–5,
   88, 109, 111, 184, 274, 288
Rowlatt Acts 11, 30, 46, 127, 168–9
Roy, Kalinath 49, 50–1, 132, 196, 206–8,
   214, 239, 320

Roy, K. C. 53–4, 113–18, 121, 123, 127, 132, 137, 148, 274
Roy, M. N. 10
Roy, Raja Ram Mohan 3, 8–10, 318
Roy, S. N. 47, 67
Rushbrook Williams, L. F. 32–3, 35, 38–40, 44, 58–60, 66, 97, 230, 283, 286–7, 290–5, 305, 308
Rustomjee, Rustom 280–1, 291

Sacramento Bee 296
Sadanand, Swaminath 94, 122, 126–55 passim, 166, 314–16
Sahni, J. N. 23, 46–7, 52, 63, 115–17, 123, 132, 198, 200, 207, 209
Saklatwala, Shapurji 144, 259, 261, 271–2, 302
Samachar 203
Samaldas, Lallubhai 232, 240
San Francisco Chronicle 308
Sanj Vartaman 138
Sapru, P. N. 125
Sapru, T. B. 22, 49, 157, 167–8, 177–8, 243
Saran, Iswar 263
Satyamurthi, S. 272–3
Savarkar, V. D. 230, 247, 266
Searchlight 23
Sen, K. C. 8, 147
Sen, Satyendra 66
Sen, U. N. 110, 114, 121, 123–4, 126, 141, 153
Servants of India Society 240
Sethna, Phiroze 139–40, 166
Seton, Sir Malcolm 106
Shah (Gilani), T. Beltie 64–5
Shiromani Akali Dal 179
Shiromani Gurdwara Prabandhak Committee (SGPC) 179–80, 183
Shivaji 8, 219, 241
Shraddhanand, Swami 320
Sikh Sudhar Committees 181
Sind Observer 208–9
Singh, Baba Kharak 179
Singh, St Nihal 250
Singh Sabha Movement 179
Sinha, Sachidananda 23
Sitaramayya, Pattabhi 249
Skeen Committee 235
Special Immigration Officer (Vancouver) 285
Spoor, Ben 253
Srinivasan, C. R. 315–16
Srinivasan, Kasturi 47, 49, 107, 125, 194, 204, 315–16
Srivastava, J. P. 212

Statesman 16, 36, 93, 95, 114, 127, 140, 148, 210–12, 268
Statesman (Montreal) 298
Statutory (Simon) Commission (1928) 15, 31, 72, 108, 164, 192, 202, 241
Stephens, Ian 48, 88, 91–3, 120, 124–5, 274
Stewart, Findlater 88
Storey, S. 313
Sunderland, J. D. 267, 279, 297, 306–7
Swadesamitran 132–3, 170
Swaraj Party 15, 63, 89, 92, 129–35, 204, 217, 231–5, 237–8
Swarajya 134, 159, 169, 182, 205, 214
Sydenham, Lord 248
Sykes, Sir Frederick 74

Tagore, Rabindranath 195, 266
Tagore, S. N. 57, 275
Tairsee, L. R. 231, 238
Tanganyika Opinion 171
Tata, Dorabji 223–4
Tata, R. D. 234
Thakurdas, Purshotamdas 36, 87, 125, 130–1, 138–40, 144, 148–9, 154, 165–6, 223–4, 233
Thomas, K. P. 67–8
Thomas, Lowell 282–4
Thomas, Norman 279
Thompson, Edward 13, 291, 303–5
Tilak, B. G. 5, 8, 12, 24, 67, 196, 214, 218–20, 222, 230, 248–9, 251, 269, 297
Tilak Memorial Swarajya Fund 160, 181, 258, 297
Times 46, 92, 121, 250, 263, 266, 268–70, 277, 289, 292
Times of India 4, 16, 23, 30, 36, 40, 75, 93, 108–9, 119–20, 138, 140–1, 171, 177–8, 198–9, 201, 210–11, 220, 308
Toronto Globe 298
Trade Disputes Act 261
Tribune 5, 17, 22, 48, 50, 58, 73, 75, 89, 94, 152, 159, 168–9, 172, 182, 206–9, 214, 216–17, 245
Turner, William 111–12, 115, 315

Umrigar, K. D. 138
United Press of America (UPA) 308–9, 311–12, 314
United Press of India (UPI) 152
United States 10, 21, 158, 277–312 passim
Usman, Sir Mohammad 125

Vanguard 255
Vincent, W. H. 37, 40, 54, 104

War Journal 65

Wedderburn, William 247–8, 253
Wedgwood, Col. 253–4
Wellesley Regulations 2–3
Wilberforce, Robert 279–80, 287–8
Willert, Arthur 277
Willingdon, Lord 89, 124
Wilson, F. W. 142, 211

Wilson, Sir Leslie 201
Wolff 99, 310

Young, Desmond 212–13
Young India 60, 158–60, 166, 214, 232
Young India (USA) 279, 297
Yugantar 269

Cambridge South Asian Studies

These monographs are published by the Syndics of Cambridge University Press in association with the Cambridge University Centre for South Asian Studies. The following books have been published in this series:

29 Ian Stone: *Canal irrigation in British India: perspectives on technological change in a peasant society*

30 Rosalind O'Hanlon: *Caste, conflict and ideology: Mahatma Jotirao Phute and low caste protest in nineteenth-century Western India*

31 Ayesha Jalal: *The sole spokesman: Jinnah, the Muslim League and the demand for Pakistan*

32 N. R. F. Charlesworth: *Peasant and imperial rule: agriculture and agrarian society in the Bombay presidency, 1850–1935*

33 Claude Markovits: *Indian business and nationalist politics 1931–39. The indigenous capitalist class and the rise of the Congress Party*

36 Sugata Bose: *Agrarian Bengal: economy, social structure and politics, 1919–1947*

37 Atuk Kohli: *The State and poverty in India: the politics of reform*

38 Franklin A. Presler: *Religion under bureaucracy: policy and administration for Hindu temples in South India*

39 Nicholas B. Dirks: *The hollow crown: ethnohistory of an Indian kingdom*

40 Robert Wade: *Village republics: economic conditions for collective action in South India*

41 Laurence W. Preston: *The Devs of Cincvad: a lineage and state in Maharashtra*

42 Farzana Shaikh: *Community and consensus in Islam: Muslim representation in colonial India 1860–1947*

43 Susan Bayly: *Saints, goddesses and kings: Muslims and Christians in South Indian society, 1700–1900*

44 Gyan Prakash: *Bonded histories; genealogies of labor servitude in colonial India*

45 Sanjay Subrahmanyam: *The political economy of commerce: Southern India 1500–1650*

46 Ayesha Jalal: *The state of martial rule: the origins of Pakistan's political economy of defence*

47 Bruce Graham: *Hindu nationalism and Indian politics: the origins and development of the Bharatiya Jana Sangh*

48 Dilesh Jayanntha: *Electoral allegiance in Sri Lanka*

49 Stephen P. Blake: *Shahjahanabad: the sovereign city in Mughal India 1639–1739*

50 Sarah F. D. Ansari: *Sufi saints and state power: the pirs of Sind, 1843–1947*

51 Rajnarayan Chandavarkar: *The origins of industrial capitalism in India: business strategies and the working classes in Bombay, 1900–1940*

52 Tapati Guha-Thakurta: *The making of a new 'Indian' art: artists, aesthetics and nationalism in Bengal c. 1850–1920*

53 John R. McLane: *Land and local kingship in eighteenth-century Bengal*

54 Ross Mallick: *Development policy of a communist government: West Bengal since 1977*

55 Dilip M. Menon: *Caste, nationalism and communism in South India: Malabar, 1900–1948*